TORAH AND LAW IN *PARADISE LOST*

TORAH AND LAW IN
PARADISE LOST

Jason P. Rosenblatt

PRINCETON UNIVERSITY PRESS   PRINCETON, NEW JERSEY

Copyright © 1994 by Princeton University Press
Published by Princeton University Press, 41 William Street,
Princeton, New Jersey 08540
In the United Kingdom: Princeton University Press,
Chichester, West Sussex
All Rights Reserved

Library of Congress Cataloging-in-Publication Data
Rosenblatt, Jason Philip, 1941–
Torah and law in Paradise lost / Jason P. Rosenblatt.
p. cm.
Includes bibliographical references (p.) and index.
ISBN: 0-691-03340-4 (acid-free paper)
1. Milton, John, 1608–1674. Paradise lost. 2. Rabbinical literature—
History and criticism. 3. Milton, John, 1608–1674—Knowledge—
Judaism. 4. Milton, John, 1608–1674—Knowledge—Law.
5. Jewish law in literature.
6. Judaism in literature. 7. Bible in literature.
8. Eden in literature. I. Title.
PR3562.R58   1994
821'.4—dc20   93-37043   CIP

This book has been composed in Laser Sabon

Princeton University Press books are printed on
acid-free paper and meet the guidelines
for permanence and durability of the Committee
on Production Guidelines for Book Longevity
of the Council on Library Resources

Printed in the United States of America

1 3 5 7 9 10 8 6 4 2

_____ **For Zipporah** _____

GRACE IS IN ALL HER STEPS, HEAV'N IN HER EYE,

IN EVERY GESTURE DIGNITY AND LOVE.

Contents

Acknowledgments

IN THIS BOOK I examine Milton's epic representations of paradise and the fallen world as the supreme mythic coordinates of the interpretive struggle between Jews and Christians over the Hebrew Bible as Torah or law. Milton regards the Bible as Torah in the 1643–45 prose tracts. There he acknowledges a debt to the magnificent Hebrew scholarship of John Selden, who respects, to an extent remarkable for the times, the self-understanding of Judaic exegesis. Those prose tracts are the principal doctrinal matrix of the middle books of *Paradise Lost*, which present the Hebrew Bible and Adam and Eve as self-sufficient entities. After the Fall, a Pauline hermeneutic reduces the Hebrew Bible to Old Testament, a captive text, and our first parents to shadowy types. Milton scholars have already pointed out Milton's radically Pauline ethos, but that ethos does not annul his Hebraism. If Milton resembles Paul, the former Pharisee, it is not least because his thought could attain harmonies only through dialectic; some of his poetry derives its power from deep internal struggles over the value and meaning of law, grace, charity, Christian liberty, and the relationships among natural law, the Mosaic law, and the gospel. Since comedy often sets up an arbitrary law and then finds a way to break or evade it without penalty, the theme of law yielding to love and the elegant evasion of *felix culpa* should make *Paradise Lost* the definitive comedy of Christian liberty. But alongside the Pauline comedy is the Hebraic tragedy of Torah degraded into law and of redemption purchased at a terrible price.

Pauline law, unlike love, cannot be renewed. It must itself end in love. But Torah includes both law and love. In acknowledging the help I have received over the years, I cannot always separate the imperatives of ethical obligation from those of an overflowing heart. I think first of Barbara Kiefer Lewalski, a "sovran Planter," who recognizes that the students whom she has nurtured are made from the materials of chaos and will revert to wilderness without constant creative ordering. She has been the audience I address ever since I wrote my first papers on Milton in her class. I also have a special intellectual and personal indebtedness to Anthony Hecht, who boosted my spirits when they were low by taking my writing seriously; to the community of Milton scholars, including Michael Lieb, Kathleen Swaim, Georgia Christopher, Albert C. Labriola, and the members of the seminar founded by Mario Di Cesare and Thomas Kranidas, for camaraderie and generosity; and to Georgetown colleagues Penn Szittya, Michael Ragussis, Joan Reuss, James Slevin, Joseph C. Sitterson, Jr., and the late Thomas F. Walsh, for sustaining fellowship.

Another sort of fellowship also sustained this project, and I am delighted to record the support I received from the Guggenheim Foundation and the National Endowment for the Humanities. Tending now toward law rather than love, I am grateful to the University of Pittsburgh Press and Bucknell University Press respectively for permission to reprint two essays from *Milton Studies*, "The Mosaic Voice in *Paradise Lost*" (7 [1975]) and "Milton's Chief Rabbi" (24 [1988]), and, from *Milton and the Middle Ages*, edited by John Mulryan, "Angelic Tact." I have also transplanted some pages from "Adam's Pisgah Vision" (*ELH* 39 [1972]). My most recent debts are to Michael Neuman, Director, Center for Text and Technology, Georgetown University; and to the editors at Princeton University Press: Robert E. Brown, literature editor; Beth Gianfagna, senior production editor; and Richard E. Jones, copy editor, whose combined skill and sensitivity have improved this book.

Finally, to end with love, I want to name my father, Rabbi Morris D. Rosenblatt, of blessed memory; my mother, Esther; my children, Noah and Raphael; and the dedicatee, my wife, Zipporah, of whom it can be said, "the torah of loving-kindness is on her tongue" (Prov. 31:26).

Abbreviations

AV	*The Holy Bible* (London, 1611). The Authorized or King James Version.
CE	*The Works of John Milton*, gen. ed. Frank Allen Patterson, 18 vols. (New York: Columbia University Press, 1931–38).
DDD	John Milton, *The Doctrine and Discipline of Divorce*
DNB	*The Dictionary of National Biography*
ELH	*Journal of English Literary History*
ELR	*English Literary Renaissance*
MLN	*Modern Language Notes*
PL	John Milton, *Paradise Lost*
PMLA	*Publications of the Modern Language Association of America*
PR	John Milton, *Paradise Regained*
SEL	*Studies in English Literature, 1500–1900*
SP	*Studies in Philology*
UTQ	*University of Toronto Quarterly*
YP	*The Complete Prose Works of John Milton*, gen. ed. Don M. Wolfe, 8 vols. (New Haven: Yale University Press, 1953–82).

TORAH AND LAW IN *PARADISE LOST*

Introduction

IN HIS GREAT EPIC Milton tries more or less successfully to turn myth into a doctrinal inevitability by representing paradise and its felt loss in terms of the transformation and supersession of the Hebrew Bible by the New Testament. An impulse more permanent than that of a lyric is required to sustain an epic muse, and the troubled relations between the Mosaic law and the gospel, elaborated throughout Milton's prose career, furnish the terms from which the representation of experience in *Paradise Lost* develops its meaning. By modeling Edenic polity upon the Hebrew Bible before the New Testament supervened and changed it into the Old Testament, Milton tries to prevent the reader from confusing Hebraic prelapsarian and Christian postlapsarian life. Such confusion could undermine the poem by blurring the distinctness of Eden and the irretrievable reality of innocence and by allowing the reader to indulge a sense of superiority to Adam and Eve by directly applying later knowledge to events before the Fall. The Edenic books are Hebraic and nontypological; when the divine voice first speaks to Eve, who has not yet seen Adam, the first epithet it uses for Adam is "no shadow": "I will bring thee where no shadow stays / Thy coming, and thy soft embraces, hee / Whose image thou art" (4.470–72).[1] Before the Fall, Adam is substantial reality; only afterward does he become a shadowy type. In a sense, this episode from book 4 rejects typology, which requires the dissolution of the image in its stronger antitype, by representing it as Eve's relationship to her shadowy reflection. In the covenantal relationship of Adam and Eve before the Fall, image is invited to enjoy heightened self-realization through a love embrace with its stronger original. Like the heroes of the Torah, Adam and Eve, immured by privilege, form a community constituted by divine law, holy place, kinship, and a direct relationship with deity. They need no mediatorial prophet, priest, or king because they are themselves good, holy, and just.

The Mosaic law is the principal source of Edenic polity before the Fall, a minister of death and condemnation only afterward. Like Paul, an ex-Pharisee and of the strictest school, Milton believes in the absolute indissolubility of the law. For Paul the law is a seamless garment that, once rent, like the veil in the temple, can never be made whole again. In the Edenic books Milton exploits the obverse of this belief. If the Mosaic law is a single, indivisible entity, then Adam and Eve can keep the entire law by keeping one law, obeying the easy terms of the single prohibition. The Mosaic law is originally benign rather than impossible to keep. In Eden it coexists with natural law, just as scriptural revelation coexists with the book of nature.

In *De doctrina Christiana*, the similarities for Milton between the Mosaic law and the prohibition in Eden are unmistakable—for example, "THE MOSAIC LAW . . . HELD A PROMISE OF LIFE FOR THE OBEDIENT AND A CURSE FOR THE DISOBEDIENT."[2] With the Fall, the efficacy of the Mosaic law, embodied in the prohibition, is lost. Milton's view on this point is more radical than that of most Protestants: true to his view of the law as a single entity that cannot be divided into disposable ceremonial and judicial components and a permanent moral one, he insists that even the Decalogue no longer binds Christians. The breach between prelapsarian and postlapsarian Eden is as irreparable as that between the Mosaic law and the gospel, which reformers like Luther never tired of elaborating:

> The world . . . braggeth of free will, of the light of reason, of the soundness of the powers and qualities of nature, and of good works as means whereby it could deserve and attain grace and peace, that is to say, forgiveness of sins and a quiet conscience. But it is impossible that the conscience should be quiet and joyful unless it have peace through grace, that is to say, through the forgiveness of sins promised in Christ. . . . But because they mingle the Law with the Gospel they must needs be perverters of the Gospel. For either Christ must remain and the Law perish, or the Law must remain and Christ perish. For Christ and the Law can by no means agree and reign together in the conscience. Where the righteousness of the Law ruleth, there cannot the righteousness of Grace rule. And again, where the righteousness of Grace reigneth, there cannot the righteousness of the Law reign; for one of them must needs give place to the other.[3]

Of course Milton concurs. "Christ, when he redeemed us from the curse, [Galatians] iii.13, redeemed us also from the causes of the curse, that is to say, from the works of the law, or from the whole law of works, which is the same thing, and this . . . does not mean merely the ceremonial law. . . . If you do no good unless you obey the law in every detail, and it is absolutely impossible to obey it in every detail, then it is ridiculous to obey it at all . . ." (*YP*, 6:531). Indeed, where Luther stops short by emphasizing the exclusively spiritual nature of liberty under the gospel—and hence its civil limitations—Milton extends the effects of Christian emancipation to include freedom "from the judgments of men, and especially from coercion and legislation in religious matters" (*YP*, 6:537–38).[4]

In Eden before the Fall, however, the reverse of both excerpts is true. The conscience is quiet and joyful without the forgiveness of sins because there is no sin. Adam and Eve can obey the single law "in every detail" because they enjoy free will, the light of reason, sound natural powers, and good works. Only after the Fall, and after an interval of despair, does the law give way to grace. Milton's dismissal of the entire Mosaic law as a result of Christ's mediation bears directly upon his handling of Eden. Before the Fall, Adam is compared with figures from the Pentateuch, most notably with Abraham and Moses, who lived in the days of easy intimacy between humankind and God. After the Fall, the Hebrew Bible's heroes, images, and events are devalued peremptorily.[5] The typological perspective introduced as a result of the Fall diminishes all merely human figures: only Christ can regain the paradise lost to Adam; only he can enter the Canaan closed to Moses. The Hebraic vision of Abraham appears in unfallen Eden (book 5), while the typological interpretation of Abraham as one who looks forward in faith to fulfillment in Christ is offered by the angel Michael after the Fall.

The reader of *Paradise Lost* finds the same sort of devaluation of Adam and Eve, their work, their innocence, and their home. Adam and Eve are naked and can only be clothed by Christ; their prayers can only reach heaven through the Son's priestly intercession. Before the Fall, Adam's own direct conversation with God suffices to grant him his wish: "Let not my words offend thee, Heav'nly Power, / My Maker, be *propitious* while I speak" (8.379–80; my emphasis). Adam's words echo those of Abraham ("Oh let not the Lord be angry, and I will speak" [Gen. 18:30]) and Moses (Exod. 32, Num. 14) when they converse directly with God. After the Fall, Adam's prayers can reach heaven only through the Son's priestly intercession:

> Now therefore bend thine ear
> To supplication, hear his sighs though mute;
> Unskilful with what words to pray, let mee
> Interpret for him, mee his Advocate
> And *propitiation*, all his works on mee
> Good or not good ingraft, my Merit those
> Shall perfet, and for these my Death shall pay.
> *(11.30–36; my emphasis)*

The Son, in his later role as Christ the Savior, transforms sighs and mute longing into articulate prayer, just as he transforms the mercy-seat of the law (*PL*, 11.2; Exod. 25:17–23) into himself by serving as the true propitiation (*PL*, 11.34; Rom. 3:25). William Guild identifies the "Mercy-Seat or Propitiatory" with Christ, and Samuel Mather interprets similarly:"The *Mercy-Seat* which was upon the Ark, was a Type of the *Passive Obedience* and Satisfaction of Jesus Christ for our Sins, whom God hath set forth to be . . . a *Propitiation*."[6] Of course the price of grace is very dear, and not only for the redeemer. The complications of priestly intercession replace the simple directness of Adam's colloquy with a God who asserts his singleness: "for none I know / Second to me or like, equal much less" (8.406–7). For Adam the decline from "propitious" to "pro-pitiation" is absolute; instead of displaying a prompt eloquence capable of achieving its own profound desire, the creation of Eve, Adam doesn't even know how to ask. Where once his "good works" (9.234) pleased God, now they must be engrafted upon Christ and perfected by him.

The Hebraic factor in the Edenic books of *Paradise Lost* does not annul Milton's radically Pauline theology.[7] Milton and Paul are in essential agreement over doctrine, but differences of motive and imaginative sympathy produce very different representations of the Mosaic law. Paul, obsessed with his inability to perform the law and with salvation by faith, has no need to explain the Mosaic law's application in history, however temporary, since he has little interest in the inner rationale of history and no need of theodicy. Milton, however, has both the interest and the need, and his unique representation of a dynamic, historical Eden, as well as his justification of God's ways, depends on his fusion of the Mosaic law and the original prohibition in Eden. More than any other great Christian poet of the seventeenth century—more even than George Herbert, who imagines in his poem "Decay" a sweet familiarity of discourse in Genesis between human beings and their heavenly father—Milton reveals in books 4 to 9 of *Paradise Lost* a generosity of spirit toward the Hebrew Bible, its God, its law, and its covenant.

The Mosaic law, like the story of Genesis 1–3 and like poetry itself, although simple in its comprehension of a vast order of consequences, is not monolithic. If Milton's *De doctrina* supplies a frame of reference for the last books of *Paradise Lost*, his great prose tracts of 1643–45 are the principal doctrinal matrix of his vision of paradise in the epic's middle books. *The Doctrine and Discipline of Divorce*, *Tetrachordon*, *Of Education*, and the *Areopagitica* all reflect, to a greater or lesser degree, Milton's felt knowledge of the saving power of the deuteronomic Mosaic law. But readers of *Paradise Lost* are familiar only with Paul's negative and limited view of the law, which appears after the Fall, when it is already obsolete. It has been the fate of the most Hebraic of great English poets to have been interpreted in this century by critics and scholars, some of them great ones, who have been conspicuously inhospitable to what Ezra Pound called his "beastly Hebraism." A. S. P. Woodhouse, Arthur Barker, and Ernest Sirluck, among others, have examined from a Pauline perspective the relations between law and gospel and have thus regarded the Hebraic factor in Milton's thought with either indifference or antipathy. Thus, for example, Woodhouse consistently applies to Milton's poetry and prose the paradigm of nature and grace. Each of these two orders of existence "is dependent on the power and providence of God, but in a manner sufficiently different to warrant the restriction of the term *religious* (which means Christian) to one order only."[8] This paradigm, consistent with Milton's doctrine of Christian liberty, helps to illuminate works as disparate as *Comus* and the last two books of *Paradise Lost*, but it is inadequate as a guide to Milton's Hebraic poetry and prose. Woodhouse insists that "Milton's plea for divorce invokes [both] the same twofold principle" of nature and grace and "the doctrine of Christian liberty."[9] Woodhouse recognizes natural law and the gospel as the only valid dispensations. When the Mosaic law occupies a central position in Milton's work, Woodhouse dissolves it, assimilating the moral law to natural law as a rational principle and the already typologized ceremonial law to the gospel, and ignoring the judicial law. Woodhouse's central texts are always Pauline, as in this discussion of book 1 of *The Faerie Queene*:

> The reader [of Spenser's Letter to Raleigh] is told that the virtue of Book I is holiness, which he would instantly recognize as a specifically Christian virtue, outside nature and belonging to the order of grace; that the armour which the Redcross Knight assumes "is the armour of a Christian man specified by Saint Paul."[10]

Woodhouse could never recognize the Hebraic ethos of *The Doctrine and Discipline of Divorce*, in which Milton refers to the Jews as God's "holy seed" and "holy people."[11] The central text of that tract is not Pauline but Mosaic, the deuteronomic law that permits divorce for the sake of charity when the common expositors of the Pauline renaissance do not. Behind Raleigh's reference and Woodhouse's "emphasis upon the Christian's armour, and especially upon the shield of faith"[12] is Paul's "sword of the Spirit" and "shield of faith" (Eph. 6:16–17). Milton picks up a different shield when he defends God's word in Deuteronomy from the detractions of canon lawyers, Catholic theologians, and erroneous biblical expositors:

> the purity and wisdom of this Law shall be the buckler of our dispute. . . . That it should not be counted a faltring dispence, a flattring permission of sin, the bil of adultery, a snare, is the expence of all this apology. And all that we solicite is, that it may be suffer'd to stand in the place where God set it amidst the firmament of his holy Laws to shine, as it was wont, upon the weaknesses and errors of men perishing els in the sincerity of their honest purposes. (*YP*, 2:351)

Milton's invented epithets flung by imaginary opponents of the Mosaic law of divorce parody the lists of Pauline epithets recited mechanically by Reformation expositors: the Mosaic law as "*a prison that shutteth up, the yoake of bondage, the power or force of sinne, the operation of wrath and of death.*"[13] Milton's defense of the Mosaic law in the divorce tracts includes a balanced critique of Paul.

The scholarship and historical insight of Arthur Barker continue to provide a basis for the understanding of Milton's thought.[14] *Milton and the Puritan Dilemma* remains the best book ever written on Milton's prose, but in it Barker views all of Milton's discussions of the law through the filter of the chapter on Christian liberty in *De doctrina*. He thus fails to realize that in the tracts of 1643–45, the Mosaic law as well as Christian liberty constitute "a demand for the freedom of the individual conscience from human ordinances."[15] In an important essay on Christian liberty, Barker's emphasis on human response ("What God consistently gives his responsive creatures is an opportunity to respond"[16]) misrepresents a doctrine based on human insufficiency and redemption by Christ—a doctrine to which human initiative is conspicuously irrelevant.

Where the prose tracts of 1643–45 reveal Milton at the height of his synthesizing powers, discovering and creating important continuities among the dispensations of natural law, the Mosaic law, and the gospel, Barker interprets them according to the nature-grace paradigm of his teacher Woodhouse. Milton speaks of the "lawfull liberty" (*YP*, 2:278) of the deuteronomic code, but, for Barker, the law can only be a burden. He thus consistently excludes it from his binary frame of reference: "If divorce according to conscience is a privilege included in Christian liberty, it is also a right to be claimed under the law of nature. At this point the demands of Christian liberty and of natural liberty are practically identical."[17]

Barker actually traces Milton's formulation of the doctrine of Christian liberty, with its corollary of freedom from the bondage of the Mosaic law, to the second edition of *Doctrine and Discipline of Divorce*, which in fact emphasizes on almost every page the perfection and contemporary applicability of that law.[18] In this tract the unabrogated Mosaic law restores freedom to those formerly under the bondage of canon law. Barker insists that "the argument from the abrogation of the Jewish Law . . . occupied the centre of his reasoning on divorce."[19] Milton endlessly asserts instead: "*Christ neither did, nor could abrogat the Law of divorce*" (*YP*, 2:281); "*Christ came not to abrogate from the Law one jot or tittle*, and denounces against them that shall so teach" (*YP*, 2:283). His closing address to Parliament includes this plea: "It must be your suffrages and Votes, O English men, that this exploded decree of God and *Moses* may scape, and come off fair without the censure of a shamefull abrogating" (*YP*, 2:351).[20]

Paul uses the element of supersession in his typology to evacuate a past for which he has no use. When he asserts that "Christ is the end of the law" (Rom. 10:4), he brazenly identifies annulment as fulfillment. Barker employs a similar hermeneutic to obliterate the separate identity of the Mosaic law, reducing it to principles that assimilate it to the law of nature. He paraphrases Milton's argument in the divorce tracts: "It was Christ's office to maintain, *not the Mosaic code*, but the law 'grounded on moral reason' and 'that unabolishable equity which it conveys to us' " [my emphasis].[21] The actual quote differs: *Moses . . . Law grounded on moral reason, was both [Christ's] office and his essence to maintain*" (*YP*, 2:264). Milton applies the word "essence" to Christ: it is his office and essence to maintain the Mosaic law. Barker seems to shift the meaning of "essence" from Christ to the law, where it becomes a summarizing abstraction distinct from the actual Mosaic code. Despite overwhelming contradictory evidence, Barker insists:

> Milton's argument [in the divorce pamphlets] rests, *not on the particular Mosaic formulation*, but on the eternal morality and equity which lay behind the law ceremonial, political, judicial, and moral; and it is this, *not the Mosaic formulation*, which still binds under the Gospel. (my emphasis).[22]

The Miltonic assertion paraphrased here without acknowledgment is more straightforward: "It is the Law that is the exacter of our obedience ev'n under the Gospel" (*YP*, 2:303).

In *The Doctrine and Discipline of Divorce*, Milton regards Christians as superior in faith but not in virtue: "Wee find . . . by experience that the Spirit of God in the Gospel hath been alwaies more effectual in the illumination of our minds to the gift of faith, then in the moving of our wills to any excellence of vertue, either above the *Jews* or the Heathen" (*YP*, 2:303). Barker comments: "I do not think that Milton ever again expressed this opinion; it contradicted his deepest convictions."[23] In fact, Milton makes this point frequently in his defense of the Jews from the charge of hardheartedness, part of his larger argument that divorce is a permanent Mosaic law and not a temporary dispensation based on the Jews' weaknesses.[24]

All of the definitions of the law that Barker purports to find in the divorce tracts will turn up in *De doctrina*. There Milton will contradict his positive arguments on the law, insisting, "It is not a less perfect life that is required from Christians but, in fact, a more perfect life than was required of those under the law" (*YP*, 6:535). Whereas Milton, in the divorce pamphlets, insists on the perpetual force of the moral and judicial Mosaic laws, in *De doctrina*, he proclaims no less forcefully death to the entire law (*YP*, 6:529). These internal quarrels and self-contradictions regarding the law constitute the principal doctrinal matrix of Milton's Hebraic paradise and his fallen Christian world.

One reads the prose tracts of 1643–45 in Ernest Sirluck's brilliant edition. Each of the editors of the individual tracts, by citing contemporary parallels of Milton's statements, naturally emphasized what is traditional and neglected what is radically Hebraic and iconoclastic. Since Milton's mission in the divorce tracts is to recover the true scriptural meaning of the law, he values contemporary scholars such as Selden, Grotius, and Fagius only for their familiarity with ancient texts—including the Targum, the Talmud, and medieval rabbinica—and with ancient languages, including Hebrew and Aramaic. The original ideas of Beza, Paraeus, Perkins, and Rivetus he generally answers or corrects. Ultimately, as Robert W. Ayers has noted, the principal nonbiblical authorities upon whom Milton appears to rely in *Doctrine and Discipline of Divorce* are not Puritan—or indeed Christian—but Jewish. And the three principal positions advanced—availability of divorce with right of remarriage for both husband and wife, broadening of grounds to include incompatibility, and removal of divorce from public to private jurisdiction—all accord precisely with Jewish divorce law.[25]

One finds even in Sirluck's invaluable general introduction the suggestion that Milton regards charity as an exclusively Christian virtue. Sirluck refers to "Christ's 'supreme dictate of charity' " (*YP*, 2:148), whereas Milton himself speaks only of "the supreme dictate of charity" (*YP*, 2:250). Similarly, when Milton appeals to charity in *The Doctrine and Discipline of Divorce* ("*Love onely is the fulfilling of every Commandment*" (*YP*, 2:258), one of his anonymous opponents accuses him of adding the word "only" to his paraphrase of Romans 13:10.[26] Milton replies to this attack in *Colasterion* (*YP*, 2:750): "Whereas hee taxes mee of adding to the Scripture in that I said, Love only is the fulfilling of every Commandment, I cited no particular Scripture, but speake a general sense, which might bee collected from many places." Indeed, throughout the tract, Milton finds charity in the Torah as well as in the gospel. He mentions the deuteronomic divorce law for the first time, in the prefatory address "To the Parlament of England, with the Assembly," as "an ancient and most necessary, most charitable, and yet most injur'd Statute of *Moses*" (*YP*, 2:224). Moses' divorce law, "being a matter of pure charity, is plainly moral, and more now in force then ever" (*YP*, 2:244). Another deuteronomic law (25:5), levirate marriage, appears to contradict the prohibition against marriage with a deceased husband's brother; yet Milton points out that the Mosaic law "preferres a speciall reason of charitie [viz., to raise up seed in the dead brother's name], before an institutive decencie" (*YP*, 2:299). Love, for Milton, is a Christian virtue, but not exclusively so. When Jesus commands us, "Thou shalt love thy neighbor as thyself" (Mark 12:31), he is quoting Leviticus (19:18), although this point seems sometimes to be forgotten or suppressed. For the rabbis, the specific commandments of the Torah were expressions of the law of love; for Paul, of course, love replaced the commandments. In the divorce tracts, Christ's apparently rigorist rejection of the charitable Mosaic law of divorce must be interpreted according to the rule of charity. The law is clear, the gospel obscure.

The scholars mentioned above have all enlarged our understanding of Milton by revealing his essential Paulinism. None of them could possibly imagine a paradise modeled on a benign Mosaic law, even though the sources of such a conception include not only Hebraists such as John Selden and John Lightfoot but also the majority of patristic and reformation expositors and even antinomians. The Hebraic factor in the Edenic books does not annul Milton's radically Pauline theology, nor does Milton's Paulinism cancel his Hebraism. The Hebrew Bible and the Pauline epistles are the principal matrices of Milton's poetry and doctrine respectively. Moreover, if Milton resembles Paul, it is not least because his thought could attain harmonies only through dialectic; some of his poetry derives its power from deep internal struggles over the value and meaning of law, grace, Christian liberty, and the relationships among natural law, the Mosaic law, and the gospel. In the following chapters, I hope to counterbalance the received critical opinion on the middle books of *Paradise Lost* and on the prose tracts of 1643–45 by demonstrating their neglected Hebraic ethos.

CHAPTER ONE

Law and Gospel in *Paradise Lost*

EDENIC-MOSAIC LAW

The famous but thoroughly commonplace list in *De doctrina Christiana* of the many sins contained in Adam and Eve's first act of disobedience concludes with two neglected, explanatory scriptural verses:

> Anyone who examines this sin carefully will admit, and rightly, that it was a most atrocious offence, and that it broke every part of the law. For what fault is there which man did not commit in committing this sin? He was to be condemned both for trusting Satan and for not trusting God; he was faithless, ungrateful, disobedient, greedy, uxorious; she, negligent of her husband's welfare; both of them committed theft, robbery with violence, murder against their children (i.e., the whole human race); each was sacrilegious and deceitful, cunningly aspiring to divinity though thoroughly unworthy of it, proud and arrogant. And so we find in Eccles. vii.29: *God has made man upright, but they have thought up numerous devices*, and in James ii.10: *whoever keeps the whole law, and yet offends in one point, is guilty of all.* (YP, 6:383–84)

Milton sounds urgent and defensive, as if worried that universal woe and death will seem incommensurate with the violation of a single dietary prohibition. Adam and Eve, disobeying one law, become "manifold in sin" (*PL*, 10.16). The primal act is death's equivalent of the original single cell from which all life is said to have derived, fertilized in a flash of lightning as the earth cooled, leaving traces of itself in all its varied progeny. Milton exploits the Preacher's choice of *adam* for "man" in the Hebrew text of Ecclesiastes 7:29 as well as his shift from singular to plural in the second clause. This rabbinic hermeneutic reinscribes the verse in an Edenic context and adds Eve as a sinner by means of binary fission. Rashi explicates *adam* in the verse ("God created Adam perfectly upright"), and both Rashi and the earlier *Midrash Qoheleth Rabbah* explain the use of the plural "they": "when Eve was created from the body of Adam, he became two people."

The paragraph's concluding verse from James asserts the strictly indissoluble unity of the Pentateuchal law, ultimately a rabbinic idea,[1] although its most famous formulations occur in the letters of Paul, who appropriates and transforms it. Taunting the Jewish Christians, less pious than the Pharisees, who yet refuse to ignore the ceremonial law, Paul insists that if they adopt Jewish law they must perform it all.[2] Paul always views the law's unity negatively, as in Galatians 3:6–14, which attempts to illustrate that the law is impossible to keep in every detail and that only faith can save. Milton cites not Paul but rather the conspicuously un-Protestant and un-Pauline James, whose assumption of the law's unity bolsters his positive declaration that works must accompany faith. The law in Milton's Eden was just, efficacious, and easy to keep. The long list of sins in *De doctrina* constitutes a complaint against Adam and Eve, not against the law itself, and so Milton appropriately cites James's positive rather than Paul's negative view of the law's unity.

The aggregate of violations implies a vast network of prohibitions, and the verse from James proves conclusively that, in order to accommodate the proliferation of sin, the simple Edenic law must give way to the complex Mosaic law. Milton's use of James to place the Fall in a Mosaic context is thoroughly commonplace. Thomas Worden describes the "covenant of works, which every carnal man and woman is bound unto by nature, and lives under, even to fulfil it in the exactest measure thereof. This covenant was made with us in the state of innocency, which requires perfect obedience in thought, word, and deed . . . constant, continual obedience to the last breath. . . . So that if a man but fails in one point of the Law of Works, he is guilty of the breach of the whole, *James* 2.10."[3] Worden, unlike Milton, has no interest in a benign prelapsarian law and covenant of works. For him, the threat of the law seems to have existed even from the beginning in paradise, and he elaborately compares the covenant of works to Pharaoh's taskmasters and "those that yet live under it to the Jews in *Egypt*, who were under the power of those task-masters."[4] He cites James 2 as if it were Galatians 3.

Sir Walter Raleigh, in his *History of the World*, merges the unwritten Edenic law and its written reformulation as Mosaic law:

> the Law of the Olde Testament, of which we now speake, is thus defined. The Law is a doctrine, which was first put into the mindes of men by God, and afterwards written by *Moses*, or by him repeated, commanding Holi-nesse and Justice, promising eternall life conditionally, that is, to the observ-ers of the law, and threatning death to those which break the law in the least. For according to S. James, *Whosoever shall keepe the whole, and faileth in one point, is guilty of all.*[5]

Raleigh includes the divine prohibition, the institution of marriage, the naming of animals, and work in the garden among the "Commande-ments which God gave unto *Adam* at the beginning."[6] He distinguishes the Mosaic law's particularity, which it shares with the Edenic prohibi-tion, from natural law's generality.[7] He connects the "Holinesse and Justice" required as a condition of the Edenic promise of eternal life to the ceremonial and judicial part of the Mosaic law: "just, or justice being referred to the Judiciall: holy, or holinesse to the Ceremoniall."[8] Finally, Raleigh's definition of the law, capped by a reference to James 2:10, evokes not only Milton's paragraph on the proliferation of sin at the Fall but also his last and most hostile definition of the Mosaic law, in *De doctrina*: "THE MOSAIC LAW WAS A WRITTEN CODE, CONSISTING OF MANY STIPULATIONS, AND INTENDED FOR THE ISRAELITES ALONE. IT HELD A PROMISE OF LIFE FOR THE OBEDIENT AND A CURSE FOR THE DISOBEDI-ENT" (*YP*, 6:517). Even at his least sympathetic, Milton recognizes that, as a conditional promise of life for obedience with a curse for disobedi-ence, Edenic law can best be understood in the context of Mosaic law.

The Reformers enlist James 2:10 to attack Roman Catholic confidence in the performance of the law and the distinction between deadly and venial sins. Calvin rails against both:

> Let the Papists brag as much as they list, can they say that they have accom-plished the hundreth part of [the commandments]? If they have kept one of Gods commandements, they have offended him in a hundred sins for it: & if there be but one fault committed, though it be never so litle a one, they be faultie in al, according as S. James saith: he that faileth in any one only point, is a breaker of the whole law.[9]

> [T]hey dare so to extenuate the transgression of the law as if it did not merit the death penalty. . . . But they ought to have weighed not simply what the law commands but who it is that commands. For in every little transgression of the divinely commanded law, God's authority is set aside. Do they deem it a small matter to violate his majesty in anything?[10]

Calvin cites James to support his refusal to distinguish between sins, sin-gle and multiple, little and great. Other Protestant exegetes reach a similar conclusion by examining the nature of Adam and Eve's (or in Milton's words "our first parents' ") sin in paradise:

> There cannot be thought any offence greater, for the time, place, persons sinning, occasions of sinning, helpes against sinne, Commandement trans-gressed, no not the matter of the sinne neither. For though the thing materi-ally considered were but eating an apple, a plum, or whatsoever fruit it might be, yet that apple was as it were a Sacrament, a visible profession of their care to forbeare all sinne by forbearing it.[11]

The common expositors, conceiving of the law as an indivisible entity, conclude that it cannot be kept, assimilating James, who decries faith without works, to Paul, who advocates it. If Milton comes closer than most other Reformers to recovering James's intention, it is not so much in his presentation of a Hebraic prelapsarian Eden, where the law is single in its unity and thus easy to keep, nor in his Pauline postlapsarian Eden, where the law multiplies uncontrollably and becomes impossible to keep, but rather precisely at the moment of catastrophe, when the Hebraic and Pauline conceptions of the law coexist in tension, as they do in the text of James. For Milton, James 2:10 realizes its full meaning at the Fall: since Adam and Eve have literally kept the entire law by obeying the single prohibition, their offense in one point makes them guilty of all.

Even the most radical exponents of the Pauline renaissance, citing James 2:10, cannot help conflating Edenic and Mosaic law. Although Bucanus constantly emphasizes discontinuities between dispensations, distinguishing between law and gospel and insisting on justification by faith alone, James encourages him to emphasize continuities instead:

> Saint James saith . . . *He that faileth in one point is guiltie of all* . . . he that breaketh one tittle, hath offended against the Maiestie of the law giver. Whereupon commeth this rule, *The whole law is one copulative*, and . . . the breach of one commaundement draweth with it the neglect and contempt of both tables, yea and of the lawgiver himselfe; because there is but one and the same lawgiver of all the precepts, and the bodie of the law is entire and unseparable.[12]

Bucanus understands the implications of James's verse, though it will remain for Milton to develop them with unprecedented intensity and thoroughness. Authorizing the continuity that runs through all dispensations are the astonishingly conservative formulations of Matthew 5:17–20, here evoked by the condemnation of anyone that "breaketh one tittle": "For verily I say unto you, Till heaven and earth pass, one jot or one tittle shall in no wise pass from the law" (5:18). The body of Edenic law, like that of the Mosaic law, "is entire and unseparable," and the violation of either is an offense against "one and the same lawgiver of all the precepts." Finally, Edenic law, like the Mosaic law, is Decalogic, so that "the breach of one commaundement draweth with it the neglect and contempt of both tables."

Although these interpretations of the law are commonplace, the direction they take in Milton's thought is not. Milton's assumption of the law's unity leads to his conception of Edenic law as Mosaic and Decalogic, and it supports a powerful urge to find continuity among dispensations, however disparate. Milton's own valuation of the law undergoes radical change between the hopeful nationalistic tracts of the 1640s, in which he views England as a second Israel under a benign moral Mosaic law, and the later *De doctrina Christiana*, where a Pauline and Lutheran antipathy to the law reflects disillusionment with human achievement. As will be seen, Milton's changing understanding of the law bears upon the central relations of *Paradise Lost*: between human freedom and God's foreknowledge, paradise and the fallen world, and the poetics of tact and forbearance in the narrator's presentation of Eden before the Fall and the grim, systematic destruction of his creation afterward. A changed conception of the law bears as well on the reader's sense of great powers unresolved below the epic's triumphant surface. The gap between prelapsarian and postlapsarian law and between law and gospel is like the gap between poetry and doctrine: at moments of wide and profound difference, one gazes down into it, and, at moments of integration, one looks across it and imagines ways that it can be bridged.

By examining under separate headings some of the theological and aesthetic implications of Milton's conception of the law's unity and their patristic, rabbinic, and Reformation sources, I shall attempt to give some degree of fixity to an entity, the law, that even within Milton's own poetry and prose is as slippery as it is immense.

THE BENIGN LAW OF PARADISE

Certain episodes in *Paradise Lost* derive their force from the powerful crosscurrents in Milton's work of positive and negative interpretations of the Mosaic law. To Adam who is under it, Edenic law before the Fall is perfectly just (5.552), "This one, this easy charge" (4.421), and "One easy prohibition" (4.433). The great progenitor praises as more delightful than angelic song the discourse of Raphael, whose narrative derives mainly from the Hebrew Bible:

> Thy words
> Attentive, and with more delighted ear
> Divine instructor, I have heard, than when
> Cherubic Songs by night from neighboring Hills
> Aereal Music send.
>
> (5.544–48)

The faint, mildly unsettling echo of earlier lines ranking demonic "discourse more sweet" over demonic song "(For Eloquence the Soul, Song charms the Sense" [2.555–56]) gives way to the more conventional sounds of praise for the Torah, beginning with Milton's own translation of Psalm I: "But in the great / Jehovah's Law is ever his delight. / And in his Law he studies day and night" (4–6). Other psalms profess delight in God's law: "Thy law [lit., *Torah*] is my delight" (119:77). The use of comparison is conventional: "The law [*Torah*] of thy mouth is better unto me than thousands of gold and silver" (119:72). Later in his mealtime symposium, shifting from music to taste, Adam praises even Raphael's words of admonition as the psalmist praises the law: "sweeter thy discourse is to my ear / Than Fruits of Palm-tree" (8.211–12). As Alexander Ross notes "Concerning the Table-behaviour of the Jews": "Let them discourse of the Divine Law, it departeth not from them, but remaineth with them, and they finde it to be sweet and wholsome meate."[13]

Such a view of the law as benign, easy, and just extends from Raphael's first appearance until the moment of his departure. The imperatives of his farewell charge to Adam and Eve, our first parents (1.29, 3.65, 4.6), like those of God's Decalogic command to the angels (5.600ff.), urge love of God and of each other:

> Be strong, live happy, and love, but first of all
> Him whom to love is to obey, and keep
> His great command; take heed lest Passion sway
> Thy Judgment to do aught, which else free Will
> Would not admit; thine and of all thy Sons
> The weal or woe in thee is plac't; beware.
>
> . . . .
>
> . . . stand fast; to stand or fall
> Free in thine own Arbitrement it lies.
> Perfet within, no outward aid require;
> And all temptations to transgress repel.
>
> (8.633–38, 640–43)

From Bishop Newton through A. W. Verity to Hughes, Bush, and Fowler, editors of *Paradise Lost* cite 1 John 5:3 as the sole source of Raphael's "keep / His great command": "For this is the love of God, that we keep his commandments."[14] Certainly the compression of manifold scriptural verses accounts for some of the power of this remarkable blessing-cum-warning, and 1 John 5:3 must be counted among them. The nature of the principal commandment in this Johannine epistle is clear: "And this is his commandment, that we should believe on the name of his Son Jesus Christ, and love one another, as he gave us commandment" (3:24). This sentiment, however, is not uppermost in Raphael's mind right now. Adam has just confessed a disturbing excess of passion for Eve, and Raphael is therefore insisting on the primacy of obedience, just as he did in the very last words of book 6, "remember, and fear to transgress" (912). Unfallen Adam and Eve can have neither knowledge nor need of Christ the redeemer. Alluding to him and thus to the sin that occasioned his redemptive act would introduce determinism into lines that stress instead our innocent progenitors' free will, perfection, and independence of mediatorial intervention. It is noteworthy that Raphael's reference to God's great command puts Milton's editors in mind of a Johannine epistle rather than of the Pentateuch, with whole blocks of chapters, especially in Deuteronomy, reiterating and amplifying the angel's message of obedience to commandment.[15]

Milton's positive portrayal of Edenic-Mosaic law in books 5 to 8 of

Paradise Lost owes much to his divorce tracts, particularly *The Doctrine and Discipline of Divorce*, his most Hebraic work. There Milton presents in a favorable light the Mosaic law that will become the source of Edenic polity, and there he provides a model of that law as easy, charitable, and permissive—more charitable, in fact, than the contemporary Christian interpretation of the law of divorce. He interprets the Deuteronomic divorce law in accord with ancient Jewish theory and practice and defends it against the accusation that it was not approved by God but merely allowed because of the hardness of Jewish hearts, "as if sin had overmaster'd the law of God, to conform her steddy and strait rule to sins crookedness, which is impossible" (*YP*, 2:314). He praises "the exact and perfect law of works, eternal and immutable" (*YP*, 2:318). Of the relation between Christ's words and the Mosaic law, Milton insists, "If we examine over all [Christ's] sayings, we shall find him not so much interpreting the Law with his words, as referring his owne words to be interpreted by the Law" (*YP*, 2:301). This important statement reverses the direction of typology from New Testament to Old and goes beyond conservatism to assert the originary power of the Hebrew Bible.

In *The Doctrine and Discipline of Divorce*, the Mosaic law rather than the Son incarnates deity:

> The hidden wayes of [God's] providence we adore & search not; but the law is his reveled will, his complete, his evident, and certain will; herein he appears to us as it were in human shape, enters into cov'nant with us, swears to keep it, binds himself like a just lawgiver to his own prescriptions, gives himself to be understood by men, *judges and is judg'd*, measures and is commensurat to right reason. (*YP*, 2:292; my emphasis)

This most Hebraic work defines the law as God's express image, and the Sinai theophany is seen as an act of divine condescension and accommodation. The most resonant phrases describe God as if he were a just king, who judges his subjects and is judged in turn by them. One is reminded that another deuteronomic law (17:14–20), limiting the rights of kings, figures in *The Tenure of Kings and Magistrates*: "that Law of *Moses* was to the King expresly, *Deut.* 17. not to think so highly of himself above his Brethren" (*YP*, 3:205). Archbishop Whitgift had reflected on the political danger following from too wide use of such verses as these from the Hebrew Bible: "To be short, all things must be transformed: lawyers must cast away their huge volumes and multitude of cases, and content themselves with the books of Moses." Slavish devotion to the precise wording of the Old Testament "tendeth to the overthrowing of states and of commonwealths."[16]

Milton is of course one of the notable agents of a transformation that Whitgift would have deplored. If even the heavenly king submits to human judgment, how dare Charles refuse? In the *Defence of the People of England*, Milton reinscribes the phrase "judges and is judg'd" in a specifically rabbinic context. Here he responds to Salmasius, who has attempted to elicit talmudic support for virtually unlimited royal prerogative:

> . . . in yet another ill-omened undertaking, you begin to give lessons on the Talmud. In a desire to prove that a king is not judged you show from the Codex of Sanhedrin that "the king neither judges nor is judged," but this conflicts with the request of that people who sought a king for the very reason that he might judge them. You try in vain to cover this over, and tell us indeed that it should be understood of kings who ruled after the captivity; but listen to Maimonides, who gives this definition of the difference between the kings of Israel and Judah: "the descendants of David judge and are judged," but says neither is true of the Israelites. (*YP*, 4:354)

In *De Synedriis*, a work of scholarship on rabbinica that refers many hundreds of times to Tractate Sanhedrin, John Selden, Milton's principal source of Jewish learning,[17] reconciles different opinions on whether that court had the power to pass judgment on the king's person. He treats in a number of different contexts the topic "Rex Israelis non judicabat, nec judicabatur, Rex Judae & judicabat & judicabatur."[18] Many times he cites both the crucial discussion in the Talmud as well as in Maimonides' *Mishneh Torah* to prove that the distinction between the kings of Israel and Judah is based on the haughtiness or violence of the former and the humility of the latter. Thus, Rabbi Joseph (in Sanhedrin 19a) holds that the kings of Israel, violent and disobedient of the Torah, are kept from judging and being judged;[19] and Maimonides emphasizes this point:

> Reges familiae Davidicae & judicabant & judicabantur: Etiam testimonium adversus eos praebere licuit. At vero de regibus Israel decrevere sapientes, eos nec judicare nec judicari, nec testimonium praebere nec in ipsos praeberi testimonium, quoniam corda eorum superba fuere, nec aliud inde manaret praeter scandalum atque abolitionem institutorum legis. [marginal note: Maimonid. Halach. *Melacim*, cap. 3. & *Sanhedrin*, cap. 2][20]

> [The kings of the House of David both judged and were judged, and it was lawful to give testimony against them. About the kings of Israel, however, the rabbis decreed that they should neither judge nor be judged, and that they should not offer testimony nor testimony be offered against them, since their hearts were proud, lest nothing spring therefrom except scandal and the abrogation of the institutes of the law.]

Milton's most Hebraic prose flashes forth from those tracts of the 1640s that present England with a vision of itself as a second Israel, a holy community capable of shaping and improving its destiny. Against the argument that a partner in an inconvenient marriage display Christian patience and submit to God's will as expressed in Christ's uncompromising sentence of indissolubility, Milton in *The Doctrine and Discipline of Divorce* bases his radical appeal to freedom on the deuteronomic law of divorce. Milton's positive conception of the Mosaic law bears upon the middle books of *Paradise Lost*, where a creator and not a redeemer concentrates blessing and achievement on independent humanity.

The virtual inclusion of the Decalogue in the Edenic prohibition (Gen. 2:17) permits Milton in *Paradise Lost* to extend Eden's temporal reach as far as Sinai, an advantage for a poet whose paradise is uniquely dynamic and whose principal characters enjoy a longer than average tenure in the state of perfection. A survey of sources should indicate not only the commonplace nature of Milton's idea that the prohibition in Eden constitutes an embryonic Mosaic law but also its adaptability to various points of view. Though the idea appears frequently in a variety of contexts, it has never before been traced and thus never been recognized as a shaping force in *Paradise Lost*. John Salkeld, in his seventeenth-century *Treatise of Paradise*, comments on Genesis 2:17: "This commandement was given to *Adam*, as the first principall foundation and ground from whence all other lawes were derived, and in which all the ten Commandments be virtually included: so that as *Adam* was the first beginning of mankinde, so this was the first ground of all other lawes."[21]

Fourteen centuries before Salkeld, in an attempt to prove that the Jews are not God's chosen people and that the Gentiles are admissible to God's law, Tertullian exploited for an anti-Jewish purpose the idea that the violation of the Edenic prohibition constitutes a violation of the ten commandments:

> God . . . gave to all nations the selfsame law. . . . For in the beginning of the world He gave to Adam himself and Eve a law, that they were not to eat of the fruit of the tree planted in the midst of paradise; but that, if they did contrariwise, by death they were to die. Which law had continued enough for them, had it been kept. For in this law given to Adam we recognize in embryo all the precepts which after-wards sprouted forth when given through Moses. . . . For the primordial law was given to Adam and Eve in paradise, as the womb of all the precepts of God. In short, if they had loved the Lord their God, they would not have contravened his precept; if they had habitually loved their neighbour—that is, themselves—they would not have believed the persuasion of the serpent, and thus would not have committed murder upon themselves, by falling from immortality, by contravening God's precept; from theft also they would have abstained, if they had not stealthily tasted of the fruit of the tree . . . nor would they have been made partners with the falsehood-asseverating devil, by believing him that they

would be "like God"; and thus they would not have offended God either, as their Father, who had fashioned them from clay of the earth, as out of the womb of a mother. . . . Therefore, in this general and primordial law of God, the observance of which, in the case of the tree's fruit, He had sanctioned, we recognize enclosed all the precepts specially of the posterior Law, which germinated when disclosed at their proper times. . . . God's law was anterior even to Moses, and was not first given in Horeb, or in Sinai and in the desert, but was more ancient; existing first in paradise, subsequently re-formed for the patriarchs, and so again for the Jews, at definite periods.[22]

For Tertullian, as for Milton, the white light of the original prohibition in Eden breaks up into countless refractive prohibitions of every color, a spectrum of offenses. Milton hints at the Decalogic nature of the prohibition when, just after the Fall, Adam tells Eve: "if such pleasure be / In things to us forbidden, it might be wish'd, / For this one Tree had been forbidden ten" (9.1024–26). After violating the easy terms of the single prohibition, Adam and Eve, in the narrator's words, are "manifold in sin" (10.16). Similarly, the serpent tempting Eve in Joseph Beaumont's *Psyche*, berating her for faintheartedness, declares:

> For my part, did ten thousand Mandates grow
> Thick in my way, to barre me from this Tree,
> Through all I'd break, and so would you, if once
> Your Heart were fir'd by my Experience.[23]

To break one commandment is to violate the entire body of the law, and one sin becomes the equivalent of ten or ten thousand. As St. Bruno observes, ten is "that number in which all numbers are contained. For number does not progress beyond ten, but that number revolved upon itself includes all other numbers."[24]

As Nicholas Gibbens demonstrates through exhaustive analysis of Adam and Eve's violation of each of the ten commandments, "[sin] consisted of manie branches: for sinne is so fruitfull and so sociable, that it will never goe alone, nor be alone."[25] For the sake of brevity, here are his comments on the breaking of the first commandment:

> . . . the first [sin] that appeareth was unthankefulnesse to God. The Lord requireth above all things a thankefull minde for his benefits received, and obedience to his word, which is the exercise thereof. For which respect unto *Adam* he enjoyed obedience, in abstaining from the fruit, which if he had zelously performed, he had reproved his wife for her transgression, and not obeyed her voice; as she likewise had chastised the Serpent, at the first sound of his rebellious words, setting before their eyes, the fulnes of Gods mercie and liberalitie bestowed alreadie on them. This unthankfulnes in them brought forth pride, in that they did not give the glorie unto God, but

thought their excellencies were worthie of all the gifts they had, and more also, if they could attaine unto them. Pride was the mother of ambition, whereby they sought to be advanced above their calling and estate. All these were sinnes against the first commandement. From these did spring neglect of Gods true worship; infidelitie, in mistrusting of his goodnes, in doubting of his threatning; contempt of the word of God; violating thereby the whole worship of God injoyned them.[26]

No one exceeds Bishop Ussher in the systematic thoroughness of his argument that although "God tryed their obedience in that fruit especially, yet were there many other most grievous sinnes, which in desiring and doing of this they did commit: insomuch that we may observe therein the grounds of the breach in a manner of every one of the ten Commandements." By subdividing each of the ten commandments, so that they fill the crisscrossed lines of some vast ledger page of sin, Ussher seems to be tempting the reader to find other patterns besides the Decalogue, such as the world, the flesh, and the devil, or the lust of the flesh, of the eyes, and the pride of life. "*What*," he asks, "*were the breach of the third* [commandment]?":

> First, presumption in venturing to dispute of Gods truth, and to enter into communication with Gods enemy, or a beast who appeared unto them, touching the word of God; with whom no such conference ought to have been entertained.
>
> Secondly, reproachfull blasphemy: by subscribing to the sayings of the Devill, in which he charged God with lying, and envying their good estate.
>
> Thirdly, superstitious conceit of the fruit of the tree; imagining it to have that vertue which God never put into it: as if by the eating thereof, such knowledge might be gotten as Satan perswaded.
>
> Fourthly, want of that zeale in *Adam* for the glory of God, which he ought to have shewed against his wife, when he understood she had transgressed Gods commandement.[27]

Rereading Milton's famous paragraph on the proliferation of sin, this time in the context of other lists such as Ussher's, he no longer sounds urgent but rather lukewarm, deficient in zeal—that is, until one remembers that the paragraph is famous only because its author returned to the theme in *Paradise Lost*. Zealous but inglorious Miltons, deficient only in art, abound during the Reformation, and the theme of lost paradise fills their biblical commentaries on Genesis and their treatises contrasting law and gospel, the covenant of works and of grace. There some of them project longing for a lost world where human beings were strong, independent, and able to achieve their own salvation. Both the topics and the tenor of most of these works presuppose profound doctrinal antipathy to the Mosaic law. As early as the *protevangelium* (Gen. 3:15), biblical expositors compare the law invidiously with the gospel, and the treatises mostly emphasize salvation by faith in Christ alone. Yet by confining their longing to an irretrievable paradise and by distinguishing carefully between the benign Mosaic law and covenant of works in Eden and their malignant postlapsarian transformation, even antinomians could praise an Edenic polity consistently regarded as Mosaic. More artfully than his Reformation predecessors and contemporaries, but as strenuously, Milton preserves the gap between the Pauline interpretations of the Mosaic law that come into play with the Fall and the operations of that law in Eden, where no stigma has yet attached itself to it.

William Whately's description of Adam and Eve in Eden is fraught with ideological implication: we cannot obey the law, though our first parents could; the terrible difference between us and them; human ingratitude in the face of divine benefits. Yet gazing across the unbridgeable gap that separates him from Eden, even Whately evinces a nostalgia in excess of ideology:

Now consider we the benefits God had bestowed upon them before their fall, the making of them after his own Image, in knowledge, righteousnesse and true holinesse, with a most beautiful, strong, swift, healthie and comely body, free from all danger of sicknesse, death, or other misery; giving them dominion over all creatures, planting so excellent a place for them as Paradise, and granting them the use of all the trees, and that of life, and putting on them so pleasant a service as that of dressing and keeping the Garden besides the hope and assurance of Eternall life upon condition of their obedience, of which Paradise it selfe and the tree of life were signes unto them. For if wee should live the life of glory by obeying the Law, so should they have done, seeing they also were under the same Covenant of workes that we be under.[28]

Though Nicholas Gibbens demonstrated our first parents' violation of each of the ten commandments, he could demonstrate with equal proficiency unfallen man's capacity to keep perfectly both tables of the law. Manifold expositions such as this of the original "human face divine" must surely have shaped the celebrations of human potential in the radical millenarianism of some of Milton's contemporaries. Gibbens celebrates man as the radiant image of God's glory, body and soul:

. . . that noble forme, wherby it was indued with life and sence, and became to have such excellent proportions, so marveilous, so beautifull, as no creature in the world may be compared with it: and the Scriptures themselves doe so greatly praise it. This very perfection of the bodie, which is as it were the perfection of all visible creatures, is of the image of Gods perfection. . . . Moreover, the sound temperature thereof, by which it would have continued for ever without corruption, carieth the savour of Gods eternitie. The strength of the bodie, wherein it was created, did evidently beare shew of the power of the Creator. . . . [I]n reason, knowledge, wisedome and memorie, which is the very expresse character of his wisdom. Of the which without doubt he received a marveilous great measure, especially of heavenly wisdome (as it were by reflection of spiritual light) in the knowledge of his Creator. . . . *[I]n righteousnes, that is in justice which concerneth the creatures, and is the summe of the second table of the Law, resembling thereby the justice, mercie and bountifulnes of God. . . . [I]n holinesse, (which is the Content of the first table) as pertaining to the worship of God, being prest, apt, and able to performe whatsoever of a creature might be expected.* (my emphasis)[29]

The Fall in Genesis 3 awakens Gibbens's imagination of destruction, and his recitation of the violated ten commandments and their endless ramifications sounds compulsive, an angry lament over loss, made more violent by the forbearance and tact that he exercised in his description of paradise: "As *Adam* was before in the similitude of God, so is he now of the likenes of the divell."[30] The language of release and disorder is Pauline, as is the paradigm: the law is a minister of wrath, death, and condemnation, but grace abounds, and Christ's sacrifice satisfies justice. Although Gibbens describes Adam at the moment of sin, his real subject—one can hardly call it a subtext—is humankind under the Mosaic law:

And for the bodilie death . . . in deed it was fulfilled, in that [Adam] was in bondage unto death, for as much as death it selfe began to wound their bodies in the day they sinned, by hunger, cold, nakednes, subjection to mortalitie, losse of native beautie and such like, that the verie life continued in so manie miseries, may seeme to be not life but a prolonged death. Thus deepe did *Adam* drinke of the wine of the wrath of God. That he died not the extremity of death, behold how grace aboundeth in the Lord; *Adam* now by sinne was made the servant unto sinne, the wages whereof is death and condemnation, the horrible paines and endlesse woes whereof no creature can endure. Wherfore when Adam must die, the justice of God requiring it, the Lord in his endles mercie translated this death unto his Sonne our Saviour, who willingly for the love hee bare to man tooke on him to indure the punishment, and making his soule an offering for sinne, the justice of God by him was fullie satisfied, the soule of *Adam* reserved from death.[31]

Like so many other nearly anonymous Reformation expositors, Gibbens is less obviously derivative when he celebrates the honeymoon in paradise before the Fall: "The body was of excellent forme, beautifull throughout, pleasant to behold, needing no clothing, either to defend cold, or to cover shame."[32] The purity of Gibbens's longing begets something resembling poetry: "The sound temperature [of the body] . . . by which it would have continued for ever without corruption, carieth the savour of Gods eternitie." This conjunction of the scientific and the spiritual evokes a description by Milton at his most Hebraic. In the Trinity Manuscript, in Milton's own hand, are four outlines for tragedies on the theme of "Paradise Lost." The third draft begins: "Moses prologuizes, recounting how he assumed his true bodie, that it corrupts not because of his [being] with god in the mount declares the like of Enoch and Eliah, besides the purity of yᵉ pl[ace] that certaine pure winds, dues, and clouds preserve it from corruption whence [ex]horts to the sight of god, tells they cannot se Adam in the state of innocence by reason of thire sin."[33] This connects the Mosaic and Edenic dispensations, suggesting that the Sinai theophany offered Moses the major benefits available originally to unfallen Adam, the sight of God and physical incorruptibility.

The Mosaic narrator of the prologue insists on the holiness and preservation of Moses' body. The explanation for this preservation depends on a conjunction of spiritual privilege and physical purity similar to that which appears elsewhere in Milton's work—in the *Apology for Smectymnuus*, where the young Milton aims to number himself among the redeemed who accompany "the Lamb with those celestial songs to others inapprehensible, but not to those who were not defiled with women" (*YP*, 1:892), and in *Paradise Lost*, figuratively, if not literally, where the narrator in heaven, like Moses on the mount, has "presum'd, / An Earthly Guest, and drawn Empyreal Air" (7.13–14) and where he struggles to soar in spite of years and adverse climate. When characters in Milton's poetry, including the narrator, declaim upon the power of chastity, the advantages of temperate diet, and the dignity of physical labor, they usually do so in a way that affirms the interdependence of body and spirit. More to the point, Milton's theological monism, explicitly derived from the Hebrew text of Genesis, accords full reverence to the body.

A possible source of Milton's sketch is the treatise *De Termino Vitae*, published in 1639 by Menasseh ben Israel, the Amsterdam rabbi whose mission to England culminated in the resettlement of the Jews. The most successful of all of Menasseh's Latin works, *De Termino Vitae* was his response to a theological problem propounded by Jan van Beverwyck (Beverovicius) to some of his friends: whether the span of human life is accidental or whether it is predetermined. The interchange of letters on this topic, published as *Epistolica Quaestio de Vitae Termino, fatali an mobili* (Dordrecht, 1634), included contributions by Hugo Grotius, whom Milton met in 1638, and by Gerhard Vos, father of Isaac Vossius, who admired Milton's anti-Salmasian polemic.[34] Menasseh's work, published independently, with a laudatory poem by Beverwyck, took the attitude that the span of life depends on constitutional, temperamental, and climatic influences. Correspondences between the treatise and Milton's sketch of a prologue include the combination of scientific and miraculous explanations for the preservation of Moses' body, the suggestion that Moses on the mount was afforded the same benefits as Adam in paradise, and the corollary idea that these benefits were taken away as a result of sin:

> . . . if *Adam* had not sinn'd, (tho his Body was compounded of a mixture of the four Elements) he might have liv'd a great many Years longer, and at last his Soul, together with his Body, might have been translated into Heav'n, as it happen'd to *Enoch* and *Elias*, and all others would have enjoyed the like privilege who had liv'd in perfect obedience to the Law. Hence the *Rabbins* believe, that when the Law was given to *Moses*, God plac'd the Israelites in the same State that Adam was in before the Fall. But that happy Condition lasted not long.[35]

Menasseh offers the scientific theory of radical moisture to explain the "augmentation" of human life, and he connects this theory with Moses' sustenance on Sinai as a result of obedience to divine law:

> Our Life may be prolong'd by observing God's Laws, and meditating thereon; so that if any one would perfectly and constantly observe the Law, it is probable that (like *Elias*) he would never die. For I believe this may be miraculously done in two ways. First by preserving the radical Moisture in its due State. Secondly, by preserving the Vertue of our Food. As to the First, it is confirmed by the Example of *Moses*, who liv'd forty Days in Mount Sinai, without Meat or Drink; then the Divine Law (which was instead of Food) preserv'd the Radical Moisture in its due Vigor and Strength.[36]

Both Milton's sketch of a prologue and Menasseh's treatise, in their concern for the condition of a human body, constitute a Hebraic affirmation of the indivisibility of body and soul. Moreover, against the Pauline inference that the Mosaic law, on the basis of which no one could be justified by works, is a law unto death (Rom. 8:2–3, Gal. 3:21), the sketch and the treatise agree with the talmudic insistence that, to the one who performs it, the Torah is *sam hayyim*, a medicine of life.[37] Participation in the divine law preserves the radical moisture necessary for life. Good works thus supplement nature, as the Mosaic law supplements natural law. It is quite a jump from Menasseh and Milton to Nicholas Gibbens, one of countless expositors of the Pauline Renaissance. Yet all three of them attribute physical incorruptibility to a sinless condition: Moses' association with the divine presence on the mount, and the "sound temperature" that carries "the savour of Gods eternitie" and that, except for sin, would have preserved Adam's body from corruption forever.

JOHN BALL AND JOHN MILTON ON
THREE ASPECTS OF THE LAW

John Ball, a Puritan divine whose *Treatise of Faith* was very popular in New England, untiringly preached the futility of works and the necessity of grace for salvation. But, in describing the benign covenant of works in paradise before the Fall, he emphasized free human obedience. With the core of Leviticus 18:5 as his central text ("*Doe this and live*"), he conflates Mosaic and Edenic law:

> This Covenant God made with man without a Mediatour: for there needed no middle person to bring man into favour and friendship with God, because man did beare the image of God, and had not offended: nor to procure acceptance to mans service, because it was pure and spotlesse. God did love man being made after his Image: and promised to accept of his obedience performed freely, willingly, intirely, according to his Commandement. The forme of this Covenant stood in the speciall Promise of good to be received from justice as a reward for his work, *Doe this and live*: and the exact and rigid exaction of perfect obedience in his own person, without the least spot or failing for matter or manner. The good that God promised was in it[s] kind a perfect systeme of good, which was to be continued so long as he continued obedient, which because it might be continued in the eye of creating power for ever, we call it happinesse, life, and everlasting happinesse.[38]

Ball "lived by faith" (*DNB*) and associated the relics of Roman Catholicism left in the national church with the ceremonial Mosaic law. He and Milton sound most alike when they lament fallen humankind, overwhelmed by evil and desperately in need of Christ's mediation. Ball's reflections on lost paradise under the law are numbingly similar to those in countless other treatises on grace and strikingly different from the passionate virtuosity of Milton's achievement in the Edenic books of his epic. But the differences that count here are those of poetics rather than doctrine. Three formulations especially make Ball's excerpt typical of countless Reformation treatises. Since all three are weighted with the gravity of implication for Milton's poetics, they deserve to be considered separately: "had not offended," "*Doe this and live*," and the redundantly Pauline "exact and rigid exaction of perfect obedience." For Ball, as for Milton, Christ was unnecessary in paradise "because man did beare the image of God, and had not offended." The difference is that, while both the Miltonic bard and Raphael in books 5 to 8 celebrate "the human face divine," they exercise strenuous tact, omitting references to the offense that will efface the image. Ball's "not [yet] offended" hints at sin and at Christ's redemption as compensation for the Fall. It introduces disunity to the surface of the text, contaminating perfection with sin, law with gospel. Milton manages to get the statue of "life in a great symbolic attitude"[39] clean away from the marble and thus to depict the state of perfection with an unmatched purity of longing.

When Protestant exegetes consider Genesis 1:26, the creation of man in God's image, their arguments usually lead inexorably to the loss of that image in the Fall and to its recovery through Christ. To emphasize past loss and future redemption is to blunt the immediacy of creation. Calvin, in the *Institutes*, cannot contemplate the original nobility of humankind without the contrast of contemporary fallen human nature. "That primal worthiness cannot come to mind without the sorry spectacle of our foulness and dishonor presenting itself by way of contrast, since in the person of the first man we have fallen from our original condition."[40] He presents the paradigm even more clearly in the argument to his commentary on creation:

> He [Adam] was endued with understanding and reason, that hee differing from brute beastes, might meditate and thinke upon the better life; and that he might go the right way unto God, whose image he bare. After this followeth the fall of Adam, whereby he separated himselfe from God, whereby it came to passe that he was deprived of all perfection. Thus Moses describeth man to be voide of all goodnesse, blinde in minde, perverse in heart, corrupte in every parte, and under the guilte of eternall death. But straite after he addeth the historie of the restoring, where Christ shineth with the benefite of redemption.[41]

Had the narrator of the epic's middle books emphasized Christian redemption occasioned by original sin, he would have degraded our first parents and determined their fall. Had he acknowledged from the outset the irrecoverability of prelapsarian paradise, instead of recovering it by recreating it, his readers would never have known the paradise whose loss can only be felt if its presence can be felt as well. The deep nostalgia to which the Miltonic bard gives way only after the Fall characterizes even Luther's initial account of innocence and paradise:

> When we must discuss Paradise now . . . let us speak of it as a historical Paradise which once was and no longer exists. We are compelled to discuss man's state of innocence in a similar way. We can recall with a sigh that it has been lost; we cannot recover it in this life.[42]

For Ball and Milton, as for most Reformation theologians, Leviticus 18:5 is the epitome of both the Edenic and Mosaic laws. Defining the law and the covenant of works as opposed to the gospel and the covenant of grace, the verse emphasizes conditionality and obedience. Thomas Cartwright sums it up neatly in his short catechism, whose most striking assertion is that the law cannot possibly be performed:

Q. What are the partes of [the Bible]?

A. The lawe & the ghospell, otherwyse called the Covenant of Woorkes and the Covenant of grace.

Q. Wiche was the fyrst?

A. The lawe, for it was geven to Adam befor his faule.

Q. What dothe ye Lawe or covenant crave of us?

A. All such duties as wer Requyred of Adam in his innocency, and requyred of all synce his faule.

Q. What is the somme of the law?

A. do this, and thowe shalt lyve.

Q. What is ment by do this?

A. Keepe all my commandementes boothe in thought woord and deede.

Q. Is any man habull to keepe the lawe?

A. No not in ye least poynt.[43]

Although Cartwright goes on to discuss the law's charge to the soul, which Adam can keep in every point, his interest lies, not in the benign original institution in Eden, but in the imperative made impossible by the Fall. This makes the gospel both inevitable and indispensable.

Bishop Ussher's dialogic formulation stresses the similarity between the prohibition in Eden and the Mosaic law:

> *What was the summe of this Law?*
> Doe this, and thou shalt live: if thou doest it not, thou shalt die the death.
> *What is meant by, Doe this?*
> Keepe all my commandements in thought, word, and deed.
> *What is ment by life, promised to those that should keepe all the Commandements?*
> The reward of blessednesse and everlasting life, *Levit.* 18.5.
> *What is meant by Death threatned to those that should transgresse?*
> In this world the curse of God, and death, with manifold miseries both of body and soule: and (where this curse is not taken away) everlasting death . . . in the world to come, *Deut.* 27.26 & 29.19, 20. & 32.22. *Levit.* 26. *Deut.* 28.[44]

John Preston explicitly conflates Eden and Sinai. "The *Covenant* of Workes runs in these termes, *Doe this, and thou shalt live*, and I will be thy God. This is the *Covenant* that was made with *Adam*, and the *Covenant* that is expressed by *Moses* in the Morall Law, *Doe this, and live*."[45]

Gulielmus Bucanus cites the conditional formula of Leviticus 18:5 ("which if a man do, he shall live in them") to underscore the superiority of the gospel's free and unconditional promises.

> [The law and gospel] differ in the forme or difference of the promises: for the promises in the law of eternal life & temporall benefits are conditional. That is they require the condition of perfect fulfilling the law, as a cause, as for

example, *If thou do these things thou shalt live in them*, where the particle, If, for because, expresseth the cause, for our obedience is required in the law as a cause. But the promises of the gospel are free, & are not given because of fulfilling the law, but freely for Christs sake.[46]

Milton's positive view of Leviticus 18:5 in a variety of contexts underscores a Hebraism that prefers both the conditional over the absolute and straightforward, unassisted human obedience over the displacements of vicarious atonement. Milton's ringing pronouncements on human freedom in the chapter of *De doctrina* entitled "OF DIVINE DECREE" (1.3) derive from the Hebrew Bible and are shaped by its ethos. It is "a rule given by God himself" that his promises must always be understood in the light of "the condition upon which the decree depends." "So we must conclude that God made no absolute decrees about anything which he left in the power of men, for men have freedom of action. The whole course of scripture shows this" (*YP*, 6:155). Eleven of the twelve biblical examples in this paragraph come from the Hebrew Bible, and it is clear that law rather than gospel has shaped Milton's thinking on the general divine decrees, whose essence is their conditionality.

Milton's identification of the Edenic-Mosaic law with the divine decrees underscores theodicy's heavy stakes: to make the law in Eden perfect. God's general decrees, perfect and conditional, must permit human freedom; "otherwise we should make [God] responsible for all the sins ever committed, and should make demons and wicked men blameless" (*YP*, 6:165). As a body of divine decrees, the Mosaic law must also be perfect; otherwise, "it makes God the direct author of sin. For although he bee not made the authour of what he silently permitts in his providence, yet in his law, the image of his will, when in plaine expression he constitutes and ordaines a fact utterly unlawfull, what wants hee to authorize it, and what wants that to be the author?" (*YP*, 2:655). More interesting here than the "author/authorize" pun is the distinction between God's providence and his law, reformulated in the epic as "eternal providence" and "the ways of God." In the Hebrew Bible the way (lit., *halakhah*) is the law: "Ye shall walk in the way which the Lord your God hath commanded you, that you may live, and that it may be well with you" (Deut. 5:30; see also 8:6, 10:12, and 11:22). It is possible to understand the relationship between God's providence and his ways in the light of other coordinates in the epic: foreknowledge and free will (divine as well as human, for God's law is "the image of his will"), birthright and merit, Christian doctrine and Hebrew poetry, the plan of providential salvation history under the gospel and the contingent, spontaneous gestures of choice under the law. Milton joins the polity of Eden and Israel within the context of these coordinates:

[God] knew that Adam would, of his own accord, fall. Thus it was certain that he would fall, but it was not necessary, because he fell of his own accord and that is irreconcilable with necessity. Similarly God foreknew that the Israelites would lapse from their true religion to alien Gods: Deut. xxxi.16. If their lapse was a necessity, caused by God's foreknowledge, then it was exceedingly unjust of him to threaten to afflict them with numerous evils, xxxi.17. It was useless for him to order a song to be written, xxxi.19, as a witness for him against the children of Israel, if in fact they sinned by necessity. But God's foreknowledge did not really have any external effect, any more than that of Moses did, xxxi.27. Indeed God testifies that he foreknew they would sin of their own accord and as a result of their own impulses. (*YP*, 6:165)

Paradise Lost is a new song of Moses, prompted by a divine spirit, witnessing for God's providence and his ways with his children.

The epitome of the law in Leviticus ("do this and live") defines not only Edenic and Mosaic but also angelic polity:

The matter or object of the divine plan was that angels and men alike should be endowed with free will, so that they could either fall or not fall. Doubtless God's actual decree bore a close resemblance to this, so that all the evils which have since happened as a result of the fall could either happen or not: if you stand firm, you will stay; if you do not, you will be thrown out: if you do not eat, you will live; if you do, you will die. (*YP*, 6:163)

The epic also binds humans and angels to what is essentially the single levitical decree. In his confidence, Adam can scarcely credit Raphael's conditional formulation, "*if ye be found / Obedient*" (5.513–14 and 501). He assures the angel: "we never shall forget to love / Our maker, and obey him whose command / Single, is yet so just" (5.550–52). Later, in the same book, Raphael models his account of the metaphorical begetting of the Son upon the Sinai theophany. The angels stand in circles around God's holy mountain just as the Israelites did when God proclaimed the law. Conditional reward and punishment as well as the sum of the two tables of the Decalogue, "the love of God and of our neighbor" (*YP*, 6:640), are compressed into a few short lines:

> Under his great Vice-gerent Reign abide
> United as one individual Soul
> For ever happy: him who disobeys
> Mee disobeys.
>
> (5.609–12)

In the divorce tracts, Milton asserts his faith in human beings as agents capable of exercising choice to improve their condition. There the Mosaic law of divorce offers escape from tyrannical custom, and the levitical epitome of the law is regarded in an entirely positive light: "*Moses* every where commends his lawes, preferrs them before all of other nations, and warrants them to be the way of life and safety to all that walke therein, *Levit.* 18" (*YP*, 2:654). Milton refers to Leviticus 18:5 in a remarkable passage in *Tetrachordon*, part of a thoroughgoing critique of Paul that has been overlooked entirely by critics and scholars. With a sympathy unmatched in other Reformation texts, Milton sees the entire verse rather than the four-word imperative "do this and live" to which it is universally reduced: "Ye shall therefore keep my statutes, and my judgments: which if a man do, he shall live in them: I am the Lord."

> The statutes and judgements of the Lord, which without exception are often told us to be such, as doing wee may live by them, are doubtles to be counted the rule of knowledge and of conscience. *For I had not known lust*, saith the Apostle, *but by the law*. But if the law come downe from the state of her incorruptible majesty to grant lust his boon, palpably it darkns and confounds both knowledge and conscience; it goes against the common office of all goodnes and friendlinesse, which is at lest to counsel and admonish; it subverts the rules of all sober education; and is it selfe a most negligent debaushing tutor. (*YP*, 2:654)

Reading Paul in the light of the Torah, Milton's position here is not far from that of Paul's original Jewish Christian opponents, who believed that only those under the Mosaic law are free from the dominion of sin. Paul of course claims that precisely the opposite is the case: sin will have no dominion over the faithful, since they are not under law but under grace. Against the argument that the Mosaic permission of divorce was a temporary concession to Israelite hard-heartedness, Milton contends throughout the divorce tracts that the purpose of the entire Mosaic law is to remove sin entirely, not merely to limit it. Law and sin can never coexist. Their antipathy is absolute, like that between order and chaos:

> It is an absurdity to say that law can measure sin, or moderate sin; sin is not a predicament [i.e., a state of being] to be measur'd and modify'd, but is alwaies an excesse. The least sinne that is, exceeds the measure of the largest law that can be good; and is as boundlesse as that vacuity beyond the world. If once it square to the measure of Law, it ceases to be an excesse, and consequently ceases to be a sinne; or else law conforming it selfe to the obliquity of sin, betraies it selfe to be not strait, but crooked, and so immediatly no law. And the improper conceit of moderating sin by law will appeare, if wee can imagin any lawgiver so senselesse as to decree that so farre a man may steale, and thus farre be drunk, that moderately he may cozen, and moderatly commit adultery. (*YP*, 2:657)

For the Pauline antipathy of law and gospel, Milton substitutes the Hebraic antipathy of law and sin.

Even when seeming to endorse Paul, Milton actually provides a detailed refutation of his arguments on the law. In Romans 7, cited explicitly by Milton, Paul spells out his notions of freedom from the law and the necessary separation of the gentiles from the Jewish community. Central to these ideas is the absolute incommensurability of law and gospel: since Christians, like Christ, have "died to sin," they have left the realm of law where sin holds sway. If anyone wants to keep the Mosaic law in any sense whatever, for that person Christ died in vain. Where Romans 7 asserts discontinuity between dispensations, Milton, drawing on Leviticus 18:5, identifies God's statutes and judgments under the Mosaic law with "the rule of knowledge and conscience." Torah thus chimes in harmoniously with natural law's twin progeny of love and the soul, knowledge and virtue (*YP*, 1:892), and with the two parts of Christian doctrine, "THE KNOWLEDGE OF GOD . . . AND CHARITY" (*YP*, 6:637). The passage from *Tetrachordon*, like all the divorce tracts and the other great prose works of 1643–45, *Of Education* and the *Areopagitica*, demonstrates the power of Milton's synthesizing imagination, which discovers and creates important continuities among natural law, the Mosaic law, and the gospel.

For Paul, the effect of the law is to intensify disastrously the dominion of sin: "the law entered, that the offense might abound" (Rom. 5:20). Romans 7 dramatizes Paul's failure to find righteousness under the law and his subsequent denunciation of it. Paul had an apocalyptic view of the law as a monolithic totality and could thus dismiss it in toto for a variety of reasons, not all of them perfectly compatible: because it is impossible to perform the entire law (the quantitative answer); because performing the law itself estranges—doing it is worse than not doing it (the qualitative answer); because of his exclusivist soteriology (only by faith in Christ, therefore not by law); and because of the exigencies of the gentile mission.[47] In context, Paul's "I had not known lust but by the law" (7:7) seems to mean not that he would not have understood lust without the law, but that he would not have experienced it.[48] He has just asserted that "the motions of sins, which were by the law, did work in our members to bring forth fruit unto death" (7:5). He will go on immediately to assert that "sin, taking occasion by the commandment, wrought in me all manner of concupiscence" (7:8). All of this is calculated to evoke in his readers a horror of the law.

In the passage from *Tetrachordon*, Milton accommodates Romans 7:7 to the statutes and judgments of Leviticus 18:5, under the Mosaic law's rule of knowledge and conscience: "*For I had not known lust*, saith the Apostle, *but by the law*. But if the law come downe from the state of her incorruptible majesty to grant lust his boon, palpably it darkns and confounds both knowledge and conscience." Distinguishing clearly between theoretical and experiential knowledge of sin, Milton accepts only the former and resoundingly dismisses the latter as a function of the law. Milton manages to be true to his Paulinism at the same time that he provides a radical critique of Paul: rejecting what appears to be the central idea elaborated in Romans 7 (that, in the hands of sin, law becomes a death-producing instrument [7:5, 10, and 13]), he holds on instead to Paul's less than enthusiastic protestation of the law's essential goodness: "the law is holy, and the commandment holy, and just, and good" (7:12). This theoretical acknowledgement of the law's divine origin and nature, added perhaps to increase Paul's credibility and persuasiveness among the Roman Jewish Christians, is eclipsed in the chapter by the devastating description of the law's actual effects. Milton's central arguments in the divorce tracts presuppose instead the permanence and indispensability of all the moral and some of the judicial Mosaic laws, whose divinity is the basis of their authority.

The excerpt from *Tetrachordon* emphasizes the good offices of the Mosaic law as educator and counselor, rejecting the notion of the law as "a most negligent debaushing tutor." The law incorporates permanently "the rules of all sober education." Since the Torah is God's "perfet Law," the argument that "*divorce was permitted for hardnesse of heart, cannot be understood by the common exposition . . .* for the Law were then but a corrupt and erroneous School-master" (YP, 2:285). Divorce is a blessed termination of an unhappy marriage, a positive commandment, and not merely "a civil immunity and free charter to live and die in a long successive adultery" (285). For Milton in the divorce tracts, the perfect Mosaic law is neither excessively lax nor, as it is in Protestant hermeneutics, excessively rigorous. Paul had invented the figure of the law as schoolmaster to solve a glaring problem in his conception of salvation history: if the law could do no more than multiply sin, why had God ever permitted it at all? His unsatisfactory answer presupposes his lack of real interest in the era of the law. Primitive, temporary, and punitive, the law "was added because of transgressions, till the seed should come to whom the promise was made" (Gal. 3:19): "the law was our schoolmaster to bring us to Christ, that we might be justified by faith. But after that faith is come, we are no longer under a schoolmaster" (Gal. 3:24–25).

For Calvin, in his commentary on Deuteronomy, the name of the book (*deutero-nomos*, second law) spells failure for the Israelites, who didn't get the lesson the first time around.

> Like as when children do not profit wel at schole, but play the grosse Asses, when they have spent a whole yeare and are never the further forewarde, they must be faine to return againe to their Apcie. And why? For notwithstanding that they have heard their schoolemaster, yet they be as ignorant as they were befoer, insomuch that insteede of learning any thing, a man shall see them continue still alwayes at one staye.[49]

The law as schoolmaster exposes the inadequacies of the student, but not as a preparatory step in a process of self-correction. Its principal purpose, according to Luther, is "to reveale unto a man his sinne, his blindnes, his misery, his impietie, ignoraunce, hatred and contempt of God, death, hel, the judgment and deserved wrath of God to the end that God might bridle and beate down this monster and this madde beaste (I meane the presumption of *mans* own righteousness) . . . [and drive] them to Christ."[50] William Perkins concurs: "The law . . . shewes us our sinnes, and that without remedy: it shewes us the damnation that is due unto us: and by this meanes, it makes us despaire of salvation in respect of our selves. . . . The law is then our schoolemaster not by the plaine teaching, but by stripes and corrections."[51]

In the excerpt from *Tetrachordon*, as in all the divorce tracts and, later, in his defense of regicide, Milton adheres to Pauline doctrine, but with a difference: while Paul asserts for polemical reasons that "the law is holy, and the commandment holy, and just, and good," Milton actually recognizes the potential saving power of the deuteronomic laws of divorce (24:1–4) and of the limits of royal prerogative (18:14–20). For both Milton and Paul the law is a schoolmaster, it brings knowledge of sin, and it is an indissoluble unity. But Paul regards the law's tutorial function as punitive, whereas Milton sees it as including "the rules of all sober education." Milton transforms the experiential lust that Paul knows only by the law into an exclusively theoretical knowledge of sin, part of the law's "rule of knowledge and conscience." The unity of the law is the linchpin of Paul's quantitative argument against it—to violate one commandment is to break the entire law. Milton sounds Pauline when he asserts that even the smallest sin is infinite: "The least sinne . . . is as boundlesse as that vacuity beyond the world." The un-Pauline conclusion Milton reaches in *Tetrachordon* is to oppose the law rather than Christ's grace to human sin. The "artillery of justice" (*YP*, 2:657) must be powerful enough to destroy sin completely rather than merely to limit it.

Schoolmaster and poet, Milton writes movingly of propaedeutics and of the integral beauty of the law, "one of the perfetest" of God's "perfet gifts" (*YP*, 2:653). Paul's failure of sympathy extends from the law to the theme of *Paradise Lost*. For Paul, the past is the era of the Mosaic law, and therefore nostalgia is an emotion entirely alien to him. He concentrates all of his enthusiasm on showing that the law has been superseded. Its individual commands need no longer be a source of disquiet, for they belong to a past that, since Christ's appearance, has lost its authority. Paul's salvation history begins with his experience of the opposition of law and gospel. He looks back with a sense of relief, not of longing.

According to Ball's description of the benign prelapsarian dispensation, God's covenantal promise of life depends on "the exact and rigid exaction of perfect obedience." Except for its redundancy, Ball's formulation is so thoroughly conventional as to be nearly anonymous. Even when, characteristically redundant, Ball celebrates the happiness of Edenic obedience, with Adam as ever in his great Task-master's eye, Paul clips his muse's wings:

> The good that God promised was in it[s] kind a perfect systeme of good, which was to be continued so long as he continued obedient, which because it might be continued in the eye of creating power for ever, we call it happinesse, life, and everlasting happinesse. But upon a supposition of *Adams* persisting in a state of obedience, to say that God would have translated him to the state of glory in Heaven, is more then any just ground will warrant; because in Scripture there is no such promise. . . . Happinesse should have been conferred upon him, or continued unto him for his works, but they had not deserved the continuance thereof: for it is impossible the creature should merit of the Creator, because when he hath done all that he can, he is an unprofitable servant, he hath done but his duty. The obedience that God required at his hands was partly naturall, to be regulated according to the Law engraven in his heart by the finger of God himselfe, consisting in the true, unfained and perfect love of God, and of his Neighbour for the Lords sake: and partly Symbolicall, which stood in obedience to the Law given for his probation and triall, whether he would submit to the good pleasure of God in an act of it selfe meerely indifferent, because he was so commanded.[52]

Ball's stinting praise derives from an inability to imagine the light of Edenic law free from the shadow of the gospel. Although Ball purports to divide Edenic obedience into natural law and symbolic precept, those two parts are in fact conventional distinctions of the Mosaic law into moral and ceremonial components. Adam's "perfect love of God, and of his neighbor" comprises the two tables of the Decalogue, the sum of the law, while his obedience to a "Symbolicall" command, "an act of it selfe meerely indifferent," indicates his compliance with a proto-ceremonial law. The limitations of such a law, when submitted to the judgment of the gospel, account for the limits placed on Adam's happiness. Good works can never achieve salvation, and even a perfect Adam would have remained "an unprofitable servant" (Matt. 25:30; Luke 17:10; Rom. 3:12). Ball repeatedly rejects the hypothesis that continued obedience to the law of God would have resulted in Adam's "translation after some number of years spent on earth."[53]

Raphael promises Adam just such a translation:

> Your bodies may at last turn all to spirit,
> Improv'd by tract of time, and wing'd ascend
> Ethereal, as wee, or may at choice
> Here or in Heav'n'ly Paradises dwell;
> If ye be found obedient.
>
> (5.497–501)

The polar opposite of Ball's grudging account of Edenic happiness, Raphael's scheme accords instead with that of Arminius, who insists that had Adam and Eve remained sinless, their descendants would have reenacted the Edenic covenant.

> If our first parents had remained in their integrity by obedience to both these laws [moral and symbolic], God would have acted with their posterity by the same compact, that is, by their yielding obedience to the moral law inscribed on their hearts, and to some symbolical or ceremonial law. . . . [I]f they had persisted in their obedience to both laws, we think it very probable that, at certain periods, men would have been translated from this natural life, by the intermediate change of the natural, mortal, and corruptible body, into a body spiritual, immortal, and incorruptible, to pass a life of immortality and bliss in heaven.[54]

By turning body to spirit and earthly existence to heavenly bliss, without rejecting either body or earth, Raphael's monism evokes Menasseh ben Israel's Hebraic identification of the law of God with the tree of life. Through obedience to Torah, "at last [Adam's] Soul, together with his Body, might have been translated into Heaven, as it happen'd to *Enoch* and *Elias*, and all others would have enjoyed the like Privilege who had liv'd in perfect Obedience to the Law."[55]

Raphael is the Hebraic angel, who begins his conversation with an implicit rejection of typology, asserting instead the interchange of matter and spirit. The conversion he describes comes not according to the Calvinistic paradigm, when human beings recognize their own insufficiency and God's supervening grace, but rather when bodies at last turn all to spirit, the result of an innate human ability to choose between right and wrong and thus to demonstrate obedience. If John Ball ruins Edenic law with Christian phrases, Raphael saves the law by ringing changes on the conventional meaning of those phrases: "To transubstantiate" (5.438) is to turn matter into angelic spirit and to promise similar transformations in the future for humankind. The word also suggests that Adam and Eve already know the real presence of the divine in a communion without sacrifice. To "convert" (5.492) matter into spirit "at last" by persisting in obedience, "Improv'd by tract of time," is to reject the jarring discontinuities of Paul's sudden conversion on the road to Damascus.[56] The primal sin will knock out the rungs of the ladder connecting earth with heaven, and the only way back to God will be through Christ: "I am the way" (John 14:6). If, in fact, Christ substitutes himself for the "way" (*halakhah*) of the Torah, prelapsarian Adam's response to Raphael's scale of perfection asserts instead the accessibility of "the way" and the ability of the unassisted individual to climb the ladder to the divine through obedience to the law: "Well hast thou taught the way that might direct / Our knowledge" (5.508–9) and "By steps we may ascend to God" (512).

Raphael's scale of perfection—an evolutionary universe becoming increasingly divine—is sufficiently rich and catholic to accommodate diversity, not only Arminius and Menasseh but also the mystical eccentricities of Boehme and Fludd, and more centrally Plato and Aristotle, Plotinus, and the Hebrew Bible ("Ye shall walk in the way which the Lord your God commanded you" [Deut. 5:30]). The New Testament verses that figure in Raphael's narrative celebrate the Son as agent of creation and not as redeemer, and they praise love without decrying the law. After the Fall, "all was lost" (9.784), including the way. When typology becomes the totalizing system of the epic's last books, the amplitude of Raphael's Hebraic poetry shrinks to the sharper focus of Michael's Christian doctrine. Richard Baxter's orthodox Protestant interpretation of Christian regeneration forces the Mosaic law into precise conformity with a Pauline paradigm. Incapable of imagining a benign Edenic–Mosaic law, Baxter explains that Christ provides the only way back to Eden, with the renewed access of regeneration replacing inaccessibility under the law.

> Surely the Lord is not now so terrible and inaccessible, nor the passage of Paradise so blocked up, as when the Law and Curse reigned? Wherefore finding, Beloved Christians, that a new and Living way is consecrated for us, through the vail, the flesh of Christ, *by which we may with boldness enter into the Holiest, by the blood of Jesus; I shall draw neer with the fuller Assurance*: and finding the flaming Sword removed, shall look . . . into the Paradise of our God.[57]

MILTON, THE REFORMERS, AND THE LAW

Differences of interest, emphasis, and nuance between Milton and Paul create a space for paradise in the epic's central books, and doctrinal similarities between them account for the peremptory devaluation of all holy places after the Fall. If Milton were only a revolutionary Christian of a Pauline stamp, there would be no place for Eden in his imaginative life. But unlike Paul, Milton has an interest in the inner workings of history and a need for theodicy. Centrally related to Milton's conceptions of both paradise and the fallen world is the scope of his thought on the meanings of the Mosaic law. By contrast, even the most comprehensive and sympathetic Protestant expositions of the benign Edenic-Mosaic law lack Milton's imaginative sympathy. For most Reformers, the law is monolithic, and it is therefore impossible, when describing Edenic polity, to avoid using strong negative terms that derive from Paul's interpretation of the Mosaic law. Musculus, emphasizing the original ease of obedience, identifies Genesis 2:15–17 as the second of four primal laws of paradise. It contains a permission to eat of all the fruit, which demonstrates God's liberality, the exception of the single tree, which demonstrates "the authoritie of Goddes majestie," and finally "a penaltie for the transgression by threatening. . . . For he is not worthie to live, that honoreth not the giver of his life, but transgresseth his commaundementes, not compelled of necessitie, beyng so easy to have bene kept."[58] When Musculus slips, shifting to the plural "commaundements" while discussing the single prohibition, he shifts the context as well, from easy paradise to rigorous Sinai, where "threatening," "death," and "transgresseth" all assume a meaning fixed by Paul.

Similarly, but self-consciously, Matthew Poole presents the serpent's temptation of Eve in Genesis 3:4 as a Pauline midrash on the rigor of the law and the grace of the gospel.

> [. . . Ye shall not surely dye.] It is not so certain as you imagine, that you shall dye. God did say so indeed for your terrour, and to keep you in awe; or, he had some mystical meaning in those words; but do not entertain such hard and unworthy thoughts of that god who is infinitely kind and gracious, that he will for such a trifle, as the eating of a little Fruit, undo you and all your Posterity, and so suddenly destroy the most excellent work of his own hands.[59]

In his *Annotations* on Genesis 3, Poole reverses Milton's alchemy, turning the poetry of book 9 of *Paradise Lost* into biblical exegesis. Poole's account of the Fall consists almost entirely of paraphrases of Milton, whom he characterizes as a "late ingenious and learned Writer," familiar with "Jewish, and other Expositors."[60] Poole's serpent, like Milton's, tempts Eve to annul prematurely the benign Edenic-Mosaic dispensation of the law by misrepresenting it as rigorous and then comparing it unfavorably to the gospel. Just as Paul changes the Torah, the tree of life, into a death-dealing instrument foreign to Judaism and then castigates the Jews for pursuing righteousness by it, so the serpent changes the single prohibition into a minister of Pauline "terror" and "awe" and chides Eve for obeying it. The "gracious" gospel opposes the terror of the law, and, under the pressure of the mediate term "mystical," the dead letter of prohibition becomes an "infinitely kind and gracious" deity's invitation to eat. The literal, abrogated, becomes anagogical, and Genesis 3 becomes Herbert's "Love (III)."

Peering at paradise through lenses ground by Paul, most Protestant exegetes are unable to imagine a place altogether different from their own—under a covenant of works genuinely benign. The harsh pronouncement of the Presbyterian Westminster Assembly seems to banish pleasure from "delicious Paradise" (4.132). "God gave to Adam a law, as a covenant of works, by which He bound him and all his posterity to personal, entire, exact, and perpetual obedience."[61] Gervase Babington emphasizes Edenic discipline: "Man schooled to obey, even in Paradise." Behind his commentary and supporting it are manifold verses from Paul, including Romans 5:20 and 7:7, on law preceding sin, and 6:23 ("the wages of sin is death"): the law "was first and before all sinne," and "eternall damnation is the due reward of the contempt of Gods commaundement by disobedience."[62] William Pemble's insistence on the separation of law and gospel bears upon the polity of the last books of *Paradise Lost*, revealing the anti-Catholic tenor of postlapsarian rejections of the law: "*Justification by works makes void the covenant of grace*"; "What Adam should have obtained by workes without Christ: now he shall receive by faith in Christ without Workes"; the "maine *Essentiall* and proper difference between the *Covenant* of workes and of Grace (that is) betweene the Law & the *Gospell*, we shall endeavour to make good against those of the *Romish Apostasy* who deny it."[63] How can Pemble appreciate wholeheartedly a paradise of law and works that evokes contemporary Roman Catholicism?

Even worse, how can Reformers regard sympathetically an Edenic prohibition that is inseparable from the Jewish ceremonial law? Milton considers "all times before Christ [to be] more or less under the ceremonial law" (*YP*, 7:284), and his Adam and Eve are bound by what is in Pauline terms an outward thing indifferent in itself and therefore related neither to the moral nor judicial laws. That aspect of the Mosaic law least binding upon a Christian enforces obedience in paradise. John Ball's description of the prohibition seems entirely incompatible with the idea of human perfection before the Fall:

> The Lord having respect to the mutability and weaknesse of mans nature, was pleased, as to try his obedience by Symbolicall precepts, so to evidence the assurance of his faithfull promise by outward seales: but when the creature shall grow to absolute perfection and unchangeableness, such symbolicall precepts and outward seales shall cease as needlesse.[64]

Adam and Eve in paradise, although sinless, are weak and mutable, under the tutelage of a temporary ceremonial law in their childhood of prescription. But "such symbolicall precepts and outward seales shall cease as needlesse." A Reformation reader could hardly be blamed for associating the cessation of the ceremonial law not with our first parents' continued obedience, but rather with Christ's sacrifice, which abolished "all the ceremonies ordained by *Moses*" and which constituted "the true and spirituall accomplishment of that externall priesthood, which was in force and had place under the lawe."[65]

For Paul, the ritual and ceremonial prescriptions of the Pentateuchal law constitute the strongest evidence of its obsolescence. Romans 8:9–17 contrasts two communities, one defined by faith that is immortal, the other defined by a law which, however spiritual in itself, is always played out in unredeemable flesh. Those who place their confidence in the works of a law associated with the flesh are condemning themselves to death, for flesh passes away. Paul had hoped to unify the community of faith by destroying the ritual distinction between Jewish Christians and gentiles. Instead, his abolition of the ceremonial law for gentile converts to Christianity made social intercourse between them and Jewish Christians no longer possible.[66] In the final, doctrinal books of *Paradise Lost*, Pauline Milton fights again the battle between Jewish and gentile Christianity. The Miltonic insistence that Paradise can never be reentered is vitally and polemically connected with the Pauline insistence that Christianity bear no traces of Judaism. Central to the epic is the record of Paul's intolerance of divided table fellowship: "When Peter came to Antioch I withstood him to his face, because he stood condemned. For before certain men came from James, he ate with the gentiles; but when they came, he drew back and separated himself, fearing the circumcision party. And with him the rest of the Jews acted insincerely" (Gal. 2:11–13). The argument against continuity between pre- and postlapsarian life is intricately and deeply tied into Paul's radical argument against conservative Jewish Christianity. In Milton's own century, the Reformers widened considerably the breach between the belief communities created by means of the ceremonial law that they associated with Judaism and Roman Catholicism. John Wollebius concedes that "the use of [the ceremonial law] before Christs death was profitable . . . but after the promulgation of the Gospel, not only was the observation of Ceremonies unwholsom, but also mortal. . . . [S]urely at this day to observe Jewish Ceremonies, were to deny Christs death and coming in the flesh."[67]

Paul makes no qualitative distinction between Edenic and Mosaic law, and Adam and Eve under a prohibition evoke inevitably the Israelites under the law. All are child heirs, not yet fit to take care of themselves and under the charge of a tutor. According to Calvin's explicitly Pauline view, "the same inheritance was appointed for them and for us, but they were not yet old enough to be able to enter upon it and manage it. The same church existed among them, but as yet in its childhood. Therefore, keeping them under this tutelage, the Lord gave, not spiritual promises unadorned and open, but ones foreshadowed, in a measure, by earthly promises." This evolutionary view of an earthly paradise that only dimly foreshadows a superior spiritual reality belies the power of the middle books of *Paradise Lost*. It determines the Fall, making our first parents' status unfree and inferior. Calvin's Paul presses for a continuous Christian revelation, with Old and New Testaments expressing faith in salvation exclusively through Christ, one by means of types and shadows, the other directly. Such a view considers neither the epic's confidence in un-fallen Adam and Eve's potential for independent achievement before the Fall nor the radical discontinuities introduced by the Fall. It aligns instead with the angel Michael's revisionist Pauline interpretation in the epic's last books of the law as inherently imperfect and never capable of effecting salvation.

The plexed artistry of *Paradise Lost* depends on the tensile strength of the law, a single prohibition in Eden that comprehends the vast legal network that figures in Milton's thought: the interrelated primary and secondary laws of nature, of nations, and of Moses. As a symbol that, in its simplicity, contains the vast order of its consequences throughout history, Edenic law in Milton's epic must both include and transcend Paul's monolithic conception of the law. The Miltonic bard calls attention to the triumph of Paul's view of the Mosaic law in book 10, when the Son pronounces judgment on the serpent. The *protevangelium* (Gen. 3:15) devalues peremptorily the literal Torah as authoritative source of law and history, turning it into the Old Testament, a mere pattern of types prefiguring Christianity, what Frank Kermode calls "a set of scattered indications of events it did not itself report."[68] The *protevangelium* activates typology, a revisionist symbolic mode that will dominate the epic from this moment on. Typology depends on disparity, between the lower, merely literal judgment on the serpent and the higher, spiritual judgment of Satan, "in mysterious terms, judg'd as then best" (10.173). Before the Fall, the Miltonic bard had diplomatically excluded from paradise the reader's determining knowledge of fallen history, thus preserving our first parents' freedom and dignity. Now, exploiting the discrepant awareness that defines the relation between Old Testament types and Christian readers, he invites the reader to indulge a sense of superiority by calling attention to the limitations of Adam and Eve's understanding of the serpent's punishment: "more to know / Concern'd not Man (since he no further knew) / Nor alter'd his offense" (169–71).

For orthodox Protestants such as Nicolas Hemmingsen, God's judgment of the sinful marks the first shift in scripture from law to gospel; here "God him selfe (proceeding from his secret seat) . . . appeared to *Adam* after the fall, and delivered first with his owne voyce, the doctrine of the *Lawe* and the *Gospell*. For in that he layd punishments upon our first parentes, for their rebellion (in perpetuall testimonie of his anger against sinners) it perteineth to the lawe: and in that he promised: *the seede of the woman, to crush the serpents head*, it is the voyce of the Gospell."[69] The Miltonic bard emphasizes our first parents' initial failure to understand the gospel promise contained in the Son's judgments. If unfallen Adam and Eve in *Paradise Lost* are more heroic than their counterparts in the earthly paradise of Reformation commentary, once fallen, they are slower

to comprehend the living voice of deity. The time between the pronouncement of the *protevangelium* and Adam's first groping attempts to understand it (10.1028–40) is the interval of a double take, in which Adam feels
the despair of his situation under the tyranny of the law.

A negative Pauline conception of the law, such as one finds in the chapter on Christian liberty in *De doctrina* (1:27), governs the last books of
the epic. Milton's revisionist Pauline doctrine reinterprets the Torah of
paradise as an inferior Old Testament law that was always destined to be
superseded:

> Albeit our first parent had lordship over sea, and land, and aire, yet there
> was a law without him, as a guard set over him. But Christ having cancell'd
> the hand writing of ordinances which was against us, *Coloss.* 2.14. and
> interpreted the fulfilling of all through charity, hath in that respect set us
> over law, in the free custody of his love, and left us victorious under the
> guidance of his living Spirit, not under the dead letter. (*YP*, 2:587–88)

Milton formulates Adam's Fall and Christ's redemption as Christian liberty from the restraints of the Mosaic law, a "law without," a prohibition
enforcing Edenic obedience. This is doctrinally identical to the chapter
promulgating Christian liberty from an adversarial law, "the hand writing of ordinances which was against us." "So long as the law exists, it
constrains, because it is a law of slavery. Constraint and slavery are as
inseparable from the law as liberty is from the gospel" (*YP*, 6:535). Such
a conception of the primal law of paradise places free will in jeopardy by
postulating a fortunate fall left inexplicit even by radical antinomians,
which focuses neither on Christ's redemption of humanity nor on Adam's
regeneration, but rather on the ultimate unsatisfactoriness of the Edenic
state and the inevitability and desirability of its destruction.

Michael, the New Testament angel, echoes the same verse (Col. 2:14)
when he tells Adam of Christ's "fulfilling that which thou didst want,
/ Obedience to the Law of God" (12.396–97), "The Law that is against
thee" (12.416). When the Son in his first act of priestly intercession presents the Father with our first parents' silent prayer of contrition, he, too,
devalues the work and prayer of innocence:

> . . . in this Golden Censer, mixt
> With Incense, I thy Priest before thee bring,
> Fruits of more pleasing savor from thy seed
> Sown with contrition in his heart, than those
> Which his own hand manuring all the Trees
> Of Paradise could have produc't, ere fall'n
> From innocence.
>
> (*11.24–30*)

In a brilliantly suggestive reading of this passage, Arnold Stein finds the Son's assertion that the fruits of contrition please God more than the fruits of innocence to be "painful . . . in its prompt dismissal of man's work, innocence, and the Garden itself—as if these had been merely second best all along."[70] The passage insists as well that the reader prefer a complex new order of Christian doctrine—the Son's intercession anticipating typologically the ultimate sacrifice that fulfills his priestly office—over the original simplicity of direct intercourse between humankind and God. Milton's model earlier in the epic for such unmediated conversation is invariably the Hebrew Bible, in particular Abraham's bold argument with God on behalf of the inhabitants of Sodom and Moses' on behalf of the sinful Israelites. But, by this late point in the epic, one cannot read the Son's offering literally in the context of the Hebrew Bible, as a priest's act of atonement in tabernacle or temple. Nor can the artifice and ceremony of the passage represent that of the ceremonial law itself. Rather, the presentation by God's "glad Son," a Priest bearing "a Golden Censer, mixt / With Incense," anticipates Christ's vicarious atonement, and the ritual ornamentation of the passage represents the elaborateness of Christian doctrine. The passage echoes the unorthodox Miltonic paradox of *felix culpa*, in which God's easy paradisiac command becomes the Pauline "Law that is against thee"—"the dead letter."

Ranking contrition above innocence, the Son introduces a system that requires preference explicitly and rejection implicitly. Typology is the system, and its principal doctrine is the supersession of the Mosaic law by the gospel. The original firstfruits of Leviticus (23:10) are inferior to the sweeter savor of Christ's advocation and propitiation (11.33–34), and the passage's principal supporting text is Luke 15, which contains both the story of the prodigal son (11–32) and Christ's insistence that there will be greater joy in heaven over one sinner who repents than over ninety-nine righteous who do not need to repent (7). In the Edenic books of the epic, when there was only Torah and not yet gospel, there was no order requiring rejection. The Son's glancing dismissal of paradise is all the more devastating in light of the narrator's emphasis in books 4 to 9 on the value of every aspect of human life before the Fall.

Part of the destructive force of *Paradise Lost* stems from Milton's reinterpretation after the Fall of his own earlier intellectual and spiritual structures. The destructive revision that occurs in the epic's last books coexists with the primal creative vision of the middle books. Occupying different books within the same encyclopedic text, they resemble the Hebrew and Greek Testaments, each of them foreign to the other, although typologists, skimping on nuance, interpret between them, smoothing over differences. Biblical texts transcend their various sources, and to read the Genesis cosmology as a response to Near Eastern mythologies or gospel narratives as midrashim on books of testimonies is to know only one of several dimensions of the meaning of these scriptural texts. Yet even polemical reactions against their sources presuppose familiarity with them, and specific departures from a prevailing cosmic outlook are instructive against the background of a general correspondence between realms of religious discourse. Similarly, Milton's *De doctrina Christiana* supplies an important dimension to the last books of *Paradise Lost*, which are heavily weighted with Christian doctrine. In his introductory epistle to the treatise, Milton adopts a Pauline persona,[71] and, not coincidentally, those chapters in book 1 whose headings derive explicitly from Paul's writings are notably hostile to the Mosaic law. Those headings are made up of terms that mark important stages in the spiritual life of any Protestant Christian: "REDEMPTION" (1.16), "RENOVATION"(17), "REGENERATION" (18), "SAVING FAITH" (20), "INGRAFTING IN CHRIST" (21), "JUSTIFICATION" (22), "ADOPTION" (23), "UNION AND COMMUNION WITH CHRIST" (24), "SALVATION," and "GLORIFICATION" (25). Of capital importance are the chapters on the Mosaic law (26) and Christian liberty (27), which examine law against gospel within the Pauline paradigm of salvation. These two latter chapters of *De doctrina*, as well as the angel Michael's severe antitheses of law and gospel (*PL*, 12.287–314), and his Pauline rejection of the Jews by distinguishing between children of one's loins and children of faith (*PL*, 12.446–50; Rom. 9:6–8)—all address the standard topics of Christian anti-Jewish polemic: the emancipation of Christians from the Mosaic law, or the annulment of the dispensation of law altogether; the repudiation of the Jewish people by God for their rejection of Christ; and the succession of the Church, the true Israel, the people of God, to all the prerogatives and promises once given to the Jews.[72]

To whom, then, does Milton address his polemic? To himself, of course—that is, to the Milton of *Doctrine and Discipline of Divorce*, *Tetrachordon*, *Of Education*, the *Areopagitica*, and the Edenic books of *Paradise Lost*. Milton's rejection and devaluation of Eden represent in mythic terms the rejection of his own Hebraism. As I shall argue in the next chapter, the primal creative vision of paradise in the middle books of Milton's epic can be understood in relation to all of the pamphlets written between 1643 and 1645, advocating, respectively, domestic liberty, educational reform, and "freedom to express oneself" (*YP*, 4:624). Though in important ways models of paradise, these tracts address themselves to problems of the present and the immediate future, not to nostalgic evocations of the past. In *Doctrine and Discipline of Divorce*, Milton calls Eden simply "another world" (*YP*, 2:316). Counseling acceptance of Moses' divorce laws, he argues that it is neither comforting nor intelligent to recall Adam and Eve in paradisiacal bliss when one is in a state of marital distress: "In such an accident it will best behove our sobernes to follow rather what moral *Sinai* prescribes equal to our strength, then fondly to think within our strength all that lost Paradise relates" (316).

Milton's positive conception of the Mosaic law in these prose tracts and in the middle books of his epic never violates the terms of the Pauline paradigm. Rather, it both includes and transcends them. Bucanus, relying entirely on quotes from the Pauline epistles, clarifies one dimension of a Protestant strategy that permits Milton to view the Mosaic law positively before the Fall, negatively afterward:

> *What Epithets and titles be given to the Law in Scripture?* Divers, but in divers respectes: For when comparison is made betweene the law and Gospell, especially in the article of Justification, then *Paule* giveth the law such termes and appellations as seeme ignominious, but this is by relation. 1. By our fault, not any fault in the Law. For he calleth it, *a Schoole-maister, a prison that shutteth up, the yoake of bondage, the power or force of sinne, the operation of wrath and of death, weake and beggerly elements of the world, the ministerie of death and condemnation, the killing letter, the hand-writing which is against us, the Testament which begetteth unto bondage.* But being considered by itself as a Doctrine published by God, it is called *a holie Lawe,* and *a holy and good commaundement, a word of life, a commandement which is unto life.*[73]

The Mosaic law governs life before the Fall, then yields to the gospel in the fallen world. Passing, along with our first parents, from a state of innocence and obedience to a condition of sin, the law itself becomes contaminated by process. From a positive, independent entity in paradise, it changes as a result of comparison with the gospel, though this is "our fault, not any fault in the Law." Bucanus goes out of his way to speak well of the law, but he is trapped inside a Pauline realm of discourse where negative epithets of the law far outweigh and outnumber positive ones. Even if one were capable of considering the law absolutely, without relation to the gospel, Pauline values might invade paradise and subvert it. Typology is the symbolic mode generated by the introduction of the gospel, and it must be excluded from paradise. It presupposes the inferiority of the law, it submits the persons, events, and images of the Hebrew Bible to the judgment of the New Testament, and it casts the shadow of determinism in the form of Christian antitype on the earlier text. Paul regards his own past and the history of his people as not only "summ'd up" by Christ but also as "mean" (*PL*, 8.473) in comparison with his incarnation and atonement. The values and emotions of the middle books of *Paradise Lost* are grounded instead in the poet's commitment to an original perfection whose unrecoverability causes pain.

Milton takes Paul's hint and develops it. He transforms Bucanus's commonplace into an extraordinary poetics of tact and forbearance that is not always adequately understood or appreciated. To describe an unrecoverable moment separate from all subsequent human history, Milton must not only separate the benign prelapsarian Mosaic law from what it will become. He must also exploit and expand the comprehensive understanding of the law that he demonstrated in the prose tracts of 1643–45. Remaining doctrinally Pauline, he must interrogate the paradigm and in the process create a new framework for the Mosaic law. This benign law must be a figure large enough to represent adequately the distinctness and reality of innocence.

Milton argues the emancipation of Christians, not from, but through the Mosaic law. The deuteronomic law permitting divorce is more charitable than the contemporary Protestant interpretation of Christ's restrictive words on the subject (Matt. 5:31–32 and 19:3–11). Instead of the annulment of the dispensation of law altogether, Milton accepts as part of God's eternal and unchanging moral law a section of the Pentateuch (Deut. 24:1–4) interpreted by most Reformers as part of the now obsolete civil law of the Jews.[74] Indeed, he argues that most of the civil law of Moses is still in force (*YP*, 2:641–42). Later, in the itemized, retrospective account of his prose production in his *Defensio Secunda* (1654), Milton reiterates the point: "this [argument for domestic liberty] was based on divine law, which Christ never overthrew, nor did he sanction any law for civil use of higher authority than the whole Mosaic law" (*CE*, 8:130–33; *YP*, 4:624). The doctrine of Christian liberty posits a condition of perpetual enmity between law and gospel, but the divorce tracts presuppose their perpetual harmony. The anonymous author of *An Answer* to the first of the four divorce pamphlets cites reprovingly Milton's view of the evil that would follow if the Mosaic law of divorce were unlawful, namely, "*That the Law and the Gospell would be subject to more then one contradiction.*"

> There is a contradiction of the Gospell to the Law; that the Gospel counts some things under its dispensation to be altogether unlawfull to be done, which the Law allowed as lawfull and pious in the time of its dispensation: this kind of contradiction we grant there is betweene the Law and Gospel many times, but is nothing to your purpose at all: for example, Circumcision . . . and a hundred the like, and yet the Gospel blames not the Law for these things in the time of its dispensation: no more will it follow in case of Divorce, if it should be allowed then and denied now.[75]

Certainly Milton's enemies attacked the *Doctrine and Discipline of Divorce* for presenting a specifically Jewish theory and practice. Of the relation between Christ's words and the Mosaic law, Milton had insisted: "If we examine over all [Christ's] sayings, we shall find him not so much interpreting the Law with his words, as referring his owne words to be interpreted by the Law" (*YP*, 2:301). Henry Hammond might well be remembering this reversal of typology when he refers to this tract as the first "in these licentious times" to plead for divorce; "and the *special* artifice made use of, was that, of bringing back *Christ* unto *Moses*, of interpreting the restraint laid on this matter in the *New Testament*, by analogie with the *Judaical permission* in the Old."[76] Alexander Ross, an antitolerationist who would later oppose the readmission of the Jews into England, dismissed succinctly Milton's argument "that a man may put away his Wife, though not for adultery; so taught the Jews."[77]

Milton's argument that divorce is an unabrogated Mosaic law resembles a more notorious argument earlier in the century regarding the Saturday-Sabbath. The religious radical Theophilus Brabourne, author of several pamphlets on liberty of conscience, advocated Sabbath observance: "To those who would say, 'this were to bringe into the Church Judaizme againe, and that strict observation of the Sabbath which they used,' " Brabourne replied, "Judaizme is when obedience is yielded to a Law Ceremoniall, but he that keepes the Sabbath day, doth it in obedience to a Law Morall."[78] Francis White, Bishop of Ely, summarizes Brabourne's defense: "*The fourth Commandement of the Decalogue, Remember the Sabbath Day to keepe it holy, & c. Exod. 20. is a Divine precept, simply and intirely morall, containing nothing legally ceremonial, in whole or in part: and therefore the weekly observation thereof, ought to be perpetuall, and to continue in full force, and vertue to the worlds end.*"[79] This argument brought Brabourne before Archbishop Laud and the High Commission, where he was pronounced "a Jew, a heretic and schismatic . . . worthy to be severely punished"; and so he was—fined, degraded, imprisoned, excommunicated, and ordered to make a public submission before he could be released from the Gatehouse.[80]

For Milton, the deuteronomic law of divorce is "*morall and perpetuall*" (*YP*, 2:262). Arguing that an unfit mate drives her spouse from religious faith, Milton proclaims: "Therefore by all the united force of the *Decalogue* she ought to be disbanded" (*YP*, 2:260). To end a bad marriage is to oppose sin and to promote "the sacred and glorious end both of the Moral and Judicial Law" (*YP*, 2:289). According to the earliest life of Milton, "In these [divorce pamphlets] hee taught the right use and design of Marriage; then the Originall and practise of Divorces among the Jews, and show'd that our Saviour, in those foure places of the Evangelists, meant not the abrogating, but rectifying the abuses of it."[81] Milton forcefully argues that Christ's purpose was not to introduce a new moral or judicial law: "Moses' Law grounded on morall reason, was both [Christ's] office and his essence to maintain" (*YP*, 2:264).

Whereas traditional Christian anti-Jewish polemic insists that God has repudiated the Jewish people, Milton defends "the *Jews*, Gods ancient people" (*YP*, 2:278). He disagrees with the argument that the Mosaic law of divorce was a concession to the hardness of Jewish hearts, even though this appears to be the gist of Christ's argument to the Pharisees in Matthew 19:8 and Mark 10:5. The Fall has hardened everyone's hearts, not only those of the Jews. Milton considers hardness to have "a twofould acceptation," "when it is in a good man taken for infirmity and imperfection," and when it denotes "the imperfection and decay of man from original righteousnesse" (*YP*, 2:661). He argues that contemporary Christians need the charitable law of divorce at least as much as the Jews did: "If wee bee wors, or but as bad, which lamentable examples confirm wee are, then have wee more, or at least as much need of this permitted law, as they to whom God expresly gave it (as they say) under a harsher covenant" (*YP*, 2:354).

Milton's expressions of philosemitism are not lifelong. At the heart of his mainly Lutheran formulation of the doctrine of Christian liberty in *De doctrina* are rejection and antipathy—gospel over law, Christian over Jew, Christ's grace over human virtue—and, as a corollary of the last proposition, the ultimate futility of human response. Luther's orthodox formulation, which included the assertion that Christ made us free, not from earthly bondage but from God's everlasting wrath, made the doctrine compatible with submission to repressive regimes. In 1659, after a long period of disillusionment with religious and political institutions, Milton would extend Christian liberty in his treatise *Of Civil Power* to include freedom not only from the Mosaic law but also from the magistrate's coercion in religious affairs. Thus he bears out the neat quip of the Erastian John Selden: "The *Puritans* who will allow no free-will at all, but God does all, yet will allow the Subject his Liberty to do, or not to do, notwithstanding the King, the God upon Earth."[82] In the great prose tracts of 1643–45, expressing a hope in institutions that often shades into Erastianism, Milton exalts "the divine testimonies of God himself, lawgiving in person to a sanctify'd people" (*YP*, 2:350). These tracts break free of Paul's (and Luther's) monolithic conception of the law, demonstrating instead a comprehensive Hebraic paradigm, in which the Mosaic law, partly universal and partly national, mediates between the universality of natural law and the particularity of the gospel. Containing both a moral law applicable to humankind and parts of a civil law still applicable to a Christian priesthood of believers, the Mosaic law in these tracts is the fulcrum upon which the forces of natural law and gospel exercise their vitality. Milton's great synthesizing power is evident everywhere in these tracts, which discover coordinates among the dispensations of eternal reason, God's immutable law, and Christ's charity, and which assert similarities among virtuous pagans, Jews, and Christians. Generally elid-

ing the obsolete ceremonial law and those judicial laws applicable only to
the Jews, the tracts emphasize continuity and kinship among God's creatures. If Christian liberty, at least as expounded in *De doctrina*, presupposes the irrelevance of human activity, the Hebraic ethos of these early
tracts posits instead our ability to imitate God "by possessing our souls of
true virtue" (*Of Education*, *YP*, 2:367), to rebuild God's temple by recovering lost truth (the *Areopagitica*), and to recover at least a portion of the
lost paradise of marital happiness according to the charitable Mosaic law
of divorce.

THE SECONDARY MOSAIC LAW IN THE FIELD OF THIS WORLD

In the tracts of 1643–45, as in the Edenic books of his great epic, Milton
asserts the perfect correspondence between God's will, incarnate in the
Mosaic law, and natural law. Here, as in Eden before the Fall, "God and
Nature bid the same" (*PL*, 6.176), and Milton speaks of "the fundamentall law book of nature, which *Moses* never thwarts but reverences" (*YP*,
2:272).

> Mariage, unless it mean a fit and tolerable mariage, is not inseparable nei-
> ther by nature nor institution. Not by nature[,] for then those Mosaick di-
> vorces had bin against nature, if separable and inseparable be contraries, as
> who doubts they be: and what is against nature is against Law, if soundest
> Philosophy abuse us not: by this reckning *Moses* should be most unmosaick,
> that is, most illegal, not to say most unnaturall. Nor is it inseparable by the
> first institution: for then no second institution in the same Law for so many
> causes could dissolve it: it being most unworthy a human (as *Plato*'s judge-
> ment is in the fourth book of his *Lawes*) much more a divine Law-giver to
> write two several decrees upon the same thing. (*YP*, 2:309–10)[83]

Itself a product of the fullest understanding of natural law, the soundest
philosophy asserts that moral law is the highest reason, implanted in nature.[84] The Mosaic law must always be in accord with nature, and Moses
the author/lawgiver, in "the same Law" of Genesis and Deuteronomy,
has instituted both marriage and divorce as laws in harmony with each
other. Although the institution of marriage in paradise (Gen. 1:27 and
2:18, and 23–24) is part of what Milton in *Tetrachordon* calls the primary law of Moses, and the deuteronomic law of divorce is part of what
he calls the secondary law of Moses, edifying footpaths connect the laws
of paradise and the fallen world, which are part of "the same Law" and
the same pentateuchal text. (Although *deuteronomy* means "second law"
and Milton's central pentateuchal texts are often deuteronomic, Milton
seems to mean by secondary law the entire Torah except for the slender

prelapsarian chapters of Genesis. In his great epic, he identifies Adam with Abraham as well as Moses.) Consonance both within and among dispensations is the principal theme of *Tetrachordon*, whose title refers to the common chord produced by the agreeable sounding of four notes, a figure of the harmony of four scriptural passages on divorce, two from the Hebrew Bible, two from the Greek.

Without losing sight of the essential agreement of the scriptural teachings on divorce, Milton maintains that, in our fallen world, the "second institution" of divorce, part of the secondary law of Moses, is actually more compassionate than marriage, part of the primary law that originates in paradise. Moreover, he associates Christianity with the mistaken belief that one can recover the perfection of the primary law.

> In the beginning, had men continu'd perfet, it had bin just that all things should have remain'd, as they began to *Adam & Eve*. But after that the sons of men grew violent and injurious, it alter'd the lore of justice, and put the goverment of things into a new frame. While man and woman were both perfet to each other, there needed no divorce; but when they both degenerated to imperfection, & oft times grew to be an intolerable evil each to other, then law *more justly* [emphasis added] did permit the alienating of that evil which mistake made proper, then it did the appropriating of that good which Nature at first made common. For if the absence of outward good be not so bad as the presence of a close evil, & that propriety, whether by cov'nant or possession, be but the attainment of some outward good, it is more natural & righteous that the law should sever us from an intimat evil, then appropriate any outward good to us from the community of nature. The Gospel indeed tending ever to that which is perfetest, aim'd at the restorement of all things, as they were in the beginning. And therefore all things were in common to those primitive Christians in the Acts, which *Ananias & Sapphira* dearly felt. . . . But who will be the man shall introduce this kind of common wealth, as christianity now goes? (*YP*, 2:665–66)

Milton distinguishes between the primary Mosaic law of marriage and the secondary Mosaic law of divorce. The Mosaic law as promulgated in Genesis, transcending natural law, permits "the appropriating of that good which Nature at first made common." This clause's best gloss is the Edenic epithalamium: "Hail wedded Love, mysterious Law, true source / Of human offspring, sole propriety / In Paradise of all things common else" (*PL*, 4.750–52). Misuse of the primary law, with its requirement of perfection from Eden's perfect inhabitants, caused a change in human nature, and it then became impossible to fulfill it. Milton clearly regards both Genesis and Deuteronomy as part of the same law, but the law that eventually governs the Edenic books of *Paradise Lost* interests him less in this excerpt than the deuteronomic divorce law, accommodated to fallen human nature, which "more justly did permit the alienating of that evil which mistake made proper." Where the Edenic law of marriage is founded on the privilege and exclusivity of private property ("sole propriety") in a world where all else is held in common, the secondary Mosaic law of divorce is founded on the relinquishing of proprietorship for the sake of common household peace.

Psalm 34:14 may be Milton's central text here: "Depart from evil, and do good; seek peace, and pursue it." "Depart" precedes "do good," for "it is more natural & righteous that the law should sever us from an intimat evil, then appropriate any outward good from the community of nature." Of course Edenic law did both: virtue was to be achieved both omissively, by abstaining from eating the fruit, and commissively, by work and by fulfilling the ends of God's "mysterious Law" of marriage. To demand perfection under either the primary Mosaic law of Genesis or the gospel is to condemn imperfect human beings to death: even Adam and Eve fell, and they were perfect; Ananias and Sapphira, good and bad like all of us, donating some of their profit and holding back some, fell down dead (Acts 5:1–10). The primary law, once benign, applies standards impossible for ordinary human beings to maintain. "If then mariage must be as in the beginning, the persons that marry must be such as then were, the institution must make good, in som tolerable sort, what it promises toeeither [sic] party. If not, it is but madnes to drag this one ordinance back to the beginning" (YP, 2:666). The secondary law of Moses is natural, righteous, and just in the fallen world. Concessions to weakness were unnecessary in paradise, and the perfection required was absolute: "Then moreover was perfetest to fulfill each law in it selfe; now is perfetest in this estate of things, to ask of charity how much law may be fulfill'd: els the fulfilling, oft times is the greatest breaking" (YP, 2:666).

Barker, recognizing that this secondary Mosaic law "of fallen human nature is clearly an impossible foundation for Christian liberty," interprets it as second best, "imperfect," especially when compared with the Pauline "liberty which is Milton's real concern."[85] Certainly the secondary law of Moses is no real concern of Milton's in the main line of his great epic's doctrine. There is a perfect primary law of Moses in paradise, and after the Fall, impossible to keep, that same primary law becomes a minister of death and condemnation. The secondary law of Moses, an alternative form of liberty, emphasizing human rights in an imperfect world, is indeed alien to Paul and to the doctrine of Christian liberty, and the postlapsarian books of the epic replace the primary law with the gospel. The Fall "alter'd the lore of justice, and put the goverment of things into a new frame."

The generous and comprehensive view of the Mosaic law in the tracts of 1643–45 is the principal model of Edenic polity. The shift in equilibrium suffered by the entire epic as a result of the Fall includes a shift from a comprehensive to a monolithic interpretation of the law. After the Fall, Milton's radical Paulinism, evident in certain books of *De doctrina*, revises and reduces the Hebraic view of the law in the early tracts and in paradise, thus making the gospel an inevitability. The sudden disappearance from the epic of the positive Mosaic law—and its unacknowledged replacement by a law identical in name but diminished in character—parallels another disappearance familiar to Miltonists. According to A. J. A. Waldock, the glorious Satan of books 1 and 2 of the epic threatens Milton's overall scheme, and he is therefore replaced by a less dangerous character: "The Satan of the address to the Sun is not a development from the old, he is not a changed Satan, he is a *new* Satan."[86] The alleged degeneration of the law (to paraphrase Waldock on Satan) is actually of the nature of an assertion that certain changes occur. The changes do not generate themselves from within; they are imposed from without. The Mosaic law does not degenerate; it is degraded.

Although Waldock regards the technique of degradation as a form of literary cheating, a sign of authorial nervousness when threatened with loss of control, the motive behind it may sometimes be difficult to assign. Adam in his soliloquy wishes that he were "Earth / Insensible" (*PL*, 10.776–77), for oblivion would provide escape from God's wrath; "his dreadful voice no more / Would Thunder in my ears" (10.779–80). But God has never thundered in his ears. The harshest sound Adam has ever heard is the Son's mild voice of judgment (10.96). Adam is here identifying the prohibition with the negative Mosaic law—specifically, with the Israelites' experience at Sinai *as interpreted in the New Testament*:

> God from the Mount of *Sinai*, whose gray top
> Shall tremble, he descending, will himself
> In Thunder, Lightning and loud Trumpet's sound
> Ordain them Laws.
>
> .　.　.　.　.　.　.　.
> But the voice of God
> To mortal ear is dreadful.
>
> (*12.227–30 and 235–36*)

For ye are not come unto the mount that might not be touched, and that burned with fire, nor unto blackness, and darkness, and tempest, and the sound of a trumpet, and the voice of words; which *voice* they that heard entreated that the word should not be spoken to them any more: for they could not endure that which was commanded . . . but ye are come unto Mount Zion . . . and to Jesus the mediator of the new covenant. (Hebrews 12:18–20 and 22–24)

The benign law whose ease of fulfillment Adam had often acknowledged has suddenly become terrible. Is this changed characterization of the law a sign enabling one to interpret Adam's argument as self-serving, ungrateful, conveniently forgetful? Or is it an example of Milton's degrading the law after the Fall, making it a mere foil to the gospel, underscoring the consolation of *felix culpa* by pretending that this inferior law operated in paradise from the beginning? The latter seems a likely explanation of another example: the Son's otherwise puzzlingly peremptory dismissal of paradise, its dispensation, and its works (11.22–36). Once the law has been reduced sufficiently, it can be dismissed without regret. The Son speaks of the dispensation of paradise as if it had always been merely the Mosaic law as understood from within a Pauline realm of discourse.

What filaments, however tenuous, stretch back from the law reduced by the Son in a scene fraught with typology to the glorious law of paradise? Had the secondary law of Moses figured doctrinally in the epic, lines of communication would have remained open between the unfallen and fallen worlds. Instead, the gap between them is as wide as that between a Hebraic and a Pauline view of the law and between law and gospel. None of these is always absolutely unbridgeable. Barker is correct about Milton's ultimate doctrinal preference of Christian liberty over the secondary law of Moses, but he underestimates the importance of that law in Milton's thought. Expounding it, a doctrinally Pauline absolutist confronts with compassion a life of mistake and the inseparability of good and evil in this imperfect world. The secondary law of Moses inspires Milton's most mature and realistic writing, and *Paradise Lost* would have been less radically nostalgic and more useful if that law had supervened after the Fall. The Decalogue, rejected in both *De doctrina* and in the postlapsarian world of the epic, is a part of the secondary Mosaic law, which reformulates the primary law of paradise, accommodating it to human imperfection. In *The Doctrine and Discipline of Divorce*, evoking the Decalogue, Milton numbers himself among the weak, grateful for the law: "it will best behove our sobernes to follow rather what moral *Sinai* prescribes equal to our strength, then fondly to think within our strength all that lost Paradise relates" (*YP*, 2:316).

When a good marriage goes bad, paradise is lost, and, in such a fallen circumstance, the justice of the secondary Mosaic law of divorce is to be preferred over futile expectations of grace. Jesus explicitly rejects divorce, appealing to the primal will of God, who created man and woman in paradise for permanent, absolutely indissoluble partnership (Mark 12:24). Paul, in a very rare citation of Jesus (1 Cor. 7:10–11), makes that rejection the basis of his own counsel that Christians not dissolve their marriages to unbelievers (1 Cor. 7:12–14). Jesus wants to recover paradise; Paul expects unbelievers to convert; and Theodore Beza, like other Reformation expositors, wants suffering spouses "to beg the gift of chastity in recompence of an injurious marriage" (*YP*, 2:690). But Milton, writing of marriage between a Christian and an unbeliever, "befriends" a far bolder speech of Beza's, which he calls "remarkable": "*what could be firmly constituted in human matters if under pretence of expecting grace from above, it should be never lawfull for us to seeke our right*" (*YP*, 2:690). The law's own mercies afford sufficient relief, while blind faith in a force higher than the law—when passivity and credulity are concomitants of that faith—simply perpetuates an intolerable situation.

The secondary Mosaic law bridges the divorce tracts and the *Areopagitica*. The deuteronomic permission to divorce resembles permission to publish. Both will help good people, and both are susceptible to abuse.

> Now that many licentious and hard-hearted men took hold of this Law to cloak thir bad purposes is nothing strange to beleeve. And these were they, not for whom *Moses* made the Law, God forbid, but whose hardnes of heart taking ill advantage by this Law he held it better to suffer as by accident . . . rather then good men should loose their just and lawfull privilege of remedy. (*YP*, 2:307)

Moses' permission must be generally available, even though wicked individuals are sure to abuse such general permission for their own particular evil ends. The licentious, freed from mistaken Reformation interpretations of Christ's restricting words, may divorce at will, or, with no Parliamentary Licensing Order to curb them, they may publish scurrilities. But the deuteronomic law of divorce will disenthrall the hapless spouse, removing the desperate occasions of blasphemy, and freedom from prepublication censorship will allow the truth to circulate freely and thus to perfect the Reformation.

The compassionate recognition of mingled good and evil in the world that characterizes Milton's exposition of the secondary law of Moses can be found in the second argument of the *Areopagitica*: "what is to be thought in generall of reading Books, what ever sort they be, and whether be more the benefit, or the harm that thence proceeds?" (*YP*, 2:507). Acts 19 reports with apparent approval the burning of magical books in Ephesus by Paul's converts: "Many of them also which used curious arts brought their books together, and burned them before all *men*: and they counted the price of them, and found *it* fifty thousand *pieces* of silver. So mightily grew the word of God and prevailed" (19–20). Milton is more reserved, recognizing that the right person might have been helped even by the Ephesian Scripts:

> As for the burning of those Ephesian books by St. *Pauls* converts, tis reply'd the books were magick, the Syriack so renders them. It was a privat act, a voluntary act, and leaves us to a voluntary imitation: the men in remorse burnt those books which were their own; the Magistrat by this exam-

ple is not appointed: these men practiz'd the books, another might perhaps have read them in some sort usefully. Good and evil we know in the field of this World grow up together almost inseparably; and the knowledge of good is so involv'd and interwoven with the knowledge of evill, and in so many cunning resemblances hardly to be discern'd, that those confused seeds which were impos'd on *Psyche* as an incessant labour to cull out, and sort asunder, were not more intermixt. It was from out the rinde of one apple tasted, that the knowledge of good and evill as two twins cleaving together leapt forth into the World. . . . As therefore the state of man now is; what wisdom can there be to choose, what continence to forbeare without the knowledge of evill? (*YP*, 2:514)

The theme of discrimination appears in a context that synthesizes classical, Hebraic, and Christian lore. The twins cleaving together might have been Castor and Pollux or Eteocles and Polyneices, but the ethos of the passage suggests that they are Jacob and Esau, the issue of a postlapsarian pentateuchal text. Indeed, the Fall splits the otherwise unified biblical text into primary and secondary laws, reflective of a new binary reality. Esau, the evil twin, was "a cunning hunter, a man of the field" (Gen. 25:27). But Jacob too learned survival "in the field of this World," and, through the "cunning resemblance" of disguise, obtained the blessing from his father Isaac to which Esau was entitled. Jacob's thorough knowledge of the habits, appearance, and tricks of speech peculiar to his evil brother allowed him to impersonate him successfully, but the deception was morally ambiguous. Who, in this episode, is good, the deceiver, or the victim? Are we wiser than Isaac, who always preferred Esau and in his blindness was unable to discern his favorite son?

Milton mingles good and evil here, as he does recurrently in the passage from *Tetrachordon* (cited above, *YP*, 2:665–66) that ranks Moses' secondary law of divorce above his primary law of marriage: "For if the absence of outward *good* be not so bad as the presence of a close *evil*, & that propriety . . . be but the attainment of some outward *good*, it is more natural & righteous that the law should sever us from an intimat *evil*, then appropriate any outward *good* to us from the community of nature" (my emphasis). Both excerpts conclude with a question that acknowledges the mixed nature of contemporary reality and dismisses the notion of absolute perfection. Grateful for the secondary law of Moses that permits divorce, Milton contrasts it with the gospel that demands perfection: "But who will be the man shall introduce this kind of common wealth, as christianity now goes?" A fallen condition is what "the state of man now is."

If the secondary law of Moses has no assigned place in the great epic's last books, its tone can still be heard occasionally in subtle counterpoint to the surgings of doctrinal piety. It is, as befits a fallen world, a mixed tone, acknowledging the inseparability of good and evil and the need to confront error with compassion. God concludes his charge to Michael, who must expel the first parents: "send them forth, though sorrowing, yet in peace" (11.117). In the very last lines, after the glorious consolations of Christian liberty and the "paradise within . . . happier far" (yet another devaluation of the epic's middle books), we find them erring, reluctant, and alone, but with hands clasped. Since the law of fallen human nature offers the prospect of life without redemption through Christ, it can at most only implicitly inform a passage in those last books whose evangelic mission is of overriding importance. The few passages that come to mind are spoken by Eve. Compassion for Adam, "afflicted" (10.863), prompts her to apply "Soft words to his fierce passion" (865). Her primary concern is neither salvation nor the kingdom of heaven but common household peace, however brief: "While yet we live, scarce one short hour perhaps, / Between us two let there be peace" (10.923–24).

In a compelling argument that unapologetically abrogates poetry with Reformation doctrine, Georgia Christopher rejects as sentimental Eve's speech and the common reader's "assumption that deliberate acts of human love can induce repentance and grace."[87] Christopher sees Eve's speech as providing at best "an unwitting but providential stimulus" to Adam's memory, and, against Eve's doctrinal blunders, she places Adam's virtuous gropings toward a correct understanding of the promise of Christ in the judgment of the serpent (10.1028–40). E. M. W. Tillyard represents the common reader, who hears in Eve's speech "a commonplace trickle of pure human sympathy" that brings with it "the first touch of regeneration"[88]—though, doubtless, that last term would provoke strong disagreement over whether and to what extent it must be understood in terms of a Pauline paradigm of salvation. For Christopher, the reader's sympathy for Eve is itself a sign of "ordinary human frailty," which is more affected by Adam's reconciliation to his spouse than by his reconciliation to his God. Recognizing the peril of preferring poetry over doctrine in the epic's last books, she concludes: "Unless the reader is willing to . . . perceive the sacramental nature of Adam's literary experience [viz., his interpretation of Gen. 3:15 as the *protevangelium*], there may appear to be a great esthetic falling off after Book IX of the epic."[89]

By replacing the primary Mosaic law of paradise with Christian liberty after the Fall, the last books of the epic assert discontinuity rather than continuity between dispensations. But Eve records the muffled vibrations of the secondary Mosaic law that accommodates legal imperatives to the fallen human condition. Her words of reconciliation briefly shift the focus of the last books of the epic, from redemption by an outside force to the consolations of a human relationship. After the lengthy typological vision and narration of Michael and Adam of a world "To good malignant, to bad men benign" (12.538), Eve offers a brief glimpse of an otherwise suppressed alternative to the epic's last books—of poetry instead of doctrine and synthesis instead of rejection.

In the last direct speech of *Paradise Lost*, Eve, no longer disconsolate, receives Adam with "words not sad":

> Whence thou return'st, and whither went'st, I know;
>
> . . . .
>
> In mee is no delay; with thee to go,
> Is to stay here; without thee here to stay,
> Is to go hence unwilling; thou to mee
> Art all things under Heav'n, all places thou,
> Who for my wilful crime art banisht hence.
> This further consolation yet secure
> I carry hence; though all by mee is lost,
> Such favor I unworthy am voutsaf't,
> By mee the Promis'd Seed shall all restore.
>
> (12.610 and 615–23)

The radically Pauline theology of the last books has systematically devalued Adam. The angel Michael has stripped him of the privilege of genetic transmission as father of the human race: his sin transmits only death (Rom. 5:14, 1 Cor. 15:22), and the distinction between the children of loins and of faith (*PL*, 12.446–50; Rom. 9:6–8) makes believing Christians the children of Abraham's faith and sinners the progeny of Adam. The redeemer is of the woman's seed; Adam, like the Jews, is of the devil's seed (*PL*, 12.394–95; John 8:44), and his progeny, in turn, are the evildoers of every generation, like those who perished in Noah's flood ("all thy offspring" [11.755]). Typology, with its tendency toward generalization and deindividualization, requires Adam to remove the tokens of his identity in order to be saved. The old Adam must be fully absorbed in the second Adam, just as the Church requires the absorption of Judaism in Christianity, the second Israel. Where the theology of the last books insists relentlessly on discontinuities between prelapsarian and postlapsarian life, Eve's healing words reach back to paradise, where Adam was "no shadow" (4.470). Her first great love lyric described her experience of temporal integration while in Adam's presence: "With thee conversing I forget all time, / All seasons and thir change, all please alike" (4.639–40). Now, after the Fall, Adam's presence transcends place: "thou to mee / Art all things under Heav'n, all places thou." In spite of doctrinal emphasis on discontinuity and devaluation, Eve proclaims the continuity of her love for Adam and the supreme value of their life together. Although Eve's rhetoric may at first sound Pauline in its use of paradox and hyperbole (leaving is really staying; the world obliterated for the sake of one man), her message is entirely antipathetic to Paul's. Adam the unworthy becomes worthy, not through a complex system of mediation that requires his own loss of identity and his redeemer's crucifixion, but simply and immediately through the transforming power of Eve's love for him.

The Fall divides the primary law of paradise from the secondary law of "the field of this World" (*YP*, 2:514), and Eve is now prepared to enter with Adam this laborious field to which they have been sentenced (10.201–8). In the divorce tracts, Milton explains how human love is the motive force behind both the primary Mosaic law of marriage and the secondary Mosaic law of divorce: "Which if it were so needfull before the fall, when man was much more perfect in himself, how much more is it needfull now against all the sorrows and casualties of this life to have an intimate and speaking help, a ready and reviving associate in marriage" (*YP*, 2:251). Indeed, Moses' laws of divorce constitute an exposition of the divine instituting command of marriage in paradise, though accommodated to "this imperfect state" (*YP*, 2:311).

Hebrews 11 is the principal source of Michael's narration, and the severe antitheses of the entire epistle, consistently devaluing the Hebrew Bible, inform the epic's final vision. But Eve's proclamation harks back to paradise and its synthesis of dispensations. Receiving Adam, who has already "descended" (12.606 and 607) and will descend further, she evokes Andromache of the white arms meeting Hektor at the Skaian gates, "whereby he would issue into the plain": "Hektor, you are father to me, and my honoured mother, / you are my brother, and you it is who are my young husband."[90]

For love of Adam, Eve renounces national affiliation ("all places thou"), and her speech, with its clear echo of Ruth, places the epic momentarily in "the field of this World." "And Ruth said, Entreat me not to leave thee, or to return from following after thee: for whither thou goest, I will go; and where thou lodgest, I will lodge: thy people shall be my people, and thy God my God" (1:16). Eve's brave, heartening charge to Adam to lead them out of paradise ("now lead on; / In mee is no delay") merits comparison with Ruth's decision to live with Naomi in a decidedly secondary world. Ruth is a widow, and Boaz will redeem her when the nearer kinsman defaults. Governed by the secondary Mosaic laws of gleaning (Lev. 23:22) and levirate marriage (Deut. 25:5–10), Ruth risks bold decisions to work out her own salvation in an alien world, one in which God does not intervene directly. Ruth, as Phyllis Trible notes, is a woman's story in a man's world,[91] and Eve's single speech is a rare Miltonic paraphrase of two brave women's speeches at critical moments in pagan epic and biblical idyll.

As Naomi is silenced by Ruth's radical break with family, country, and faith, so is Adam silenced by a love that ranks him above paradise: "So spake our Mother *Eve*, and *Adam* heard / Well pleas'd, but answer'd not" (12.624–25). Is Hebrew poetry or Christian doctrine the principal source of Adam's pleasure? "Well pleas'd" recalls the second Adam, "my beloved, in whom my soul is well pleased" (Matt. 12:18). Michael has told Adam to speak with Eve "chiefly" about "The great deliverance by her Seed to come / (For by the Woman's Seed) on all Mankind" (12.600–1). And Eve's very last words, after her profession of love for Adam, are of "This further consolation," "By mee the Promis'd Seed shall all restore" (620 and 623). Eve's postscript, "This further consolation," may be deliberately played down, the capital theme of paradise regained remembered only as an afterthought, the Miltonic bard's ironic counterbalance at the epic's conclusion of the almost parenthetical "with loss of Eden" in the opening invocation.[92] Or the real burden of Eve's speech may not be here, in her perfunctory recapitulation of a doctrinal lesson, but rather in her radical affirmation of faith in the only Adam she knows.

According to the midrashic *Pirke de-Rabbi Nathan*,

> When Rabban Johanan ben Zakkai's son died, his disciples came to comfort him. Rabbi Eliezer entered, sat down before him, and said to him, "Master, by your leave, may I say something to you?"
>
> "Speak," he answered.
>
> Rabbi Eliezer said, "Adam had a son who died, yet he allowed himself to be comforted concerning him. And how do we know that he allowed himself to be comforted concerning him? For it is said: 'Adam knew his wife again' [Gen. 4:25]. You, too, should be comforted."[93]

Adam and Eve "hand in hand" (12.648) may also find consolation in the renewal of desire. Worlds apart from Michael's doctrinal consolations in the epic's last books, this midrash emphasizes merely human grief and comfort. Indeed, it is the degree of sympathy for Adam's plight (rather than a more predictable insistence on its irrelevance) that makes R. Johanan's harsh rejection of R. Eliezer's offered comfort completely unexpected: "Is it not enough that I grieve over my own that you remind me of Adam's grief?" Whether Adam's reconciliation with Eve or with Christ is the truer consolation depends in part on the degree to which the Christian scheme of redemption has been emotionally integrated into Eve's final speech. It is finally for each reader to decide whether Adam's beloved, in whom his soul is well pleased, is his wife, his redeemer, or both.

THE GOSPEL AS HEIR OF THE LAW

It is not Eve, but Adam and Michael who dominate the epic's last books, the doctrinal matrix of which is decidedly not the secondary law of Moses, but rather the New Testament, particularly the epistles of Paul. Michael's last speech to Adam evokes the Mosaic law by emphasizing command and obedience and by identifying an emblem of the law's inaccessibility:

> . . . the hour precise
> Exacts our parting hence; and see the Guards,
> By mee encampt on yonder Hill, expect
> Their motion, at whose Front a flaming Sword,
> In signal of remove, waves fiercely round;
> We may no longer stay: go, waken *Eve.*
>
> *(12.589–94)*

In the divorce tracts, Milton spoke positively of an unabrogated secondary Mosaic "Law that is the exacter of our obedience ev'n under the Gospel" (*YP,* 2:303). In Michael's peremptory lines, the *gan eden* of Genesis (literally, the garden of pleasure, delicacy), a paradise combining pleasure and an easily performable law, has turned into the Mosaic law itself, no longer benign but a law of wrath (Rom. 4:15). The hour "exacts" departure, the angelic guards await the order to move, and Raphael, under orders himself, commands Adam to waken Eve and accompany her into exile. Immediately following Eve's last speech, the Miltonic bard's comparison of the angels to mist gathering ground at a laborer's heel (12.628–32) recalls the sentences of hard labor (10.201–8) and of the *protevangelium* ("thou bruise his heel" [10.181]) that first turned Torah into Old Testament. The flaming sword waving fiercely round "[i]n signal of remove" from paradise reminds Christians insistently of the primary Mosaic law and its inaccessibility. "The brandisht Sword of God . . . blaz'd / Fierce as a Comet," already beginning to parch the temperate climate of paradise (633–36). From a distance, Adam and Eve regard this emblem of the wrath-working law:

> They looking back, all th' Eastern side beheld
> Of Paradise, so late thir happy seat,
> Wav'd over by that flaming Brand, the Gate
> With dreadful Faces throng'd, and fiery Arms.
>
> *(641–44)*

Before the Fall, Raphael, the angel of the Hebrew Bible, visited Adam and Eve as a "glorious Shape," "another Morn / Ris'n on mid-noon"

(5.309 and 310–11). But now the faces of the cherubim occupying paradise are "dreadful." Henry Ainsworth comments on the "fiery Arms" of
the angels, which terrify:

> Such spiritually is the use of the Law and doctrine thereof, which terrifieth
> the conscience, and by the works whereof, no flesh can be justified, *Rom.*
> 3.20. but it serveth to drive men unto Christ, that they may be made righ-
> teous by faith, *Gal.* 3.24.[94]

The *"fierie Law"* is so called "to shew the nature and effect of the Law,
which is *like fire, Jer.* 23.29."[95] John Salkeld cites Ambrose, for whom the
fiery arms symbolize a baptism of fire in Christ for those who want to
return to the law. He also cites Rupertus, who affirms

> *that therefore this fire was put before Paradise that those who should
> passe to everlasting glory might passe immaculate. . . . But this fire* (saith
> Rupertus) *which is put before Paradise maketh it altogether inaccessible, by
> reason of the vehement heate it sendeth forth, which diffuseth it selfe very
> farre.*[96]

The flaming sword preventing access to the garden is the mythic correlative of the Pauline doctrine that "Christ is the end of the law" (Rom.
10:4), he who has cut off any route by which believers might return to
that law. Paul's audacious pun on "end" asserts that Christ fulfills the law
by abrogating it. For Paul, Christ did not merely override the Mosaic law.
By the agency of that law, he was made a curse in the place of sinners,
and, by his dying, he has ransomed and redeemed them. This means,
however, that one can no longer attain salvation by means of obedience
to the law. The righteousness that Christ effects cancels all human righteousness, making it instead the possession only of those who believe
(Rom. 10:4).

   The correlative in Milton's poetics of the flaming sword that protects
paradise is the barrier, transparent but impermeable, that keeps Hebraic
Eden separate from the fallen world of Christian experience. Under the
Edenic-Mosaic law of paradise, the Miltonic bard can compare Eve with
Sarah, and Adam with Abraham, Moses, and David, but he must refrain
from using typology, which would taint prelapsarian life with determi-
nacy. To introduce prematurely into paradise Paul's message of faith in
Christ and freedom from the law—the two fundamental innovations that
distinguish Christianity from Judaism—would be to degrade our first
parents, making them sinful adumbrations of the second Adam and Eve,
Mary and Christ. From the standpoint of Christianity, Adam and Eve
are like the Jews. In the characteristically forthright explanation of
Yeshayahu Leibowitz,

The Church could be reconciled to the continued existence of the Jewish people only to the extent that this existence was severed from the proper existence of mankind, that of the Christian world, whose members are the "true Jews." . . . Christianity regards itself as the legitimate heir of Judaism, and the heir cannot take possession of his inheritance while the testator is still alive.[97]

In the final books of the epic, Adam, who in his innocence knew the Son only as his creator and as the hero of the war in heaven, acknowledges him as his redeemer and so converts to Pauline Christianity. Behind the wall of paradise, in the epic's middle books, the Miltonic bard tries to keep inoperative postlapsarian experience, particularly the Christian experience of salvation in a crucified messiah. The attempt to block off the fallen reader's experience bears directly on the question of free will in paradise. As Arnold Stein has noted, Milton attempts to create in the Edenic books a suggestive pattern of foreknowledge that refrains from overt influence or necessity, in which presentiments of the Fall (such as Eve's dream and Adam's disclosure of excessive passion) do not transgress the boundary of innocence.[98] The narrator would like the reader to view the Fall, when it comes, as understandable but not inevitable, not determined by internal necessity. This problem of making Adam and Eve incline toward sinful behavior while yet remaining sinless is related to the narrator's problem of telling an oft-told story, the outcome of which is foreknown, without appearing to manipulate his characters. Milton discourages the direct application of postlapsarian experience and interpretation to events before the Fall by creating a paradise governed by the Hebrew Bible, where perfect creatures under a benign law of life speak directly with their Creator-God. After the Fall, Torah becomes a captive text, the Old Testament, and the narrator, who has been holding back, lets go, degrading our first parents, the law, and, like Paul, bankrupting the world for the sake of Christ. Moreover, what were in paradise regarded merely as presentiments and tendencies develop quickly into full-blown causes leading to inevitable evil consequences, which God, the narrator, and the angel Michael elaborate throughout the last books. The grimly methodical devaluation of the law of human freedom that Milton had regarded positively in the tracts of 1643–45 reflects the disillusionment of a great idealist, for whom England had been a second Israel.

Theological and aesthetic implications of Milton's changing conceptions of the law proliferate almost as uncontrollably as original sin itself. I should like to conclude by summarizing some doctrinal points and by touching very briefly on some of the implications that are developed in the next chapters. Milton is writing a Pauline theodicy on the theme of lost paradise governed by a benign proto-Mosaic law, though Paul himself would have found such a theme uncongenial. Paul believes passionately in the paradise within of death to the world in Christ, and he never looks back longingly at the state of innocence. Paul regards the Pentateuchal law as a strictly indissoluble unity, never working out explicitly or consciously distinctions between its moral and ceremonial components, although he seems to be thinking of the former when he speaks of the law's holiness and of the latter when he speaks of its inferiority . (To differentiate methodically between individual legal prescriptions, assigning a higher value to some than to others, as Milton does in the divorce tracts, is generally to try to rescue the principle of the law.) For Paul, the period of the entire Mosaic law was meant to be a temporary time of slavery, lasting only until the appearance of Christ. God wished to make sin all the more powerful by means of the law, in order that he might then destroy it all the more completely. The ultimate purpose of the law, then, is to convince those under it that they are unable to fulfill it. Paul understands the Old Testament as a Christian Bible, which preaches salvation through faith and which relegates Torah to an inferior position. Hence Abraham, who lived before the time of the law, "believed in the Lord; and he counted it to him for righteousness" (Gen. 15:6; Rom. 4:3; Gal. 3:6).[99]

Between 1643 and 1645, the period of the great prose tracts and of the *Poems*, Milton felt and recorded what Paul never did, the saving power of the Pentateuchal law. The concealed problem in Paul's conception of salvation history is why the fatal law was ever permitted at all, if it could do no more than multiply sin. But Milton's prose and poetry, throughout his career, transcribe his living appreciation of the spirit and content of Torah. Milton's confidence in unmediated human achievement, the indispensability of human response and initiative, the identification of his country with Israel as a holy community, the literary achievement of the Hebrew Bible itself separate from its doctrinal manipulations into a pattern of prediction and fulfillment, its concessions to fallen human nature in the field of this world—these enable Milton to understand the Hebrew scriptures in themselves in a way that Paul never could. Paul stripped away the literal text and understood the Old Testament, as he saw it, from within, as a Christian Bible. This Milton does in the last two books of *Paradise Lost*, where his explicit Paulinism devalues a paradise and a law that Paul never knew and, therefore, never missed. They are entirely different from the Hebraic paradise and the law of the epic's middle books.

Since there is no qualitative difference between the prohibition in Eden and the rest of the Mosaic law, Milton must avoid the hint that the law's purpose is to convince the people that they are unable to fulfill it. After the Fall, Michael reminds Adam that Christ will destroy evil "by fulfilling that which thou didst want, / Obedience to the Law of God, impos'd / On penalty of death" (12.396–98). Before the Fall, a Pauline conception of the law would taint paradise with determinism, making the Fall not merely a foregone conclusion, but the very purpose of the instituting prohibition. The heavy stakes in a theodicy require a perfect law. Otherwise, as Milton reminds the reader, God would be made "the direct author of sin" (*YP*, 2:655).

Where the purpose of the law's somber interlude remains a problem for Paul, Milton's solution in *Paradise Lost* is to create a paradise that combines the primary and secondary laws of Moses and the fate of our first parents and Israel. Milton conflates the expulsion from paradise and exile from the promised land (*PL*, 9.1121; Ps. 137:1). Once Adam and Eve have broken the law, there is no point in putting them under it again, especially since sin has already proliferated uncontrollably ("manifold in sin" [10.16]; "So many laws argue so many sins" [12.283]) and since their ability to perform it has become impaired. Our first parents leave paradise as proto-Christians—no longer under the law—whose limitations the angel Michael has emphasized (12.285–314) in response to Adam's Pauline question about its purpose (280–84).

Countless Reformation expositors emphasize continuity between the original law of paradise and its renewal at Sinai, the primary and secondary laws of Moses.[100] All of them regard the law with some degree of hostility, contrasting the covenant of works with the covenant of grace and, within the covenant of works, the easily performable law before the Fall and the less easily performable one afterwards. William Pemble explains:

> By the *Covenant of Workes*, wee understand that we call in one word the Law: Namely, that meanes of bringing man to *Salvation*, which is by perfect obedience unto the will of God. Hereof there are also two severall administrations. 1. The first is with *Adam* before his Fall. When *Immortality* and *Happinesse* was promised to man, and confirmed by an externall *Symbole* of the *Tree of life*: upon condition that he continued obedient to God, as well in all other things; as in that particular Commandement of not eating of the *Tree of knowledge of good and evill*. 2. The second administration of this covenant was the renuing thereof with the *Israelites* at Mount *Sinai*: where . . . God revived the law, by a compendious and full declaration of all duties required of man, towards God or his neighbour, expressed in the Decalogue. According to the tenor of which law God entred into covenant with the *Israelites*, promising to be their God; in bestowing upon them all blessings of life and happinesse, upon condition that they would be his people, obeying all things that hee had commanded. Which condition they accepted of, promising an absolute obedience. *All things which the Lord hath said we*

will doe. Exod. 19.24. & also submitting themselves to all punishment in case they disobeyed; saying Amen to the curse of the law. Cursed bee every one that confirmeth not all the words of this law to doe them: and all the people shall say Amen. Deut. 27.26.[101]

Most of the expositors follow a strict Pauline argument, concentrating on the discovery that the Old Testament, although in a hidden and prefatory manner, yet speaks of salvation through the covenant of grace. Joseph Mede contrasts the open and hidden covenants:

> For all the time under the Law, the open and apparent Covenant was the Covenant of Works, to make them the more to see their own misery and condemnation, and so to long after Christ who was yet to come, and at whose comming this obligation should be quite cancelled. Yet neverthelesse, together with this open Covenant, there was a secret and hidden Covenant, which was the Covenant of *Grace*, that they might not be altogether without the meanes of salvation whilst Christ yet tarryed.[102]

Few expositors are as humane as Jeremy Taylor, who cannot entirely conceal his uneasiness with the Pauline scheme. Despite human inability to fulfill the commandments, they multiplied, and even before Sinai "they were very many: And still God held over mans head the Covenant of Works." "Until man had sinned he was not the subject of mercy: and if he had not then receiv'd mercy, the infliction had been too severe and unjust, since the Covenant was beyond the measures of man, after it began to multiply into particular laws, and man by accident was lessen'd in his strengths."[103]

Milton's unique solution to the Pauline problem of the law's purpose is to strengthen the bond between the laws of Eden and Moses by placing both the original prohibition and the promulgation of the Mosaic law within the state of innocence. Indeed, the chronology of *Paradise Lost* begins with the metaphorical begetting of the Son as ruler over the angels, which Raphael narrates as Sinai theophany. God's emphatically legal declaration ("Hear my Decree, which unrevok'd shall stand") compresses into just two lines the two tables of the law, the love of God ("Under his great Vice-gerent Reign" [5.609]) and of our neighbor ("abide / United as one individual Soul" [609–10]). Satan arouses his rebel troops by complaining that God means to "introduce / Law and edict on us" (5.797–98). Abdiel, who "divine commands obey'd" with zeal (806), spells out the difference for Satan between the benign Mosaic law of heaven and the Pauline Mosaic law of hell:

> . . . henceforth
> No more be troubl'd how to quit the yoke
> Of God's *Messiah*: those indulgent Laws

> Will not be now voutsaf'd, other decrees
> Against thee are gone forth without recall;
> That Golden Sceptre which thou didst reject
> Is now an Iron Rod to bruise and break
> Thy disobedience.
>
> (5.881–88)

Identifying Adam and Eve with heroes of the Hebrew Bible and placing the angels in heaven under the "Golden Sceptre" of the law, Milton presents that law as benign and perfect. Fallen Adam and Eve can be saved by the hidden covenant of faith in Christ, instead of by the iron rod of a law whose commandments are beyond their ability to perform. The dual aspect of the Edenic-Mosaic law before and after the Fall of humankind and the angels allows Milton to solve a related problem: how to reconcile belief in an original state of perfection with belief in an evolutionary deity whose successive dispensations (natural law, Mosaic law, gospel) manifest divine benevolence ever more clearly and fully. Milton associates Hebraic paradise with the benign law, which requires neither the sacrifice nor the rejection that will later characterize Christianity. Adam's love entire includes, but cannot be summed up by, his love for Eve, and his love of God does not trivialize his love of Eve. The higher includes the lower. The postlapsarian Mosaic law, what Paul calls a minister of death and condemnation, will be superseded by the gospel, a sign of the improvable perfection of divine providence.

In light of Milton's heavy doctrinal reliance on Paul, his strenuous effort to keep him out of paradise is remarkably successful. But there are moments of failure, such as the explanation of Raphael's mission in the argument of book 5: "God *to render man inexcusable sends Raphael to admonish him of his obedience, of his free estate, of his enemy near at hand; who he is, and why his enemy, and whatever else may avail* Adam *to know.*" "*Raphael* the sociable Spirit" (5.221), "Divine Interpreter" (7.72), and the benevolent guest who reveals the secrets of the Hebrew Bible becomes here a personification of the Mosaic law according to Paul. Raphael's purpose—and the law's—is to prepare, admonish, and forewarn (5.245) those who cannot be helped because they are doomed. For Paul, "they are without excuse" (Rom. 1:20), "Therefore thou art inexcusable, O man" (Rom. 2:1). The Mosaic law leaves those who live by it "without excuse."[104] Sir Walter Raleigh describes without remorse the purpose of the Mosaic law:

> This Law, it pleased God to ingrave in stone . . . that so these Children of *Israel*, though bred among an Idolatrous people in *Egypt*, might be without excuse: the slight defences of ignorance being taken from them.[105]

The . . . end of the Law, is to render us inexcusable before God: who knowing so perfect a law, do not keepe it; the law requiring a perfect and intire,
not a broken or halfe obedience: but both inward and outward righteousnesse, and performances of duty to God and Men.[106]

Milton, writing in *De doctrina* that "THOSE WHO DO NOT BELIEVE ARE
DEPRIVED OF ALL EXCUSE (*YP*, 6:454), cites, in addition to Romans, John
15:22: "If I had not come and spoken unto them, they had not had sin;
but now they have no cloak for their sin." The old Adam, like the old
Israel, enjoys advantages given early by God. But the Jews' failure to recognize the messiah reflects a moral and spiritual delinquency exposed in
the most Judeophobic of the four gospels. Within the framework of the
gospel, to call unfallen Adam inexcusable is to make him already guilty.
Perhaps William Empson intuits a relationship between Raphael in the
argument of book 5 and Paul's conception of the law when he claims
"that Adam and Eve would not have fallen unless God had sent Raphael
to talk to them."[107] It has already been seen how Eve briefly and undis-
ruptively introduces the secondary Mosaic law into the Pauline postlapsarian world of book 12. But when the gospel invades the law—as it will
with particularly catastrophic results in book 9—the epic's equilibrium is
threatened.

As a concluding example of Paul's sometimes uncontrollable presence
in Milton's work, it is worth considering briefly the last line of the epic's
opening invocation: "justify the ways of God to men" (1.26). Those editors of Milton bold enough to comment on the line invoke Paul's conception of justification by faith in Christ. J. B. Broadbent cites Romans 8,[108]
and Alastair Fowler refers somewhat vaguely to the biblical meaning of
"justify," which "implies spiritual rather than rational understanding."[109] Pauline justification has been translated variously—including,
but not limited to, "righteoused," "acquitted," and "put into a right relationship with" God—but it never depends on human obedience: "if justification were through the law, then Christ died to no purpose" (Gal.
2:21).

The Reformers define "justify" in two incompatible ways: as Hebraic
legal justice that requires obedience to the law and demands punishment
as satisfaction for its violation, and as evangelical justification by faith
alone. These two meanings in a single word compress the polity of Eden
and of the fallen world. William Pemble emphasizes the incompatibility
of the legal and evangelical meanings:

> the law gives life unto the just upon condition of perfect Obedience in all
> things: the Gospell gives life unto sinners upon condition, they repent &
> beleive [sic] in Christ Jesus. Whence it is plaine that in the point of justifica-
> tion these two are incompatible, & that therefore . . . justification by the
> workes of the law, makes voide the covenant of grace.[110]

Arminius places justification in paradise:

> The condition of the law . . . as it was delivered to Adam, excludes the neces-
> sity of making the promise and announcing the Gospel; and, on the other
> hand, the necessity of making the promise and announcing the Gospel, de-
> clares, that man has not obeyed the law which was given to him. For justifi-
> cation cannot be at once both "of grace" and "of debt"; nor can it, at the
> same time, admit and exclude "boasting" (Gal. ii, 17; Rom. iv, 4, 5; iii,
> 27).[111]

Even in *De doctrina*, Milton's generally conventional Pauline discussion of justification appears to distinguish between the legal relationship
of God the Father and the Son ("Filial obedience: as a sacrifice / Glad to
be offer'd, he attends the will / Of his great Father" [*PL*, 3.269–70] and
the evangelical one between the Son and humankind ("his meek aspect
/ Silent yet spake, and breath'd immortal love / To mortal men" [3.266–
68]).

> It is evident that our justification is freely given so far as we are concerned,
> but it is not free from Christ's point of view. He paid the price, and imputed
> our sins to himself, and of his own free will washed them away and expiated
> them. We receive his righteousness, imputed to us, as a gift. We pay nothing
> for it, we merely have to believe. Thus the Father is appeased, and pro-
> nounces all believers righteous. There could not be a simpler or more equita-
> ble method of satisfaction. (*YP*, 6:486)

Gulielmus Bucanus, who recognizes that the verb "justify" appears far
more often in the Hebrew Bible than in the New Testament, enumerates
some of its legal meanings:

> It is used in the Scripture for a word of lawe, and signifieth to impute Jus-
> tice[,] . . . to accompt a man righteous, to repute a man to be just,
> to absolve and acquite a man from the crimes objected against him, to
> discharge a man, or by sentence to pronounce him just, to make & ac-
> knowledge a man to be just, which signification the Hebrew word *hizdik*
> agreeth with, and is everie where in the Scripture opposed to the word of
> condemning.[112]

Once one has the Reformation definitions of "justify," one may try,
like Malvolio, yet another Puritan, to fit Milton's apparently Hebraic
legal assertion into a Pauline framework. The bard prays for the ability to
justify God's ways to humankind. Elsewhere, not here, he celebrates the
appeasement of God the Father through the Son's sacrifice (3.403–15).
Looking for a reading that actually makes sense, it is recalled that, in the
Defence of the People of England, Milton inscribes the phrase "judges
and is judged" in a specifically rabbinic context, where it applies to the
royal descendants of David (*YP*, 4:354). Further, in *The Doctrine and*

Discipline of Divorce, Milton describes God himself submitting to human judgment. In that treatise, the Mosaic law rather than the Son incarnates deity:

> the law is [God's] reveled will, . . . herein he appears to us as it were in human shape, enters into cov'nant with us, swears to keep it, binds himself like a just lawgiver to his own prescriptions, gives himself to be understood by men, *judges and is judg'd*, measures and is commensurat to right reason. (*YP*, 2:292; my emphasis)

One might perhaps proffer the suggestion that to justify the ways of God to men is to judge God as a king willing to be judged, who "gives himself to be understood by men."[113] God's justice might best be understood as legal rather than evangelical, inherent rather than imputed. The arrogation by Paul himself of Hebrew concepts such as love and faith constitutes an entirely successful act of piracy. But the example of "justify" suggests that readers are so conditioned to read all of Milton typologically that they cede to Paul not only the last books of the epic, which are rightfully his, but the entire poem from the outset. An exclusively Pauline reading of Milton forgets, or suppresses, his Hebraic past, even when that past furnishes the plain sense of a given text. Because the gospel succeeds the law in Milton's great epic, one may well concede the superiority of its doctrinal consolations. We also succeed our first parents, but our sense of superiority over them has been attained, if at all, only at the cost of innocence, and in the coin of our mortality and misery, so that it is at best a doubtful "superiority." It is, in the bard's words, "Knowledge of Good bought dear by knowing ill" (4.222).

CHAPTER TWO

Milton's Hebraic Monism

To PARAPHRASE Coleridge on the effect of reading Fielding after Richardson, to read book 4 of *Paradise Lost* after book 3 is to emerge "from a sick room heated by stoves, into an open lawn, on a breezy day in May."[1] Heaven, of course, has its own poetic splendors, including a strikingly monistic description of beatitude among the Spirits as at once perceptible through the senses and intelligible to the mind:

> Thus while God spake, ambrosial fragrance fill'd
> All Heav'n, and in the blessed Spirits elect
> Sense of new joy ineffable diffus'd.
>
> (3.135–37)

But Pauline dualism dominates the doctrinal heart of Book 3. In this "sickroom," the Son is the patient who elects to undergo slow torture, and the Father is something worse than the surgeon who guarantees recovery "after unconsciousness had finally supervened."[2] Pious readers have attempted to explain every apparently objectionable phrase in God's encyclopedic sermon on human depravity and Christian salvation: the defensive "whose fault? / Whose but his own?" (3.96–97), the snarl, "ingrate, he had of mee / All he could have" (97–98), the coy equivocation of the omniscient deity's "if I foreknew" (117), and the ultimate appeal to a hyper-Pauline travesty of the law, "Die hee or Justice must" (210). Some readers will prefer, above all explanations, the refreshment and lucidity of paradise, where a creator concentrates blessing on human beings who do not yet need to know the terrible price of redemption. In the aftermath of turbulence, the Miltonic bard takes one back to a time before suffering, human or divine, became necessary and to a place of clarity and repose.

Milton's monistic belief in the continuity of body, mind, and spirit finds passionate expression in paradise, where it sounds poetic rather than doctrinal. In the state of perfection, where "smiles from Reason flow" (9.239), and with "delight to Reason join'd" (9.243), the intelligence shines into the senses. After the Fall, Michael's various warnings to Adam presuppose disjunction and dualism: "Judge not what is best / By Pleasure, though to Nature seeming meet" (11.603–4). The right order of ascending value in paradise includes the lower in the higher, creation not disparaged as "mean" in comparison with Eve, but rather "in her

summ'd up, in her contain'd" (8.473).[3] Paradise, at once a privileged
zone and the entire inhabited earth, is uniquely suited to monistic inclusiveness. Divine blessings are both particular and universal, since
Adam and Eve are the world's king and queen and its total human population. There is no conflict in paradise between monogamous and polyga-
mous conceptions of marriage or between monarchy and republicanism.
With the Fall and the subsequent expulsion from Eden comes the dissociation of particularity from universality, resulting in a competitive desire
among individuals and rival nations for privilege, election, covenant, and
dominion.

Since Milton's monism is inclusive by definition, it is appropriate that
no one so far has been able to talk about it as a principle separate from his
poetry. Recent sweeping discourse on the nexus of religion and literature
evokes for readers of *Paradise Lost* Raphael's speeches on angelic diges-
tion and degree, the central texts of Milton's monism, in which the higher
being is not higher by virtue of any exclusion but by virtue of greater
inclusiveness:

> and food alike those pure
> Intelligential substances require
> As doth your Rational; and both contain
> Within them every lower faculty
> Of sense, whereby they hear, see, smell, touch, taste,
> Tasting concoct, digest, assimilate,
> And corporeal to incorporeal turn.
>
> (5.407–13)

Whereas Raphael describes the cosmos as a great plant, Nathan A. Scott
speaks of the power of poetry to unite the deepest things in ourselves and
in our world as though they were "but a taproot uniting the human reality with the ultimate ground of all reality."[4] In book 5 of *Paradise Lost*,
every item in the hierarchy of existence is sustained and comprehended by
its superior, and the chain of causes terminates in the first cause:[5] "In
contemplation of created things / By steps we may ascend to God" (511–
12). The coalescence in Milton's paradise of matter, mind, and spirit
evokes an awareness of the vitally fluid unity of the world and attests to
an infinitude both beyond that world and bound up with it.

Genesis 2, the most monistic of all Western texts,[6] is the source of Milton's conception of the indivisibility of body and soul. Regarding the creation of man as a "living soul" (Gen. 2:7), he insists:

We must interpret this as meaning that man is a living being, intrinsically
and properly one and individual. He is not double or separable: not, as is
commonly thought, produced from and composed of two different and dis-

tinct elements, soul and body. On the contrary, the whole man is the soul, and the soul the man: a body, in other words, or individual substance, animated, sensitive, and rational. (*De doctrina Christiana*, YP, 6:318)

Milton is sufficiently competent in Hebrew philology to find nine texts in *Tanakh* featuring the word *nephesh*, in which "all properties of the body are attributed to the soul as well" (*YP*, 6:318). Noting that the account of Adam begetting Seth (Gen. 5:3) uses the same words *zelem* (image) and *d'muth* (likeness) as that of God creating *adam* (Gen. 1:26), Milton concludes that we and God resemble each other externally as well as internally:

> If *God is said to have created man in his own image, after his own likeness*, Gen. i. 26, and not only his mind but also his external appearance (unless the same words mean something different when they are used again in Gen. v.3: *Adam begot his son after his own likeness, in his own image*), and if God attributes to himself again and again a human shape and form, why should we be afraid of assigning to him something he assigns to himself, provided we believe that what is imperfect and weak in us is, when ascribed to God, utterly perfect and utterly beautiful. (*YP*, 6:135–36)

Milton's readers have registered resistance to some of the implications of a monism that is unmistakably Hebraic in its origin and nature. Where Milton proves from Leviticus 21:11 ("*animas mortuas*" [dead souls]) that the soul like the body is subject to death, Sumner's translation relies instead on the Authorized Version's "dead body."[7] Milton's Hebraic monistic texts—particularly the prose tracts of 1643–45 and the middle books of *Paradise Lost*—are entirely incompatible with the Pauline epistles, which are among the most dualistic of Western texts. The monistic prose tracts employ a specific comparatist historical-philological exegesis to demonstrate the vitally fluid unity of natural law, the Mosaic law, and a gospel from which Paul's devaluation of the law has been excised.

In order to find theoretical justification for Milton's transfer of Christian liberty from the religious to the political arena, Arthur Barker attempts to co-opt Milton's monism and to assimilate it to an impermeable Pauline doctrine. From its opening paragraph contrasting gospel and law, grace and works, life to the regenerate and "ETERNAL DEATH TO UNBE-LIEVERS" (*YP*, 6:521), Milton's chapter on Christian liberty is founded on Pauline duality. Barker attempts to establish an impossible continuity between the prose tracts of 1643–45 and this chapter by deleting the Mosaic law from the former and by adding natural law to the latter. Obliterating differences between these texts, he can then trace Milton's first formulation of his heterodox doctrine of Christian liberty to the divorce tracts. According to Barker, the "important" "effect of Milton's monism on his interpretation of Christian liberty"[8] includes a conception of morality for the regenerate free from the law and under the gospel as "a spiritual and *natural*, not a legal, morality."[9]

His motive for applying Milton's monism to the Pauline chapters of *De doctrina* soon becomes clear. "Since redemption included the restoration of the whole man, not merely of the soul as distinct from the body, Milton applied the privileges of Christian liberty to the natural as well as the spiritual sphere, and so associated himself with the extreme Puritan revolutionaries."[10] Attempting to graft a monist conception of natural liberty upon Milton's Pauline conception of Christian liberty, Barker would create a single entity of nature and grace, all of humankind and the regenerate. There would then be no essential difference between the liberty Milton affirms in *De doctrina* 1:xxvii, and that affirmed by an extreme Puritan revolutionary, such as the Leveller Richard Overton:

> By naturall birth, all men are equally and alike borne to like propriety, liberty, and freedome, and as we are delivered of God by the hand of nature into this world, every one with a naturall, innate freedome and propriety (as it were writ in the table of every mans heart, never to be obliterated) even so are we to live, every one equally and alike to enjoy his Birthright and priviledge; even all whereof God by nature hath made him free. . . . Every man by nature being a King, Priest and Prophet in his owne naturall circuite and compass, whereof no second may partake, but by deputation, commission, and free consent from him, whose naturall right and freedome it is. . . . For by nature we are the sons of *Adam* and from him have legitimatly derived a natural propriety, right and freedome, which only we require.[11]

When Barker describes Milton's view of morality for the regenerate under the gospel as "a spiritual and natural, not a legal, morality," he attempts to pit a unified gospel and natural law against the Mosaic law. But there is no place at all for nature in the Pauline chapters of *De doctrina*, which are driven entirely by dualistic and hierarchical oppositions of Old and New Testaments. Basic inequality is built into the chapter on Christian liberty, which presupposes distinctions rejected by Overton between nature and grace and between Christians and other human beings. Overton's monistic text evokes an inward Mosaic law ("writ in the table of every mans heart") and Christ's threefold mediatorial office as Milton conceives of it in *De doctrina*, 1:xv ("King, Priest and Prophet"), but he refers the Mosaic and the evangelical back to the natural that contains them both. One finds authentic affinity between Overton and the Milton of the divorce tracts, who refers to "the fundamentall law book of nature, which *Moses* never thwarts, but reverences" (*YP*, 2:272). The law "writt'n by *Moses*," "character'd in us by nature" and never abrogated by Christ, "is to force nothing against the faultles proprieties of nature"

(*YP*, 2:237). Milton asserts a harmony of dispensations, in which natural law's universal moral reason is the basis of the Mosaic law governing God's holy nation—a law maintained by Christ for the individual regenerate Christian: "Christ bidding to forsake wife for religion, meant . . . divorce as *Moses* meant it, whose Law grounded on morall reason, was both his office and his essence to maintain" (*YP*, 2:264).

Scholars have drawn a specific analogy between Overton's argument on the mortality of the soul, which he infers from Genesis 2:7, and Milton's monistic argument to the same effect.[12] Overton asserts on the title page of the second edition of *Mans Mortalitie* "that whole Man (as a *rationall* Creature) is a Compound wholly mortall, contrary to that common distinction of *Soule* and *Body*." Milton is likely to have known Overton's argument; Overton certainly knew George Wither's translation of Nemesius on *The Nature of Man*, which includes references to what "[t]he *Hebrewes* affirme."[13] Wither prefixed to this book a dedicatory epistle to John Selden, the great Hebraist, whose name will be inseparable from most of what follows in this chapter.

Borrowing an analogy from the Miltonic curriculum as set forth in *Of Education* (1644), one can proceed toward a detailed understanding of Milton's specifically Hebraic monism in the tracts of 1643–45. The curriculum stresses the ascent from specific details regarding matter, plants, and living creatures to a comprehensive understanding of the organic arts of logic, rhetoric, and poetry, which is "made subsequent [to rhetoric in the educational scheme], or indeed rather precedent [in value], as being less suttle and fine, but more simple, sensuous and passionate" (*YP*, 2:403). Poetry thus affects the senses more directly than rhetoric. Balachandra Rajan's important exposition suggests that Milton subordinates the transcendentalist ideal of the knowledge of goodness in a state of pure being to the informed action generated by that goodness: "We possess our souls of heavenly virtue not to escape, but to redeem our bodies: and at this point of emergence of knowledge into action the hierarchic values are reversed. . . . [W]e measure our utterance by its capacity to change."[14]

This chapter, like Milton's curriculum, attempts to ascend slowly, by steps, from the details of Milton's knowledge of Hebrew to a more comprehensive understanding of his Hebraic monism. The details are essential, in part because Milton's monism resembles its opposite. Readers of *Paradise Lost* remember how often apparent equivalents separated only by "or" turn out to be opposites: the Pauline antipathy of law and gospel as symbolized by "*Sinai*" or "*Sion*" (1. 7, 10); Arianism opposed to orthodox trinitarianism in "offspring of Heav'n first-born / Or of th' Eternal Coeternal beam" (3.1–2); creation rejected or accepted: "what seem'd fair in all the World, seem'd now / Mean, or in her summ'd up" (8.472–

73). Milton's commitment to what might be called the principle of trans-position manifests itself in contradictory ways. Transposing terms from natural law to the Mosaic law and thence to the higher key of the gospel may eventuate in a global typological system, a hermeneutics of supersession that destroys the identity of what precedes it under the pretext of fulfilling it. St. Augustine's formulation asserts textual continuity: "In the Old Testament there is a concealment of the New, in the New Testament there is a revelation of the Old."[15] But, as Jill Robbins has noted, traditional Christian relationships of obscurity and clarity, promise and fulfill-ment—like those of old and new, carnal and spiritual, elect and repro-bate—"already include an account of the Judaic in [their] assertion of the *figural* relationship between the two testaments" and thus occlude "the truth claim of the Hebrew Bible that would be independent of the Gos-pel."[16] When Milton contrasts Sinai and Sion, he invokes the Sinai the-ophany as described in Exodus to prefigure the inferior status of the law, citing the Old Testament as an authority to discredit itself.

I shall argue that John Selden's Hebraic and even rabbinic scholarship is a principal source of Milton's monistic approach in the 1643–45 tracts to natural law, the Mosaic law, and the gospel. In a monistic as opposed to a typological scheme of transposition, the gospel, instead of disparag-ing what precedes it, engages in a reverse motion of spirit, returning to a Mosaic law "grounded on [the] morall reason" of natural law (*YP*, 2:264). Frequently in these tracts Milton brings the Mosaic law back to natural law:

> Marriage, unless it mean a fit and tolerable marriage, is not inseparable nei-ther by nature nor institution. Not by nature for then those Mosaic divorces had bin against nature, if separable and inseparable be contraries, as who doubts they be: and what is against nature is against Law, if soundest Philos-ophy abuse us not: by this reckning *Moses* should be most unmosaick, that is, most illegal, not to say most unnaturall. (*YP*, 2:310)

Just as frequently, he brings the gospel back to the Mosaic law: "If we examine over all [Christ's] sayings, we shall find him not so much inter-preting the Law with his words, as referring his owne words to be inter-preted by the Law" (*YP*, 2:301). Submitting the divine gospel to a natural law that he, like Selden, regarded as equally divine, Milton proclaims: "The great and almost only commandment of the Gospel, is to command nothing against the good of man" (*YP*, 2:638–39). Asserting the human measure of natural law, the Mosaic law, and the gospel, the Milton of the divorce tracts identifies the most serious sins as those against nature.

Selden's scholarship affects Milton's exegesis in the prose tracts, and that Hebraic exegesis contributes to the foundation of paradise. It is im-portant to recognize the degree to which the sense of play and freedom in paradise results from the redeemer's not yet having come upon the scene. Instead of the "Die hee or Justice must" mentality, which requires multiple victims (not only Christ, but also all persons and texts who would escape this mentality), paradise offers a covenantal relationship between Adam and a God who asserts, "[I] am alone / From all Eternity, for none I know / Second to mee or like, equal much less" (8.405–7). In *De doctrina*, 1:v, Milton insists repeatedly on God's single indivisible essence:

> The numerical significance of "one" and of "two" must be unalterable and the same for God as for man. It would have been a waste of time for God to thunder forth so repeatedly that first commandment which said that he was the one and only God, if it could nevertheless be maintained that another God existed as well, who ought himself to be thought of as the only God. Two distinct things cannot be of the same essence. God is one being, not two. One being has one essence, and also one subsistence—by which is meant simply a substantial essence. If you were to ascribe two subsistences or two persons to one essence, it would be a contradiction in terms. You would be saying that the essence was at once one and not one. (*YP*, 6:212)

Milton's penchant for triadic structures as well as his commitment to a principle of transposition might seem to make him sympathetic to orthodox trinitarianism. A Son begotten from a Father and a Spirit proceeding from Father and Son—this paradoxical doctrine of divine mutuality and unity seems compatible with aspects of Raphael's speech on degree. Certainly orthodox Miltonists have adopted extreme measures to dissociate Milton from his antitrinitarianism.[17] Yet Milton's insistence on God's single, indivisible essence (distinct, separate, and particular) seems ultimately to ally him with a monist principle of transposition. The higher includes the lower without any sort of turning away or disparagement, since Milton doesn't want to risk obliterating individual identity. Neither syncretistic nor typological, Milton rejects a hermeneutics of supersession for the sake of what, it is argued later, is a Hebraic mon(othe)ist exegesis. The covenant that this one God establishes with Adam during their long conversation (8.296–499) compresses the two models of *brith* contained in the Hebrew Bible: the Abrahamic (Gen. 15 and 17) and the Davidic (2 Sam. 7; Ps. 89), which are concerned respectively with the gift of the land and the gift of kingship and dynasty: "all the Earth / To thee and to thy Race I give; as Lords / Possess it, and all things that therein live" (8.338–40). Both promissory and obligatory, this primal covenant entails mutual responsibility, most notably Adam's loyalty to the great command, "The Pledge of thy Obedience and thy Faith" (325). The God who promises blessings with a "gracious purpose" (337)—not grace deriving from sacrifice, but rather the Hebrew Bible's *hanan* of graciousness and favor—this same God joins obedience to the life-giving commandment and faith, just as they are joined in the Torah. Paul was the first to tear them asunder into polarities, creating in Galatians 3 a contradiction between Deuteronomy 27:26 (stressing obedience) and Habakkuk 2:4 (stressing faith). For the converted Paul, faith based on spiritual absorption into the risen Christ replaced observance of Torah, thus removing obedience as a possibility for humankind. This entirely new duality is repeated in Romans 10, when Paul contrasts the righteousness of Torah (Lev. 18:5) with the righteousness of faith (Deut. 30:12–14), thus setting up a contradiction that would never have occurred to a believing Jew, for whom both passages would have applied to Torah as revealed on Mount Sinai.[18] In Milton's paradise, obedience to two or more kinds of righteousness are set alongside each other, not, as they will be after the Fall, played off against each other.

The sense of playfulness and freedom in the absence of sacrifice characterizes Adam's account of his first moments of life:

> As new wak't from soundest sleep
> Soft on the flow'ry herb I found me laid
> In Balmy Sweat, which with his Beams the Sun
> Soon dri'd, and on the reeking moisture fed.
>
> (8.253–56)

Geoffrey Hartman's answerably playful comments on this passage stress the "entirely unhurtful, sympathetic, even symbiotic relation" between the ethereal and the earthly: "The sun feeding on Adam fortifies him."[19] The sun feeds on Adam's sweat like a mare licking her foal, and this, unlike the Fall, is a feeding "which is not a theft or a wounding."[20] The mutuality of the passage anticipates the lengthier "celestial Colloquy sublime" (8.455) that unites Adam's "earthly" with God's "Heav'nly" (453) nature. The union of ethereal nature and creaturely function to benefit both may also be said to figure forth the conjunction of high and low implicit in covenant. Richard Sibbes expresses the superiority of New Testament over Old in terms of the difference between testament and covenant. Testament is to be preferred precisely because it requires the death of the testator and because its benefits, absolute rather than conditional, are completely one-sided:

First, *A testament indeed is a covenant, and something more*. It is a covenant sealed by death. The testator must die before it can be of force. So all the good that is conveyed to us by the testament it is by the death of the testator, Christ . . . for "without blood there is no redemption," Heb. ix.22; without the death of Christ there could be no satisfaction, and without satisfaction, there could be no peace with God.

Secondly, *A testament bequeatheth good things merely of love*. . . . A covenant requireth something to be done. In a testament, there is nothing but receiving the legacies given. In covenants, ofttimes it is for the mutual good one of another, but a testament is merely for their good for whom the testament is made, to whom the legacies are bequeathed; for when they are dead, what can they receive from them? . . . what can God receive of us?[21]

William Pemble uses covenant and testament as synecdoches for the Hebrew Bible and the Old Testament respectively: the text as a literal, independent narrative is covenantal, but read typologically, as a prefiguring of the New, it too becomes a testament, which requires death as its seal. Both testaments preach "*[r]emission of sinnes*, and *salvation* bequeathed as a Legacy unto the Church: and this bequest ratified by the death of the *Testator, typically* slaine in the Sacrifices, for confirmation of the Old. *Really* put to death in his owne *Person*, For the *Sanction* of the *New Testament*.[22] The primal covenant of book 8, innocent of the Fall and of the crucifixion, requires neither wounding nor sacrifice, but rather only obedience and faith for the fulfillment of blessings to Adam and Eve of boundless space, time, and progeny.

There are textual as well as doctrinal explanations for the joy in mere being characteristic of Milton's paradise and for the unease and anxiety in the epic's last books. Paul's epistles as well as Hebrews, the principal sources of the postlapsarian books, can be read only with reference to the Old Testament in a hermeneutics of supersession, but Genesis 1–2, the source of Milton's paradise and, not coincidentally, of his most forceful monistic arguments on the indivisibility of soul and body, can be understood without reference to the dualistic and hierarchical oppositions that constitute Pauline interpretation. Nietzsche has remarked the bad faith accompanying "the unheard of philological farce in regard to the Old Testament . . . the attempt to withdraw the Old Testament from the Jews by asserting that it contains nothing but Christian doctrine and belongs in truth to the Christians as the true people of Israel . . . a process which cannot possibly have been compatible with a good conscience."[23] When Christian hermeneutics suppresses the self-understanding of Judaic exegesis, its "uneasy relation to this suppressed possibility" results in discontent.[24] Newborn Adam springing lightly to his feet, "[b]y quick instinctive motion" (8.259), knows a joy that precedes earth's wound at the Fall, Christ's agony, and the hurt inflicted upon the Hebrew Bible.

Before arguing that John Selden (1584–1654) is an important influence on Milton's specific knowledge of Hebraica and on his monism, it is important to underscore the rare degree to which he honors the self-understanding of Judaic exegesis. According to Jonathan Ziskind, "Selden may be regarded as the first modern western scholar, Jew or gentile, to analyze the practices of [the Karaites],"[25] a sect that he called the *Scripturarii* and compared to certain Christians guided "by the simplicity of the sacred words rather than someone else's traditions" (*a sacri sermonis simplicitate quam Traditiones ipsas alienas*).[26] Selden relied mostly on classic rabbinic texts and their commentaries in order to understand the Jewish laws of marriage and divorce, and he was thus unaware of the development since the twelfth century of closer public regulation of these laws under rabbinic authority. His ignorance of increased regulation and of the emergence of the rabbi as a professional, officiating clergyman has been seen as a flaw in his scholarship.[27] But for this most independent of scholars, who inscribed, in Greek, on all his books the motto "in all things, above all things, Liberty," the recovery of ancient Jewish laws, ceremonies, and institutions, from the time before they had become encrusted with coercive regulations never mentioned in the original texts, led to a liberal conception of the religion. Selden was a pioneer of the science of comparative religion and a linguistic prodigy. His rabbinical works, the result of a love of learning for its own sake, are marked by an expansiveness of spirit as well as of scholarship. His broad conception of Judaism as a legal and religious system and his mastery of a humanist philological method contribute to the boldness, inclusiveness, and complexity of his investigations. Frank Manuel asserts that casting odium on the ceremonies of the Jews living in Christian Europe is a "covert secondary intent in writing about Judaism" and that a defensive attitude toward rabbinica is evident among the Christian Hebraists with "the rarest of exceptions—John Selden perhaps."[28] Selden was freer than most of his contemporaries of blatantly ideological motives, although his motives are traceable, and they accord to a remarkable degree with Milton's in the 1640s.

Selden's worldly-wise toleration of the Jews should be measured against the legacy in seventeenth-century England of medieval patterns of diabolization based ultimately on John 8:44. Catholics could always convert, but, as David S. Katz has noted, "the demonological, supernatural element in the early modern attitude to the Jews . . . renders it quite different from other forms of opposition to religious minorities and outcasts."[29] The content of Katz's study *Philo-Semitism and the Readmission of the Jews to England* subverts the optimism of the title. The principal motives behind even the most Judeophilic arguments for readmission were either opportunistic and economic, such as Sir Thomas Sherley's early "project for Jews" (1607), conversionist, such as John Weemse's plea for immigration rather than genuine religious toleration, with Romans 10:4 as his central text ("how shall they believe in him of whom they have not heard?"), or millenarian, such as Thomas Brightman's humane request that the Gentiles end their "hatefull and spightfull" treatment so that the Jews might become a "Christian Nation."[30] When Joseph Mede, a champion of apocalyptic millenarianism, responds sympathetically to Henry Finch's tolerationist argument in *The Calling of the Jewes* (1621), he confesses that it accords with his own long-held view: "God forgive me if it be a sin, but I have thought so many a day." Mede's asking God to forgive him for not condemning the Jews is the contrite version of Huck Finn's defiant decision to tear up the letter that would have betrayed Jim the runaway slave: "All right, then, I'll *go* to hell."[31] In both cases the generous heart overcomes the condemning conscience, but not without a struggle that reveals the depth of prejudice in the culture at large. Katz's study reveals that the Jews are eventually admitted formally to England not as a result of Menasseh ben Israel's mission or of the Whitehall Conference convened by members of Cromwell's Council of State, but rather because they had already let themselves in "through the entrance reserved for tradesmen."[32]

Selden's remarks on Christianity as a Jewish sect give a foretaste of his wit and sophistication. Selden recognizes that Christianity originated in Judea and that Christians preserved for some time the civil rites and ceremonies of the Jews.

> In the High Church of *Jerusalem*, the Christians were but another Sect of *Jews*, that did believe the *Messias* was come. To be called was nothing else, but to become a Christian, to have the name of a Christian, it being their own Language, for amongst the *Jews*, when they made a Doctor of Law, 'twas said he was called.[33]

Selden stresses throughout his rabbinic scholarship the depth of Christianity's relationship to first-century Judaism, but his tone changes when he discusses contemporary Jews.

> Talk what you will of the Jews, that they are Cursed, they thrive where e're they come[;] they are able to oblige the Prince of their Country by lending him money[;] none of them beg, they keep together, and for their being hated, my life for yours, Christians hate one another as much![34]

Selden has a highly developed sense of irony, and this ingenious defense relies for its effectiveness on a hostile attitude toward an imaginary opponent of the Jews. As will be seen later, the main intent of one of Selden's immense scholarly books may be deliberately tucked away in a parenthesis, and the key phrase in this brief monologue is the casually brutal "my life for yours." As soon as his opponent takes the bet, Selden wins, exposing the bloody-mindedness of one Christian Englishman willing to take the life of another in order to prove that Jews hate one another more than Christians do.

It has seemed worth anticipating the argument that John Selden is an important source of Milton's knowledge of Hebrew in order to stress Selden's transmission of an uncommonly generous view of Judaism. Far more than most other literate and mobile Englishmen of his time, Selden belonged to a plurality of discursive communities. As Richard Helgerson has observed, he constructed his identity *"within* particular forms and communities" and "also *across* them,"[35] as a member of Camden's Society of Antiquaries, annotator of Drayton's *Poly-Olbion*, expert on Roman civil law, Coke's parliamentary collaborator on behalf of the common law, pioneer of comparative religion, and student of international law. Whatever ideological motives lay behind even his most apparently dispassionate discourse, Selden wrote always as a scholar and never as a theologian. Although he accepted the rabbinic view of the seven Noachide commandments as a divinely given natural law incumbent on all of humankind, his description of the Mosaic law can serve as an example of his tough-minded conception of religious institutions:

> God at the first gave Laws to all Mankind, but afterwards he gave peculiar Laws to the Jews, which they were only to observe. Just as we have the Common Law for all *England*, and yet you have some Corporations, that, besides that, have peculiar Laws and priviledges to themselves.[36]

The commonplace identification (and not only among Puritans) of seventeenth-century England with biblical Israel stresses continuity between Old and New Testament dispensations, but usually to reformulate Augustine's point: "In the Old Testament there is a concealment of the New, in the New Testament there is a revelation of the Old." Selden's homely comparison between the special laws of the Hebrews and the peculiar laws and privileges of English corporations is innocent of conversionist or millenarian motives. His stupendous Hebrew scholarship respects to an extent remarkable for the times the self-understanding of Judaic exegesis. In the thicket of detailed argument regarding Milton's knowledge of Hebrew, one might try to keep in mind that the prose tracts published between 1643 and 1645, which constitute the doctrinal matrix of the middle books of *Paradise Lost*, are informed by an unusually generous conception of Judaism.

MILTON'S CHIEF RABBI

Although the first systematic analyses of Milton's debt to Jewish exegesis appeared in the 1920s, in the work of Denis Saurat, Harris Fletcher, and E. C. Baldwin, the first hint of such a debt appears in 1683, in Matthew Poole's *Annotations upon the Holy Bible*.[37] In his commentary on the third chapter of Genesis, the author of *Synopsis Criticorum*, whose eclecticism generally extends to those authorized patristic, scholastic, and Reformation sources one expects to find in the most exhaustive scriptural commentaries of that century, considers the question "How the Serpent could speak, and what the Woman conceived of his speech, and why she was not affrighted, but continued the discourse with it."

> A late ingenious and learned Writer represents the matter thus, in which there is nothing absurd or incredible: The Serpent makes his address to the Woman with a short speech, and salutes her as the Empress of the World, &c. She is not affrighted, because there was as yet no cause of fear, no sin, and therefore no danger, but wonders and enquires what this meant, and whether he was not a brute Creature, and how he came to have speech, and understanding? The Serpent replies, that he was no better than a brute, and did indeed want both these gifts, but by eating of a certain fruit in this Garden he got both. She asked what Fruit and Tree that was? Which when he shewed her, she replied, This, no doubt, is an excellent fruit, and likely to make the eater of it wise; but God hath forbidden us this Fruit: To which the Serpent replies, as it here follows in the Text. It is true, this discourse is not in the Text; but it is confessed by Jewish, and other Expositors, that these words, *Yea, hath God said, & c.* are a short and abrupt sentence, and that they were but the close of a foregoing discourse; which might well enough be either this now mentioned, or some other of a like nature. And that expression which follows [,] *v.6 When the Woman saw, i.e.* understood, *that it was a Tree to be desired to make one wise*, may seem to imply, both that the Serpent told her, and that she believed, that the speech and understanding of the Serpent was the effect of the eating of that Fruit; and therefore that if it raised him from a brute Beast to the degree of a reasonable Creature, it would elevate her from the humane to a kind of divine nature or condition.[38]

Of interest both here and in the rest of Poole's extensive annotations on this crucial chapter is the characterization of Milton as "ingenious and learned" expositor rather than poet and, implicitly, of books 9 and 10 of *Paradise Lost* as biblical exegesis rather than epic. In this excerpt, as elsewhere in the annotations on Genesis 3, Poole appears to have Milton's great argument at his elbow, next to the Bible itself. He begins with the serpent's "short speech" (9.532–48) and subsequent salutation to the "Empress of this fair World, resplendent *Eve*" (9.568), and ends by paraphrasing the serpent's argument of proportional elevation ("I of brute human, yee of human Gods," [9.712]), which he regards as a gloss of "When the woman saw" (Gen. 3:6).

Of some relevance to the question of Milton's knowledge of extrabiblical Hebraica is Poole's view of the long dialogue between Satan and Eve as a sort of *midrash* on Genesis 3:1, for which he appeals to "Jewish, and other Expositors." Poole needed to look no further than Rashi's *Commentary* on this verse for the interpretation of the serpent's question as merely "the close of a foregoing discourse": "although he [the serpent] saw them [Adam and Eve] eating from other fruits yet he entered into a long conversation with her so that she should answer him, and so that he might then have an opportunity to talk about that *particular* tree."[39]

From the seventeenth through the nineteenth centuries, Milton's biographers assumed his familiarity with Hebrew, though, unlike Poole, they would have limited his use of it to the Old Testament. John Aubrey notes: "He was an early riser. Yea, after he lost his sight. He had a man read to him: the first thing he read was the Hebrew bible."[40] David Masson, unsurprisingly, discusses in tandem Milton's competence in Hebrew and Greek and concludes circumspectly: "There is evidence of his acquaintance with Greek authors, and of his having more than ventured on Hebrew."[41] Masson's magisterial study established Milton as a dogmatic Puritan, the sort who would have applied his Hebrew learning to the study of Scripture alone.

Poole's early invocation of Jewish expositors in connection with Milton is not unique. Another Bible scholar, Richard Laurence, in his 1819 edition of the apocryphal *Ascension of Isaiah*, mentioned Milton's debt to rabbinical literature, including the midrash *Pirke de-Rabbi Eliezer*.[42] Still, such invocations are rare, and they are echoed only in the twentieth century, when literary scholars belatedly develop the hints given by biblical scholars. As if making up for lost time, these scholars tend to exaggerate Milton's linguistic competence. Their extravagant claims are by now familiar to Miltonists: Denis Saurat's sweeping assertion that, except for his materialism and mortalism, "the whole of Milton's philosophy is found in the Kabbalah,"[43] E. C. Baldwin's citations of midrashic sources for some of Milton's ideas in *Paradise Lost*, and Harris Fletcher's book-length argument that Milton read Buxtorf's edition of the *Biblia Rabbinica* with the commentaries of Rashi, Ibn Ezra, Levi ben Gerson, and David Kimchi.

That these studies were, at the time of publication (between 1925 and 1930), regarded as more or less persuasive may have something to do with the anti-Puritan climate of opinion in the 1920s. The program to create a new conception of the poet as the last great exemplar of Renaissance humanism, rather than as merely a Puritan, extended into the area of Milton's Hebrew readings. Emphasis was now placed not on the Bible but on arcane rabbinic materials that would demonstrate the poet's breadth of learning, daring originality, and unorthodoxy. Of course Milton's general reputation for broad learning has in the past lent credibility to theories assuming his familiarity with all manner of obscure material. Exhibiting the range of his learning through allusion, borrowed image, or outright name-dropping, Milton remains among the most compliant of all major English poets for a source study.

Inevitably, reaction set in, and more recent evaluations of these studies of Milton and Hebraica contain accusations of bad faith. Saurat was said to have relied on a faulty translation of the *Zohar*. Baldwin never considered the problem of the inaccessibility to Milton of the many extra-biblical sources he cited, and Baldwin himself relied not on the original sources, but rather on Louis Ginzberg's compilation *The Legends of the Jews*. Finally, Fletcher lacked the proficiency required to handle the Buxtorf Bible.[44] This sort of corrective scholarship goes far toward replacing Milton on his sectarian perch, but at least it stops short of accusing Milton himself of bad faith.

Such an accusation is strongly implicit in the most recent studies of Milton's use of the extra-biblical Hebraic sources he cites in his prose. Milton excoriates lazy scholars who, ignoring direct sources, rely instead on "an English concordance and a *topic folio*, the gatherings and savings of a sober graduatship, a *Harmony* and a *Catena* . . . not to reck'n up the infinit helps of interlinearies, breviaries, *synopses*, and other loitering gear" (*YP*, 2:546). Yet if there is, at present, a consensus on the subject of Milton's rabbinic learning, it is the skeptical one that Milton took his information from concordances, lexicons, and phrase books—in short, from seventeenth-century versions of Cliff's Notes.[45] The scholar who refers approvingly in *Doctrine and Discipline of Divorce* to medieval Hebrew commentaries on the Bible and to Maimonides' *Guide for the Perplexed*, who in *Tetrachordon* indicates his awareness of the controversy between Hillel and Shammai regarding divorce at will at the end of the talmudic Tractate Gittin, and who cites Tractate Sanhedrin a number of times in his first *Defence of the People of England*, is now accused of having "employed . . . dubious scholarship."[46]

I should like to argue for an intermediate position on the question of Milton's Hebrew learning. I still maintain that Milton's competence in biblical Hebrew would have enabled him to read Rashi's *Commentary*, which appeared in more editions of the Hebrew Bible than any other.[47] Rashi's lucidity, the simplicity of his diction, his analytic approach to Scripture, which allies him to a tradition of literal exposition originating in the Middle Ages and culminating in the great exegetical works of the Reformation—all would have made him Milton's most accessible primary rabbinic source. Yet of course Rashi's *Commentary*, despite its likely influence on *Paradise Lost*, cannot account for other rabbinic presences in Milton's prose and poetry, such as the Talmud, Midrash, and Maimonides.

I hope to fortify with evidence the claim made earlier in this chapter that John Selden, the most learned person in England in the seventeenth century and the author of a half dozen immense rabbinical works, is the principal source of Milton's Jewish learning. In a Latin tortuous enough to discourage casual readers, Selden explores thoroughly the Jewish position on natural law, marriage and divorce, the division of authority between clergy and laity, the limitations of royal power, and manifold other topics that concerned Milton. To read Selden is to become something of an expert in Jewish learning. This means that, while Milton may indeed have lacked the linguistic competence to tackle the Talmud directly, his knowledge of rabbinic sources would nonetheless have been extensive.

Scholars celebrated for their own broad and deep learning gladly conceded Selden's superiority and conferred titles on him. For Ben Jonson, who praised his "unweary'd paine / Of Gathering" and his "Bountie in pouring out againe," Selden was "Monarch in Letters"; for Grotius, he was the "glory of the English nation"; and for John Lightfoot, he was "the great Mr. Selden, the Learnedst man upon the earth."[48] According to the *DNB*, most of "Selden's work as an orientalist consisted in the exposition of Jewish, or rather rabbinical, law. . . . The acquaintance with the original of the Old Testament and the ancient versions and commentaries which all these works display is very great. Their author's familiarity with rabbinical literature was such as has been acquired by few non-Israelite scholars." It is certain that Selden relied not merely on secondary materials, such as those of the Johann Buxtorfs, father and son, but read both the Babylonian and Jerusalem Talmud as well as the varied works of post-Talmudic rabbinical literature that crowded his library.[49] And Maimonides' *Code* was his favorite source.

Milton shows himself to be familiar with Selden's *History of Tithes* (1617) in *The Likeliest Means to Remove Hirelings*,[50] and *De Dis Syriis* (1617) may have provided some of the names of pagan deities in the *Nativity Ode*,[51] but three other works contribute a great deal more to the Hebraic factor in his prose and poetry. The first, *De Jure Naturali et Gentium, Juxta Disciplinam Ebraeorum* (London: Richard Bishop, 1640), 847 folio pages, treats, from a rabbinic perspective, universal and particular law—that is, those commandments given by pre-Mosaic revelation to the whole of the human race and those specifically given to Israel and only binding upon them. Among other things, this comprehensive and minutely detailed work provided Milton with the principal rabbinic comparisons of Edenic, natural, and Mosaic laws and thus helped to shape the polity of paradise in his great epic. Moreover, in a prefatory statement explaining his method in *De Jure*, Selden typically appeals to precedent for publishing opposed and disagreeing views as a means of distinguishing more readily between truth and falsehood. In the *Areopagitica*, addressing Parliament, Milton also employs this firmly established usage and points to Selden, M.P. for the University of Oxford, to authorize it:

> Wherof what better witnes can ye expect I should produce, then one of your own now sitting in Parlament, the chief of learned men reputed in this Land, Mr. *Selden*, whose volume of naturall & national laws proves, not only by

great autorities brought together, but by exquisite reasons and theorems, almost mathematically demonstrative, that all opinions, yea errors, known, read, and collated, are of main service & assistance toward the speedy attainment of what is truest. (*YP*, 2:513)

The final argument of Milton's *Doctrine and Discipline of Divorce* is that divorce should not be restrained by law, "*it being against the Law of nature and of Nations. The larger proof wherof referr'd to Mr.* Seldens *Book* De jure naturali & gentium" (*YP*, 2:350). Milton concludes by recommending *De Jure* as the sequel to his own tract on divorce for the reader "who so desires to know at large with least pains, and expects not heer overlong rehersals of that which is by others already so judiciously gather'd" (350). Having begun his tract with an attack on custom, he ends it by contrasting the divine natural and civil laws of *De Jure* with the principles of canon law, which are based in great part on custom (*consuetudo*). By insisting that Christ's purpose in the gospels was not to bring a new morality into religion (264), Milton implicitly rejects the *fontes iuris canonici scripti*—the laws contained in the New Testament, the decrees of synods, and the constitutions of popes. It is not surprising that in such a work Milton should recommend Selden to his reader:

> let him hast'n to be acquainted with that noble volume written by our learned *Selden, Of the law of nature & of Nations*, a work more useful and more worthy to be perus'd, whosoever studies to be a great man in wisdom, equity, and justice, then all those *decretals* and *sumles sums*, which the *Pontificial Clerks* have doted on. (350–51)

Regarding marriage and divorce, the rabbinical work by Selden of greatest influence on Milton is the *Uxor Ebraica, seu De Nuptiis & Divortiis ex Iure Civili, Id Est, Divino & Talmudico, Veterum Ebraeorum* (London: Richard Bishop, 1646), 621 quarto pages, an exhaustive summary of the Jewish law of marriage and divorce and of the status of the married woman under Jewish law. Five times in *De Jure* Selden indicates that *Uxor Ebraica* is ready for the press,[52] and Eivion Owen has already argued persuasively that Milton had access to the manuscript before writing *Tetrachordon*.[53] Masson believes that in 1643 or 1644, when Milton had paid Selden the compliments quoted above, he "first made Selden's personal acquaintance."[54]

Milton praises the *Uxor Ebraica* whenever he names it, and he names it often, in contexts that indicate its importance to him. The man who married Katherine Woodcock in a civil ceremony performed by an alderman and a justice of the peace[55] appeals to "Selden . . . in his Uxor Heb. Book 2. c[hapter] 28, all of it, and [chapter] 29" for evidence "[t]hat the ministers of the Church had no right, among the earliest Christians, to share in the celebration of either contracts or nuptials."[56] In a striking

passage of *The Likeliest Means to Remove Hirelings*, composed a year
after Katherine's death, he expands upon this point:

> As for marriages that ministers should meddle with them, as not sanctifi'd or
> legitimat without their celebration, I finde no ground in scripture either of
> precept or example. Likeliest it is (which our *Selden* hath well observd, *1. 2,
> c. 28, ux. Eb.*) that in imitation of heathen priests who were wont at nuptials
> to use many rites and ceremonies, and especially, judging it would be profit-
> able, and the increase of thir autoritie, not to be spectators only in busines of
> such concernment to the life of man, they insinuated that marriage was not
> holy without their benediction, and for the better colour, made it a sacra-
> ment; being of it self a civil ordinance, a houshold contract, a thing indiffer-
> ent and free to the whole race of mankinde, not as religious, but as men: best,
> indeed, undertaken to religious ends. . . . Yet not therefor invalid or unholy
> without a minister and his pretended necessary hallowing, more then any
> other act, enterprise or contract of civil life, which ought all to be don also
> in the Lord and to his glorie. (*YP*, 7:299)

For Selden, Christianity originated as "a reformed Judaism," and he emphasizes the retention by the early Christians of Hebrew rituals: "Now
among the ancient Hebrews, although there were blessings introduced at
both betrothals and marriages, nonetheless, there is no evidence that it
was necessary for a priest or Levite to be present." "At the beginning of
Christianity, much in imitation of the Jews, it is certain that ministers did
not have to be present at marriages."[57]

A section of the *Uxor* of capital importance to Milton is the account of
the schools of Hillel and Shammai, which Selden compares with the Pro-
culian and Sabinian schools of Roman law. This appears in a discussion
that attempts to reconcile the Talmudic-rabbinic view of divorce with
Christ's statements in the New Testament. Milton refers to this section in
places where the acknowledged presence of an external authority is rare,
in *De doctrina Christiana*, in which Scripture, in conjunction with the
author's spirit, generally claims exclusive interpretive rights, and in the
autobiographical section of the *Defensio Secunda*, an itemized, retrospective account of his own prose production.[58]

In the *Uxor*, as in all of Selden's rabbinical scholarship, the arguments
seem to turn of their own weight, without being pushed, and the conclusion is always understated. Selden provides overwhelming evidence that
the rigors of canon law on divorce contradict the more liberal laws
among pagans, Jews, and early Christians. Finally, on the very last page,
he concludes in a sentence fragment, parenthetically:

> Indeed, among our British people (who by act of Parliament enacted more
> than a century ago relaxed the degrees of affinity and consanguinity estab-
> lished by the pontifical law, retaining only what is in Scripture, but never-

theless kept in its entirety the pontifical teaching on divorce after the Reformation) . . . a provincial synod of clerics [declared] . . . that no court may make a judgment on deprivation of bed and board unless in addition neither spouse be permitted a remarriage.[59]

Even this, his most definitive statement on contemporary domestic law, leaves it up to the reader to infer inevitably the need to reform the laws of divorce, especially in light of England's great divorce from Rome.

Milton echoes the *Uxor* even when it errs (rarely). Selden, paraphrasing Plutarch, cites "the divorce of Papiria, the wife of Aemilius Paulus, who was reproached by his friends because he sent away a very fine wife. Exhibiting his shoe, he answered, 'Is it not pretty? Is it not new? None of you knows where it pinches my foot.' "[60] In fact, Plutarch attributes the remark to an anonymous Roman and then applies it to the situation of Aemilius Paulus, noting that "no documentary grounds for the divorce have come down to us."[61] Milton, improving on Selden stylistically, follows him in attributing the remark to "*Paulus Emilius*, beeing demanded why he would put away his wife for no visible reason[:] *This Shoo*, said he, and held it out on his foot, *is a neat shoo, a new shoo, and yet none of you know where it wrings me*" (YP, 2:348).

Although this chapter concentrates on the *Uxor*'s influence on Milton's views of divorce, it is tempting to speculate on further influences. Selden observes the scholarly courtesies, but his direct quotations from Paolo Sarpi's *Historia del Concilio Tridentino*, like Milton's in the *Doctrine and Discipline of Divorce* and the *Areopagitica*, are not cited as such in the *Uxor*.[62] The never-repeated format of Milton's first divorce tract—the division into books and short chapters, with headnotes for each chapter—resembles that of both *De Jure Naturali* and *Uxor Ebraica*. Finally, Milton on polygamy relies on biblical permissiveness: "Let no one dare to say that it is fornication or adultery. . . . For God . . . loved the patriarchs above all, and declared that they were very dear to him" (*De doctrina* 1.10, YP, 6:366). Although Selden applies rabbinic advice and admonition to the more liberal biblical texts ("One could marry as many wives as he wished . . . provided that he has what suffices for them"[63]—a proviso that could keep a man from marrying at all), he may have furnished Milton with evidence that the Ethiopian woman whom Moses is said to have married (Num.12:1) was not his first wife, Zipporah, but a second one. Along with the overwhelming majority opinion ("all the Christian versions") that "the Ethiopian woman" designates Zipporah, Selden records Josephus's view that this was a new wife, Tharbis, daughter of the king of Ethiopia. Milton includes Moses in his list of polygamists, "for he had married a Cushite. It is incredible that Zipporah, who had been named so often before, should suddenly be given this new title of Cushite" (YP, 6:366).

The third rabbinical work, which may have influenced Milton almost as much as the other two, although it has never been mentioned in connection with him, is *De Synedriis et Praefecturis Juridicis Veterum Ebraeorum* (London: Jacob Flesher, 1650, 1653, and 1655), published in three quarto books and occupying 1,132 huge folio columns in the *Opera Omnia*.[64] *De Synedriis*, a work of stupendous erudition, deals primarily with the constitution of Jewish courts, including the Sanhedrin, which, as Selden notes pointedly, was not priestly in composition. Like the *Uxor*, it demonstrates the function of the Jewish polity in sacred and secular affairs because of Christianity's roots in Judaism and because the early church copied Jewish practices. Selden's understated argument is thoroughly Erastian, demonstrating that matters under the jurisdiction of ecclesiastical courts in England were decided by ancient Jewish courts that could well be called secular. Selden attacks the position on excommunication taken by the Presbyterians, who "insist upon it more positively and advance it further in their own interest than . . . others; having inveighed against this power in papal and episcopal hands, they have, as it were, cut it into pieces and portioned it out among themselves."[65] This, the last of Selden's Jewish books, is a retitled version of the *History of Presbyters and Presbyteries* promised in the *Uxor* (1:xv, p. 117). It draws on Selden's experiences as a lay member of the Westminster Assembly, where he delighted in confuting Presbyterian claims of *jure divino* right to uncontrolled spiritual jurisdiction. According to the eyewitness testimony of Whitelock, a friend and fellow divine,

> Mr. Selden spake admirably, and confuted divers of them in their own learning. And sometimes when they had cited a text of scripture to prove their assertion, he would tell them, "Perhaps in your little pocket-bibles with gilt leaves" (which they would often pull out and read) "the translation may be thus, but the Greek or the Hebrew signifies thus and thus," and so would totally silence them.[66]

The *DNB* also notes that "Selden proved a thorn in the sides of the Westminster divines, for he liked the claims of presbytery no better than those of episcopacy; and according to Fuller (*Church History*, bk. xi. sect.ix. par.54), he used his talents rather 'to perplex than inform' his auditors."

Like the other two works that influenced Milton, *De Synedriis* cites primary rabbinic sources in their original Hebrew and Aramaic and then translates them into Latin. Organized like the Talmud itself, in a style that is not so much digressive as voluminous, it begins by exploring a single topic's ramifications and ends by drawing those now interrelated topics into its plenum of discourse. There is no index in the edition of *De Synedriis* that Milton used (nor is there any in the editions of the other two rabbinical works discussed here that were published in Milton's lifetime), and he could not have predicted where he might find the topic he was looking for, whether it was the seven Noachide commandments, pre-Mosaic courts of justice, capital punishment, the Christian doctrine of the Trinity and the Kabbalah, the seventy elders endowed with the divine spirit who formed the great Sanhedrin or Supreme Court in Israel, or limitations on royal authority.

The inconvenience of using Selden, the talmudic thoroughness of his arguments, and the length of his rabbinical works are stressed in order to counter the implicit charge of bad faith brought against Milton by scholars investigating his knowledge and use of rabbinic materials. A close look at the most recent essays on this subject, one by Leonard Mendelsohn and two by Golda Werman,[67] should reveal that Milton's familiarity with extra-biblical Hebraica is less casual than they acknowledge and should strengthen the possibility of a connection between Milton and Selden. These skeptical scholars are more persuasive than Fletcher et al., in part because they are more familiar with the primary sources; moreover, they are both correct in their general opinion that Milton relied on some intermediate Latin sources for most of his rabbinic citations. Yet it may be unfair to conclude from this that Milton's scholarship is "dubious"; that, though he chides Salmasius for turning over phrase books, lexicons, and glossaries, he is guilty of the same practice; that his understanding of the rabbinic material in the prose tracts is "superficial"; and that he derived his material "by way of casual gleanings . . . rather than from a deep study of the sources."[68]

In order to prove that Milton could not read the Talmud, Mendelsohn concentrates exclusively on the references to Tractate Sanhedrin in the *Defence of the People of England*. Mendelsohn does not attempt to supply the identity of Milton's sources—he is, for example, unaware that Milton's citation of Talmudic and Maimonidean opinion on the limits of royal prerogative derives (as was noted in the preceding chapter) from *De Synedriis*. Were Mendelsohn familiar with Selden, he would recognize him as an initiate, capable of satisfying the criteria for scholarship that he himself has set down, such as understanding the Talmud's "peculiar terminology, its abundant abbreviated and contracted words, and its host of other stylistic peculiarities."[69] Thus, for example, regarding kings of the House of Israel neither judging nor being judged, Selden quotes the following narrative evidence from Tractate Sanhedrin, which, in the original, is indeed as elliptical as Mendelsohn would claim it is. When the slave of King Alexander Jannaeus killed a man, the leader of the Sanhedrin, Simeon ben Shetah, required his presence at court. The two leaders fell into an argument over whether the king should stand or be seated, Jannaeus maintaining that he would respect the wishes of the whole court in the matter.

He [Simeon ben Shetah] turned to his right, and they [the judges] bent their faces down to the ground [as a result of fear and said nothing]; also when he turned to his left, they looked down to the ground. Then Simeon ben Shetah said to them, "Are you masters of thought? [You are calculating according to your own interests and thus remain silent.] Let the Master of Thoughts come and call you to account." Immediately, Gabriel came and struck them down to the ground, and they died. At that moment [when the rabbis saw that the Sanhedrin lacked the power to control the king], it was declared that a king [not of the House of David] may neither judge nor be judged, testify nor testify against [because of the danger in the matter].[70]

Selden cites the original text, then translates into Latin, consistently filling in gaps and identifying the antecedents of pronouns:

Simeon Ben Shatach *princeps synedrii* monuit collegas ut rem animadverterent atque in judicium vocarent. . . . Conversus *princeps synedrii* in dextram, vidit omnes oculos in solum defixisse. Idem, in sinistram conversus, vidit. . . . Confestim Gabriel advenit, & eos humi afflixit, adeo ut omnes morerentur. (Selden's italics.)[71]

[Simeon ben Shetah, the leader of the Sanhedrin, pointed out to his colleagues that they should consider the matter and bring it before the court. . . . When he turned to the right, the leader of the Sanhedrin saw all eyes fastened on the ground. Likewise, when he turned to the left, he saw [the same thing]. . . . Immediately Gabriel appeared and dashed them down to the ground so that all would die.]

In the *First Defence*, Milton derides this story, which after all supports his opponent Salmasius's contention that kings are exempt from judgment, although the tone seems to indicate that this exemption derives from a collective failure of nerve. The text is problematic, and Gabriel's smiting has also been interpreted (without the brackets provided in the English translation) as punishment for daring to require a king of Israel to stand. Milton is ungracious, but his comment does indicate an understanding of the literal account:

You say on my behalf that Aristobulus first and then Jannaeus surnamed Alexander did not receive that royal right [not to be judged] from the Sanhedrin which is the guardian and interpreter of rights, but rather by a gradual usurpation on their own account against the opposition of the council. To please these kings that fine tale about "Gabriel smiting" the leaders of the Sanhedrin was made up, and this great right of the king not to be judged, on which you seem to depend so much, was by your own confession derived from that old wives' tale or even worse, being but a rabbinical fable. (*YP*, 4:355)

Mendelsohn criticizes Milton for assuming that Gabriel smote the leaders of the Sanhedrin:

> Whoever it was who consulted the Talmud directly was . . . misled by the indefinite pronoun references "them" and "they." Actually these pronouns refer not to the principal men, but to everyone else. All present, *except the principal men*, were slain. If Milton did confront this passage in the original, he was confused by the pronoun reference, though such confusion would argue against familiarity with Talmudic style. . . . [I]t is much more probable that he never encountered this passage either in the original or in an accurate translation. (my emphasis)[72]

One might argue that Milton's reading of the story is as valid as Mendelsohn's (the text does not indicate that the principal men were spared) and that the peremptory tone of the latter's essay unfairly diminishes Milton. Another Talmudic passage, less susceptible of definitive interpretation than Mendelsohn concedes, deals with a basic point of difference regarding royal power: "R. Jose said: 'Whatever is enumerated in the chapter of the king, the king is permitted to do.' R. Judah said: 'This chapter was intended only to put fear into them [the people, so that they should receive the king's rule with fear]."[73]

In replying to Salmasius, Milton identifies "the chapter of the king" as Deuteronomy 17, which deals with royal responsibility as well as privilege, rather than 1 Samuel 8, which deals exclusively with privilege.

> You then turn to the rabbis and cite two of them with no better luck than you had before, for it is obvious that the chapter about the king which Rabbi Joses spoke of as containing the rights of kings is in Deuteronomy and not in Samuel; and Rabbi Judas declared quite correctly, contradicting you, that the passage in Samuel concerns only his putting fear into the people. (*YP*, 4:353).

Mendelsohn finds Milton's reading of this passage to be "inept"; for him it is "obvious" that R. Jose's "chapter about the king" is 1 Samuel 8, and any "doubt as to the source would be resolved by Rashi, who summarizes all the evidence for assigning the passage to Samuel."[74] Moreover, he continues, Milton might have consulted Kimchi on 1 Samuel 8:9, in the Buxtorf Bible that Fletcher claims he knew, for a full explanation of the disagreement between R. Jose and R. Judah. Mendelsohn is overstating the case when he asserts that the Talmudic text only appears to be ambiguous and that there is no rabbinic warrant for identifying R. Jose's chapter about the king as Deuteronomy 17. Rav Meir Abulafia, the most renowned Spanish rabbi of the first half of the thirteenth century, in his commentary on Sanhedrin, *Yad Ramah*, holds that the chapter on the king is not 1 Samuel 8, but (as Milton would have it) Deuteronomy 17.

According to this minority opinion, even the chapter in Deuteronomy does not deal with kingship as a positive commandment, but rather threatens the people so that, if they set a king over themselves, his awe will be upon them. This view interprets the similar phrasing in both chapters, reflecting a desire for a king "like as all the nations that are about me" (Deut. 17:14; 1 Sam. 8:5), to suggest that both intend to put fear into the people. The point here is that a rabbinic opinion unacknowledged by Mendelsohn but hardly inept interprets Deuteronomy 17 as permitting rather than commanding the appointment of a king.

When Mendelsohn claims that Deuteronomy 17 lists only limitations on a king's power and not privileges, he is ignoring the extensive discussion in Tractate Sanhedrin, in exactly the same textual neighborhood he is visiting, of the privileges of kingship implicit in that chapter.[75] Finally, it is disingenuous to attack Milton for not inferring the full positions of R. Jose and R. Judah from either Rashi's brief comment or Kimchi's elliptical one.[76]

In her recent learned essay on Milton's Hebraica, Golda Werman never resorts to verbal overkill, although she too assumes that Milton's exclusive reliance on translation makes his understanding of rabbinic material superficial. Yet, if Milton read, say, Selden's comprehensive survey of opinion on whether the king was subject to stripes from the Sanhedrin— ranging from Maimonides to contemporaries such as Grotius, Petit, and Casaubon—then there are reserves of knowledge behind even the following reproach to Salmasius:

> That Hebrew kings can be judged and even condemned to the lash is shown at length by Sichard from the rabbinical writings; and it is to him that you owe all this matter, though you are not ashamed to howl against him. (*YP*, 4:355)

Werman reads this not as an accusation of intellectual dishonesty but only of ingratitude toward the translator, upon whose compendium Milton, as well as Salmasius, relied for this information.[77] Yet, even setting aside this reproach's similarity in spirit to earlier attacks on sciolism,[78] Milton's well-placed confidence in his own proficiency in Hebrew,[79] and a tone suggesting that the author has himself consulted a more reliable source, Milton would have found in Selden's *De Synedriis* both the information itself and evidence that Salmasius drew upon Schickard.

Against Grotius, who supposes that by "stripes" the rabbinic authorities meant only some symbolic or voluntary penance undergone by the king for his sins, Selden quotes Maimonides, who clearly states that flogging is the punishment for violating the deuteronomic prohibition against the abuse of royal power. His note following the quotation refers to "Maimonid. Hal. *Melakim*, cap. 3, section 4 . . . & videsis Guil. Shickardum in Jure Regio, cap. 2. theorem 7. pag. 60."[80] In fact, Selden, who seems to have read all sources primary and secondary, cites Schickhard on other Talmudic passages that Salmasius uses.[81] More important, Selden also quotes at length from Salmasius's "In Defensione Regia, cap. 2" on the question of flogging the king.[82]

Between Salmasius's *Defensio Regia* (1649) and Milton's response to it, *Pro Populo Defensio* (1651), comes Selden's *De Synedriis* (1650), whose rhetorical contours one can trace in *The First Defence*. Thus, for example, Milton accuses Salmasius of twisting David's words in Psalm 17 ("let my sentence come forth from thy presence"):

> Therefore, so Barnachmani has it, "none but God judges a king." But rather it seems more likely that David wrote these words when he was being harassed by Saul and, though already anointed of God, did not refuse even the judgment of Jonathan. . . . Now comes that old argument which is the masterpiece of our courtiers: "Against thee only have I sinned." (*YP*, 4:361)

Selden cites the same texts in the same order: "Hebraei Barnachmoni sententia exstat in dictis Rabbinorum, titulo de judicibus, nulla creatura judicat regem, sed Deus benedictus," Psalm 54 ("tibi soli peccavit"), and, in the same column, Salmasius's "*In Defensione Regia*, cap. 2."[83]

In March 1649, Milton was ordered to answer the *Eikon Basilike*; it has been suggested that Cromwell had earlier invited Selden to answer it, but that he refused.[84] A similar statement was made about Selden and a reply to Salmasius. In May 1650, Gui Patin wrote from Paris to Dr. Charles Spon that Selden had written a reply to Salmasius but that it was suppressed while being printed.[85] If any of this is true, one might conjecture that *De Synedriis* contains a great deal of the material necessary for a response to Salmasius. With Selden at his elbow during the composition of *The First Defence*, Milton would have enjoyed the tactical advantage of reading and evaluating Salmasius's opinion on a given topic in the broad context of other arguments, ancient and contemporary.

The problem of how and why Milton used a source bears upon a second essay by Professor Werman in which, taking a hint from a note by D. C. Allen, she argues that a Latin translation by Willem Vorstius of the midrashic *Pirke de-Rabbi Eliezer* is a source of material in *Paradise Lost*.[86] Some difficulties that must be overcome if her thesis is to be accepted include convincing the reader that Milton would have been drawn to this source, demonstrating that an idea in the source actually appears in the epic, and proving that the material in question does not also appear in a more accessible source. Professor Werman's scholarship is sound; nevertheless, she does not always overcome these difficulties.[87]

The most striking image not of Christian provenance found by both Werman and Allen in the *Pirke* and the epic is that of the nuptial bower.

> . . . it was a place
> Chos'n by the sovran Planter, when he fram'd
> All things to man's delightful use; the roof
> Of thickest covert was inwoven shade
> Laurel and Myrtle, and what higher grew
> Of firm and fragrant leaf; on either side
> *Acanthus*, and each odorous bushy shrub
> Fenc'd up the verdant wall; each beauteous flow'r,
> *Iris* all hues, Roses, and Jessamin
> Rear'd high thir flourisht heads between, and wrought
> Mosaic.
>
> (PL, 4.690–700)

The *Pirke* speaks of "ten wedding canopies" made by God for Adam from precious stones, pearls, and gold, and Vorstius renders *huppah* (canopy) as *thalamus*, which can mean a bride's room or marriage bed.[88] Almost as if to concede tacitly that the union between the Pirke's *huppah* and the Edenic bower needs bolstering, Professor Werman cites a Talmudic text in which *huppah* unequivocally means a wedding chamber, although she doesn't indicate how Milton would have known that text.[89]

Milton would have found in Selden's writings numerous discussions of *huppah*, including but not limited to the text in *Pirke* as well as the Talmudic text cited by Werman. An entire chapter of *Uxor Ebraica* discusses entry into the *huppah* ("introductionem in chuppam, id est, in thalamum nuptialem") and rehearses at length the rabbinic argument that leading a betrothed woman into the bower rather than matrimonial blessings effects matrimony: "Non benedictio sponsorum facit seu perficit nuptias, sed deductio in thalamum."[90] "To the Nuptial Bow'r / I led her blushing like the Morn" (8.510–11), Adam recounts, and perhaps this silent act solemnized his marriage to his blushing bride.

The bower is in fact the principal emblem of the wedding.

> Here in close recess
> With Flowers, Garlands, and sweet-smelling Herbs
> Espoused *Eve* deckt first her Nuptial Bed,
> And heav'nly Choirs the Hymenaean sung,
> What day the genial Angel to our Sire
> Brought her in naked beauty . . .
>
> (4.708–13)

In books by Selden that Milton praised, one finds extensive rabbinic commentary on the bower itself and on nuptial garlands.[91] The most convincing sections of Werman's essay on the *Pirke de-Rabbi Eliezer*'s influence on *Paradise Lost* deal with domestic matters (marriage in the garden, work in Eden), and Selden refers often to this midrash when he discusses marriage.[92]

According to the law of economy of means, Milton found midrashic commentary on the nuptial bower not in a separate volume of the *Pirke* but rather in works by Selden, who cites in addition to this midrash all the major rabbinic sources to which Milton refers or alludes—other *midrashim*, the Talmud, the commentaries of the *Biblia Rabbinica*, Maimonides, even the *Zohar*. This does not necessarily mean that Milton was a one-stop shopper in Selden's supermarket of Hebraic materials. In the *Doctrine and Discipline of Divorce* alone, for example, he refers favorably to Buxtorf's translation of Maimonides' *Guide for the Perplexed* and to specifically rabbinic elements in works by Paulus Fagius and Hugo Grotius.[93] But the presence of rabbinic materials cited by Milton—including hundreds of references to Maimonides and a great many to Grotius as well—in the work of a scholar he singles out for praise does mean that Selden should be recognized as a major Miltonic source. The existence of Selden's work casts doubt on some recent conclusions reached by two Miltonists genuinely familiar with rabbinic learning; had it been noticed, as perhaps it should have been, when the topic of Milton's Hebraica was broached, then the claims of Saurat, Fletcher, et al., checked against the materials gathered by Selden, might have proved to have been more permanently persuasive.

Anyone who wants to enlarge even by one title the already vast wilderness of Miltonic sources should refer first to Selden and then perhaps to Grotius, Fagius, and the other Latin compendia of Hebraic scholarship cited by Milton. Unlike those other compendia, either indexed or at least organized by scriptural chapter and verse, Selden's work is difficult to plunder. One can glance at a work that is amenable to use as a dictionary of rabbinic ideas or as a repository of specific sources, but the reader drawn to Selden must be patient. The reward of that long, slow gaze is to penetrate beyond such details as this chapter has concerned itself with so far, to the heart of Selden's thought.

PHARISEES SELDEN AND MILTON ON DIVORCE

Milton's interpretation of Deuteronomy's divorce law in accord with ancient Jewish theory and practice is an important example of rabbinic influence mediated by Selden. The title page of the second edition of *Doctrine and Discipline of Divorce*, asserting that the true doctrine has been "Restor'd" "from . . . bondage," might seem at first to be employing the rhetoric of Christian liberty; as it turns out, however, each of Milton's title page changes—including a reference to "that which the Law of God allowes" and the addition of a verse from the Hebrew Bible (Prov. 18:13)—underscores the harmony of law and gospel. In this tract the unabrogated Mosaic law restores freedom to those formerly under the bondage of canon law.

As chastity in *Comus* incorporates all virtues and as the single dietary prohibition in the Edenic books of *Paradise Lost* contains all laws, so does the brief Mosaic pronouncement on divorce (Deut. 24:1–2) in Milton's first tract on that subject represent the entire Torah. Most interpreters of the New Testament hold that Jesus dissociated himself directly from a regulation of the Torah on one occasion only: when, in defiance of Pharisaic interrogation (Matt. 19:3–9), he rejected explicitly and categorically the deuteronomic right of divorce. But in *Doctrine and Discipline of Divorce* Milton forces Christ's words into compliance with that deuteronomic right and thus becomes in effect a defender of the entire Mosaic law.

When Milton refers on the title page to restoring the doctrine and discipline of divorce from bondage and to recovering the "long-lost meaning" of scriptural passages, "Seasonable to be now thought on in the Reformation intended," he hints at the persona he will be adopting in the body of the tract: that of a new Josiah. Like "good Josiah" (*PL*.1.418), whose discovery and consequent implementation of the "book of the law of the Lord given by Moses" (2 Chron. 34; 2 Kings 22), after years of idolatrous neglect, made him an obvious symbolic figure to Protestant Reformers, Milton sees himself as a moral archaeologist, picking up shards of truth buried for years in custom and error: "Bringing in my hands an ancient and most necessary, most charitable, and yet most injur'd Statute of *Moses* . . . thrown aside with much inconsiderat neglect, under the rubbish of Canonicall ignorance: as once the whole law was by some such like conveyance in *Josiahs* time" (*YP*, 2:224).

Milton keeps Josiah's reformative activities in mind when he refers to himself as "the sole advocate of a discount'nanc't truth" (224), and later, in the *Areopagitica*, his figure stands as a conspicuous exception to the lament that "revolutions of ages do not oft recover the losse of a rejected truth, for the want of which whole Nations fare the worse" (*YP*, 2:493). Of capital importance for Milton was the belief that the book of the law discovered and defended by Josiah was Deuteronomy, which made their missions identical.

Beginning in *Doctrine and Discipline of Divorce*, continuing in *Tetrachordon*, and concluding in *De doctrina Christiana*, Milton's Hebraic argument for divorce becomes increasingly more rabbinic in nature. This development coincides with his increasing reliance on the rabbinic authorities cited by Selden, first in *De Jure Naturali* and then in *Uxor Ebraica*. Milton and Selden refer to the same rabbinic commentaries on

Judges, who assert that the Hebrew word *zonah* need not refer to a prostitute,[94] and they appeal to Maimonides for the argument that divorce can restore household peace.[95] More important, one can identify as exclusively rabbinic the central argument in all of Milton's discussions of divorce: that Christ's pronouncement on divorce can be accommodated to the deuteronomic permission.

The Mosaic law authorizes a husband to write a bill of divorce if, through "some uncleanness" (*ervath davar*), his wife should fail to find favor in his eyes (Deut. 24:1); Christ, while speaking to the Pharisees, appears to reject this law and to grant divorce only "for fornication" (Matt. 19:9). Rabbinic discussions of these two key phrases, which appear at first to restrict the grounds of divorce to unchastity and sexual offense, widen their meaning to include any kind of obnoxious behavior.

In *Uxor Ebraica*, Selden quotes the entire talmudic dispute over the meaning of the deuteronomic phrase *ervath davar*, which led to a fundamental break in the religious schools of Palestine in the first century B.C.E. The School of Shammai, emphasizing *ervah* (shame, nakedness, unchastity), permitted divorce when fornication occurred because it made the continuation of marriage impossible. The School of Hillel, emphasizing *davar* (a thing), argued that divorce should be granted for any *thing*—that is, for any sort of cause. Selden, who reads Matthew 19 in the light of this talmudic text (Gittin 90a), demonstrates the consistency of Christ's position with that of an advocate of the School of Shammai. He also points out that the Pharisees whom Christ reproved in this chapter belonged to the School of Hillel.[96]

The light shed by the Talmud on first-century Judaism allows Selden to contextualize Christ's pronouncement on divorce: "While that well-known controversy between the schools of Hillel and Shammai was raging in Jerusalem, Christ taught that a wife should not be divorced for any reason one pleases, or that he who sends her away 'except for the reason of fornication' commits a grave sin and causes his wife to commit adultery."[97] Positing a Semitic original for the gospels and retroverting Greek passages into Hebrew or Aramaic, Selden solves numerous textual difficulties. He distinguishes between Aramaic (which he, like Milton, calls "Syriac") and rabbinic Hebrew, concluding that Christ probably used the latter, "since he was addressing the pharisees, the foremost theologians and jurists of the time." This rabbinic or Talmudic dialect ("Rabinica seu Talmudica dialectus") he compares to the scholastic Latin still used at Oxford in disputations by students of theology and jurisprudence. Selden reveals extraordinary sensitivity to the style of Talmudic disputation by posing, in its original Hebrew, the Hillelite question most likely put to Christ by the Pharisees: "Is it permitted for a man to dismiss his wife for any cause?" He then reads Christ's pronouncement in

Matthew as an answer in Talmudic Hebrew that accords with the school of Shammai:

> To a question asked in that way, the most appropriate response for someone who rejects the Hillelite opinion and embraces the Shammaite would be . . . "If a man sends his wife away except because of baseness or except because of a matter of baseness."[98]

But then, extending his argument much further, Selden proves through exhaustive citation and analysis that "fornication" (Matt. 19:9 and also 15:19) is the translation of the Hebrew word *ervah* (and the Aramaic word *z'nuth*) that both the Hebrew Bible and rabbinic sources apply generically to any form of turpitude: "since *porneia* and *ervah* have the same meaning . . . may not that phrase of the schools of the time, 'except for the cause of baseness,' that occurred so frequently in the discussions about divorce, be equated with 'except for the cause of fornication' whether in the Greek version of the Gospel or in the words of Christ?"[99] Selden thus identifies the Gospel's ground of divorce, "fornication," with that of the Mosaic Law, "some uncleanness," finding in both terms a vastly inclusive meaning. The practical result of narrowing considerably the gap between Hillel's most permissive and Christ's (only apparently) most restrictive interpretations is that divorce can be granted for virtually any cause at variance with marital harmony.

In what Milton would have called "this plain and Christian *Talmud*, vindicating the Law of God from irreverent and unwary expositions" (*YP*, 2:635), Selden examines the word *porneia*, conceding that, once, he too would have concurred with the church fathers, who "wanted nothing included in the force of that word but the violation of a marriage by illicit cohabitation." Finding the word to be "very rare in ancient Greek in whatever form," he notes that Demosthenes uses it "for that form of lewdness known as pederasty." The word is used frequently in the Greek version of the Hebrew Bible, and Selden cites Philo as a contemporary of Christ ("Philone, Christo satis coaevo") who defines fornication as simple defloration, copulation from the trade of prostitution, and adultery. Finally, in a passage that Milton knew, Selden cites numerous texts from the Hebrew Bible to expand considerably the application of *porneia* to include all instances of *ervah* and *z'nuth*.

> The wider or secondary definition [of fornication] . . . inclines toward sin and baseness of any kind and denotes a deviation or rather a serious transgression, and so by metalepsis it becomes a clear act of lustfulness toward others inherent in the corrupt nature of man. With regard to idolatry there is recurrent mention of the phrase "they whore after their gods" (Ex. 34:15; Lev. 17:7; 20:5; 1 Ch. 5:25, etc.). With regard to magic and soothsayers . . . "to go a whoring after them" (Lev. 20:6). The Greek used here is "to forni-

cate after." All the sins of the Jerusalemites or Judaeans that are graver and more numerous than those of the Sodomites and the Samaritans (Ezek. 16:36–58) are several times indicated by the word *z'nuth* or fornication. And it is not only idolatry but also other abominations and basenesses whereby the people brought iniquity upon themselves. Hosea said, "The land hath committed great whoredoms from the Lord." . . . Clearly what is discussed is widespread impiety and sin, not just adultery.[100]

One can trace this two-pronged argument for reconciling Christ and Moses in all of Milton's major discussions of divorce, although it becomes progressively more explicit.

> The cause of divorce mention'd in the Law is translated *some uncleannesse*; but in the Hebrew it sounds *nakednes of ought*, or *any reall nakednes*: which by all the learned interpreters is refer'd to the mind as well as the body. (*Doctrine and Discipline of Divorce*, YP, 2:244)

> For the language of Scripture signifies by fornication . . . not only the trespas of body . . . but signifies also any notable disobedience, or intractable cariage of the wife to the husband. . . . [Fornication] signifies the apparent alienation of mind . . . to any point of will worship, though to the true God; some times it notes the love of earthly things, or worldly pleasures though in a right beleever, some times the least suspicion of unwitting idolatry. As *Num*. 15.39. willfull disobedience to any the least of Gods commandements is call'd fornication. *Psal*. 73.26, 27. a distrust only in God, and withdrawing from the neernes of zeal and confidence which ought to be, is call'd fornication. (*Tetrachordon*, YP, 2:672–73)

> As Selden demonstrated particularly well in his *Uxor Hebraea*, with the help of numerous Rabbinical texts,[101] the word *fornication*, if it is considered in the light of the idiom of oriental languages, does not mean only adultery. It can mean also either what is called *some shameful thing* (i.e., the lack of some quality which might reasonably be required in a wife), Deut. xxiv. 1, or it can signify anything which is found to be persistently at variance with love, fidelity, help and society. . . . I have proved this elsewhere, . . . and Selden has demonstrated the same thing. It would be almost laughable to tell the Pharisees, when they asked whether it was lawful to send away one's wife for every cause, that it was not lawful except in the case of adultery. Because everyone already knew that it was not merely lawful but one's duty to send away an adulteress, and not simply to divorce her but to send her to her death. So the word *fornication* must be interpreted in a much broader sense than that of adultery. (*De doctrina Christiana* 1:10, YP, 6:378)

In this last excerpt Milton relies on the two-pronged argument that interprets "some shameful thing" broadly, in the light of tractate Gittin 90a, and then identifies it with *porneia* or "fornication," also broadly interpreted. The critical biblical argument for divorce thus depends ultimately on rabbinic interpretations of two key phrases, one in Hebrew, and the other, as Milton asserts, not Attic but Hebraic, a word that "the Evangelist heer *Hebraizes*" (*Tetrachordon*, YP, 2:671). The source of the excerpt's final argument—that Christ's exception *parektos logou porneias* could not possibly refer to adultery, since an adulteress was not divorced but put to death—is John Selden: "Indeed, adultery, lawfully proved in court, was a capital case and was not punished by divorce."[102]

The elliptical Hebrew text of Malachi 2:16, which permits opposed readings, is a shibboleth dividing proponents of divorce from those who advocate Christian patience. Rejecting the apparently more authoritative reading (*AV*: "For the LORD, the God of Israel, saith that he hateth putting away"), Milton chooses an alternative more to his liking ("*he who hates let him divorce*" [YP, 2:257]), appealing, with some exaggeration, to "the best interpreters, all the ancient, and most of the modern" (2:749). Milton quotes the verse in *De doctrina*, 1.10, to refute those who claim that the sacred law of divorce is a concession to hard-heartedness:

> Mal. ii.16: *whoever hates* or *because he hates, let him send her away.* . . . God enacted this law . . . not in order to make any concessions to the hard-heartedness of husbands, but to rescue the wretched wives from any hard-heartedness which might occur. . . . [T]hat a woman who is not loved but justly neglected, a woman who is loathed and hated, should, in obedience to the harshest of laws, be kept beneath the yoke of a crushing slavery (for that is what marriage is without love), by a man who has no love or liking for her: that is a hardship harder than any divorce. (*YP*, 6:375)

After recording the dispute between the schools of Hillel and Shammai regarding divorce, tractate Gittin concludes with a discussion of the various meanings of Malachi 2:16 (including "he that sends his wife away is hated"). At least twice in the *Uxor Ebraica*, Selden cites both the verse in its Talmudic context and Rashi's commentary on it, which emphasizes charity: "Our sages dispute the matter in tractate *Gittin*. Some of them say, 'If you hate her, send her away with a bill of divorcement, that she might marry another. . . . If you hate her, then put her away; but act not cruelly by retaining her in the home, if you are estranged from her." Selden paraphrases closely: "It is understood as if the prophet later warned about injuries that would be unjustly inflicted on the wife of one's youth . . . and it would be better if he hates her that he should divorce her with a document rather than keep her while afflicted and hated."[103]

Both the style and the meaning of the passage from *De doctrina* seem to reflect the *Uxor*'s influence: the scholarly scrupulousness characteristic of Selden ("*whoever hates* or *because he hates*") and the portrayal of marriage in certain circumstances as "the harshest of laws" and of divorce as a charitable release from affliction. Selden, a bachelor, called marriage a "desperate thing" and complained that "of all actions of a man's life, his marriage does least concern other people; yet of all actions of our life, 'tis most meddled with by other people."[104]

Of the 122 occurrences of the word "charity" in Milton's prose, ninety-two are found in the divorce tracts,[105] but, ever since their appearance, the tracts have been criticized for their lack of Christian charity. The anonymous author of *An Answer* specifically chastises Milton for failing to realize that the entire judicial Mosaic law, including divorce, is abrogated and that Christ came "to shew the law of the Gospell to require more mutuall love and passing by injuries then the law." The author then personates Christ:

> During . . . [the old] dispensation, this law of Divorce was a good positive law: But now whosoever will be my follower and professe himself to have received the plenteous grace of the Gospell, he must be so farre from using hardship or unkindnesse to his Wife, or others to whom he is neerly bound, that he must not revenge wrong done from strangers & enemies, but pray for them, and bless them: he must be so farre from turning his Wife out of doores for her ill cariage, yea although it should proceed to cursing and persecuting him, that he must use all mildnesse, and love, and godly means to reforme her; . . . you will finde the drift of Christ, to give as it were new inlargements of lawes under the Gospell, requiring more spiritualness in observation, then the Mosaical government.[106]

Milton recognizes perfectly well that he is being accused of lacking charity, and, in his answer, he suggests that the Mosaic law may in some instances be more forgiving than the law of love:

> Charity indeed bids us forgive our enemies, yet doth not force us to continue freindship and familiarity with those freinds who have bin fals or unworthy towards us; but is contented in our peace with them, at a fair distance. . . . No more doth Charity command, nor can her rule compell, to retain in neerest union of wedloc, one whose other grossest faults, or disabilities to perform what was covnanted, are the just causes of as much greevance and dissention in a Family, as the private act of adultery. (*Colasterion, YP,* 2:731–32)

Such is Samson's peace with Dalila, at a fair distance:

> *Dalila*. Let me approach at least, and touch thy hand.
> *Samson*. Not for thy life, lest fierce remembrance wake
> My sudden rage to tear thee joint by joint.
> At distance I forgive thee, go with that.
>
> (951–54)

The enemies of divorce associate it with a nation lacking in patience and charity. For Anthony Ascham, in his generally good-natured little treatise on marriage, the Jews seek improvement through change, whereas Christians meet difficulties with patience. "Why then is it not as lawfull to change a [spouse] as a place or a howse, which is incommodious or infectious or falling into Ruine? Seeing in all other Contracts in which the Iudgment is surprizd by some deceit or hidden fault, wee may recover ease and freedome. This indeed the Iews argued."[107]

At stake in all of Milton's writings on divorce is the true meaning of charity. Georgia Christopher has argued that Milton in *Comus* altered the famous triad of 1 Corinthians 13:13 to "faith, hope, and chastity" in order to avoid suspicion of a *fides charitate formata*: "The idea of charity as the 'form' of faith would have seemed to him a papist legalism, for then love could be said to produce faith—an arrangement thought to be tantamount to salvation by human love and works."[108] According to Christopher, charity represents works, just as chastity is a Lutheran metaphor for faith. But in the divorce tracts, Milton could hold to various positions (including the efficacy of works, and charity as the sum of the law) resembling those of Roman Catholicism without fear of suspicion, since, of course, divorce was forbidden by canon law, the institution most vilified in all of Milton's tracts of 1643–45.

Milton recognizes and repudiates the pervasive use of charity as a code word in anti-divorce polemic to condemn Jews for hardheartedness, the opposite of Christian love. Whether defending the Jews from the charge of hardheartedness (*YP*, 2:284 and 354) or appealing to "an ancient and most necessary, most charitable, and yet most injur'd Statute of Moses" (*YP*, 2:224), Milton reveals a comprehensive understanding of charity as both Hebraic and Christian. He identifies as extremes to be avoided both the Pharisees who interrogated Christ, hardhearted to women in their very licentiousness, and those who would make Christian patience a "compulsive Law": "Let not therfore under the name of fulfilling Charity, such an unmercifull, and more then legal yoke, bee padlockt upon the neck of any Christian" (*YP*, 2:732).

David Paraeus comments on 1 Corinthians 7:10–11 ("Let not the wife depart from the husband . . . and let not the husband put away his wife"):

> Those who retain or imitate the hardheartedness of the Jews reveal themselves strangers to the spirit of Christ. . . . The Church is to correct such a one by excluding him from the company of the faithful, the Christian magistrate by subjecting him to imprisonment or fine, in accordance with the precept of the Lord, "If he neglect to hear the Church [*ecclesia*], let him be unto thee as a heathen" [Matt. 15:17], and of the Apostle, "Put away from yourselves that wicked person."[109]

Paraeus would reinforce with ecclesiastical and civil power the rigid distinction between the charity of Christian marriage and the hardheartedness of Jewish divorce, a distinction that breaks down even as he formulates it. His first proof text is of capital importance to all religious factions in the seventeenth century for its authorization of excommunication, while the second grounds civil power in the gospel. Milton answers Paraeus authoritatively that no judicial Mosaic law ever becomes obsolete under the gospel—"the Gospel hath not the least influence upon judicial Courts" (YP, 2:352)—and that the emotions permitted by the Mosaic law (which Paraeus argued should be subdued under the gospel) are "meerly natural and blameles affections" (352).

> Paraeus on the Corinthians would prove that hardnes of heart in divorce is no more now to be permitted, but to be amerc't with fine and imprisonment. I am not willing to discover the forgettings of reverend men, yet here I must. What article or clause of the whole new Cov'nant can Paraeus bring to exasperat the judicial Law, upon any infirmity [of that law] under the Gospel? (352)[110]

Although Milton consistently displaces upon the Pharisees who interrogated Christ the hardheartedness with which opponents of divorce characterize the Mosaic law and the Jewish people, his own juridical position is identical to that of Hillel, the most permissive (hardhearted?) of all the Pharisees, who allows divorce "both for any reason whatsoever and because of baseness."[111] Milton keeps these two reasons side by side, deliberately refusing to distinguish between immoral behavior and an unpleasing nature, "grossest faults, or disabilities" (YP, 2:732), "wilfulnes or inability" (589). Unfitness according to the law of nature corresponds for Milton to *ervath davar* under the Mosaic law and to fornication under the gospel: in "the Hebrew Text . . . *the nakednes of any thing*" refers to "any defect, annoyance, or ill quality in nature, which . . . was unalterably distastful" (620), and "fornication is to be understood as the language of Christ understands it . . . when to be a tolerable wife is either naturally not in their power, or obstinatly not in their will" (673).

Contemporary readers have joined the anonymous author of *An Answer* in regarding as unchristian Milton's view of unalterable unfitness providing grounds for divorce.[112] In the divorce tracts, where "God and Nature bid the same" (*PL*, 6.176), sins against grace (such as religious despair) derive from and are subsidiary to sins against nature, and Hillel's view that one can divorce a wife at will achieves primacy over Christ's forbiddance of divorce without exception (Mark 10:11–12 and Luke 16:18, most contemporary scholars regarding Matthew's "saving for the cause of fornication" as a later addition). For Milton, "enthrallment to one who either cannot, or will not bee mutual . . . is the ignoblest, and the lowest slavery that a human shape can bee put to" (*YP*, 2:625–26). His notion of natural sympathy and antipathy draws on analogies of elemental attraction and astronomical conjunction:

> For Nature hath her *Zodiac* also, keeps her great annual circuit over human things as truly as the Sun and Planets in the firmament; hath her *anomalies*, hath her obliquities in ascensions and declinations, accesses and recesses, as blamelessly as they in heaven. And sitting in her planetary Orb with two rains in each hand, one strait, the other loos, tempers the cours of minds as well as bodies to several conjunctions and oppositions, freindly or unfreindly aspects, consenting oftest with reason, but never contrary. (*YP*, 2:680–81)

An important chapter of the *Uxor Ebraica* recapitulates the law of divorce according to "the law of the Hebrews, of Nature, and of the Ancient Pagans" and introduces "the Passages in the Gospels on Divorce." Surveying the transmission among the ancients of extremely liberal laws and practices of dissolving matrimony, Selden cites from Ptolemy's *Tetrabiblos* a passage on cosmic affinity and antipathy that Milton may well have adapted in *Tetrachordon*:

> Regarding the unrestricted practice of divorce and right of divorce among the most ancient pagans in the East, there is a famous passage in Claudius Ptolemy that derives from the astrological works of the Chaldeans and Egyptians and that deals with marriage and divorce. The words are as follows: "The cohabitation of spouses shall be permanent [or "a marriage is never dissolved"] when it would happen that each of their natal luminaries were harmoniously configured, . . . when the figures of the bodies form a triangle or a hexagon and especially when a reciprocal change takes place—that is, when the sun of one is in line with the moon of the other or vice versa. . . . They are dissolved on trivial grounds and are mutually separated when the ordained positions of the heavenly bodies should happen to be either in unconnected signs or in a diagonal or square to each other."[113]

Milton's critics are probably correct when they accuse him of being unchristian in the divorce tracts. The charity to which he appeals may be closer to Selden's Rashi than to Matthew's Christ: "act not cruelly by retaining her in the home, if you are estranged from her," but "send her away . . . that she might marry another," rather than "Moses because of the hardness of your hearts suffered you to put away your wives: but from the beginning it was not so (19:8)." To expect fallen humanity, bereft of innocence, to be as perfect as Adam and Eve were in paradise in "the beginning" is to expect, as pharaoh did, a tally of bricks, but this time without the straw, in equal number to what they were "heretofore" (Ex. 5:7–8).

Christ may have forbidden divorce to prevent its abuse by the licentious Pharisees, but Milton, like Hillel, would permit anyone to sue for divorce for any reason. "The law of *Moses* is manifest to fixe no limit therein at all, or such at lest as impeaches the fraudulent no more than if it were not set; only requires the dismissive writing without other caution, leaves that to the inner man, and the barre of conscience" (*Tetrachordon*, YP, 2:657). The identical juridical position of Milton and the Pharisees resonates in the sonnet "On the Detraction which followed upon my Writing Certain Treatises":

> But this is got by casting Pearl to Hogs,
> That bawl for freedom in their senseless mood,
> And still revolt when truth would set them free.
> License they mean when they cry liberty.
>
> (*ll.8–11*)

Christ, tempted by the Pharisees, did not cast his pearls before swine: his was "not so much a teaching, as an intangling. . . . Neither was it seasonable to talke of honest and conscientious liberty among them who had abused legall and civil liberty to uncivil licence" (*Tetrachordon*, YP, 2:642–43). Christ forbade divorce in order to curb the freedom of his licentious opponents. But Milton did cast his pearls before his swinish countrymen, hoping to free them through the Mosaic law of divorce ("the known rule of ancient liberty"). As Christ accused the Pharisees of abusing legal liberty for the sake of uncivil license, so, perhaps, does Milton accuse contemporary libertines who mistake promiscuity for liberty, although the line echoes most strongly the numerous Presbyterian accusations against Milton for introducing "licentious[ness]" under the guise of liberty.[114] For Milton, as for the most extreme among the Pharisees, "this law [of divorce] bounded no man; he might put away whatever found not favour in his eyes" (YP, 2:656–57).

After the execution of Charles I, royalists associated regicides with the Jews, as when Abraham Cowley helped to spread the rumor that Cromwell intended "to sell St. *Pauls* to them for a Synagogue . . . to reward that Nation which had given the first noble example of crucifying their King."[115] The attacks on Milton following the divorce tracts for "Judaizing" were more personal,[116] and his later attempts to distance himself from the Jews may follow in part an ancient paradigm of bitterly criticizing a source from whom one has drawn heavily, especially when that source is already defamed. Livy criticized Valerius Antius, and Jerome, whose mastery of Jewish tradition was unmatched among the church fathers, occasionally repeated the invectives of his predecessors Tertullian, Cyprian, Eusebius, and Origen, although this did not protect him from the accusation that he was attempting to Judaize the Church of Christ.[117] Milton in the *First Defence* derided a Talmudic story as an "old wives' tale" and "a rabbinical fable" (YP, 4:355). Jay Braverman, recounting Jerome's acknowledged debt to his Hebrew teacher and rabbinic tradition, notes the traditional nature of his tendency to "speak disparagingly of the Jewish midrashim as perverted exegesis or old wives' tales."[118]

The ostensible enemies in the divorce tracts, canon law and the Pharisees, pose no real challenge to Milton. The actual enemies of Pharisee Milton are the pronouncements of Christ and Paul against divorce and Paul's message of death to the law. Milton's thoroughgoing critique and revision of Paul, any one of whose multifarious attacks on the Mosaic law is a potential threat to the law of divorce, eclipses even the various reinscriptions in the divorce tracts of Christ's apparent intention in the synoptic gospels. Paul believes that God intended to condemn by the law because he intended to save everyone in another way. His repeated insistence that the Mosaic law was given not to restrain transgressions, but rather *in order that* (Greek, *hina*) they be increased (Gal. 3:10–14, 22, and 24) is opposed variously in the divorce tracts: the law removes sin (*YP*, 2:657–58); the secondary Mosaic law of divorce in a fallen world can renew, *so far as is possible*, the primary Mosaic law of paradise (Gen. 1 and 2): it can "restore the much wrong'd and over-sorrow'd state of matrimony, not onely to those mercifull and life-giving remedies of *Moses*, but, as much as may be, to that serene and blisfull condition it was in at the beginning" (*YP*, 2:240). The postlapsarian secondary law allows one to recover as much "in execution, as reason, and present nature can bear" (2:666). For Paul, "the law entered, that the offense might abound" (Rom. 5:20); the law precipitates transgressions, actualizing and exposing human rebellion against God. Milton reinterprets the verse by separating rather than identifying law and sin.

> That it could not be the end of the Law, whether Moral or Judiciall to licence a sin, I prove easily out of *Rom. 5.20. The Law enter'd that the offence might abound*, that is, that sin might be made abundantly manifest to be hainous and displeasing to God, that so his offer'd grace might be the more esteem'd. Now if the Law in stead of aggravating and terrifying sin, shall give out licence, it foils it selfe, and turns recreant from its own end: it forestalls the pure grace of Christ which is through righteousnesse, with impure indulgences which are through sin. And instead of discovering sin, for *by the Law is the knowledge therof*, saith S. Paul, and that by certain and true light for men to walk in safely, it holds out fals and dazling fires to stumble men: or like those miserable flies to run into with delight, and be burnt. (*YP*, 2:287).

That the offense might abound means "that sin might be made abundantly manifest to be hainous and displeasing to God." What Milton rejects as travesty is the common exposition of Paul's meaning: that indeed the purpose of the law is to increase sin, and that knowledge of sin means concrete experience of sin, actualizing sin. The image of law as *ignis fatuus*, or as a deadly flame drawing a moth to its death, is much closer to Paul's apparent intention than that of a "certain and true light for men to walk in safely." In Romans 6, the Mosaic law is virtually the same as sin. Paul, who could not reconcile the New Testament and the Hebrew Bible, instinctively related them by having the old lead up to the new negatively, the law condemning, Christ saving. The Miltonic excerpt describes a law that leads not to sin but to the acceptance of grace.

Romans 7:11 may allude to the Fall: "sin, taking occasion by the commandment, deceived me, and by it slew me." In Paul's dualistic view, sin is a power capable of wresting the law from God and using it to deceive human beings. Bucanus offers a commercial analogy to prove that the impossibility of performing the law after the Fall is no excuse: "Even as if one should lend any man money, and the debter should by his negligence and fault spend or lose it, and is no more able to pay, notwithstanding the creditor can not bee proved to deale unjustly, if he demaund the lent money of him & his heires."[119] In a refutation of Paul no less powerful and passionate for being indirect, Milton considers for a moment hypothetically

> both [the] moral and judicial [Mosaic laws] full of malice and deadly purpose conspir'd to let the dettor Israelite the seed of *Abraham* run on upon a banckrout score, flatter'd with insufficient and insnaring discharges, that so he might be hal'd to a more cruel forfeit for all the indulgent arrears which those judicial acquitments had ingaged him in. No no, this cannot be, that the Law whose integrity and faithfulnesse is next to God, should be either the shamelesse broker of our impurities, or the intended instrument of our destruction. (*YP*, 2:323)

This rejected Pauline interpretation of the law as a ruinous Mafia-style loan will revive after the Fall in Adam's soliloquy.

Milton handles in various ways the killing Pauline letter on marriage and divorce. Arguing, against the majority view, that the Jewish law of divorce in Deuteronomy is a command and not a mere permission, he proposes obversely that the problematic verses of 1 Corinthians 7:12–14, condemning divorce between a Christian and an unbeliever, are a permission and not a command: "whether this be a command or an advice [to stay married to an unbeliever], we must look that it be so understood as not to contradict the least point of morall religion that God hath formerly commanded, otherwise what doe we, but set the morall Law and the Gospel at civill war together: and who then shall be able to serve those two masters?" (*YP*, 2:268). Submitting Paul to Moses' correction, Milton insists that "the moral reason of divorcing stands to eternity, which neither Apostle nor Angel from heaven can countermand" (2:681), and, in order to prove that "this heer spoken by *Paul*, not by the Lord[,] cannot be a command," cites "[f]irst, the law of *Moses, Exod.* 34.16. *Deut.* 7.3.6" (2:681). Milton also sets the word itself against the word, making Paul's general stricture in 2 Corinthians 6:14 appear to be a specific rejection of marriage with an unbeliever ("Mis-yoke not together with Infidels") and thus a refutation of the apparent meaning of 1 Corinthians 7 (2:262).

Milton sometimes consciously rejects the accepted meaning of a Pauline verse. The burning in *"It is better to marry then to burne"* (1 Cor. 7:9; *YP*, 2:250) is neither the fire of lust nor of hell, but rather of one lonely soul's longing for conversation with "a fit soule . . . in the cheerful society of wedlock" (2:250–51). Often assuming a higher innocence, Milton acts as if Paul's condemnation of the Mosaic law were actually approbation: "If the Law be silent to declare sin, the people must needs generally goe astray, for the Apostle himselfe saith, *he had not known lust but by the Law* [Rom. 7:7]" (2:290). More times than can be enumerated here Milton rejects the virtual equation of sin and the Mosaic law in Romans 6 and the first verses of Romans 7: "For sin shall not have dominion over you: for ye are not under the law" (6:14), and "ye also are become dead to the law" (7:4). Milton argues instead that the Mosaic law is a law of life; it contains statutes that God approves; it saves; and it has not expired (2:653–54, 662, and [for an audacious recasting of Rom. 7:10] 297). To maintain that "the wages of sin is death" (6:23) is to interpret limitingly "the uncorrupt and majestick law of God, bearing in her hand the wages of life and death" (2:321).

Paul virtually equates the law with sin and the flesh, to which a Christian is dead. But Milton, in his role as Josiah, recovers the law and repudiates the Reformation position ultimately derivable from Paul that God permitted the imperfect Mosaic law of divorce because of the people's hard-heartedness. The Pauline view operates in the great epic after the Fall ("Law can discover sin, but not remove" [12.290]), and it lies behind the myth of Sin's birth after the promulgation of God's decree (no sin without law). According to the Hebraic view of the law's sufficiency in paradise, "sure sin can have no tenure by law at all" (2:288).

> If the Law allow sin, it enters into a kind of covnant with sin, and if it doe, there is not a greater sinner in the world then the Law it selfe. The Law, to use an allegory somthing different from that in *Philo Judaeus* concerning *Amaleck,* though haply more significant, the Law is the *Israelite,* and hath this absolute charge given it Deut. 25. *To blot out the memory of* sin *the Amalekite from under heav'n, not to forget it.* Again, the Law is the *Israelite,* and hath this expresse repeated command, *to make no cov'nant with* sin *the Canaanite,* but to expell him, lest he prove a snare. (2:288)

As evidence that the Torah is perfect and would not allow hard-heartedness, Milton cites not merely underlying principles but specific deuteronomic laws: divorce (Deut. 24) and the limitations of royal prerogative

(17); prohibitions of usury (23:9–10; *YP*, 2:289 and 320) and of worshipping God "in high places" (12:2; *YP*, 2:289); and the commandments of levirate marriage (25:5; *YP*, 2:299), blotting out Amalek (25:17), and destroying the seven nations (Deut. 7:1–2; *YP*, 2:288). Allegory in contemporary discourse is regarded as a fallen mode, artificial and hence intrinsically inauthentic, though it should perhaps be admired instead for calling attention to its own fictiveness. Unlike typology, in which the literal stands in relation to the figurative as shadow to substance, Milton's various allegories of the Mosaic law in the *Doctrine and Discipline of Divorce* employ a hermeneutic of alternation rather than supersession, as when marriage between unequals coexists with the ceremonial prohibition against plowing with diverse animals (Deut. 22:10): "He that lov'd not to see the disparity of severall cattell at the plow, cannot be pleas'd with any vast unmeetnes in mariage" (2:277).

Finally, it seems worth mentioning that a Hebraic rather than Pauline conception of God can be traced in the *Doctrine and Discipline of Divorce*. The theology of the divorce tracts bears upon Milton's paradise in the epic, which combines the primary Mosaic law (Gen. 1 and 2) with some aspects of the postlapsarian secondary Mosaic law, as when Adam and Eve work hard, make mistakes, and know pain. It is as important to keep Paul's central tenets out of the divorce tracts as it is to banish them from paradise. In these tracts, treating as choice what others before him had treated as necessity, Milton exhorts radical change for the improvement of the human condition and thus asserts faith in human beings as agents capable in some measure of controlling their lives. The secondary Mosaic law of divorce is a gift from a benign God who pities our misery and wants us to achieve happiness. Echoing the theodical invocation of *Paradise Lost*, with one huge difference, Milton insists that we have only ourselves to blame for our woe, which is remediable not through Christ's redemptive sacrifice but through the divine law:

> If any therfore who shall hap to read this discourse, hath bin through misadventure ill ingag'd in this contracted evill heer complain'd of . . . let him not op'n his lips against the providence of heav'n, or tax the waies of God and his divine Truth; for they are equal, easy, and not burdensome; nor do they ever crosse the just and reasonable desires of men, nor involve this our portion of mortall life, into a necessity of sadnes and malecontent, by Laws commanding over the unreducible *antipathies* of nature sooner or later to be found: but allow us to remedy and shake off those evills into which human error hath led us through the middest of our best intentions. (2:342)

In the divorce tracts, God is not the stern judge who demands the sacrifice of earthly pleasures, but a force of mercy who offers us, through his Torah, the freedom from misery that custom in the form of canon law would prevent us from exercising (2:222–27). This view of the world as imperfect but improvable carries over into the *Areopagitica* as well, where parliamentary legislation takes the place of the Mosaic law: "For this is not the liberty which wee can hope, that no grievance ever should arise in the Commonwealth, that let no man in this World expect; but when complaints are freely heard, deeply consider'd, and speedily reform'd, then is the utmost bound of civill liberty attain'd, that wise men look for" (2:487).

John Ziesler, in his study of Pauline Christianity, contrasts Paul's absolutist understanding of the law as a single entity that must never be transgressed with the Jewish view of Torah in the first century, a view that accords with Milton's of the secondary Mosaic law in the 1643–45 tracts:

> Palestinian Judaism . . . did *not* suppose that people could earn God's favour. On the contrary, his favour was freely given, without any deserving on Israel's part, in election and covenant. The role of the Law was to show the nation how to live within that covenant in order to maintain . . . the relation to Yahweh. . . . Moreover, perfect obedience was not expected, and there were means of atonement and forgiveness for the inevitable lapses, so long as there was a fundamental intention to be within God's people, and his covenant.[120]

It is by now a commonplace that, for Puritans, the identification of England and New England with biblical Israel as holy nations entering into a covenantal relationship with God was a thoroughgoing and comprehensive procedure. Milton often makes this identification in *Tetrachordon*, where the fusion of Moses, the law, and the commonwealth (2:618–19 and 625) is downright Erastian, and in the *Areopagitica*: "the favour and love of heav'n we have great argument to think in a peculiar manner propitious and propending towards us. Why else was this Nation chos'n before any other, that out of her as out of *Sion* should be proclaim'd and sounded forth the first tidings and trumpet of Reformation to all *Europ*" (2:255). Milton alludes to Isaiah 2:3 ("out of Zion shall go forth the law, and the word of the Lord from Jerusalem"), comparing England, the first nation to hear the trumpet of Reformation, with Israel, the first to hear the divine word. Far from commonplace are Milton's generous conception of God the Father, his forgiving view of humankind, and his description of the law as a means of maintaining human happiness as well as a relationship to the divine. These take one from the prose tracts of the mid-1640s to the very first human speech in *Paradise Lost*, where grace is very different from what it will become:

> needs must the Power
> That made us, and for us this ample World
> Be infinitely good, and of his good

As liberal and free as infinite,
That rais'd us from the dust and plac't us here
In all this happiness . . .

. . . .

        hee who requires
From us no other service than to keep
This one, this easy charge.

                                    (4.412–17 and 419–21)

MOSAIC AND PARLIAMENTARY LAW IN THE *AREOPAGITICA*

The discontinuities and surprising continuities between the *Areopagitica* (1644) and the Hebraic divorce tracts that encompass it represent Milton's self-struggle over Torah and law. One of the many surprises of the *Areopagitica* is Milton's effort, at times noticeably strained, to portray the Mosaic law as an institution preserving liberty and freedom of choice. Pauline verses are crucial to the argument of the tract, and terms ordinarily used to vilify the law, to the gospel's advantage, abound here: "tutor" (*YP*, 2:531), "Pedagogue" (531), "perpetuall childhood of prescription" (514), "an abrogated and mercilesse law" (559). But Milton applies these terms to the Parliamentary Licensing Order, which he associates with Roman Catholicism, the Anglican Church's "apishly Romanizing" prelates, and even Roman civil law, but *never* with the Mosaic law.

Milton cites, at a key moment in his second argument, "what is to be thought in generall of reading Books, what ever sort they be" (*YP*, 2:507), one Pauline verse that abolishes the dietary distinctions of the Jewish ceremonial law ("Rise *Peter*, kill and eat" [Acts 10:13; *YP*, 2:512]) and two additional verses that can be interpreted similarly: "Prove all things, hold fast that which is good" (1 Thes. 5:21; *YP*, 2:511–12) and "To the pure all things are pure" (Tit. 1:15; 512), to which Milton adds, "Not only meats and drinks, but all kinde of knowledge whether of good or evill." Milton echoes Raphael's warning to Adam and Eve: "Knowledge is as food, and needs no less / Her Temperance over Appetite" (*PL*, 7.126–27). In paradise, food that is knowledge is forbidden by divine law; knowledge that is like food is subject to discretion in the form of temperance. In the *Areopagitica*, Milton distinguishes between digesting books and foods, stressing the "remarkable" freedom to know implicit in the Pauline verses:

For books are as meats and viands are; some of good, some of evill substance; and yet God in that unapocryphall vision, said without exception, Rise *Peter*, kill and eat, leaving the choice to each mans discretion. . . . Bad meats will scarce breed good nourishment in the healthiest concoction; but herein the difference is of bad books, that they to a discreet and judicious Reader serve in many respects to discover, to confute, to forewarn, and to illustrate. (512)

Perhaps in order to make this great tract even more interesting and contemporary, Ernest Sirluck discounts the importance of Milton's appeal to scriptural authority. The primary function of the citations is actually "to free the issue from the influence" of authority: "It is true that the principle [of temperance] is itself introduced by citations from Scripture, but only in order to prepare a favorable atmosphere for its reception, not as establishing its authority: Scripture had been proved too available an arsenal for the proponents of the contrary principle for a skillful controversialist to resubmit the issue to this kind of arbitration once he had succeeded in freeing it" ("Introduction," YP, 2:165). But Milton's surprise ("and yet," "without exception") and delight in Paul's boldness (citing Tit. 1:15 as "another remarkable saying of the same Author" [512] and Acts 10:15 as "that unapocryphall vision") suggest that scripture was more than a smoke screen in the wars of truth. Milton himself might not have appreciated the argument that the *Areopagitica* commands respect precisely because it derives its convictions from some other source than the Bible.[121]

Milton finds bold conceptual force in the Pauline verses themselves, and his second argument adapts and extends a topic based on these verses in the systematic theology of the Pauline renaissance. These verses turn up in chapters on "the Holy Scriptures," with the ostensible purpose of rejecting the Roman Catholic distinction between the clergy, which is privileged to search the scriptures, and the laity, which is not. Wolfgang Musculus, in his *Common Places*, quotes 1 Thessalonians 5:21 in his chapter "of holye Scriptures," to support the argument that "the Scripture is profitable for a triall":

> Whereas the Apostle sayeth: Trye all thyngs, and holde that which is good. And, let the man prove himselfe: it can not be done without diligent looking upon the holy scriptures. For as the same Apostle sayth: Whatsoever is reproved, is opened by the lyghte, and the same which lurketh in darkenesse, is not revealed but by lighte.[122]

Pauline verses authorized to abolish distinctions between forbidden and permitted foods and, more important, between Jew and gentile are used by Reformers to abolish distinctions between clergy and laity and to proclaim throughout the land the liberty to search the scriptures. According to William Walwyn, Paul asserts the competence of ordinary people.

The . . . interest of the Divine is to preserve amongst the people the distinction of Clergie & Laity, though not now in those termes. . . . Because otherwise if the people did not believe so, they would examine all that was said, and not take things upon trust from their Ministers . . . : they would then try al things, & what they found to be truth, they would imbrace as from God, for God is the authour of truth; what they found to be otherwise, they would reject. . . . He that bade us to try all things, and hold fast that which was good, did suppose that men have faculties and abilities wherewithall to try all things, or else the counsel had bin given in vaine.[123]

In his adaptation of this argument in the *Areopagitica*, Milton widens the freedom to read the Bible to include the freedom to read any text. The ability of any regenerate Christian to interpret scripture with no aid except that of the Holy Spirit and to arrive at a truth obscured and complicated by privileged ecclesiasts is modified slightly to become an argument for individual freedom against the imposition of censorship. Milton himself had applied 1 Thessalonians 5:21 to the Bible alone in *Of Reformation*.

If we will but purge with sovrain eyesalve that intellectual ray which *God* hath planted in us, then we would beleeve the Scriptures protesting their own plainnes, and perspicuity, calling to them to be instructed, not only the *wise*, and *learned*, but the *simple*, the *poor*, the *babes*, foretelling an extraordinary effusion of *Gods* Spirit upon every age, and sexe, attributing to all men, and requiring from them the ability of searching, trying, examining all things, and by the Spirit discerning that which is good; and as the Scriptures themselves pronounce their own plainnes, so doe the Fathers testifie of them. (*YP*, 1:566)

When, in the final, most nationalistic argument of the *Areopagitica*, Milton praises England's flourishing publishing industry, he applies the same verse, still within a Reformation context, to any of the graver products of "the industry of a life wholly dedicated to studious labours": "[writers] sitting by their studious lamps, musing, searching, revolving new notions and idea's wherewith to present, as with their homage and their fealty the approaching Reformation: others as fast reading, *trying all things*, assenting to the force of reason and convincement" (*YP*, 2:554; my emphasis).

Behind the great defense of books in the proposition ("For books are not absolutely dead things" [492]) stands the authority of the Bible. Families of images recapitulate salvation history from the account of creation in Genesis 1–2 to the gospels: books are the progeny of the soul, vials storing the distilled essence of the originating intellect, the image of God in the eye. Josiah's discovery of Deuteronomy "recover[s] the losse of a rejected truth" (493). If "a good Book is the pretious life-blood of a master spirit, imbalm'd and treasur'd up on purpose to a life beyond life" (493), then the New Testament is the good book that contains the essence of Christ, the master spirit whose lifeblood was spilled on the cross and whom Joseph of Arimathea entombed with myrrh and aloes. Censorship is homicide, martyrdom, and massacre (493) in a context of religious persecution. Reciprocally, the *Areopagitica* becomes a sort of Bible. Milton defends the "textual Chetiv," the original transcription of the Masoretic text of the Hebrew Bible, against the "marginal Keri" (517), the amended text to be read aloud. He distinguishes between *keri* and his own *chetiv*, proclamation and writing, in the opening sentence, setting those who "direct their Speech" over against those, like himself, who "write that which they foresee may advance the publick good" (486). Later he adds that "writing is more publick then preaching; and more easie to refutation, if need be" (548).

What matters is that books, like the Bible itself, whether heard or read, be available. Giovanni Diodati's Protestant translator exults, "Every man amongst us may be a *Rabbi*, learned in the Lawes, conversant in the Scriptures, and speaking the language of Canaan, here is nothing withheld that God hath revealed for the benefit of the meanest."[124] Musculus, in his explicitly anti-Catholic section on "the readyng of Holy Scriptures," cites "Josephus writing against Appion of the custome of the Israelites": "Every weeke all people come togither to heare the law. Eache of us demaunded of the lawes, can easilier recite them than tell his owne name. For we have them all written in our mindes, even strayght from our first perseverance."[125] Milton remembers the freedom of the ancient Israelites in his own chapter "OF THE HOLY SCRIPTURE": "No one should be forbidden to read the scriptures. On the contrary, it is very proper that all sorts and conditions of men should read them or hear them regularly. This includes the king, Deut. xvii.19; magistrates, Josh. i.8; and every kind of person, Deut. xxxi.9–11, etc." (*YP*, 6:577).

Milton's justly renowned insistence on trial—"I cannot praise a fugitive and cloister'd vertue, unexercis'd & unbreath'd"; "that which purifies us is triall, and triall is by what is contrary"—derives from the Bible's "try all things" and from Reformation elaborations on the theme that "the Scripture is profitable for a triall." To be unexercised and unbreathed is to submit one's own convictions to the authority of the church. When Musculus attacks the principle of implicit faith, he finds "the unexercised," willing to surrender responsibility, to be its most likely victims. He further cites Ephesians 6 (on warfaring Christians) to oppose the armor of the Bible to the temptations of evil: "And how can they have thys armure, whyche doe not make themselves acquaynted wyth the holy Scriptures, by readying and exercisyng. . . . It is over true that Chrysostome sayeth: We goe into the fielde without armure, and how shall we overcome?"[126]

Musculus quotes Chrysostom to rebuke those lay persons ignorant of scripture who protest, "I am no Cloyster man, I have wyfe and chyldren, and charge of householde":

> You say that the reading of holy Scriptures doth belong to Cloyster men onely, whereas it is muche more necessary for you than for them. For they that be conversant in the middes of the fielde, and do dayly receyve wound upon wounde, they have more neede of Gods medicine.[127]

Paul's verses are the very life of Milton's Puritan argument in the *Areopagitica*, but, surprisingly, there are no contrasts between law and gospel. Milton conspicuously refrains from using arguments that appear frequently in his first, antiprelatical tracts. In Galatians, Paul describes the law as a divinely appointed guardian whose day is now over; therefore, to remain in its guardianship now that the freedom of Christ and of his Spirit has arrived is anachronistic bondage. To remain under the tutelage of the law is to reject the freedom of the sons of God (Gal. 4:5). Milton uses Pauline language of teacher-pupil, father- (or patriarch-)child, overseer-slave (*YP*, 2:531–33), but he displaces the law-gospel conflict onto Laud and the Roman Catholics on one side and God's Englishmen on the other.

Milton's interventions—adaptations and displacements that recover even the Jewish ceremonial law—become particularly evident when he cites John Selden. Milton had dedicated *The Doctrine and Discipline of Divorce* "To the Parlament of *England* with the Assembly" and the *Areopagitica* only to the Parliament. Selden, as member of Parliament for Oxford and a lay member of the Westminster Assembly, is the only dedicatee to be named in either work. Milton calls Selden as a witness to testify to the importance of studying all opinions in a case. Selden often cites the complete talmudic discussion rather than the Maimonidean codification of a particular law because the former contains the diverse opinions that give the law meaning. In *De Jure Naturali*, Selden asserts that the collation of all opinions, including errors, on philosophical, theological, and legal disputations, is the method of the Talmud. His ultimate source of this view is biblical: "In the multitude of counselors there is safety" (Prov. 11:14 and 24:6).[128] According to Milton, even bad books can be instructive to a discreet and judicious reader.

> Wherof what better witnes can ye expect I should produce, then one of your own now sitting in Parlament, the chief of learned men reputed in this Land, Mr. *Selden*, whose volume of naturall & national laws proves, not only by

great autorities brought together, but by exquisite reasons and theorems almost mathematically demonstrative, that all opinions, yea errors, known, read, and collated, are of main service & assistance toward the speedy attainment of what is truest. I conceive therefore, that when God did enlarge the universall diet of mans body, saving ever the rules of temperance, he then also, *as before* [my emphasis], left arbitrary the dyeting and repasting of our minds. . . . How great a vertue is temperance, how much of moment through the whole life of man? yet God committs the managing so great a trust, without particular Law or prescription, wholly to the demeanour of every grown man. And therefore when he himself tabl'd the Jews from heaven, that Omer which was every mans daily portion of Manna, is computed to have bin more then might have well suffic'd the heartiest feeder thrice as many meals. For those actions which enter into a man, rather than issue out of him, and therefore defile not, God uses not to captivat under a perpetuall childhood of prescription, but trusts him with the gift of reason to be his own chooser. (*YP*, 2:513–14)

This invocation of Milton's chief rabbi ("the chief of learned men reputed in this Land, Mr. *Selden*") includes an extraordinary insistence not only on intellectual liberty under the Mosaic law but also on dietary freedom under the ceremonial law. In *De doctrina Christiana*'s chapter on Christian liberty, Milton interprets the New Testament verses that immediately precede this passage as evidence that ceremonial food laws (Acts 10:13; *YP*, 6:540) and indeed the entire Mosaic law, including the Decalogue, have been abrogated (Tit. 1:15; *YP*, 6:526). But in this passage, in the same paragraph that refers to the dietary prohibition in paradise, he risks an allusion to Jesus' attack on Jewish sacred food hygiene: "there is nothing from without a man, that entering into him can defile him: but the things which come out of him, those are they that defile the man" (Mark 7:15). People should worry, not about the natural foods they put into themselves, which Jesus declares clean, but about the envy, murder, adultery, and deceit, spewed from the human heart, that really defile. John Drury notes the shocking sacrilege of Jesus' pronouncement: "This is profanation with a vengeance, bringing the walls of ritualized purity tumbling down to disclose the real source of our troubles with one another, the real dirt."[129] Such an ethos would be inimical to Milton's Hebraic paradise, where evil is loosed upon the world as a result of "one apple tasted" (*YP*, 2:514).

When Milton, in a passage framed by these verses, speaks of God in the gospel "enlarg[ing] the universall diet of mans body," one expects him to continue, "he then also did enlarge the dyeting and repasting of our minds." But he does not. He asserts instead continuity between gospel ("then") and Torah ("as before"), which allow "every mature man

. . . to exercise his owne leading capacity." At this point, imagining intellectual freedom to be the paragraph's topic, one may reasonably assume that a figurative, "spiritual" reading of the introductory Pauline verses, centering on inward freedom, has replaced the "carnal" proclamation of dietary freedom. Surprisingly, Milton cites Exodus 16, the tabling of the wandering Israelites in the desert with a precise measure (an omer, less than two quarts) of manna, as an example of Jewish dietary freedom under the law: "And therefore when he himself tabl'd the Jews from heaven, that Omer which was every mans daily portion of Manna, is computed to have bin more then might have well suffic'd the heartiest feeder thrice as many meals." The proliferation of ligatures in the excerpt—"then also, as before," "For," "therefore" (twice)—and in the entire paragraph attest to the continuation from the divorce tracts of a monist hermeneutic harmonizing natural law, Mosaic law, and gospel.

Continuities between auxiliary elements of the other tracts of 1643–45 and the *Areopagitica* blur the single large discontinuity—from an insistence on the continuing relevance of the deuteronomic law of divorce to what would seem to be an elaboration of Pauline Christian liberty to include freedom from the external authority of a censor. The invocation of John Selden in tracts advocating parliamentary reform of existing divorce laws and the repeal of its own Licensing Order signals the continuing theme of Erastianism. In 1645, Robert Baillie complained: "The most of the House of Commons are downright Erastians: they are lyke to create us much more woe than all the sectaries of England. . . . L'Emperour promised to write against Selden, for the Jewish ecclesiastick Sanhedrim, and their excommunication. This man is the head of the Erastians: his glory is most in the Jewish learning; he avows every where, that the Jewish State and Church was all one, and that so in England it must be, that the Parliament is the Church."[130]

Sidrach Simpson, preaching "before Sundry of the House of Commons," distinguishes between the Christian elect and the nation of Israel: "On the Church of the *Jewes*, the Common-Wealth had great dependance. . . . In the new Testament, the Common-wealth hath not such dependance . . . , the Churches now consist not of Nations, but pickt persons."[131] Milton, in the divorce tracts, shades into Erastianism, associating the Mosaic law with nationhood and emphasizing "the holines and moral perfection which [God] intended by his Law to teach this people" (YP, 2:619):

> Yee are the childern of the Lord your God, the Lord hath chosen thee to be
> a peculiar people to himself above all the nations upon the earth. . . . surely
> this great Nation is a wise and understanding people. For what Nation is

ther so great, who hath God so nigh to them? and what Nation that hath
Statutes and Judgements so righteous as all this Law which I set before you
this day? (YP, 2:618–19)[132]

Joining the deuteronomic law of divorce and parliamentary law, Milton argues that to withhold divorce from a suffering partner is to throw him into "such a dull dejection, as renders him either infamous, or useles to the service of God and his country. Which the Law ought to prevent as a thing pernicious to the Common wealth; and what better prevention then this which *Moses* us'd?" (625). In the Hebraic fourth argument of the *Areopagitica*, Milton's major tropes—the building of Solomon's temple, the Nazarite Samson, the city of refuge, the new Israel in which all the Lord's people are prophets—portray England as a holy nation and incline toward Erastianism. Even the attack on Roman Catholicism for "extirpat[ing] . . . civill supremacies" (565) reveals an awareness of the clerical theocratic tendencies inherent in the Presbyterian program.[133]

Milton's displacements of Pauline attacks on the law, evident in the divorce tracts, continue in the *Areopagitica*. Ephesians 2:3, in the *Doctrine and Discipline of Divorce*, applies not to non-Christians, as Paul intended, but to the unhappy children of angry parents whatever their religion: "the offspring of a former ill-twisted wedlock, begott'n only out of a bestiall necessitie without any true love or contentment, or joy to their parents, so that in some sense we may call them the *childern of wrath*" (YP, 2:259–60). Citing models for contemporary London from the wisest commonwealths—ancient Greece and biblical Israel—Milton derogates licensing and its enforcers in Pauline terms usually reserved for the Jews: "perpetuall childhood of prescription" (513), "the tuition, . . . the correction of his patriarchal licencer" (533) (a reference to Laud and his ostensible ambition to erect a Patriarchate of the Western Church), "the wardship of an overseeing fist" (533).

> What advantage is it to be a man over it is to be a boy at school, if we have
> only scapt the ferular, to come under the fescu of an *Imprimatur*? if serious
> and elaborat writings, as if they were no more then the theam of a Grammar
> lad under his Pedagogue must not be utter'd without the cursory eyes of a
> temporizing and extemporizing licencer. (531)

Milton rebukes those whose "faith and religion" reside in the Laudian Church's Convocation house and in Henry VII's Chapel in Westminster, which are insufficient "to edifie the meanest Christian who desires to walk in the Spirit, and not in the letter of human trust" (567). The sheer number of these Pauline displacements suggests that, while the *Areopagitica* holds up the Hebrew Bible as a model of the book, Milton may want, at least subliminally, to condemn all licensers (including Parliament, if it does not repeal the order) as Judaizers.

Of course it is also true that the theology of the *Areopagitica* resembles that of the divorce tracts in its emphasis on national self-renewal rather than on Christ's resurrection. Jesus is consistently portrayed as victim rather than redeemer. He is the master spirit who has shed his life's blood, and, although Truth herself is only his servant, few can read of her "mangl'd body" (549) and of "our obsequies to the torn body of our martyr'd Saint" (550) without recalling the crucifixion. Typology is absent from the tract: no "Joshua, whom the gentiles Jesus call" but rather Joshua the servant of Moses. Christology is conspicuously absent from passages that could evoke it through sheer nuance:

> Methinks I see [England] as an Eagle muing her mighty youth, and kindling her undazl'd eyes at the full midday beam; purging and unscaling her long abused sight at the fountain it self of heav'nly radiance. (558)

Just as England is the eagle, so might Christ have been the sun, as in Bishop Haymo's reading of the passage's Hebraic source, Psalm 103:5 ("thy youth is renewed like the eagle's"):

> The nature of the eagle is such that in old age its beak and claws grow so large that it is unable to refresh itself with food. And indeed it then ascends toward the sun, until its feathers are burned away by the heat, and thence it falls into living water. . . . So we, filled with many sins, when we are held in the old age of Adam, draw near to Christ, who is the true sun, by whose warmth and infusion of grace our sins are burned away.[134]

The final example of displacement—of the secondary, postlapsarian Mosaic law of the divorce tracts upon Parliamentary law—is perhaps the most important and the most indeterminate. The divorce tracts distinguish the law of paradise, "tending ever to that which is perfetest," from the Mosaic law that considers "what can be . . . not only what should be" (*YP*, 2:665). Interpreting Christ's "But from the beginning it was not so," Milton notes that the Fall "alter'd the lore of justice, and put the goverment of things into a new frame" (665). In the fallen world, the Mosaic law of divorce is more perfect than the law of marriage established in paradise. With a similarly ironic glance at Genesis ("the midst of the garden"[2:9]), Milton, in the *Areopagitica*, looks to Parliament "to ordain wisely as in this world of evil, in the midd'st whereof God hath plac't us unavoidably" (526). "[T]hat no grievance should ever arise in the Commonwealth, that let no man in this World expect"—it is a hope more suited to paradise. "[B]ut when complaints are freely heard, deeply consider'd, and speedily reform'd, then is the utmost bound of civill liberty attain'd, that wise men look for" (487).

In the divorce tracts, Milton asks Parliament to adopt the Mosaic law as the law of the land. In the *Areopagitica*, Milton looks for intellectual freedom within the broad limits of the law. Like the lawyer in the gospel, he asks, "What is written in the law? How do you read it?" (Luke 10:26). He turns for an answer to *Tanakh* and the example of Solomon:

> *Salomon* informs us that much reading is a wearines to the flesh; but neither he, nor other inspir'd author tells us that such, or such reading is unlawfull: yet certainly had God thought good to limit us herein, it had bin much more expedient to have told us what was unlawfull, then what was wearisome. (514)

In 1651, Milton himself would serve as a licenser of books, a state censor,[135] and he concludes the *Areopagitica* by asking Parliament to regulate publication by means of an earlier, less restrictive order (569). In a sense, then, he maintains the most important continuity with the divorce tracts: urging Parliament not to abandon law altogether but to adopt more humane regulations.

This tract has generated widely divergent readings. Milton is for some a poet of democratic liberalism and for others a prophet of revolutionary absolutism. Those who view liberty and authority as irreconcilable opposites might associate his Pauline Christian liberty with unrestrained tolerance and his defense of the law with authoritarianism. But the *Areopagitica* employs a monist hermeneutic in which natural law, the Mosaic law, and the gospel accord with a libertarian position on censorship. Milton uses a doctrinally unorthodox version of Christian liberty prevalent in Reformation texts on the Holy Scriptures to obliterate clerical privilege and to defend the universal right to read, a right that also exists under the Mosaic law. The essence of Christian liberty—rejection of the law of works and redemption in Christ—is alien to the ethos of this tract. At the same time, the extensive use of Pauline terms—displaced though they may be—and the sense of strain detectable in the defense of the Jewish ceremonial law anticipate the eventual rejection of Milton's Hebraism in the final books of *Paradise Lost*.

TOWARD A MONIST AESTHETIC

Young John Selden's learned notes on Sir John Fortescue's fifteenth-century classic *De Laudibus Legum Angliae* contain the seeds of a monist aesthetic. Fortescue's insular, common-law fantasy of an English constitution of immemorial antiquity, resisting and superseding all foreign influence, can be read as a secular counterpart of Pauline typology: a hierarchical system, founded upon the principle of rejection, that exalts the greater by despising the lesser. At a moment of crisis in constitutional history, when proponents of the uniqueness and antiquity of English law were pressing their claims with particular intensity, Selden proposes instead a sophisticated alternative interpretation, the harmonious combination of feudal laws and Saxon customs to produce a potent, vital constitution. Applying the philological method of continental legal historians to the understanding of English common law, Selden portrays the ancient constitution as ever-developing:

> But questionelesse the *Saxons* made a mixture of the *British* customes with their own; the *Danes* with the old *British*, the *Saxon*, and their own; and the *Normans* the like. The old laws of the Saxons mencion the *Danish* law (*Danelage*), the *Mercian* law (*Mercenlage*), and the *Westsaxon* law (*Westsaxonlage*) of which also some Counties were governed by one, some by another. All these being considered by *William* I. comparing them with the laws of *Norway*. . . . They were you see called St. *Edward*'s laws, and to this day are. But cleerly, divers Norman customes were in practice first mixt with them, and to these times continue. As succeeding ages, so new nations . . . bring alwaies some alteration.[136]

Arguing that time and new nations alter the ancient constitution, Selden combines cosmopolitanism and nationalism and anticipates a monist (and decidedly nonmonolithic) aesthetics of inclusion, accommodating both historical continuity and change, in which the higher includes the lower.

Selden applies his comparatist historico-philological method of interpretation to a great range of texts in the fields of history, jurisprudence, and theology. As a believer in the divinely revealed nature of both the Mosaic and natural laws ("*Gods Law*, that is . . . the *Divine morall Law* [and] the *Divine naturall Law*, which should bind all men and ever"),[137] he regards the Mosaic law precisely as Milton does, as God's "reveled will, his complete, his evident, and certain will; [w]herein he appears to us as it were in human shape . . . measures and is commensurat to right reason" (*YP*, 2:292). Free from the prejudice against Pharisaism that made other Christian scholars shun the study of Jewish law, Selden values most the juristic character of Judaism. Throughout his rabbinical works he refers to the rabbis of the Talmud as jurists (*jurisconsulti*) or teachers of the law (*magistri*) rather than as theologians or clerics. For Selden, the sacred Mosaic law of the Hebrew Bible, combined with ancestral customs and rabbinic sanctions, constitutes the civil law of the Jews, comparable to "Roman or Caesarean" law and to "English law for the English of today."[138] Ziskind has noted that Selden saw the Bible as the Romans saw the Twelve Tables, the *leges* of the popular assemblies, or the various codes—that is, as basic statements of the law—and that he saw both the

Babylonian and Jerusalem recensions of the Talmud, containing the discussions of jurists, as similar to Justinian's *Digest*.

> In fact, in the preface to his first work on Jewish law, *De Successionibus in Bona Defunctorum*, Selden calls the Talmud the "Pandects," which is the alternative name for the *Digest*, and he goes on to cite from the Mishnah and Maimonides the line of transmission of Jewish juristic interpretation from Moses at Sinai to the period following the destruction of the Temple in Jerusalem in 70 A.D. by the Romans.[139]

In the rabbinic scholarship that Milton knew, Selden reveals the legitimate common ground of Graeco-Roman culture, Judaism, and early Christianity. He demonstrates the extent to which the first Christians, who were also Jews, freely and openly borrowed from the culture of their Jewish and gentile neighbors. Relying on the sheer weight of scholarship, without polemic, he subtly pleads the case of reform, proving that Christian ideas on marriage, divorce, and church government were originally broader and less parochial than what they have become. Selden's scholarship is indispensable if one is to recover the substance of Milton's thought regarding these institutions. Selden is chief among "the wise and right understanding handfull of men" (*YP*, 2:232) that Milton addresses: "my errand is to find out the choisest and the learnedest, who have this high gift of wisdom to answer solidly, or to be convinc't. I crave it from the piety, the learning and the prudence which is hous'd in this place [Parliament]. It might perhaps more fitly have bin writt'n in another tongue" (233)—like Selden's own scholarship. In the *Second Defence* (1654), Milton regrets having published his divorce tracts in English.

According to Milton, "antiquaries affirm that divorce proceeded among the *Jews* without knowledge of the Magistrate, only with hands and seales under the testimony of some Rabbies to be then present" (*YP*, 2:317). Selden brings rabbinic law on this matter to bear on Matthew 1:18–19: "Then Joseph her husband, being a just man, and not willing to make her a public example, was minded to put her away privily." Joseph wanted to send Mary away quietly, without court clamor or the disgrace of loss or diminution of dowry, but the divorce document required witnesses, "which could not be dispensed with," since an act of cohabitation that today would be adulterous and punished with a capital sentence could tomorrow be permissible if it led to marriage. Since no document ever mentions the reason for the divorce, "the grounds remained in the conscience of the husband."[140]

Selden discusses at length in *De Jure* and the *Uxor Ebraica* "the contracting of a marriage among gentiles . . . who subsequently become proselytes and are transferred to the Jewish church or polity" (*De Contractu Sponsalitio seu Nuptiali Gentilium . . . qui postea Proselyti fierent seu in Judaicam Ecclesiam seu Rempublicam transirent*).

Now a convert as well as a freedman, as soon as he comes into Judaism . . . they say that he was regarded as reborn, as a "recently born baby"; that he became Jewish and thus the things which were altogether in the past, such as blood and affinity, were poured away. Accordingly, Tacitus put it most aptly when he said of those proselytes, "The first thing they are taught is to hold the gods in contempt and to remove themselves from their homeland, parents, children, and brothers and to hold them of no account."[141]

When Milton's Samson reminds Dalila of her failure to remember this point, he actually names Selden's *De Jure Naturali et Gentium*:

> Why then
> Didst thou at first receive me for thy husband,
> Then, as since then, thy country's foe profest?
> Being once a wife, for me thou was to leave
> Parents and country; . . .
>
> . . . .
> . . . if aught against my life
> Thy country sought of thee, it sought unjustly,
> Against *the law of nature, law of nations,*
> No more thy country.
>
> (882–86; 888–91; *my emphasis*)

Pagan and Hebrew customs and rituals of betrothal and marriage found a place in early Christianity. Selden devotes an entire chapter to the responsibilities of the wedding attendants ("*Paranymphi*") to lead the couple into the wedding chamber and to see to the matter of the bride's virginity. He distinguishes between the customs of ancient Judaea, where the "comrade" or "nuptial companion" (Aramaic: *re'uhah shushvina*) spent the entire night in the bedroom, and those of Galilee, where the paranymph would retire. In accord with the latter custom, "St. Augustine says, 'As soon as the husband begins to fondle his wife, he looks for a room that is removed from witnesses, household slaves, and even attendants, and anyone else to whom friendship might have permitted access' (*Civ. Dei.* XIV. 18)."[142] When the Bible briefly notes Samson's loss of the woman of Timna, it never mentions a groomsman or paranymph: "But Samson's wife was given to his companion, whom he had used as his friend" (Judg. 14:20). Selden's Talmud-based discussion of the paranymph, emphasizing his intimacy with the newlyweds, introduces a note of irony and a hint of tribal night games to the chorus's taunting of Samson: "the *Timnian* bride / . . . so soon preferr'd / Thy Paranymph, worthless to thee compar'd, / Successor in thy bed" (1019–22).

Eve before the Fall is Milton's *Uxor Hebraica*. When Adam "led her blushing like the Morn" to the nuptial bower (8.510–11), this act ("deductio in Thalamum") effected matrimony. One of Selden's proof texts is the parable of the wise and foolish virgins; while the latter went to buy oil for their lamps, "the groom came, and those women who were prepared entered with him to the wedding, and the door was closed" (Matt. 25:10). Entering the *huppah* (the *thalamum nuptialem*) together was the decisive act.[143] Nature and the supernatural perform the ceremony in paradise (the "Ev'ning Star . . . light[s] the bridal Lamp" for this wise virgin [8.519–20]):

> heav'nly Choirs the Hymenaean sung,
> What day the genial Angel to our Sire
> Brought her in naked beauty.
>
> (4.711–13)

According to Selden, "Gods of marriage are mentioned as being invoked at the marriage rites, especially Hymenaeus," and, in his chapter on paranymphs, citing the midrash on Genesis, *Bereshith Rabbah*, he limits the search for the "genial Angel": "Among the ancient Hebrews, Michael and Gabriel were called by the term 'attendants of Adam.' "[144]

To understand the Miltonic bard's lyric epithalamium "Hail, Wedded Love" and the relation of the "mysterious Law" of marriage (4.750) to the law of paradise, one must turn from Selden's *Uxor* to *De Jure Naturali et Gentium*, which sets forth "for the first time" the rabbinic position on the subject of natural law. I have already argued that, in his great epic, Milton places Adam and Eve under both natural law and an originally benign, proto-Mosaic law. *De Jure* is the principal source of Milton's natural law thinking, and, in it, Selden relies almost exclusively on rabbinic tradition based ultimately on the Talmud. Selden's idea that the prohibition formula in Genesis constitutes an embryonic Mosaic law is more or less commonplace. Absolutely original, however, is his belief, based on the Talmud, that natural law consists not merely of innate rational principles that are intuitively obvious, but also of specific divine pronouncements uttered at a point in historical time.

In the most thoroughgoing analysis of Edenic polity in the seventeenth century, Selden accepts the rabbinic identification of natural law with the Adamic and Noachide laws, considered by rabbinic tradition as the minimal moral duties enjoined by the Bible on all humankind. Besides citing Maimonides' *Code* and numerous other sources, he quotes in its entirety the *locus classicus* in Tractate Sanhedrin (56a–b), which includes the traditional enumeration of the Noachide laws: the prohibitions of idolatry and blasphemy, the injunction to establish a legal system, commandments against bloodshed, sexual sins, and theft, and a seventh law, not applicable to Adam but added after the flood and based on Genesis 9:4, forbidding anyone to eat flesh cut from a living animal. Selden devotes an entire book of *De Jure* to each of the Noachide commandments, and he follows the order set by Maimonides, which emphasizes their Decalogic nature. The first two, like the first table of the law, deal with the relations between human beings and God, while the rest govern relations among human beings.

Selden includes R. Johanan's elaborate inference of these precepts from seven key words in Genesis 2:16. The entire discussion, which at times conflates Edenic polity with laws pronounced to the sons of Noah, with the ten precepts given to the Israelites at Marah, and with the Decalogue, relies on the mode of Talmudic interpretation known as *gezerah shawah*. This permits one to infer a rule from the use of a common scriptural expression in two verses; thus, R. Johanan infers from the similar use of the word "the Lord" in the original Edenic commandment (Gen. 2:16) and, in the later verse, "he that blasphemeth the name of the Lord . . . shall surely be put to death" (Lev. 24:16) a primordial prohibition against blasphemy.[145]

Hugo Grotius's great work on international law, *De Jure Belli ac Pacis*, which influenced Selden's natural law thinking, also cites Tractate Sanhedrin on the Noachide rules binding on all humankind.[146] Milton, who read both Grotius and Selden, may have these laws in mind in *Eikonoklastes*: "The first express Law of God giv'n to mankind, was that to *Noah*, as a law in general to all the Sons of men. And by that most ancient and universal Law, *whosoever sheddeth mans blood, by man shall his blood be shed*" (YP, 3:586). But Grotius's reference is tangential, and Milton's is more scriptural than rabbinic. It remains for Selden to develop the argument that natural law was divinely given and discoverable by human reason with divine assistance.

The thrust of Selden's rabbinic discussion is universalist. Selden blurs distinctions between the Edenic, Mosaic, and natural laws. All of these laws oblige because they are God's command and because he will punish disobedience. To conflate these laws is to recognize that moral progress is the privilege and obligation of all humankind. Selden identifies the rabbinic Adamic and Noachide laws with natural law and asserts that this law is coeval with the beginning of humankind and that God's "most holy voice" pronounced it.[147]

Although Selden spoke of a faculty, the *intellectus agens*, by which humankind could perceive the principles of natural law, his belief that God pronounced this law at the beginning of time derives in large part from his skepticism regarding the power of unaided human reason. He puts the matter cogently in his *Table Talk*:

> I cannot fancy to myself what the law of nature means, but the law of God.
> How should I know I ought not to steal, I ought not to commit adultery,
> unless some body had told me so? Surely 'tis because I have been told so. 'Tis

not because I think I ought not to do them, nor because you think I ought not; if so, our minds might change. Whence then comes the restraint? From a higher power, nothing else can bind. I cannot bind myself, for I may untie myself again; nor an equal cannot bind me, for we may untie one another. It must be a superior power, even God Almighty.[148]

God's voice and the *intellectus agens* are the means by which one becomes aware of natural law: "The principles of this law were enjoined upon the human race by God's most holy voice both at the very beginning of things and at the restoration of the human race after the Flood." At the same time, Selden countenances the view that the principles of natural law were "given to the human race at its very creation, and that every rational soul was then naturally endowed with a faculty by which those things that had been ordained and which were always to be observed, were revealed and made manifest, like principles or theorems in demonstrative matters, to every man whose mind was not depraved, who was not corrupted, and who intuited rightly and diligently enough."[149]

Jeremy Taylor's chapters "OF THE LAW OF NATURE" in *Ductor Dubitantium*" are largely a translation of Selden's *De Jure*. He emphasizes God's continual necessary assistance (not mere reason but reason guided by God) when he describes God as the sun, the human conscience as the eye, and the *intellectus agens* as light.

> Philo says, the law of nature is a law "engraven in an immortal understanding by an immortal nature." In this whole affair, God is as the sun, and the conscience as the eye: or else God or some angel from Him being the *intellectus agens* did inform our reason, supplying the place of natural faculties and being a continual monitor (as the Jews generally believe. . . .) And the Gloss and Gulielmus Parisiensis, and before them Maimonides, from whom I suppose they had it, affirm this to be the meaning of David in the fourth psalm, "Offer the sacrifice of righteousness;" it follows *Quis monstrabit*, "who will shew us any good?" who will tell us what is justice, and declare the measures of good and evil? He answers, *Signatum est super nos lumen vultus tui Domine*, "Thou hast consigned the light of Thy countenance upon us," *ut scilicet*, as it is in another psalm, *in lumine tuo videamus lumen*, "that in Thy light we may see light."[150]

Selden distinguishes between two forms of divine law, the main topics of *De Jure* and the *Uxor Ebraica*, respectively: "natural law, which we have seen is coeval with the very beginning of mankind, and positive law, which was introduced at a particular time."[151] The latter, which includes the Mosaic law as the civil law of the Jews, is binding only on particular persons. If *De Jure*'s theoretical purpose is to redefine natural law along non-Thomistic lines, its practical purpose is to redefine church-state relations in accordance with rabbinic thought by distinguishing between divine law incumbent on all humanity (Noachide law) and divine positive law (the Mosaic law as the civil law of the Jews) binding upon particular persons. According to Selden, unnecessary confusion results when the latter is conceived of as applicable to those for whom it was not intended, such as bishops who "run to the text for something done amongst the Jews that nothing concerns England."[152] But *De Jure* emphasizes connections between these laws far more than it does differences. Regarding divorce, for example:

> Let us first review what the Hebrew jurists and theologians determined about divorce in the Noachide law, the law for all humankind before the Mosaic law, and after the Mosaic law was given the law for all humankind except the Jews. . . . Divorce was permitted to either party of the union without the introduction of a document or any other object to withdraw from or plainly to dissolve a marriage or life partnership that was previously contracted. The words of the Talmud are, "Each of the spouses sends the other away."[153]

Were Parliament to reform contemporary laws of divorce so that they more closely approximated the Mosaic law of Deuteronomy, these civil and Mosaic laws would, in turn, accord more fully with divorce by mutual consent according to the rabbinic conception of natural law.

Selden's views on the relation between natural law and positive law influence Milton's conception of Edenic polity as formulated in *De doctrina*. When these principles turn up in the great epic at moments of interpretive uncertainty embodied as myth, they will have been elaborated almost beyond recognition, and readers may be surprised to recall their unremarkable doctrinal provenance. Selden used indifferently the *intellectus agens* and the voice of God pronouncing the Noachide precepts as the two sources of universal natural law. Milton associates the former with natural law and the latter with a Mosaic positive law. Since this positive law applies to Adam and Eve as the only human beings, the boundaries for Milton between natural and positive law in paradise are fluid. He opens his chapter "OF THE FALL OF OUR FIRST PARENTS" in *De doctrina* by citing the prohibition formula in paradise (Gen. 2:16–17) as an unwritten, embryonic Mosaic law: "SIN, as defined by the apostle, is . . . the breaking of the law, 1 John iii.4. Here the word *law* means primarily that law which is innate and implanted in man's mind; and secondly it means the law which proceeded from the mouth of God; Gen. ii.17: *do not eat of this*: for the law written down by Moses is of a much later date" (*YP*, 6:382).

As Milton sees it, then, the First Letter of John defines sin as the transgression of both natural law ("innate and implanted in man's mind") and of an external, oral law ("the law which proceeded from the mouth of God") that precedes the written Mosaic code. Earlier in the *De doctrina*,

Milton cites the Edenic prohibition formula as part of a demonstration that the divine decree of predestination is conditional. He conflates the Mosaic and prelapsarian dispensations and distinguishes them from salvation under the gospel, by identifying them as based on obedience: "scripture . . . offers salvation and eternal life to all equally, on condition of obedience to the Old Testament and faith in the New. . . . [T]he decree, as it was made public, is everywhere conditional: Gen.ii.17: *do not eat of this, for on the day you eat it you will die*" (*YP*, 6:177–78).

De doctrina, begun early as a "Theological Index" (now lost) and completed decades later, is a balkanized text, representing different stages in Milton's theological development, suggesting that Adam and Eve were under a commandment but not a covenant (*YP*, 6:351) and asserting in the very next chapter that God entered into a covenant (*foedere*) with them in paradise (*YP*, 6:385). The chapter "OF THE SPECIAL GOVERN-MENT OF MAN BEFORE THE FALL: DEALING ALSO WITH THE SABBATH AND MARRIAGE" yokes together three heterogeneous topics with nothing in common but the Hebraic and sometimes even rabbinic exegesis that Milton applies to them. Given the Paulinism of surrounding chapters, that is enough to unify them.

Milton asserts in this chapter that God's command in Eden supersedes natural law.

> Man was made in the image of God, and the whole law of nature was so implanted and innate in him that he was in need of no command. It follows, then, that if he received any additional commands, *whether about the tree of knowledge or about marriage*, these had nothing to do with the law of nature, which is itself sufficient to teach whatever is in accord with right reason (i.e., whatever is intrinsically good). These commands, then, were simply a matter of what is called positive right. Positive right comes into play when God, or anyone else invested with lawful power, commands or forbids things which, if he had not commanded or forbidden them, would in themselves have been neither good nor bad, and would therefore have put no one under any obligation. (*YP*, 6:353; my emphasis)

> It was necessary that one thing should be either forbidden or commanded, and above all something which was in itself neither good nor evil, so that man's obedience might in this way be made evident. For man was by nature *good* and *holy*, and was naturally disposed to do *right*, so it was certainly not necessary to bind him by the requirements of any covenant to do something which he would do of his own accord. (*YP*, 6:352; my emphasis)

In the first quotation, Milton asserts that the divine commands in Eden regarding both the tree of knowledge and marriage had nothing to do with natural law, which operates in accord with right reason but which, presumably, is incapable of comprehending supernatural revelation. In the second, he implies that the prohibition is a sort of covenant binding prelapsarian man to obey something that is morally indifferent in order to test his obedience. Since Adam, following natural law, is already good, holy, and disposed to do right, the Edenic commandment must operate beyond the limits of that law. Although William Ames, in *Conscience* (1639), and other contemporary theologians discuss positive laws, Milton's definition of the divine commandment as a positive right derives from Selden. The phrase "God or anyone else invested with lawful powers" is Selden's signature, evoking countless passages from *De Jure* and the *Uxor Ebraica* (including its opening paragraph) on the Mosaic law as the civil law of the Hebrews, comparable to Attic law, Roman civil law, and the "law for the English of today."

Both of these excerpts reveal Milton's commitment to the principle of transposition. This principle sometimes employs a negative typology, contrasting an inferior type with the Christian antitype that supersedes and reverses it, to emphasize discontinuity, changes in the decorum governing a particular dispensation and differences in God's relationship with humans, angels, and the Son. In these two excerpts, however, Milton employs a positive typology (congruity rather than disparity), transferring terms from one dispensation to another in order to emphasize God's continuous ways with all his creatures. Thus, the precepts of natural law require behavior that is good, holy, and just. When Milton writes of the Mosaic law, he differentiates among the moral, ceremonial, and judicial laws, each of them a precise counterpart to a precept of natural law (goodness, holiness, justice). When he turns to the gospel, he devotes an entire chapter of *De doctrina Christiana* (1.15) to the triple function of Christ's mediatorial office, "PROPHETIC, PRIESTLY AND KINGLY," each of these in turn corresponding to a mode of behavior under natural law and to a division of the Mosaic law.

When Milton refers in the first excerpt to the commands in paradise beyond natural law, the two examples he offers—those concerning the tree of knowledge and marriage—suggest the importance to him of finding precise Edenic counterparts to postlapsarian dispensations. The ends of natural law are wisdom and virtue, as Plato attests in a passage that Milton knew well. In the *Symposium*, Socrates distinguishes between those people whose creative instinct is physical and those whose creative desire is of the soul. The latter "long to beget spiritually, not physically, the progeny which it is the nature of the soul to create and bring to birth. If you ask what that progeny is, it is wisdom and virtue in general."[154] Writing in *An Apology* of happiness both individual and communal, Milton places these remarks in a framework of platonic idealism and ethical doctrine: "the first and chiefest office of love, begins and ends in the soule, producing those happy twins of her divine generation knowledge and vertue." (*YP*, 1:892; see also *Animadversions*, *YP*, 1:719).

The tree of knowledge, a pledge of the relationship between humankind and God, and marriage, a pledge of the relationship between human beings, are the Edenic prototypes of knowledge and virtue. Under the Mosaic law, the counterparts of the two pledges (Edenic) and the twin progeny of the soul (natural law) are the two tables of the Decalogue, which reduce the commandments to faith and performance. Milton asserts that the law and the gospel, correctly understood, are entirely compatible: "The works of the faithful are the works of the Holy Spirit itself. These never run contrary to the love of God and of our neighbor . . . which is the sum of the law" (*De Doctrina Christiana*, 2.1; *YP*, 6:640). With the advent of Christ, the two tables of the law are in turn transposed to a higher key. To begin the second book of *De doctrina Christiana*, Milton defines the two parts of Christian theology: "The first book dealt with FAITH and THE KNOWLEDGE OF GOD. This second book is about THE WORSHIP OF GOD and CHARITY" (*YP*, 6:637). The two commands that extend beyond natural law, concerning the tree of knowledge and marriage, constitute an Edenic equivalent for Milton of the central imperatives of natural law, the Mosaic law, and the gospel, resembling most closely "the love of God and of our neighbor."

The aesthetic counterpart of this theological principle of transposition is the tripartite crescendo movement in Milton's poetry: the development of the idea of *katharos* in the successive quatrains of the twenty-third sonnet, which begin with Euripides' *Alcestis*, extend to the levitical rites of purification after childbirth under "the old Law," and conclude with a vision of absolute purity in a Christian heaven;[155] and the continuous but developing sense of the pastoral in *Lycidas*, narrated by a shepherd whose consolation is measured at least in part by the progression from classical aesthetics (64–84), through Hebraic-prophetic ethics (113–31), to the limitless reward of a Christian heaven purged of evil (165–85). *Paradise Lost* employs a global negative typology. Its first four books derive primarily from pagan authors, who are governed by natural law— and even book 4 owes more to the happy garden of classical literature than it does to the earthly paradise of biblical commentary. The middle books draw most heavily upon Hebraic revelation beyond nature's law, provided by the "Divine Interpreter" Raphael. The last books systematically debase the others by submitting both natural law and the Mosaic law to the judgment of Christian experience. *Paradise Lost* is a radically nostalgic work that insists relentlessly on the discontinuity between Christianity and earlier dispensations and thus between postlapsarian life and paradise before the Fall.

Related to the doctrinal continuity of Edenic law, Mosaic law, and the gospel is the geographical triad of Eden, Jerusalem, and contemporary England. In the cavalcade of pagan deities, for example (*Paradise Lost*, book 1), the devil-gods, all with animal associations, profane God's temple in Jerusalem, enacting their great commander's original defilement of paradise, and anticipating the Sons of Belial, contemporary courtiers of Charles II who have ruined Milton's holy city. Josiah Nichols, in *Abraham's Faith*, emphasizes continuity among the dispensations of Eden, Israel, and England in order to attack canon law as a conspicuous and aberrant disruption of that continuity. A virulently anti-Catholic tract, *Abraham's Faith* surveys various Christian doctrines, beginning with the Trinity, finding them progressively revealed, from Edenic obscurity to New Testament clarity "in these last times":

> as touching the manifestation of the spirit, marke with me, that the same promise, which to Adam was generall in the seede of the woman, was more speciall to Abraham to be in his seede, and in his posteritie more certaine in Juda. . . . Howbeit that grace of revelation, which was in the Apostles, excelled all the rest . . . and therefore in comparison of the clere manifestation of the gospel, now in these last times, to the more obscure revelation of former ages, it is called a mistery had since the world began and from all ages, but now is made manifest to his saints, and this most abundantly in all wisedome and understanding.[156]

For Nichols, such continuity is a witness against the "new broached" religion of Catholicism. Acknowledging differences in ceremonies and forms of government, he insists that, "from the beginning of the world," the true church remains the same "in one rule of faith & religion": "the religion and faith publikely professed in this Realme, and maintained by the righteous scepter and sword of our dread soveraign and gracious Queene Elizabeth, is of the onely truth, most aunocient, catholicke, and unchangeable."[157]

Whether positive, emphasizing congruity, or negative, emphasizing disparity, typology allows one to sum up Milton and the dispensations that govern his major poetry and prose: the universal natural law, the national Mosaic law, and the gospel speaking to the elect individual, a congregation of one—or the pagan id, the Hebraic superego, and the Christian ego. A certain practical reconciliation is possible even between the Mosaic law of the divorce tracts and the Christian liberty of *De doctrina*'s Pauline chapters. The law for Milton can be reduced to a few essentials accentuating the negative: refrain from the Noachide transgressions ("concerning the seven commandments, they are thought of as 'sit and do nothing' [*sheb ve'al ta'aseh*, an idiom for exercising restraint]"[Sanhedrin, 58b]); don't eat the fruit; remove a tyrant; dissolve a

marriage. Christian liberty requires only faith in Christ as the fulfillment
of the law. The common ground between them is freedom from institutional coercion. Certain passages on Christian liberty actually reach back
to the tracts of 1643–45. There Milton had argued that permission to
divorce and to publish would help good people, but would also be susceptible to abuse by the wicked. In the treatise *Of Civil Power*, Milton
evokes Christian liberty to prevent the magistrate from prosecuting the
wicked and licentious, "lest while he goes about to take away the scandal
. . . he take away our liberty, which is the certain and the sacred gift of
God, neither to be touchd by him, nor to be parted with by us" (*YP*,
7:267). But the tracts of 1643–45 advocate freedom from church power,
while *Of Civil Power* would remove magisterial power from religious
matters.

At the beginning of this chapter, it was noted that Milton's Hebraic
monism resembles its opposite, Pauline dualism. Their differences are
open for inspection in the monist divorce tracts of 1643–45, which demonstrate continuity among natural law, Mosaic law, and the gospel, and
in the Pauline chapters of *De doctrina*, which betray an aggressive hermeneutics of supersession. Typology allows one to see all of history neatly,
as in a quip. Milton's detailed monism, derivable at least in part from
Selden's painstaking, comparatist, historico-philological scholarship, is
devoted to establishing continuity, finding resemblances, and charting development, but not to obliterating the identity of what comes before. De-
claring the holiness of matter, which proceeds from God, Milton fore-
stalls an objection:

> But, you will say, body cannot emanate from spirit. My reply is, much less
> can it emanate from nothing. Moreover spirit, being the more excellent sub-
> stance, virtually, as they say, and eminently contains within itself what is
> clearly the inferior substance; in the same way as the spiritual and rational
> faculty contains the corporeal, that is, the sentient and vegetative faculty.
> (*YP*, 6:309)

The right order of ascending value in the poem includes the lower in the
higher, and the tendency to reject is at odds with the purposes of divine
creation. The rejection of the law as the essence of typology is the great
epic's principal analogue of the rejection of the law as the essence of the
Fall.

Selden scrupulously avoids the fiction of complete unity, and he never
fuses the Graeco-Roman, Hebraic, and Christian cultures that he studies;
his comparatist approach can thus appear to be dualistic. Typology,
swallowing what precedes it under the pretext of fulfilling it, can appear
to be monistic. The Miltonic principle of transposition can be monistic or
typological, and to distinguish between these antithetical impulses re-

quires a detailed reading of Milton's poetry—a poetry more resonant than a quip and more concise than Selden's conscientious but prolix scholarship. The Miltonic bard, like Eve, is "guided by [God's] voice, nor uninform'd / Of nuptial Sanctity and marriage Rites" (8.486–87), and one is apt to find monism whenever the Miltonic bard celebrates an institution with the comedic inclusiveness of marriage. Even within the godhead, "Two distinct things cannot be of the same essence" (*YP*, 6:212), but the mutual attraction between a man and a woman can be comprehended under the rubrics of natural law, the primary Mosaic law of paradise (Gen. 1:28 and 2:18), civil law (Roman and Jewish), and Christian marriage:

> Our Maker bids increase, who bids abstain
> But our Destroyer, foe to God and man?
> Hail wedded Love, mysterious Law, true source
> Of human offspring, sole propriety
> In Paradise of all things common else.
> By thee adulterous lust was driv'n from men
> Among the bestial herds to range, by thee
> Founded in Reason, Loyal, Just, and Pure,
> Relations dear, and all the Charities
> Of Father, Son, and Brother first were known.
> Far be it, that I should write thee sin or blame,
> Or think thee unbefitting holiest place,
> Perpetual Fountain of Domestic sweets,
> Whose bed is undefil'd and chaste pronounc't,
> Present or past, as Saints and Patriarchs us'd.
> Here Love his golden shafts imploys, here lights
> His constant Lamp, and waves his purple wings,
> Reigns here and revels.
>
> (4.748–65)

Pagan, Hebraic, and Christian sources lie behind this lyric epithalamium, from Ovid (763; *Met.* 1, 468), through Genesis (748; 1:28), to the New Testament (750: Eph. 5:31–32; 761: Heb. 13:4: "Marriage is honourable in all, and the bed undefiled"). Less obvious, perhaps, is Selden's crucial definition of marriage under natural law, characteristically relegated to parentheses:

According to the Noachide or natural law, which for the Hebrews was the law prior to Moses and equally binding on other people and the human race (what is plainly implicit is not to steal or enter upon what is someone else's), they decided that a lawful marriage takes place by the mutual consent of a man and woman to live together.[158]

Marriage is "sole propriety / In Paradise of all things common else," for "what is plainly implicit is not to steal or enter upon what is someone else's." The emphasis on "Father, Son, and Brother" accords with the first book of the *Uxor*, an incredibly detailed discussion of degrees of affinity and consanguinity according to rabbinic law based on the Hebrew Bible. Nor is the Talmudic view of sacred carnality irrelevant here: "This too is Torah" is the judgment of Tractate Berachot (62a) on married sexual activity. According to Tractate Yebamoth (34b), a husband and wife may enjoy intercourse in the manner that best suits their needs; everything is permitted to them. And Rashi, commenting on Ketubot 62b, recommends that scholars and their wives enjoy sexual intercourse on Sabbath eve, because the Sabbath is created for pleasure, rest, and enjoyment. Even without notes, a reader can sense an ethos of cultural inclusiveness in these lines, Christian *Saints* living together with Hebraic *Patriarchs*.

Monist inclusiveness occurs where it occurs, sometimes in a single unexpected word, as in one of the most dualistic passages of *Paradise Lost*, where Michael teaches Adam to dissociate the spiritual from the physical, Christians from Jews, and the children of faith from the children of loins:

> Not only to the Sons of *Abraham*'s Loins
> Salvation shall be Preacht, but to the Sons
> Of *Abraham*'s Faith wherever through the world.
>
> (12.447–49)

The principal source is Romans 9:6–8, which disenfranchises the Jews: "it is not the children of the flesh who are the children of God, but the children of the promise are reckoned as descendants." But Michael grafts an earlier, more irenic text (Rom. 4:16) upon Romans 9, and "only" comes as a complete and welcome surprise.

God the Father is concise and resonant when he praises the redeemer of humankind, "By Merit more than Birthright Son of God" (3.309). The Miltonic coordinates of merit and birthright are limitless: good works (merit) and grace (birthright), free will and determinism, Cromwellian republicanism and divine right monarchy, and Raphael's fluid hierarchy of "active spheres assign'd" (5.477), "nearer to [God] plac'd or nearer tending" (5.476). God prefers merit over birthright: the redeemer's best claim to sonship is his goodness: "Found worthiest to be so by being Good, / Far more than Great or High" (3.310–11). But of course he is son by birthright as well as merit. A concluding analogue of merit and birthright may be the spontaneous gestures of original poetry and the principles of inherited doctrine. These take one full circle to the passionate monism on display in the middle books of the great epic (merit) and to the Pauline dualism of the final vision (birthright). For some readers, typology is a delusion, discovering order where there is none. For others, Miltonic typology attests to a masterful intelligence able to see pattern and repetition transcending any historical moment. For such a reader Christianity is merit, Judaism birthright—the birthright sold by Esau to Jacob, the younger brother who supplants him, for a mess of pottage. Perhaps merit and birthright are reconciled at last in the person of Milton, a poet of genius and a master of tradition.

CHAPTER THREE

Moses Traditions and the Miltonic Bard

ATTEMPTS TO ISOLATE the component parts of the epic narrator of *Paradise Lost* demonstrate the value of a rhetorical approach to narrative and to the narrating personae that stand between Milton and his readers. Recognizing that the role of inspired poet-narrator is in some sense an artifact, critics have been attentive to those voices that Milton himself invented—the night bird, the blind bard, and the Christian poet who defines himself with reference to the characters in his poem.[1] A presence felt early in the poem—inherited rather than invented—is that of Moses, although the example he sets in the Bible and in Milton's work of fortunate beginnings and incomplete endings is reflected in the tendency of critics to relate him to the epic voice only in the first quarter of *Paradise Lost*. Although he stands between biblical Israel and God, to whom there is "no access / Without Mediator, whose high Office now / *Moses* in figure bears" (12.239–41), Moses is the figure who ultimately falls short.

James Holly Hanford, Moses' strongest advocate, limits his appearance in *Paradise Lost* to the invocations of books 1 and 3. Hanford elaborates the importance of two of the four drafts of a tragedy on the theme of paradise lost that have been preserved in the Trinity Manuscript.[2] These jottings, set down within a year of Milton's return from the Continent in 1639, assign a prominent role to Moses, who is first among "the Persons" in the second draft and who serves as prologue in the third draft. Hanford regards Moses' role of Platonic philosopher in the third draft as a paradigm of his role in *Paradise Lost*. He characterizes Moses as the inhabitant of a Hellenistic universe, whose symbolic office is exclusively that of hierophant, interpreting inaccessible divine truth to the unpurged faculties of his audience. Hanford concludes his study by observing that Milton's exalted notion of Moses' character presents similar problems in both the third draft and the epic poem. Gabriel, whose gift of perfect vision is the result of an angelic nature that requires no special explanations, supplants the more difficult Moses as prologue in Milton's fourth draft in the Trinity Manuscript. Similarly, argues Hanford, Milton's early invocation in *Paradise Lost* of the inspired "Shepherd, who first taught the chosen Seed" (1.8) is succeeded by the invocation of a less troublesome model of divinity: "Milton loses sight of Moses and elaborates the Platonic and poetic symbolism of Urania."[3]

Hanford's suggestive note invites anyone attempting to understand the character of Moses in *Paradise Lost* to examine the Hellenistic tradition that portrays him as a sort of all-knower and bringer of gnosis. Following Hanford's suggestion, D. C. Allen searches Philo for a mystical interpretation of the Sinai theophany. Allen conceives of Moses' role in the epic as that of illuminator, and the relevant biblical verse is Exodus 20:21: "And the people stood afar off, and Moses drew near unto the thick darkness where God was." The oxymoron "bright darkness," implied and expressed in the writings of Philo and of Alexandrian Christian theologians interested in mysticism, conveys the notion that the divine light "hides itself in the dark and one must enter the cloud to find it."[4] Allen demonstrates that Moses and the blind narrator apprehend divinity in darkness.

Hanford and Allen begin their search for the source of the inspired poet-narrator in the Hellenistic Jewish apologetics of Philo and Josephus—specifically, in their accounts of the life of Moses. There one finds a portrayal of the "the divine (and) holy Moses,"[5] whose mediatorial office is unexcelled and whose human limitations are seldom—and then only grudgingly—admitted. It would, of course, be a mistake to suggest that wholly approving interpretations of Moses' life are limited to non-Christian sources. Although more restrained than Philo and Josephus, patristic interpreters such as Origen, Eusebius, Theodoret, Gregory of Nyssa, and others present Moses as a mediator whose exemplary life is set before the faithful as an ideal. Moreover, the extensive historical and allegorical tradition of Moses as poet-prophet extends into Milton's England and sheds light on the first two invocations of *Paradise Lost*.

Placing Moses within an essentially Hellenistic perspective and elevating him to virtually godlike status, Milton relies on some of the Platonic and Hebraic sources that he presents in a positive light in the prose tracts of 1643–45. This positive view of Moses bears directly on the prelapsarian books of the epic. Most of Milton's contemporary English Protestants ignored the valuable, inclusive tradition outlined by Hanford and Allen and understood Moses typologically, as a sinner excluded from the Canaan regained by Christ, as the imperfect "Minister / Of Law" (*PL* 12.308–9), and, at best, as a "Mediator . . . to introduce / One greater, of whose day he shall foretell" (12.240–42). This is the postlapsarian view of Moses that Milton presents in the Pauline chapters of *De doctrina Christiana*.

It should be noted at the outset that the boundaries between various Moses traditions in patristic writings are sometimes fluid. St. Augustine, for example, treats two central, conflicting points of view in one breath when he states: "There is no doubt that Moses . . . represents two different persons. In the first instance he is an image of the one who participates in the divine truth (for he entered the cloud on Mt. Sinai); but secondly he represents the Jews, who set themselves against the image of the grace of Christ. They did not understand and did not join in the covenant."[6] If a shift from predominantly Platonic and Hebraic to typological symbolism marks the transition from Edenic perfection to sin in *Paradise Lost*, then these shifts might be assisted by the recognition of a changed emphasis upon the character of Moses. Although lines ought not be drawn too sharply, it is generally true that the early invocations depend on the Platonic and Hebraic view of Moses as poet and prophet, inspired author of the Pentateuch, and "image of the one who participates in the divine truth."

Among the changes signaled by the opening lines of the lyrical prologue to book 9 is an altered conception of the role of Moses:

> No more of talk where God or angel Guest
> With Man, as with his Friend, familiar us'd
> To sit indulgent . . .
>
> . . . .
>
> . . . I now must change
> Those Notes to Tragic; foul distrust, and breach
> Disloyal on the part of Man, revolt,
> And disobedience.
>
> (9.1–3, 5–8)

Todd notes that "Milton was here instructed . . . by the divine historian himself, *Exod.* xxxiii.11 'And the Lord spake unto Moses face to face, *as a man speaketh to his friend.*' "[7] The inspired narrator of the Pentateuch, then, is describing his own relationship with God, a relationship now rendered inappropriate to the poet's concerns by the introduction of sin. The fallen narrator replaces Raphael, himself the "Divine / Historian" (8.6–7), because "now" fallen readers require communication with someone acquainted with distrust and disobedience. Later in the poem, Moses is united with Adam as a sinner excluded from sacred ground by sin (12.307–14), and, in *De doctrina*, Milton identifies Moses' sin at the waters of Meribah (Num. 20:10–11) as "distrust of God" (*YP*, 6:658). Whereas Adam and Eve fall, Moses is the single historical figure who spans the abyss between perfection and sin—unique and inimitable as a result of his communion with God, yet, somehow, like Milton's fallen Christian readers in their sinfulness and in their dependence on Christ's redemptive force. This is the paradox that the inspired narrator of *Paradise Lost* attempts to embody. Although he prays for the inward illumination to "see and tell / Of things invisible to mortal sight" (3.54–55), he admits to kinship with his readers as a sinner who requires one greater man to "restore us" from a state of "woe" (1.3; 9.11).

Since the paradox can be understood largely in terms of a changed dependency on negative rather than positive Moses traditions, the complex of attitudes toward Moses that characterizes these different traditions is examined in this chapter. The portrait of Moses as illuminator is traced first, and traced somewhat lightly, since it offers an interpretation of Moses' role in the early invocations of *Paradise Lost* that has already been recognized.

This portrait is shown to best advantage in a setting where the threat of continued and necessarily damaging comparisions of Moses to Christ is absent. Milton provides such a setting in the *Areopagitica*, where he attests to the sufficiency of the individual to separate good from evil by exercising his gift of reason. At the very start of the second argument, Moses is cited as an example of an individual "skilfull in all the learning of the Aegyptians, Caldeans, and Greeks, which could not probably be without reading their books of all sorts" (*YP*, 2:507–8). In addition to relying on the summary account of Moses' education that appears in the New Testament ("And Moses was learned in all the wisdom of the Egyptians" [Acts 7:22]), Milton would have known the fuller account in the work of Philo, whom he calls "a writer of weight . . . who wrote a lengthy commentary on all the Mosaic law and was most learned in its lore" (*YP*, 4:345; and see 2:593 and 646–47). Philo includes prosodic principles among the subjects that Moses learned from the three cultures:

> Arithmetic, geometry, the lore of metre, rhythm and harmony, and the whole subject of music as shown by the use of instruments or in textbooks and treatises of a more special character, were imparted to him by learned Egyptians. These further instructed him in the philosophy conveyed in symbols, as displayed in the so-called holy inscriptions. . . . He had Greeks to teach him the rest of the regular school course, and the inhabitants of the neighbouring countries for Assyrian letters and the Chaldean science of the heavenly bodies.[8]

Drawing on his youthful instruction in poetry and music, Moses would have sung a hymn to God and an ode to Israel (Exod. 15 and Deut. 32), both composed in structurally classical hexameter verse. Israel Baroway has already charted the underground patristic stream that carried the myth of scriptural prosody from Philo and Josephus to the early modern literary critics.[9] Transmission of the myth is also aided by the spirit of controversy, which has thrived on the association of Moses and sacred scripture with classical prosody. Although their ends require different emphases, Philo's coreligionist Flavius Josephus confuted the grammarian and anti-Semite Apion with an argument substantially similar to one used later by Sidney against the Puritan attack of Gosson. Josephus dignified Moses by attesting to his composition of an "Ode in Hexameter verse, containing the prayses of God, and a thanksgiving for the favour he had done to them [the Israelites]."[10] Sidney's justification of literature and figurative expression in general depends partly on the support of "Moses and Deborah in their Hymns," which demonstrate that the chief among poems, "both in antiquity and excellency, were they that did imitate the unconceivable excellencies of God."[11] In this same spirit of self-justification, Milton writes of "those frequent songs throughout the law and prophets" that surpass the odes and hymns of Pindarus and Callimachus (*YP*, 1:816; and see *PR*, 4.334–49).

The deliverance at the waters of the Red Sea prompted Moses' first song, "the most auncient song that is extant in the world,"[12] and the seventeenth-century exegete William Attersoll strictly discriminates the lofty style of the song in expounding the doctrine that "Poetry is ancient and commendable":

> Poetry is ancient in the Church of God, and commendable among the godly. The setting forth of the workes of God, not onely truly, soundly, and simply in a plaine forme & frame of words, but strictly, poetically, artificially, is worthy of praise and commendation. . . . See the examples of Moses singing the praises of God after their deliverance out of Egypt, after the overthrow of Pharaoh, and after their passage over the red sea; he footed it not in a low, but in a lofty stile, praising God in verses, not in prose, for the greater efficacy of the matter, and the better expressing of their affections. The like we might say of his sweet song sung not long before his death, Deut. 31, 19, 22 & 32, 1, 2, &c. which he taught the children of Israel.[13]

Milton promises a poem composed in lofty style when he adopts a distinctive Mosaic personality in *Animadversions*. There he prays to God for the perfection of the Reformation in a mood of chiliastic exaltation.

> O perfect, and accomplish thy glorious acts; for men may leave their works unfinisht, but thou art a God, thy nature is perfection; shouldst thou bring us thus far onward from *Egypt* to destroy us in this Wildernesse though wee deserve; yet thy great name would suffer in the rejoycing of thine enemies, and the deluded hope of all thy servants. When thou hast settl'd peace in the Church, and righteous judgement in the Kingdome, then shall all thy Saints addresse their voyces of joy, and triumph to thee, standing on the shoare of that red Sea into which our enemies had almost driven us. And he that now for haste snatches up a plain ungarnish't present as a thanke-offering to thee, which could not bee deferr'd in regard of thy so many late deliverances wrought for us one upon another, may then perhaps take up a Harp, and sing thee an elaborate Song to Generations. (*YP*, 1:706).

Although such a victory and such hosannas are not forthcoming, the narrator of *Paradise Lost*, speaking more softly than the youthful Milton, records at least a limited sort of Exodus deliverance. Fisch and Shawcross have already pointed out intimations of the Exodus myth in the epic.[14] One might also recall Milton's announcement, in the conclusion to his defense of "The Verse," that his Heroic Verse without Rime sets an example, "the first in *English*, of ancient liberty recover'd to Heroic Poem from the troublesome and modern bondage of Riming." Moreover, faint echoes occasionally sound in passages not overtly concerned with the Exodus. Thus the invocation to book 3 suggests a comparison between the narrator, borne by his muse, and the Israelites' flight from Egypt on eagles' wings (Exod. 19:4). The narrator has "Escap't the *Stygian* Pool, though long detain'd / In that obscure sojourn" (3.14–15). The latter books of the epic refer to the lengthy "sojourn" in Egypt (12.159 and 190–92), and the first Exodus simile in the poem compares Satan's broken legions in the fiery lake to Pharaoh's army beheld by "The Sojourners of *Goshen*" (1.309). The narrator's sense of relief here—of escape—is explained at least partly by reference to the dramatic context of the Exodus.

The vibrations of the Sinai theophany are recorded rather more emphatically than those of the exodus in the early invocations of *Paradise Lost*. The Hebrew Bible insists on the united functions of prophet and legislator (Exod. 20, 21, and 34), and the Apocrypha embellishes the argument that Moses' mystic ascent authenticates his role as lawgiver. An apocalyptic tenor characterizes God's account of Moses' visions: "I brought him up on to Mount Sinai; and kept him with me for many days. I told him of many wonders, showing him the secrets of the ages and the end of time, and instructed him what to make known and what to conceal" (2 Esd. 14:4–5). Jesus the son of Sirach, in his praise of famous men, also sees the ascent of Sinai as the occasion for the revelation of mysteries:

> He gave him commandments for his people
>   and showed him a vision of his own glory.
> For his loyalty and humility he consecrated him,
>   choosing him out of all mankind.
> He let him hear his voice and led him into the dark cloud.
> Face to face, he gave him the commandments,
>   a law that brings life and knowledge.
>
> (*Sir.* 45:3–5)

Philo's interpretation of the Sinai ascent as Moses' induction into kingship and prophecy is of some importance in understanding the Hellenistic conception of the mediatorial office—a conception that must at least have influenced Milton in the Trinity Manuscript drafts of the "Paradise Lost" tragedy. Moses is assigned an intermediary status between God and the rest of humankind:

For he was named god and king of the whole nation, and entered, we are told, into the darkness where God was, that is, into the unseen, invisible, incorporeal and archetypal essence of existing things. Thus he beheld what is hidden from the sight of mortal nature, and, in himself and his life displayed for all to see, he has set before us, like some well-wrought picture, a piece of work beautiful and godlike, a model for those who are willing to copy it. Happy are they who imprint, or strive to imprint, that image in their souls.[15]

Whereas Philo treats Moses as supreme prophet, priest, and king,[16] Josephus, somewhat more moderately, stresses the roles of author-editor and legislator. Just as Moses was a lawgiver, so was he devoted to natural philosophy. This is evident from his method in the Pentateuch of prefixing the Genesis cosmogony to the legal prescriptions of the other books. The prophet "deemed it above all necessary, for one who would order his own life aright and also legislate for others, first to study the nature of God, and then, having contemplated his works with the eye of reason, to imitate so far as possible that best of all models and endeavour to follow it."[17] Moses' narrative method is a paradigm for Josephus, who states: "I therefore entreat my readers to examine my work from this point of view."[18]

Milton acknowledges the influence of Josephus in shaping his understanding of the merged functions of author and legislator. He realizes that the purpose of divine inspiration is not only to "see and tell / Of things invisible to mortal sight" but also to "justify the ways of God to men." Thus he writes in the preface to book 1 of *Reason of Church-Government*:

> *Moses* therefore the only Lawgiver that we can believe to have been visibly taught of God, knowing how vaine it was to write lawes to men whose hearts were not first season'd with the knowledge of God and of his workes, began from the book of Genesis, as a prologue to his lawes; which *Josephus* right well hath noted. That the nation of the Jewes, reading therein the universall goodnesse of God to all creatures in the Creation, and his peculiar favour to them in his election of *Abraham* their ancestor, from whom they could derive so many blessings upon themselves, might be mov'd to obey sincerely by knowing so good a reason of their obedience. (*YP*, 1:747).

In Milton's view, all knowledge—even the inspired wisdom of poetic song—must be regarded as the base upon which virtuous action is founded, and the poetry of creation is only the preface to legal instruction. The Hebraic divorce tracts insist that the voice of Moses promulgating the law is the voice of God: "the prudence of *Moses*, or rather that mercifull decree of God" is "the perfect, the pure, the righteous law of God" (*YP*, 2:281). But even in *Reason of Church-Government* Milton explains why laws bear the name of a divinity: "all the ancient lawgivers were either truly inspired as *Moses*, or were such men as with authority anough might give it out to be so, as *Minos*, *Lycurgus*, *Numa*, because they wisely forethought that men would never quietly submit to such a discipline as had not more of Gods hand in it than mans" (*YP*, 1:753–54).

Jeremy Taylor translates the ultimate source of this view, Selden's *De Jure*:

> It were impossible that all the world should acknowledge any lawgiver but God; for nothing else could be greater than all mankind, nor be trusted in all cases, nor feared but He alone. And therefore the heathen princes when they gave their laws, gave them in the name of a deity. So Numa, Lycurgus, and others; which was not a design to scare fools and credulous people, but in some instances (excepting only that they named a false god) was a real truth; that is, in all those things which commanded natural justice, honesty and decencie: for these were really the laws of the true God.[19]

Milton as textual scholar justifies the editorial insertion of a description of the Sabbath into the second chapter of Genesis by appealing to Moses' primary role as lawgiver. Separating commemoration from event, Milton notes the scriptural anachronism of referring to the institution of the Sabbath before the account of the promulgation of the law and concludes: "Moses . . . inserted this sentence from the fourth commandment in what was, as it were, an opportune place. Thus he seized an opportunity of reminding the people for the reason, which was, so to speak, topical at this point in his narrative, but which God had really given many years later to show why he wanted the Sabbath to be observed by his people, with whom he had at long last made a solemn covenant" (*YP*, 6:354).

In works close to Milton, Moses' Sinai ascent becomes the source of apocalyptic knowledge as well as legal regulation. Indeed, both Clement of Alexandria, whom Milton cites early in his *Commonplace Book*, and Eusebius, the poet's favorite church historian, present fragments of a verse drama by Ezekiel, an otherwise unknown author, in which Moses himself narrates the ascent as a dream-vision. Standing before "a mighty throne that reached to heaven's high vault," Moses surveys the prospect:

> Thence I looked forth
> Upon the earth's wide circle, and beneath
> The earth itself, and high above the heaven.
> Then at my feet, behold! a thousand stars
> Began to fall, and I their number told,
> As they passed by me like an armed host.[20]

In the interpretation of the dream that follows, Moses learns of his combined role of legislator and seer.[21]

The narrator of book 3 of *Paradise Lost* assumes a role analogous to that of Moses. Dealing with what Isabel MacCaffrey calls "divine episte- mology, the ways whereby men can know, or come to know, God,"[22] he aspires to a vision of the timeless realm of light. The poet evokes the Sinai theophany by modulating the significance of "cloud" and "ever-during dark." The Sinai narrative employs the imagery of covering: Moses is enveloped by the thick cloud (Exod. 19:9), shaded by the hand of God (Exod. 33:22), and concealed by the veil (Exod. 34:33–35). These images suggest at once initiation and revelation as well as obstruction and con- cealment. A consideration of the invocation to book 3 should indicate a relationship between the Miltonic bard and Moses by bringing into simi- lar play the varied meanings of the imagery of concealment.

The poet's ascent to knowledge is first described as a "flight / Through utter and through middle darkness borne / With other notes than to th' *Orphean* Lyre" (15–17). Then, both clinically and poetically, the narra- tor describes the cloud covering his eyes: "So thick a drop serene hath quencht thir Orbs, / Or dim suffusion veil'd" (25–26). "Drop serene" is a literal translation of *gutta serena*, the medical term for the form of blindness that Milton suffered. The term furnished the poet with some consolation, and in the *Second Defence* he wrote that his eyes were "as clear and bright, without a cloud, as the eyes of men who see most keenly" (*YP* 4:583). Yet the consolation here is immediately canceled when the alternate description of blindness, "or dim suffusion veil'd," evokes the image of a cloud covering the eyes.

The association of darkness and song appears soon after in the descrip- tion of the bird: "as the wakeful Bird / Sings darkling, and in shadiest Covert hid / Tunes her nocturnal Note" (38–40). This somewhat fuller consolation is also canceled immediately, by the dissociation of the bird, who is in tune with nature and who knows when night comes, from the speaker:

> Thus with the Year
> Seasons return, but not to me returns
> Day, or the sweet approach of Ev'n or Morn,
> Or sight of vernal bloom, or Summer's Rose,
> Or flocks, or herds, or human face divine;
> But cloud instead, and ever-during dark
> Surrounds me, from the cheerful ways of men
> Cut off, and for the Book of knowledge fair
> Presented with a Universal blanc
> Of Nature's works to me expung'd and ras'd,
> And wisdom at one entrance quite shut out.

> *(40–50)*

The "cloud" and "ever-during dark" surrounding the poet are not, at this point, transmitters of consolatory wisdom, and the invocation ends with the prayer that the Celestial Light

> Shine inward, and the mind through all her powers
> Irradiate, there plant eyes, all mist from thence
> Purge and disperse, that I may see and tell
> Of things invisible to mortal sight.
>
> (52–55)

The speaker must wait longer for the next consolation, which comes in the form of a dark mystery at the upper limit of human poetic vision. Through a sort of divine peripeteia, the speaker's prayer for illumination is answered in an unexpected way when he joins the angels in the next apostrophe to the divine light of God the Father:

> Fountain of Light, thyself invisible
> Amidst the glorious brightness where thou sit'st
> Thron'd inaccessible, but when thou shad'st
> The full blaze of thy beams, and through a cloud
> Drawn round about thee like a radiant Shrine,
> Dark with excessive bright thy skirts appear,
> Yet dazzle Heav'n, that brightest Seraphim
> Approach not, but with both wings veil thir eyes.
>
> (375–82)

"Fountain of Light" recalls the eighth line of the invocation to book 3, though it has been reinterpreted. The cloud that blinds the poet becomes the vehicle of the beatific vision. The blind speaker, "from the cheerful ways of men / Cut off," imitates the Father who sits "Thron'd inaccessible." Surrounded by a cloud and by ever-during dark, the bard is like God, who draws a cloud about him, and like the dazzled seraphim, who voluntarily veil their eyes. Here, indeed, the oxymoron "Dark with excessive bright" alludes to Moses, who "drew near unto the thick darkness where God was." The bard also evokes Exodus 33:18–23, where God reveals himself in a cloud to Moses alone atop Mount Horeb, while the Israelites (the "society of men") watch from a distance and wonder. The epic narrator ascends the mount of inspiration and, after praying and waiting, he is granted a veiled glimpse of eternity. The beatific vision becomes a function of his blindness.

The radical alterations of meaning of the cloud image in book 3 enable it to represent fully the paradox that divine mysteries are apprehended in darkness. When the epic narrator is associated with Moses, the cloud becomes a symbol of authenticity as well. God tells Moses: "Lo, I come unto thee in a thick cloud, that the people may hear when I speak with thee, and believe thee for ever" (Exod. 19:9). For Milton, too, the cloud of blindness becomes a mark of inspirational authenticity.

The complex of attitudes toward Moses examined so far affirms, among other things, the possibilities of human endeavor. Primarily Hebraic or Platonic rather than Christian, these traditions offer a decidedly positive conception of Moses' symbolic role in Milton's work. Moses' genuine achievements without the aid of Christ's mediation are recalled most often in Milton's prose tracts of the 1640s. These represent Milton's part in a program for achieving religious, political, and domestic freedom. Attacking abuses of institutional authority, Milton sought to transfer power and freedom to his regenerate countrymen. The example of Moses' reproof to Joshua (Num. 11:29) sustained Milton in his hope that the culmination of the Reformation could be achieved. In a passage in the *Areopagitica* preceded by the announcement that "great reformation is expected," Milton foresaw a holy community in England: "For now the time seems come, wherein *Moses* the great Prophet may sit in heav'n rejoycing to see that memorable and glorious wish of his fulfill'd, when not only our sev'nty Elders, but all the Lords people are become Prophets. No marvell then though some men, and some good men too perhaps, but young in goodnesse, as *Joshua* then was, envy them" (*YP*, 2:555–56)[23] That this is one of Milton's noblest visions of human capability is dramatized by Blake's selection of the verse on which it is based as the epigraph for his brief epic, *Milton*. Blake's Milton is redeemed by becoming a liberating prophet.

Milton's later, altered opinions regarding unmediated human achievement are reflected in the final books of *Paradise Lost*, in *Paradise Regained*, and in the Pauline chapters of *De doctrina*. The disinclination to expect redemption in the material world through solitary human action is marked by a relentless emphasis on the need for divine intervention. Fallen human history becomes the record of "supernal Grace contending / With sinfulness of Men" (11.359–60).

As a poet, Milton chooses to exploit his fallen opinions of humankind by expressing them in *Paradise Lost* as a consequence of Adam's fall. In paradise, before the Fall, Raphael offers himself as a model of perfection, advising that Adam can alter his own nature from human to angelic simply by obedience. It is only a matter of time, he suggests, "Till body up to spirit work" (5.478). He underscores his claim that the body's work is to be mediated only by the action of time (497–98), adding the postscript "If ye be found obedient" (501).

After the Fall it becomes clear that the verses treating Eden were written in the subjunctive mood and that Raphael's postscript must now be reinterpreted as an unsettling codicil. In the soteriology of the last books,

Christ replaces Raphael as a pattern for Adam—a pattern ultimately matchless. As an earlier Adam had twice repeated the word "obedience" (5.514), incredulous at the thought that his could be doubted, so a newly startled Adam hears the word repeated by Michael (12.403 and 408), who discloses the effects of a sin so terrible that only Christ can atone for it.

Adam is told that Christ must destroy Satan's work

> In thee and in thy Seed: nor can this be,
> But by fulfilling that which thou didst want,
> Obedience to the Law of God, impos'd
> On penalty of death, and suffering death,
> The penalty to thy transgression due,
> And due to theirs which out of thine will grow.
>
> (12.395–400)

In the passage that follows immediately (401–50), Michael dispels the fallacy of simple self-reliance. The complex system of imputations—of human sin to Christ, of Christ's righteousness to all believers, and of Adam's sin to all his descendants—is founded on the mediateness of vicarious substitution.

Michael, unlike Raphael, treats the progression from body to spirit in a context of the relation of law to justification by faith—a context that forecloses the possibility of redemption without Christ's intervention.

> So Law appears imperfet, and but giv'n
> With purpose to resign them in full time
> Up to a better Cov'nant, disciplin'd
> From shadowy Types to Truth, *from Flesh to Spirit,*
> From imposition of strict Laws, to free
> Acceptance of large Grace, from servile fear
> To filial, works of Law to works of Faith.
>
> (12.300–6; *my emphasis*)

Michael evokes Christ's redemptive reenactment of a mission uncompleted by Moses: to bring humankind home safe from wandering to "eternal Paradise of rest" (12.314). In Michael's presentation of history, Moses is the minister of a law that brings the awareness of sin, but not the power to overcome it. Only Christ has the power to enter Canaan and to regain paradise.

Milton's increased dependency on typological Moses traditions in the later books of *Paradise Lost* results in a diminished Moses. The degrading of events and personages from the Hebrew Bible is dramatized by a reexamination of the images of "cloud" and "ever-during dark." In emphasizing the limitations of the law, the Pauline epistles systematically distort and degrade Moses' Sinai ascent. Moses, the minister of the law, is involved in obscurities of vision and language:

> Seeing then that we have such hope [of glory], we use great plainness of speech: And not as Moses, which put a veil over his face, that the children of Israel could not steadfastly look to the end of that which is abolished: But their minds were blinded: for until this day remaineth the same veil untaken away in the reading of the old testament; which veil is done away in Christ. But even unto this day, when Moses is read, the veil is upon their heart. Nevertheless, when it shall turn to the Lord, the veil shall be taken away. Now the Lord is that Spirit: and where the Spirit of the Lord is, there is liberty. But we all, with open face beholding as in a glass the glory of the Lord, are changed into the same image from glory to glory even as by the Spirit of the Lord. (2 Cor.3:12–18)

Paul identifies Moses with the covenant that has passed away ("when Moses is read") and contrasts him with the new covenant in Jesus. This passage alludes constantly to Exodus 34:29–35, although Paul distorts the biblical text by suggesting that Moses' veil was meant to conceal the loss of his glory from the Israelites. Paul's purge of Moses is complete. The last verse, with its image of a mirror and its theme of transformation by beholding, is an ironic reminder of the very similar passage in Philo dealing with the establishment of *Moses* as a paradigm of virtue.

The passage from Corinthians proves that the imagery of covering is not possessed of an inalienably sublime meaning. In Hebrews 12:18–22, the verses' antitheses oppose terror to serenity, clouds and darkness to light, Sinai to Zion, the law to the gospel. Samuel Mather interprets both sets of verses while discussing Moses as a type in regard of his dispensation ("a type of the Law"): "There was a *darkness* also in that Dispensation, *Heb.* 12.18. *Ye are not come unto blackness, and darkness, and Tempest.* Hence *Moses* had a Veil upon his Face, *Exod.* 34.29, 30, 33. But there was a further Mystery in this Veil; it signifieth a spiritual Veil, a Covering upon the Heart, 2 *Cor.* 3.13, 14. a Veil upon their Mind, *Act.* 13.27. they understood not the Prophets though Read every Sabbath-day."[24]

Typologists saw Moses' thick cloud as equivalent to the "shadows and figures" of the Old Testament which are then opposed to the clarity of the gospel.[25] That Moses embodies the obscurities and the limitations of the old law is brought home when one recalls some of the titles, and the still more revealing subtitles, popular among seventeenth-century Protestants: William Guild's *Moses Unvailed, or, Those Figures Which Served unto the Patterne and Shaddow of Heavenly Things* (London, 1620); Thomas Godwin's *Moses and Aaron: Civil and Ecclesiastical Rites, used by the ancient Hebrews: observed and at large opened* (London, 1625); and Thomas Taylor's *Moses and Aaron, or, The Types and Shadows of the Old Testament Opened and Explained* (London, 1653).

William Guild endlessly compresses images opposing "Evangelicall light" to "Legal obscuritie." In his epistle dedicatory to the Bishop of Winchester, he remarks that "Moses covered with a vaile stood before the people: Even so (Right Reverend) in the detection of the glorious worke of mans Redemption, mysticall promises went before mercifull performance, darke shadowes were the fore-runners of that bright substance, obscure types were harbingers to that glorious Anti-type the Messiah."[26]

The New Testament verses and their various interpretations all agree that Christ and the new dispensation he embodies must be reached without clouds and darkness. This is evident when one returns to book 3—not to the invocation but to the exposition of Christian doctrine. The Son, participating in the heavenly dialogue with God the Father, foresees his final ascension after defeating death:

> Then with the multitude of my redeem'd
> Shall enter Heav'n long absent, and return,
> Father, to see thy face, wherein no cloud
> Of anger shall remain, but peace assur'd,
> And reconcilement; wrath shall be no more
> Thenceforth, but in thy presence Joy entire.
>
> (260–65)

The opposition of the old and new dispensations is subtly but definitely suggested by the association of "cloud" with anger and of anger with wrath. In *De doctrina Christiana*, opposing the covenant of grace to the Mosaic law, Milton quotes successively Romans 4:15 ("the law worketh wrath") and 5:20 ("moreover the law entered, that the offence might abound; but where sin abounded, grace did much more abound") (*YP*, 6:518). Similarly, in the Pauline postlapsarian books of *Paradise Lost*, wrath is used as a virtual synonym of law ("over wrath grace shall abound" [12.478]), and this meaning is not absent from God's reply to the Son, whom he addresses as "the only peace / Found out for mankind under wrath" (3.274–75).

In the same book, just after his veiled vision of God the Father, the epic narrator addresses the Son as

> Divine Similitude,
> In whose conspicuous count'nance, without cloud
> Made visible, th' Almighty Father shines,
> Whom else no Creature can behold.
>
> (384–87)

Thomas Taylor reinforces the Mosaic allusion: "Never was God so clearly seene by the eye of flesh as to *Moses*, who talked face to face: But never did creature see his face but Christ, Joh. 1.18."[27]

God the Father is covered by a cloud before Moses in the Bible and before the Miltonic bard in the poem. When he is alone with the Son, he is "without Cloud, serene" (11.45). The Son of God experiences the ultimate perfection from which even Moses and the narrator are excluded. Unlike the Son, they cannot experience a totally unmediated vision of divinity. "Without Cloud, serene" describes the calm of the Father, whose countenance is not darkened by the Son's desire to mitigate human punishment. It alludes to the clouds of mystery that can be removed when the Father and Son deliberate together; it recalls by contrast the limitations of Moses' mediatorial office and of the law that works wrath; and, finally, it returns to the invocation's "*gutta serena*," the "drop serene" and "dim suffusion" that cloud the eyes of a blind narrator.

In the Pauline chapters of *De doctrina*, Milton emphasizes the relative obscurity and indistinctness of Moses' law. He distinguishes between the plainness and light of the gospel (as in his quotation from 2 Cor. 3:11 "we use great plainness of speech; and not as Moses" [*YP*, 6:522]) and "the obscurity necessarily arising from the figurative language of the prophets" (*CE*, 14 and 291; *YP*, 6:255). Moses was the first to announce the new dispensation of the covenant of grace, though obscurely and indistinctly. Afterward Christ clarified the law's obscurity and revealed the true Mosaic intention (*CE*, 16, 99, 103, and 113). Into the turmoil of misunderstanding and misinterpretation that confuses Moses' words, Christ always descends. He is Moses' only authoritative interpreter.

Just as Christ is required to complete Moses' meaning, so is he required to complete his mission. The exclusively positive features of Moses' life are disclosed in those accounts which stress his marvelous birth. Milton interprets Moses' life as an example of fortunate beginnings ("that Shepherd, who first taught the chosen Seed, / In the Beginning") and incomplete endings ("and therefore shall not Moses . . . his people into *Canaan* lead" (12.307 and 309). In *An Apology against A Pamphlet*, he draws on Hebrews to reduce Moses' life to faith in fulfillment through Christ:

> What reward had the faith of *Moses* an eye to? He that had forsaken all the greatnesse of *Egypt*, and chose a troublesome journey in his old age through the Wildernesse, and yet arriv'd not at his journies end: His faithfull eyes were fixt upon that incorruptible reward, promis'd to *Abraham* and his seed in the *Messiah*, hee sought a heav'nly reward which could make him happy, and never hurt him, and to such a reward every good man may have a respect. (*YP*, 1:950)

In the invocations of *Paradise Lost*, the narrator asks the Holy Spirit to clarify his obscurity ("What in me is dark / Illumine") and to find him an audience that will understand the true intent of his words ("fit audience find, though few"). The narrator prays for the successful end to his journey: the completion of a great epic poem. The confidence of the beginning gives way to fear that the poet will fall short. The sense of strain is explicit in the lyrical prologue to book 9, where the narrator prays for style answerable to his great argument and fears lest

> an age too late, or cold
> Climate, or Years damp my intended wing
> Deprest; and much they may, if all be mine,
> Not hers who brings it nightly to my Ear.

> (44–47)

Here the immense effort of flight is evoked by the image of a bird, which manages to support itself only by the ceaseless beating of its wings. The fear that cultural decline, cold climate, and old age may prevent his success is aggravated by the narrator's acute sense of the possibility of the withholding of inspiration. A waning of the narrator's powers is suggested by the transition from references to sight in the opening invocations to the reference to hearing in this prologue. The narrator no longer sees the holy light; he must depend entirely on the narration of his muse.

The Miltonic bard retells Moses' historical narrative and, in his fallen state, depends on the Holy Spirit to transform that narrative by revealing its true meaning. The poem, then, is an implicit prayer for understanding. Milton himself reminds us: "It is not necessary that our prayers should be always audible; the silent supplication of the mind, whispers, even groans and inarticulate exclamations in private prayer, are available. *Exod* xiv.15. 'Jehovah said unto Moses, Wherefore criest thou unto me?' though he was saying nothing with his lips, and only praying inwardly" (*YP*, 6:671). In *Paradise Lost*, the Son hears the prayer of our first parents, who "sighs now breath'd / Unutterable" (11.5–6), and he intercedes on their behalf as "Advocate / And *propitiation*" (11.33–34). Before the Fall, Adam, like Abraham and Moses (Gen. 18, Exod. 32, Num. 14), enjoys direct, gracious conversation with God the Father: "Heav'nly Power, / My Maker, be *propitious* while I speak" (8.379–80; my emphases).

Hebraic and Platonic Moses traditions bearing on prelapsarian life and on the Miltonic bard's office as poet-legislator stress the knowledge, power, and literary skill of the composer of the Pentateuch, of its songs (Exod. 15, Deut. 32), and even of some of the most beautiful psalms (e.g., Psalm 90, "A Prayer of Moses the man of God"). The introduction of sin increases anxiety about the communicability of religious doctrine, apparent in the slow advances toward an understanding of God's judgment on the serpent and in the oblique and partial rendering of the new dispensation, "obscurely . . . foretold" (12.543) in a few lines near the end of the poem. The Miltonic bard, involved in the necessary obscurities of figurative language, can be understood at least partly in relation to the negative typology of Moses, whose own cloudy formulations in the Old Testament must be understood by the Christian reader with the help of the Holy Spirit.

Moses shares with our first parents fortunate beginnings, incomplete endings, and exclusion from the promised land (paradise or Canaan). Where Hebraic and Platonic Moses traditions emphasize eloquence, typology emphasizes the silence of prayer that only Christ can understand. In paradise, Adam and Eve offer up to God a glorious psalm of praise, presented in its entirety, the result of prompt eloquence (5.153–208). Based on Psalms 19, 104, and 148, the great morning hymn not only omits mentioning the Son of God, it also reminds readers of his absence in its decidedly literal and non-Christological invocation of the sun and of the "Sons of Light, / Angels" (5.171–74 and 160–61). The fallen penitential hymn of book 10, interior and unrecorded, must be interpreted by Christ (11.30–36). The motto of the Sternhold and Hopkins psalter best expresses the difference: "James 5. *If any be afflicted, let him pray: and if any be merry, let him sing Psalms.*"[28]

When the Son offers up our first parents' prayer, "Sown with contrition" (11.27), he too draws on a psalm, though, inevitably, he appropriates it, as do countless Christian commentaries that distinguish between a psalm's literal, Hebraic words and those same words "personating Christ":

> The sacrifices of God are a broken spirit:
> a broken and a contrite heart, O God,
> thou wilt not despise.
>
> *(51:17)*

After the Fall, inarticulate Adam cannot pray, and the Son must intercede—his is the only sacrifice that matters. In the Hebrew text itself, the psalmist prays and offers a sacrifice in which God delights (51:16).

Adam's first speech in book 11 is inadequate precisely because he fails to recognize that Torah has irreversibly become law.

> *Eve,* easily may Faith admit, that all
> The good which we enjoy from Heav'n descends;
> But that from us aught should ascend to Heav'n
> So prevalent as to concern the mind
> Of God high-blest, or to incline his will,
> Hard to belief may seem; yet this will Prayer,
> Or one short sigh of human breath, up-borne
> Ev'n to the Seat of God. For since I sought

By Prayer th' offended Deity to appease,
Kneel'd and before him humbl'd all my heart,
Methought I saw him placable and mild,
Bending his ear; persuasion in me grew
That I was heard with favor; peace return'd
Home to my Breast, and to my memory
His promise, that thy Seed shall bruise our Foe;
Which then not minded in dismay, yet now
Assures me that the bitterness of death
Is past, and we shall live.

(141–58)

All of Adam's assertions would have been true under the benign Edenic law: good descending from heaven, human initiative affecting heaven, the power of prayer, the sufficiency of human beings to appease offended deity, and the assurance that he will live. Unaware of Christ's present and future priestly intercessions on his behalf (his prayers would have missed the way otherwise), he knows nothing of the terrible price that someone else will pay for his sin. Nor has he heard God's very recent harsh judgment of him: "His heart I know, how variable and vain / Self-left" (92–93). Adam speaks as if he had never fallen and as if God will respond to his penitential prayer as he did to the psalmic hymn, when as a gift he sent down Raphael, the divine interpreter. But God responds only to the Son. From his facile beginning ("easily") to his brutally ironic conclusion, Adam's speech is false, a fact underscored by the scriptural echo not of Abraham, Moses, or David, but of Agag, king of the Amalekites, the nation whose memory God commands the Israelites to obliterate (Deut. 25:17). Agag's last words, uttered one brief moment before Samuel hacks him to pieces, are a lie: "Surely the bitterness of death is past" (1 Sam. 15:32).

Prelapsarian Hebraic-Platonic and postlapsarian typological Moses traditions help to relate the Miltonic bard to Moses and to our first parents. They suggest that the Hebrew Bible may be the principal metaphor of language in the epic—external, comprehensive, and simple, efficacious before the Fall, inadequate afterwards—and that the gospel may be the principal metaphor of silence and interiority, governing the last books of the epic and pointing toward *Paradise Regained*.

CHAPTER FOUR.

Angelic Tact: Raphael on Creation

RAPHAEL'S ACCOUNT of creation in book 7 of *Paradise Lost* owes much more to the genre of biblical commentary than it does to hexameral poetry. Genesis is used to organize the bombastic verse of Sylvester's *Du Bartas* only to the extent that it keeps it from swelling indefinitely. In *Paradise Lost*, however, Raphael, even more than the Mosaic bard, is a "Divine Interpreter," who joins a careful rendition of the divine word in Genesis 1 and 2 with an interlinear interpretation of that word. Raphael's dual office here is that of the Hebrew Bible and its commentary. The direct paraphrases of scripture in book 7 are usually even more concise than their principal source, the King James Bible, and the interlinear poetic commentary, free of blatant ideology, celebrates the beauty of the book of nature. Raphael's doctrinal statements are so subtle that it is easy to overlook them, but, occasionally, they betray their generic origins in commentaries on Genesis. In this brief chapter I look at Raphael's exposition in book 7 of two angelic celebrations and of two acts of creation: the angelic hymns celebrating the creation of the *Ur-Licht* on the first day and the Sabbath on the seventh, and the creation of the sun on the fourth day and of humankind on the sixth.

Raphael, unlike Luther and Calvin, forbears emphasizing Christ's re-creation. He resists strategies that would diminish the physical, present creation by signaling the ultimate inconsequentiality of its loss. Although faith in Christ's redemption of humankind compensates for the Fall, it also weakens the attraction of an earthly paradise. The result, in book 7, of the poet's forbearance is the celebration of a visible, palpable universe—a celebration that is, in comparison with Christian commentaries on Genesis, purer in its sense of longing. Raphael's restraint and patience throughout books 5 to 8, as he educates pupils who he knows will undo his best efforts, relate to his patience as exemplar of a Hebrew Bible destined to be abrogated. He is one more Miltonic hero who will not complete his task, but who is not excused from performing it.

The first selection from book 7, the hymn of the angels upon beholding the *Ur-Licht* of the first day, maintains a position in the exegetical controversy over when the angels were created. According to St. Augustine, the creation of the angels on the first day is indicated by the term *light* in the command "Let there be light."[1] Rashi, the eleventh-century rabbinical exegete, infers the creation of the angels after the first day from Genesis 1:5 (lit., "and it was evening, and it was morning, one day"): "Why is it written 'one' [rather than 'the first']? Because the Holy One, blessed be He, was alone in the universe, the angels not having been created until the second day."[2] Luther also believes that the angels were created on the second day and treats as an "invention" the "account of a very great battle," presumably before creation, in which "the good angels withstood the evil ones."[3]

Willet, in his *Hexapla in Genesin*, surveys various opinions in considering "Why Moses omitteth the creation of the angels." He rejects Basil and Damascene, who claim "that the angels were created long before the visible world," as well as Gennadius and Achacius, who "thinke the Angels to have been created the same day with man."[4] Willet worries about the earlier date, "least the Angels beeing made before the sixe daies work beganne, should be thought to have ministered unto God in the creation." Willet concludes: "to mee it seemeth more probable, that they were created upon the fourth day, when the starres and other ornaments of heaven were made."[5]

Raphael's poetic elaboration of Genesis 1:4–5, while avoiding reference to the controversy, is nonetheless pointed. Here are the verses and their commentary:

> God saw the Light was good;
> And light from darkness by the Hemisphere
> Divided: Light the Day, and Darkness Night
> He nam'd. Thus was the first Day Ev'n and Morn:
> Nor pass'd uncelebrated, nor unsung
> By the Celestial Choirs, when Orient Light
> Exhaling first from Darkness they beheld;
> Birth-day of Heav'n and Earth; with joy and shout
> The hollow Universal Orb they fill'd
> And touch'd thir Golden Harps, and hymning prais'd
> God and his works, Creator him they sung,
> Both when first Ev'ning was, and when first Morn.

(7.249–60)

The poetic commentary begins by registering disagreement through litotes: "Nor pass'd uncelebrated nor unsung." The angels' song is ipso facto proof of their existence at this point. That they behold "Orient Light / Exhaling first from Darkness" proves that they were created before heaven and earth and before the primal light. The consistency of this view with Milton's theology is substantiated by the chapter treating creation in *De doctrina*. There Milton disagrees with "most people," who understand the angels to have been created on the first day: "But that they were created on the first or any one of the six days is asserted by the general mob of theologians with, as usual, quite unjustifiable confidence. . . . The fact that they *shouted* for *joy* before God at the creation, as we read in Job 38:7, proves that they were then already created, not that they were first created at that time" (*YP*, 6:312). The angel Raphael buttresses his opinion on angelic creation by including the verse from Job in his commentary: the angels who fill the universe with "joy and shout" (256) are Job's sons of God who "shouted for joy."

The book's second angelic hymn contains a less demonstrable example of Milton's disagreement with received opinion, similarly registered by an initial use of understatement. Raphael elaborates on Genesis 2:3, a description of the first Sabbath, when God the Father,

> Now resting, bless'd and hallow'd the Sev'nth day,
> As resting on that day from all his work,
> But not in silence holy kept; the Harp
> Had work and rested not, the solemn Pipe,
> And Dulcimer, all Organs of sweet stop,
> All sounds on Fret by String or Golden Wire
> Temper'd soft Tunings, intermixt with Voice
> Choral or Unison.
>
> (7.592–99)

"But not in silence holy kept; the Harp / Had work and rested not"—this may be an implied rejection of the custom not to play musical instruments on the Sabbath. Milton's angels, who sing and play in company with the music of the spheres and thereby keep the Sabbath, differ markedly from the sober Sunday worshipers in the Reformed Church, as described in Sylvester's *Du Bartas*:

> For, by th' Almightie this great Holy-day
> Was not ordain'd to daunce, and maske, and play.
>
> . . . .
>
> God would, that men should in a certaine place
> This Day assemble as before his face,
> Lending an humble and an attentive eare
> To learne his great Names deere-dread loving-feare.[6]

Raphael emphasizes joy rather than fear, the heavenly choir rather than the heavenly host. Indeed, considering his mission to provide literal exposition, Raphael's deletion of the word *host* (Gen. 2:1) is singular. Luther, commenting on the word, tells us that Moses "uses military terminology in this passage and calls the stars and the luminaries of heaven the army or host of heaven."[7]

The long angelic Sabbath hymn contains no allusion to Christ and his resurrection. This, too, is consistent with Milton's theology. Milton rejects Sunday as the Lord's Day: "If [Sunday] is the day of the Lord's resurrection, why, may I ask, is that day to be considered the Lord's Day any more than the day of his birth or the day of his death or the day of his ascension? Why should we consider it more important or more solemn than the day on which the Holy Spirit was sent to us?" (*YP*, 6:712).

Raphael's elaboration of the creation of the sun on the fourth day offers more interesting (though indirect) evidence of Milton's familiarity with exegetical tradition than do some other examples in book 7, such as the painstaking but silent reconciliation of various contradictory verses from the two distinct accounts of creation in Genesis 1 and 2—e.g., do birds emerge from water (Gen. 1:20) or from earth (Gen. 2:19)? Mud seems to be Raphael's compromise, "the tepid Caves, and Fens and shores" (417). This is precisely the sort of literal detail about the creation of nature that occupies Rashi, who comes up with the same answer. The example of the sun nourishing the stars and planets is important for what it omits—namely, an emphasis on the Christology of creation. St. Basil, drawing upon Philippians 2:15, notes that holy men are lights in the world, who participate in Christ, "the true Light of the World."[8] St. Ambrose develops the comparison between Christ and the sun in his commentary on the fourth day: "The Son made the sun, for it was fitting that the 'Sun of Justice' should make the sun of the world."[9]

In his poem "Faith," George Herbert demonstrates the Christological implications of the sun's gift of light to the lesser heavenly bodies.

> When creatures had no reall light
> Inherent in them, thou didst make the sunne
> Impute a lustre, and allow them bright;
> And in this shew, what Christ hath done.[10]

Herbert's bright sun symbolizes the imputation of Christ's righteousness to all believers. Raphael's description of the sun, however, is notably literal and scientific rather than homiletic.

> Of Light by far the greater part [God] took,
> Transplanted from her cloudy shrine, and plac'd
> In the Sun's Orb, made porous to receive
> And drink the liquid Light, firm to retain
> Her gather'd beams, great Palace now of Light.
> Hither as to thir Fountain other stars
> Repairing, in thir gold'n Urns draw Light,
> And hence the Morning Planet gilds her horns;
> By tincture or reflection they augment
> Thir small peculiar . . .
>
> (7.359–68)

This is one example of Raphael's deliberate reticence in book 7, his decision not to intimate Christian redemption. He will not use verbal irony or even prefigurative language to share a secret with the reader at our first parents' expense. Raphael celebrates the glory of humankind, "the Master work" (505), and so he forbears alluding to Christ's redemption, necessitated by Adam's Fall.

Patristic and Reformation exegetes generally find occasion to introduce Christ's redemption into their account of the hexameron. Although St. Basil's nine homilies on creation constitute a word-for-word commentary on Genesis 1:1–26, the significance of their delivery within the Holy Week would not have been lost on the auditory. Willet, in his commentary on Genesis, mentions the "synode holden in Palestina by Theophilus[,] Bishop of Cesarea, wherein it was agreed, that the world was made in the Spring, and that Christ was crucified the same day that Adam was created; at which time he also transgressed, that the first Adam herein might be a type of the second."[11]

St. Ambrose, whose sermons on creation, delivered during Holy Week, freely adapt St. Basil's text, notes the springtime occurrence of creation, the miracle at the Red Sea, and Christ's redemption of humankind.

> The sons of Israel left Egypt in the season of spring and passed through the sea, being baptized in the cloud and in the sea, as the Apostle said. At that time each year the *Pasch* of Jesus Christ is celebrated, that is to say, the passing over from vices to virtues, from the desires of the flesh to grace and sobriety of mind, from the unleavened bread of malice and wickedness to truth and sincerity. Accordingly, the regenerated are thus addressed: "This month shall be to you the beginning of months; it is for you the first in the months of the year."[12]

It is just, concludes Ambrose, that creation took place in the time in which the re-creation would occur.[13]

Raphael's description of the gathering of the waters on the third day evokes the miracle at the Red Sea, but only through a restrained, allusive use of imagery:

> Part rise in crystal Wall, or ridge direct,
> For haste; such flight the great commander impress'd
> On the swift floods.
>
> (293–95)

Raphael draws no connection between the Passover and New Testament redemption. His description here differs markedly from that of Michael, the typologizing angel, who will find resonant implications of Christian redemption in his explicit account of the Exodus in book 12.

Christian expositors of Genesis 1:26 ("And God said, Let us make man in our image") take the plural *Elohim* and "Let us" as evidence of the mystery of the trinity.[14] Although, in his speech at the beginning of the book, God "to his Son thus spake" (138); here he "to his Son thus audibly spake" (518). The audibility of God's speech to the Son seems to refute the overwhelming majority of exegetes who declare that the trinity deliberated with itself.[15] The adverb suffices to bring the account into accord with Milton's position in *De doctrina*: "The word Elohim, although it is plural in number, is applied even to a single angel, (in case we should think that the use of the plural means that there are, in God, more persons than one)" (*YP*, 6:234). Not surprisingly, Rashi is one of the few exegetes to learn a nontrinitarian lesson from the plurality of persons:

> Let us make man. We learn from this the humility of the Holy One, blessed be He. Since man is in the image of the angels and they might be jealous of him, therefore he consulted them. . . . Even though there is a place for the heretics to rebel [because of the plural Elohim], Scripture doesn't leave out the teaching of proper behavior and the virtue of humility, that the great one consults and takes permission from the lesser one.[16]

Christian commentary on the creation of humankind in God's image usually leads inexorably to the loss of that image in the Fall and to its recovery through Christ. To emphasize past loss and future redemption is to blunt the immediacy of creation. Calvin, in the argument to his commentary on creation, presents the paradigm:

> [Adam] was endued with understanding and reason, that hee differing from brute beastes, might meditate and thinke upon the better life; and that he might go the right way unto God, whose image he bare. After this followeth the fall of Adam, whereby he separated himselfe from God, whereby it came to passe that he was deprived of all perfection. Thus Moses describeth man to be voide of all goodnesse, blinde in minde, perverse in heart, corrupte in every parte, and under the guilte of eternall death. But straite after he addeth the historie of the restoring, where Christ shineth with the benefite of redemption.[17]

Luther's nostalgia for lost innocence and paradise is explicit:

> when we must discuss Paradise now, after the Flood, let us speak of it as a historical Paradise which once was and no longer exists. We are compelled to discuss man's state of innocence in a similar way. We can recall with a sigh that it has been lost; we cannot recover it in this life.[18]

Raphael possesses an exquisite sense of decorum. Talking to our first parents in their state of innocence, he emphasizes their unlimited capacity to achieve virtue unmediated by any force outside themselves:

There wanted yet the Master work, the end
Of all yet done; a Creature who not prone
And Brute as other Creatures, but endu'd
With Sanctity of Reason, might erect
His Stature, and upright with Front serene
Govern the rest, self-knowing, and from thence
Magnanimous to correspond with Heav'n,
But grateful to acknowledge whence his good
Descends, thither with heart and voice and eyes
Directed in Devotion, to adore
And worship God Supreme who made him chief
Of all his works.

(505–16)

Of course the Christian reader, who knows what is to come, is likely to find Raphael's account all the more poignant for the purity of its celebration. Yet this is accomplished with utmost tact—without the italics that would constitute a wink in the reader's direction.

The mood of Raphael's commentary in book 7 is in a sense more Hebraic than Christian. Indeed, without making extravagant claims of influence, one might suggest that, in its refusal to intimate the Fall and the Passion, Raphael's commentary resembles those of the medieval rabbinical exegetes, most notably Rashi's. Raphael's exposition is literal rather than figurative; the angel celebrates external vision ("this World / Of Heav'n and Earth *conspicuous*" [62–63]) rather than inward illumination, and he underscores the glory of unmediated human potentiality.

For a glimpse at what the creation account might have been in less skillful hands than Raphael's, one can turn to the poem that marks Milton's attaining poetic majority. Theologically conservative as it is, the *Nativity Ode* conveys an account of creation informed with a Christian ethos of guilt. The nativity—and its associations with sin and with atonement through crucifixion—diminishes Nature:

She woos the gentle Air
To hide her guilty front with innocent Snow,
And on her naked shame,
Pollute with sinful blame,
The Saintly Veil of Maiden white to throw.

(38–42)

The magnificent temple of the sun (7.243–49 and 359–65) resembles in no way the sun of the *Ode*, who "hid his head for shame, / As his inferior flame, / The new-enlight'n'd world no more should need" (80–82).

Finally, and inevitably when one considers a poem entitled *Paradise Lost*, Raphael's account of creation is revised and complicated by the

Fall, which necessitates the redemption available only through Christ's mediation. When the reader turns to the beginning of book 3, a postlapsarian invocation by a blind narrator, one discovers a complete reversal of Raphael's emphases. Where Raphael celebrates the creation of Light, "first of things, quintessence pure" (7.243–44), the Miltonic bard invokes the Son of God as "holy Light, offspring of Heav'n first-born" (3.1). Raphael celebrates a visible, material world:

> Earth now
> Seem'd like to Heav'n, a seat where Gods might dwell,
> Or *wander* with delight, and love to *haunt*
> Her sacred Shades.
>
> (7.328–31; *my emphasis*)

The blind narrator's haunts are immaterial, a world of words:

> Yet not the more
> Cease I to *wander* where the Muses *haunt*
> Clear Spring, or Shady Grove, or Sunny Hill,
> Smit with the love of sacred Song.
>
> (3.26–29; *my emphasis*)

Raphael sings the wonder of six evenings and mornings. He describes at length the vernal bloom of the third day, the "flocks / Pasturing" (7.461–62) and the "broad Herds" upspringing (7.462) on the sixth day, and, at last, the creation of humankind in God's image. The blind narrator compresses the six-days' creation into three short lines and complains that it is lost to him:

> . . . the sweet approach of Ev'n or Morn,
> Or sight of vernal bloom, or Summer's Rose,
> Or flocks, or herds, or human face divine.
>
> (3.42–44)

The way back to God is lost with the Fall. Now Christ is the Way, and his mediation is necessary if paradise is to be restored. Blind to the visible creation, the fallen narrator substitutes inward vision for eyesight, figure for letter, Christ for Adam, re-creation for creation, word for world, and, in so doing, he complicates Raphael's beautiful commentary.

CHAPTER FIVE

Book 9: The Unfortunate Redemption

THE ARGUMENT OF John Traske's little *Treatise of Libertie from Judaisme, or, An Acknowledgement of True Christian Libertie*[1] resembles those of countless others on the topic in the seventeenth century. Traske's central text, not surprisingly, is Romans 7:1–7, which allegorically represents the Mosaic law as a husband whose death sets his wife free. Traske adds the figure of divorce to that of death: "We are divorced from the flesh, and so free from it, yea dead thereto, and so at liberty from the Law. . . . By this similitude is our Divorce exemplified, yea, our freedome from the Law."[2]

Traske, once chief among English Judaizers and archadherent of the ceremonial as well as moral laws of Moses, now echoes Paul in calling the entire law "wraths minister" and rejecting even the Decalogue.[3] Only the prefatory material belies the zeal of Traske's argument, starting with the subtitle's "Acknowledgement," which implies reluctance, and culminating in the dedicatory epistle to his "HOLY AND TENDER MOTHER, THE CHURCH OF ENGLAND," who had clapped her wayward son in prison to reconsider the relations between law and gospel:

> At last perceiving that solitarinesse was best for mee, she inclosed mee awhile to contemplate what I had formerly done . . . and so continuing about a yeeres space; even till that set time, wherein God was pleased to withdraw the cloudie veile from mine eies; and the first thing I understood, was my Mothers great Authoritie; this was I throughly setled in . . . ere I came to see my foule failings, in those points of *Judaisme*.[4]

The large irony of Traske's imprisonment for resisting Christian liberty might at least qualify the assumption that this doctrine, of crucial significance in Puritan revolutionary theory, always supports individual liberty and freedom of conscience.[5] In what sounds like the doctrine of implicit faith, acceptance of institutional authority seems not only to have preceded but also to have caused Traske's change of mind. Once he had boldly proclaimed the efficacy of works under the Mosaic law. As penance he praises meekness above all other virtues, hinting even in his penitence at the coercion that stopped his pen and that substituted the authorized words of others for his own: "By [meekness], the penne that is truely guided, is kept from dropping down any poyson . . . to grieve any . . . and by it men are holpen to read things written, with such respect, as if they had been written with their owne pen."[6]

Knowing the circumstances of its composition invests this otherwise nondescript treatise with pathos. For Traske's old crime of "Judaizing in matters of dayes and meates,"[7] Star Chamber enforcers had nailed him to the pillory by his ears, burned the letter "J" into his forehead, and whipped him across England.[8] Meek "John Traske: of late stumbling, now happily running againe in the Race of Christianitie"[9] would seem to have little in common with defiant John Milton, who claimed that a truth accepted on the authority of cleric or assembly became for that very reason a heresy. Yet Traske's treatise is virtually identical doctrinally to Milton's chapter "OF THE GOSPEL, AND CHRISTIAN LIBERTY" in *De doctrina Christiana*. Milton too bases his rejection of the entire Mosaic law on Romans 7:

> vii.6: *but now we are delivered from the law, since that in which we were held is dead, so that we may serve in newness of spirit, and not in the oldness of the letter.* At the beginning of the same chapter Paul shows that we are released from the law in the same way as a wife is released from her dead husband. Also vii.7: *I did not know sin except through the law;* that is, the whole law, *for I should not have known lust if the law had not said, Do not lust* [Thou shalt not covet[10]]. . . . The law referred to here is the decalogue, so it follows that we are released from the decalogue too (*YP*, 6:525).
>
> It was certainly not merely the ceremonial law through which the desires of sin flourished in our members to bring forth fruit to death, Rom. vii. 5. But it is that law to which we are dead, vii.4, and which is dead to us, vii.6, and from which we are therefore freed as a wife from her dead husband, vii.3. It follows that we are freed not only from the ceremonial law but from the whole Mosaic law, vii.7, as above (*YP*, 6:529).

Related to these doctrinal correspondences, but instinct with poetic implication, is Traske's unsuccessfully suppressed nostalgia for a lost paradise that he associates with the Mosaic law. Adherence to this law presupposes a degree of human dignity, independence, and potential for achievement that the doctrine of Christian liberty denies. Humankind's first estate in paradise is part of a constellation of vanished felicities associated with the Mosaic law; one of these felicities, according to Traske, is the seventh-day Sabbath.

> Now then as with the destruction of Israels common-wealth, the holy temple, which served their use was destroyed, and the holinesse vanished: and Canaans blessednesse is also gone: as it stood distinguished from other lands: And *all mans holinesse, and happinesse naturall is now vanished*: the

Jewes prerogative, above all nations abolished: So also the holinesse, and blessednesse of that seventh day, is *vanished*, and quite done away, *with the death and destruction of man himselfe*. Indeed had man to this day, retained, and continued in his first estate, that day had retained its first blessednesse, and continued its holinesse still: but as little comfort as man hath left in himselfe at this day, of any holinesse or blisse, by vertue of creation, so little benefit shall man find in that daies observation, on that ground, and in that manner as it was injoined.[11]

The Fall, the destruction of the Temple, and the abrogation of the fourth commandment of the Decalogue—all bring to an end a time of natural holiness, blessedness, and bliss. Is Traske trying to convince his readers or himself that this time is over? Even at the time, Dorothy Coome Traske, who had been imprisoned far longer than her husband John, was still openly observing the Saturday Sabbath—and Traske's own most scandalous offense, a corollary of his belief that many of the Mosaic laws applied to Christians as well as Jews, had been his seventh-day Sabbath observance. Traske argues in the *Treatise* that the Mosaic law is still "of force" but that only Christ can fulfill it. Accepting Christ's fulfilment of the law's terms is the heart of Christian liberty, which seems to induce in Traske not overwhelming love and gratitude but a profound sense of human insufficiency:

> Whosoever dare, either oppose [the doctrine of Christian liberty], or scorne it, or at all limit it in any fleshly manner, as by forbearing of meates, or by legall observation of dayes: they are they, who at least ignorantly, doe scorne *Gods love*, set light by *Christs Merit*, and doe set themselves against the *Truth of Gods grace*. . . . And yet notwithstanding, the Law Morall stands firme, not abolished, but established by the doctrine, and of it we say, that *hee that observeth the whole Law and faileth in one point, is guilty of all*, Jam.2.10. And *except our righteousnesse doe exceed that of the Scribes and Pharisees, there is no entrance for us into the Kingdome of God*, Mat.5.20. But this exceeding righteousnesse is not ours, but Christs; as is before showed, for that *all ours is as filthy rags*, Isay 64.5.[12]

To oppose Christian liberty by "forbearing of meates" is to return to the Mosaic law and to pretend to go back further still, to Eden, where it was possible to observe the whole law. Traske compares "that Law of difference of things for food, *Levit.11. Deut.14*" to the "difference . . . put even in Paradise, between things for food."[13] Describing the Christian liberty he enjoyed in prison, Traske has no real complaints about the food or the conditions: "at that time had I libertie to heare the Word preached: the use of my Bookes, Food and Raiment enough, (unlesse by the mistake or default of the Jailours other things fell out)."[14] The mild, cryptic pa-

renthesis fails to state that his diet in prison was only "bread and water
. . . and that indeed was his fare, but of swine's flesh he might have eaten
his fill every day, for so it was ordred."[15] The mind is its own place, and
it is impossible to know which dream of freedom might have nurtured
Traske in his cell: death to the law and the world in Christ, or a return to
Eden, a time of natural blessedness under a law of difference. For his
jailors, the meat offered and resisted is an example of increase inaugu-
rated by Christian liberty. Traske himself, at the conclusion of his *Treatise*, employs a telling metonymy of Christian liberty as diminution rather
than increase. He entreats his readers "to pray fervently for mee . . . that
as I have been stout for *Moses* and *Christ* together: so I may bee as reso-
lute for Christ alone."[16]

Traske's only innovation in the *Treatise*—adding divorce to widow-
hood in Romans 7 as a second figure of Christian liberty—similarly hints
at his ambivalence toward the gospel. Certainly other Christians in the
seventeenth century, John Milton among them, found the right of divorce
under the Mosaic law to be more charitable than the Church's interpretation of divorce under the gospel. Of course Traske must have been thinking only of the spirit of divorce and not of the letter. Luther's warning to
keep them separate was a Reformation commonplace: "because they
mingle the Law with the Gospel they must needs be perverters of the
Gospel. For either Christ must remain and the Law perish, or the Law
must remain and Christ perish."[17] Traske's imprisoned voice and the
wounds on his body testify to the catastrophic effect of mixing law and
gospel, of being "stout for *Moses* and *Christ* together."

Traske's *Treatise* is, mutatis mutandis, his *Paradise Lost*, just as Milton's great epic is his own profoundly ambivalent treatise on Christian
liberty. Turning now to book 9 of the epic and soon to the catastrophe
itself, one should keep in mind Traske's nostalgia for a time of original
holiness, blessedness, and bliss and especially his punishment for violating Luther's warning. The breach between prelapsarian and postlapsarian Eden is as unbridgeable as that between law and gospel, and our first
parents, like Traske, attest to the catastrophic effect of violating the Reformers' warning—but with a difference: in book 9, the unfortunate redemption precedes the fortunate fall. Our first parents fail to preserve the
sanctity of the law from contamination by a demonic parody of the gospel and by the premature introduction of an ethos that is in part genuinely
Pauline.

The opening lines of this book announce fallings off and disjunctions.
The fallen narrator implicitly contrasts his own belated vocation ("beginning late" [9.25]) with the timely Edenic labors of Adam and Eve, "begun
/ Early" (224–25). He is downright in describing the withdrawal of the
divine from the human:

No more of talk where God or angel guest
With man, as with his friend, familiar used
To sit indulgent, and with him partake
Rural repast, permitting him the while
Venial discourse unblamed.

(9.1–5)

The Hebrew Bible records relationships of direct discourse and sweet intimacy between human creatures and their divine creator: "the LORD spake unto Moses face to face, as a man speaketh unto his friend" (Exod. 33:11). In Greco-Roman pagan literature, Moses is *"familiaris dei."*[18] At the deep level of the Fall, however, the traditional machinery of harmonistics does not work, and, instead of confluent and reciprocal relationships of Greek, Hebrew, and Christian, there are chasms and gulfs. "No more of talk" foretells the end of the law and of the benign original covenant of works, negotiated directly between humankind and God. As Thomas Blake points out in *Vindiciae Foederis*, "the first Covenant between God and man was immediate, no Mediator intervening, no daysman standing between them to make them one."[19]

Arminius holds sin in Eden to have been of particular enormity because "it was a transgression of such a law as had been imposed to try whether man was willing to be subject to the law of God . . . [and] [b]ecause he committed that sin . . . almost under the eyes of God himself, *who conversed with him in a familiar manner*" (my emphasis).[20] A change in the relation between human beings and God prompts the narrator to change the mode of his epic from pastoral "to tragic" (9.6), and it prompts Arminius to argue for a corresponding change in the mode of religion:

> The first relation, and that which was the first foundation of the primitive religion, was the relation between God and man—between God as the Creator, and man as created after the image and in a state of innocency; wherefore the religion built upon that relation was that of . . . righteousness and legal obedience. But that relation was changed, through the sin of man, who after this was no longer innocent and acceptable to God, but a transgressor and doomed to damnation. Therefore, after the commission of sin, either man could have had no hope of access to God . . . since he had violated and abrogated the divine worship; or a new relation of man to his Creator was to be founded by God, through his gracious restoration of man, and a new religion was to be instituted on that relation.[21]

As if fearful of an interval of despair, Reformation theologians such as Blake and Arminius do not wait an instant before describing the covenant of grace that compensates for the lost covenant of works. They acknowledge that the price of grace is dear, not only for Christ, the agent of reconciliation, but for human beings, who sacrifice a relationship of immediacy with the divine. For the second covenant, according to Blake, "man being fallen by sin, a Mediator was necessary, that God and man now in that distance, should be reconciled."[22] Arminius also points out that fallen Adam was in no condition to negotiate the terms of the latter covenant.[23] In *Paradise Lost* the Fall will lead in books 10 to 12 to a shift in covenant from works to grace and in symbolic mode from Hebraic to typological. But, for now, the patient narrator, who wants his readers to feel the loss of paradise, avoids even a hint of the doctrinal consolation that constitutes a major part of Reformation covenant theology. When Bucanus wonders why "*Angels, [who] were wont in old time to appeare often to the Fathers in the forme of men, and to converse and talke with them familiarly, now . . . do it no more,*" his answer deplores the nostalgia that prompted the question: only in its childhood did the Church require confirmations, and Christ now prefers "that our conversation should be in heaven, and not with the Angels upon the earth visibly."[24] The Miltonic narrator's peremptory, almost childlike "No more" and the prefixes of departure and deprivation that follow *dis*obedience—"foul *dis*trust, and breach *dis*loyal" (9.6–7), "*dis*tance and *dis*taste" (9.9)—give loss and nostalgia their full due.

Defining the Christian heroism that will replace Edenic virtue, the narrator disjoins power from goodness. His rejection of heroic warfare (9.28–31) implicitly devalues his own recent account of angelic heroism and the Son's triumph over evil in the war in heaven. Now he prefers Christ's "better fortitude / Of patience and heroic martyrdom" (31–32). But, writing in *The Tenure of Kings and Magistrates* shortly after the execution of the king, Milton had celebrated virtue as strength conjoined with goodness rather than as saintly ataraxia not of this world. He had then pronounced Parliament's struggle with King Charles "worthy of heroic ages" and praised those of its members who were "endu'd with fortitude and Heroick vertue" (*YP*, 3:191). *The Tenure* celebrates the "better fortitude" of executing justice rather than suffering martyrdom: future nations studying the actions of Parliament and the Military Council "henceforth may learn a better fortitude, to dare execute highest Justice on them that shall by force of Armes endeavour the oppressing and bereaving of Religion and thir liberty at home" (*YP*, 3:238). Milton is alluding here to the penultimate psalm, a song of triumph:

> Let the high praises of God be in their mouth, and a two-edged sword in their hand; to execute vengeance upon the heathen, and punishments upon the people; to bind their kings with chains, and their nobles with fetters of iron; to execute upon them the judgment written: this honor have all his saints. Praise ye the LORD. (149:6–9)

In the decidedly Hebraic context of *The Tenure*, these verses, surely interpreted as a defense of regicide, oppose another psalmic verse, 51:4, crucial to royalist arguments that the king is accountable to God alone:

> some would perswade us that this absurd opinion was King *Davids*; because in the 51 *Psalm* he cries out to God, *Against thee onely have I sinn'd*; as if David had imagin'd that to murder *Uriah* and adulterate his Wife, had bin no sinn against his Neighbour, when as that Law of *Moses* was to the King expresly, *Deut.* 17. not to think so highly of himself above his Brethren. (*YP*, 3:205)

Milton underscores the Hebraic ethos of *The Tenure* by submitting David's "pathetical words of a Psalme" to the judgment of the Mosaic law limiting the king's privileges, which furnishes "abundantly more certain rules to goe by" (*YP*, 3:205). As the deuteronomic law of divorce subsists at the heart of Milton's divorce tracts, Deuteronomy 17 is a central text of *The Tenure of Kings and Magistrates*. Milton's Hebraic arguments in both tracts bear upon his insistence on the rich potentialities of human activity in Eden.

When the Miltonic narrator shifts the mode of his epic from the pastoral of "rural repast" and the comedic symposium of "venial discourse" to the tragedy of the Fall,[25] he overwhelms the *hortus conclusus* of Genesis 2–3 with apocalyptic struggle. Until they fall, however, Adam and Eve live in a world human in scale. The Satan they know as a result of the psychic disturbance he caused Eve resembles the adversary *satan* of the Hebrew Bible more than he does the devil of later writings, and Christ the redeemer they know not at all. Only later will the gigantic proportions of the struggle between Christ and Satan eclipse the human proportions of earthly struggle against resistible temptation. In prelapsarian Eden, Adam and Eve live according to the easy terms of a benign original covenant of works that presupposes virtue as power.[26] According to William Whately, writing from the perspective of the covenant of grace, the paradise within requires evangelical obedience, the earthly paradise of Genesis legal and exact obedience:

> For by trusting in Christ we shall goe to Heaven in the way of Evangelicall obedience . . . as sure as they [i.e., Adam and Eve] or we should have done in the way of Legall obedience, if they and we had remained innocent; and God will as surely inable us to this Evangelicall obedience, if we seeke to him for grace and the renewing of his Image in us, as hee had inabled him to Legall and exact obedience. In truth Christ hath made the way to life eternall as easie to us in the path of the Gospell, as it was to him in the path of the Law, for wee have grace to keepe us from loving and serving sinne *as sure as hee had power to abstaine from committing sinne* (my emphasis).[27]

Whately, like Milton an alumnus of Christ's College, Cambridge, was a Puritan divine whose constant refrain was justification by faith alone, one's own righteousness being "no better then a menstruous rag, in respect of justification."[28] But even the most thoroughgoing apostles of the covenant of grace can indulge in nostalgic evocations of Eden under the covenant of works without compromising ideologies that verge on antinomianism. They isolate doctrine from emotion by insisting, first, on the absolute incompatibility of the two covenants, which are "opposite . . . in kind, so that at one and the same time, man cannot be under the Covenant of workes and the covenant of grace."[29] Then, after finding in the Old Testament the earliest possible entry point for the second covenant, usually Genesis 3:15, the *protevangelium*, they clear a small space in paradise for the original covenant.

Edward Leigh lists various differences, "in kind: [the original] was a Covenant of amity betweene the Creator and the creature; this of Reconciliation betweene enemies. . . . In the conditions: workes are required in the first, faith in the other. *Adam* was to make that good of himselfe, and by his owne power: In the Covenant of grace, God giveth what he requireth, and accepteth what he giveth. . . . In the object: [the covenant of works] is extended to all men, [the covenant of grace] belongs to some certaine men by a singular reason; for although it is often promiscuously propounded, yet by a special propriety it belongs to them to which it is intended by God."[30]

As long as they insisted that the original covenant no longer obtains, Protestants could praise its universality and the human amity and power its terms made possible. For John Ball, works can only be prelapsarian: "Neither can it be proved, that God ever made the covenant of works with the creature fallen: but whensoever the Scripture speaks of Gods entring into Covenant with man fallen and plunged into sinne, and for sinne deserving wrath, it must be understood of the Covenant of Grace."[31]

Despite a general uniformity in the sermons and treatises on the topic, admiration for Adam and Eve under the covenant of works may be mixed not only with gratitude to the creator who first set its terms and to the redeemer who reconciled sinners to the creator by submitting to the terms of a new covenant, but also with fury at the presumption of sinners after the Fall who dare to imagine that they, like their first parents, can perform works. John Cotton condemns all who "take delight and comfort . . . in their obedience," which is a "snare":

> but what followed upon the delight which they tooke in God, and in holy duties, it made them ready to expostulate with God, why he did not answer them according to their works: the delight which they found did so fill their

hearts with Assurance of the grace of God, that they looked at their duties, as so many tokens of the love of God unto their soules; and then when men come to finde more comfort in their obedience, than in the grace of God in Jesus Christ, it maketh them ready to expostulate with God touching the worth of their owne righteousness. . . . [T]he disobedience of the Law leaves them without excuse, that so disobey it. Againe, the obedience of it and comfort in that obedience doth harden the hearts of others from Christ.[32]

Cotton sees the law of God after the Fall catching all who live by it in a double bind: those who disobey it are left without excuse, while those who obey it avoid Christ out of hardheartedness. The Miltonic narrator, writing of Eden, longs for what Cotton condemns: delight in achievement filling our hearts with assurance of God's grace. The angel Raphael has advised Adam, "Ofttimes nothing profits more / Than self-esteem, grounded on just and right / Well managed" (8.571–73). William Whately's description of Adam and Eve in Eden, although cited earlier, might forgivably be reprised at least in part to serve as *mise-en-scène* for book 9 of *Paradise Lost*:

Now consider we the benefits God had bestowed upon them before their fall, the making of them after his own Image, in knowledge, righteousnesse and true holinesse, with a most beautiful, strong, swift, healthie and comely body, free from all danger of sicknesse, death, or other misery . . . besides the hope and assurance of Eternall life upon condition of their obedience, of which Paradise it selfe and the tree of life were signes unto them. For if wee should live the life of glory by obeying the Law, so should they have done, seeing they also were under the same Covenant of workes that we be under.[33]

This is how one finds our first parents, who "looked at their duties as so many tokens of the love of God unto their soules," God's priests at "earth's great altar" (9.195), joining "their vocal worship to the quire /Of creatures wanting voice" (199). For Reformers such as William Ames, the covenant of works is merely a straw man for the covenant of grace, an exact abstract equivalent of those sinful Old Testament heroes whom typologists contrast witheringly with Christ. Ames prefers to regard the first relation as a "transaction," reserving "covenant" for the latter, where the culminating fullness of Christ and his dispensation becomes known.[34] In Milton's hands, the original benign Edenic covenant of works becomes not merely a primitive document in the evolving account of humankind's relationship with God but rather a genuine covenant asserting human dignity and participation in creation.[35] If the Miltonic narrator is a Protestant, he is the only one in seventeenth-century England who has constructed a scene of some length (205–384)—the first domestic quarrel—

that evokes the covenant of works without the covenant of grace. Moreover, throughout the discussion, the adequacy of the entirely human is
never in doubt, so long as the numbers suffice. For Eve, work grows, "till
more hands / Aid us" (207–8), but those are the hands of their own children, not of a divine redeemer. Eve believes that she can resist temptation
alone. Adam pronounces Satan "Hopeless to circumvent us joined, where
each / To other speedy aid might lend" (259–60). Later, when Adam
replies to Eve with "healing words" (290), he assumes the role of the
angel Raphael, whose name means "God's healing."

Eve, worrying about the relative inefficiency of labor without children
to help, introduces a note of anxiety about their "day's work brought to
little, though begun early" (9.224). Portraying herself as a laborer hired
on set terms, Eve toils from "early in the morning" (Matt. 20:1), concerned lest the hour of supper come unearned (225). Were she somehow
to have divined Matthew's parable of the laborers in the vineyard, she
might at first have resented the eleventh-hour latecomers, although she
would have been relieved to think that God might not after all be the great
quantifier she imagines him to be. Eve's specific worries evoke Sonnet 19
and a couple of its less comforting scriptural sources, including John 9:4:
"I must work the works of him that sent me, while it is day: the night
cometh, when no man can work." Adam's countertext is decidedly Hebraic: "thou shalt eat the labor of thine hands: happy shalt thou be, and
it shall be well with thee" (Psalm 128:2). In his reply, after conceding
Eve's responsibility to promote "good works" (9.234), Adam explains
the covenant of works as he understands it:

> Yet not so strictly hath our Lord impos'd
> Labor, as to debar us when we need
> Refreshment, whether food, or talk between,
> Food of the mind, or this sweet intercourse
> Of looks and smiles, for smiles from Reason flow.
>
> (9.235–39)

Conversing with Adam, unsmiling Eve reveals a conception of the original covenant of works that, though unfallen, is closer than Adam's to
what that covenant will become after the Fall. Her anxiety sounds like the
"bondage to works" that Ames warns against. Adam characterizes their
responsibilities as "easy" (4.421 and 433). Although Eve does not demur,
she understands her situation under the Edenic covenant of works and
law of obedience as already in some sense "a childhood of prescription."
At least this is how Eve later remembers her unfallen condition, when she
accuses Adam of having been, perhaps like the easy prohibition itself,
"Too facile" (9.1158) and complains, "Being as I am, why didst not thou,
the head, / Command me absolutely not to go [?]" (9.1155–56). Eve

wishes that Adam had been more severe in restraining her before the Fall, when it counted, and less severe now, but Adam's harsher response reflects the difference between Eve's sinless "Desire of wand'ring" (1136) and her transgression (1169). When Eve was innocent and Adam mild, he had incorporated not only Raphael's healing words but also his mission, which was identical to that of the Mosaic law. God had charged his Hebraic angel to warn Adam of danger, lest "he pretend / Surprisal, unadmonished, unforewarned" (5.244–45). This in turn became Adam's mission to Eve in the state of innocence:

> And am I now upbraided as the cause
> Of thy transgressing? Not enough severe,
> It seems, in thy restraint. What could I more?
> I *warned* thee, I *admonished* thee, *foretold*
> The danger. . . .
>
> (9.1168–74; *my emphasis*)

Once sin is introduced into the world, the purpose of the law becomes condemnation, and Adam unstintingly fulfills this purpose as well, even employing the cadences of the Reformers' wrathful deity ("Would thou hadst hearkened to my words" [9.1134]), conveniently neglecting the enormity of his own sin. Originally, the covenant of works and Edenic law were benign, but Eve hints at a potential discontent with both of them that makes her vulnerable to temptation. She imagines the original covenant to be more rigorous than it is, requiring unremitting labor and obedience to absolute commands from Adam as well as God.

Eve brings to her conversation with Satan a sensibility that is incipiently Pauline. Like the former Pharisee of the strictest school, Eve wants to do more and ends up not with less but with nothing. She increases the scope of the prohibition to include even touching the fruit and ends up eating it; she separates from Adam in order to get more work done and ends up doing no gardening at all—indeed, ruining the garden. Hers is compulsive perfectionism grounded in a suspicion of inadequacy. For her, but not for Adam, there will be some relief in laying down the burden of the law. Paul, in Galatians, tells the Jewish Christians that they are debtors to do the whole law (5:3), and Luther, commenting on the verse, describes feelingly his own performance anxiety:

> The more men try to satisfy the Law, the more they transgress it. The more someone tries to bring peace to his conscience through his own righteousness, the more disquieted he makes it. When I was a monk, I made a great effort to live according to the requirements of the monastic rule. I made a practice of confessing and reciting all my sins, but always with prior contrition; I went to confession frequently, and I performed the assigned penances faithfully. Nevertheless, my conscience could never achieve certainty but

was always in doubt and said: "You have not done this correctly. You were
not contrite enough. You omitted this in your confession." Therefore the
longer I tried to heal my uncertain, weak, and troubled conscience . . . the
more uncertain, weak, and troubled I continually made it. . . . For as Paul
says, it is impossible for the conscience to find peace through the works of
the Law.[36]

One recalls that, in *De doctrina Christiana*, Milton refers to two commands in Eden that supersede natural law, those concerning the tree of
knowledge and marriage (*YP*, 6:353). They are the prototypes of the two
tables of the Decalogue, "the love of God and of our neighbor . . . which
is the sum of the law" (*YP*, 6:640). For unfallen Adam, who is decidedly
un-Pauline in his theology, the law does not require a static or pedantic
perfectionism, but supposes a covenant relationship in which human mistakes are forgiven and where God applies a measure of grace. Before Eve
leaves him to work alone, Adam reminds her of this law and warns her of
their foe's possible assault on it:

> Whether his first design be to withdraw
> Our fealty from God, or to disturb
> Conjugal love, than which perhaps no bliss
> Enjoyed by us excites his envy more.
>
> (9.261–64)

The love of God and of each other sums up the benign Edenic law. Eve,
asseverating that her "firm faith and love" cannot be "shaken or seduced" (286–87), shows her understanding of this law in her slightly ruf-
fled reply to Adam's warning:

> But that thou shouldst my firmness therefore doubt
> To God or thee, because we have a foe
> May tempt it, I expected not to hear.
>
> (279–81)

Later, in her solipsistic violation of the law, Eve disregards ethical impulse and social conscience: "Eve / Intent now wholly on her taste, naught
else / Regarded" (785–87). Concentrating on her own experience, Eve
displays the lineaments of romantic religion that Leo Baeck finds in Paul:

Romanticism . . . has an antipathy against any practical idea which might
dominate life, demanding free, creative obedience for its commandments
and showing a clearly determined way to the goals of action. Romanticism
would like to "recover from purpose." . . . In the religious activity demanded by classical religion, man finds himself directed toward others; in
mere religious experience, in this devotion devoid of any commandment, he
seeks everything in himself. He is concerned only with himself, satisfied with
himself, concentrated on himself to the point of religious vanity, of a coquet-

tishness of faith. . . . Nothing could be more opposed to the aspirations of a social conscience than this romantic piety which always seeks only itself and its salvation.[37]

Eve's quantification of works, her perfectionism, and her desire for solitude—all are sinless, although all hint at a terrible resolution in "the end of the law" (Romans 10:4). Satan will ruin Eve by mingling law and gospel, introducing prematurely into a Hebraic dispensation language associated with Christ the Redeemer, who is as yet unknown to our first parents. In Hebraic Eden, Satan's New Testament promises will sound to Eve irresistibly like wish fulfilment and fantasy gratification. The Fall, a quick snatching at immortality, parodies the Christian conversion experience in its suddenness and violates not only the Hebraic prohibition, but also the ethos of the covenant of works. Humankind is to be "under long obedience tried" (7.159), "till by degrees of merit raised" (7.157).

Satan opens the conversation by praising Eve in the terms of worship that he withheld conspicuously from the Son in book 5. Now, in Eve's presence, "Oft he bow'd" (9.524), "Fawning, and lick'd the ground whereon she trod" (526), though, in that earlier book, anticipating the Son's royal progress, he presented himself as a grand republican, refusing to pay "Knee-tribute . . . prostration vile" (5.782). According to Satan, Eve appears as "the Heav'n of mildness" (9.534), yet her "awful brow, more awful thus retired" (537), inspires fear. In the only other use of the word "mildness" in Milton's poetry, the Son clears up the confusion by reminding the Father, "[I] can put on/ Thy terrors, as I put thy mildness on, / Image of thee in all things" (6.734–36).

The rhetorical effect of Satan's first compliments is to induce dissatisfaction in Eve by presenting her with the difference between her present situation and the one she deserves. What makes these satanic compliments incredibly brazen is their source in the distinction between the Son of God and Christ the Redeemer. In the desired future that Satan projects, Eve would displace the Son of God, "Fairest resemblance of thy Maker fair" (538), "adored and served / By angels numberless, thy daily train" (547–48). The crèche that Satan builds in Eve's mind represents her current situation:

> here
> In this enclosure wild, these beasts among,
> Beholders rude, and shallow to discern
> Half what in thee is fair.
>
> (542–45)

In a rare instance of discrepant awareness before the Fall, the reader, but not Eve, recalls the nativity scene and the humiliation of Christ's incarnation. Satan presents the Son's current status in heaven as Eve's future;

Eve's imagined present, mere satanic hyperbole, becomes Christ's actual future condition on earth. Her decision to reject obedience for the experience that Satan promises will necessitate the Son's slow and patient transfer from immortality to mortality to reverse the course of sin.

Upon reaching the tree, Eve reveals her complete understanding of the Hebraic nature of the prohibition:

> of this tree we may not taste nor touch;
> God so commanded, and left that command
> Sole daughter of his voice; the rest, we live
> Law to ourselves, our reason is our law.
>
> (651–54)

To eat the fruit is not to violate an innate rational principle that is intuitively obvious, but rather to transgress a specific divine pronouncement transcending natural law and uttered at a specific point in historical time. Milton, glossing this passage in *De doctrina Christiana*, distinguishes between natural law ("our reason is our law") and positive right, which "comes into play when God . . . commands or forbids things which, if he had not commanded or forbidden them, would in themselves have been neither good nor bad, and would therefore have put no one under any obligation" (*YP*, 6:353).

This distinction between natural law and positive right sounds like Maimonides' distinction between "rational law," prohibiting "things which all people commonly agree are evils," and "statutes . . . which you have no right to subject to criticism, which the nations of the world attack, and which Satan denounces." Maimonides identifies these statutes with the ceremonial law:

> When . . . the rabbis maintain that he who overcomes his desire has more merit and a greater reward [than he who has no temptation], they say so only in reference to laws that are ceremonial prohibitions. This is quite true, since were it not for the Law, they would not at all be considered transgressions. Therefore, the rabbis say that man should permit his soul to entertain the natural inclination for these things, but that the Law alone should restrain him from them.[38]

Lest Maimonides be considered too arcane a source, one should remember that Eve's phrase for the divine echo, "daughter of his voice," translates literally *bat kol*, a specifically rabbinic term that Selden traces back to Maimonides as well as to the Jerusalem Talmud.[39] More important, Selden quotes in Hebrew and Latin the entire lengthy Talmudic passage distinguishing between rational and ceremonial laws that Maimonides paraphrases. This Talmudic passage ("Tit. Joma [i.e., Yoma]. cap 6. fol. 67.b") identifies universal rational law with the Noachide laws, specifically naming the prohibitions against idolatry, sexual sins, homicide, robbery, and blasphemy (*"veluti de Cultu extraneo, Revelatione Tur-pitudinum, Homicidio, Rapina seu Furto, & Maledictione Nominis"*), and it places Jewish dietary prohibitions first in its list of ceremonial laws denounced by Satan.[40]

Eve's formulaic separation of natural law from the divine command is unexceptionable. Containing her first actual quotation of scripture in her conversation with Satan, it is also ominous: "the rest, we live / Law to ourselves, our reason is our law" (653–54). In Romans 2:12–14 Paul distinguishes between Jews and Jewish Christians under the Mosaic law and the Gentiles without it: "For when the Gentiles, which have not the law, do by nature the things contained in the law, these, having not the law, are a law unto themselves" (2:14). Eve is under the divine command ("as many as have sinned in the law shall be judged by the law" [2:12]). She has heard the divine echo, though "not the hearers of the law are just before God, but the doers of the law shall be justified" (2:13). By introducing her lengthy quotation of the prohibition formula (659–63) with the verse from Romans, Eve cues Satan to subvert the divine command by wrenching it from its immediate context in Genesis and reinscribing it in a New Testament context.

Satan follows Eve's cue and sticks to the Talmudic and Maimonidean script ("statutes . . . which Satan denounces") by undermining the ceremonial law, though under the guise of interpreting it. Satan offers two contradictory interpretations of this law, which have nothing in common except their New Testament origin. In the first, the prohibition equals the dead letter of the ceremonial law, which God wants Eve to set aside, as Christ did when he performed works of charity on the Sabbath:

> will God incense his ire
> For such a petty trespass, and not praise
> Rather your dauntless virtue, whom the pain
> Of death denounced, whatever thing death be,
> Deterred not from achieving what might lead
> To happier life, knowledge of good and evil?
>
> (692–97)

Suggesting that God will approve of Eve's eating the fruit, Satan submits the dietary prohibition to the judgment of the gospel, where it becomes a law to be abrogated. His central text here is the episode of hungry Peter's vision at Jaffa, "Rise, Peter; kill, and eat" (Acts 10:13), which abolishes the distinction between clean and unclean foods. Milton's contemporary polemics provides a corrective judgment: Satan treats as dispensable what is in fact an indispensable law. In *Doctrine and Discipline of Divorce*, Milton had attacked the canon law position that the deuteronomic law of divorce, which he regarded as a divine command permanently binding, was only a temporary permission, a concession to the hard-heartedness of the Jews: "that God . . . should enact a dispensation as long liv'd as a law whereby to live in priviledg'd adultery for hardnes of heart . . . is the most deadly and Scorpion like gift that the enemy of mankind could have given to any miserable sinner, and is rather such a dispence as that which the serpent gave to our first parents" (*YP*, 2:300). Satan can thus be regarded here as a prototype of the canon law apologist offering license, in the form of dispensation and indulgence, for uncontrolled behavior.

In Satan's second interpretation, God is both impotent and malevolent, and he has imposed the prohibition "to keep ye low and ignorant" (704). To this conception of a creator-God, the only deity Eve knows, Satan opposes a new conception of salvation that derives great force from a tightly compressed series of Pauline verses:

> So ye shall die perhaps, by putting off
> Human, to put on Gods, death to be wished,
> Though threatened, which no worse than this can bring.
>
> (713–15)

In this presentation of salvation free of charge, the scope of demonic mischief is almost infinite. Satan abuses Pauline doctrine by denuding it of its Christological import and by linking it to mechanical process. If "this corruptible must put on incorruption, and this mortal shall have put on immortality" (1 Cor. 15:53), it is only because Christ, the life-giving spirit, dies to redeem the sin of the first Adam. But in prelapsarian Eden, only one Adam exists, and Eve is married to him. Satan distorts every Pauline echo in this passage,[41] prematurely introducing New Testament doctrine into a Hebraic dispensation where it is glaringly inappropriate. The resurrection of the dead offers comfort only after the Fall, not now, when Eve's immortality is contingent upon continued obedience to the divine commandment. Where Paul, in Colossians 3, confounds distinctions between Greek and Jew, circumcised and uncircumcised, slave and free man, Satan confounds the necessary distinctions between human beings and God and between Edenic and Gospel conceptions of immortality, transformation, and salvation. The common theme that runs through all the relevant Pauline verses, to live in God's image, imitating him as his likeness, becomes in Satan's mouth an exhortation to attain godship.

Satan first presents a benevolent God who tests Eve's courage and her obedience to the living spirit rather than the dead letter and who wants her to abrogate the dietary prohibition, and then a malevolent, impotent God who fears her dying into divinity. Satan's entire temptation of Eve is an arabesque, nowhere more dizzying than in the quick arguments that come between the two contradictory presentations. These arguments—

beginning in Plato and culminating in Paul—deflect Eve's attention from the saving letter of the proto-Mosaic law. Distorting the meaning of the qualities that he names, Satan praises Eve's "dauntless virtue" (694) leading to "knowledge" (697). In the *Symposium*, Socrates commends those whose creative desire is of the soul and identifies the progeny of the soul as "wisdom and virtue,"[42] which are the ends of natural law. For Milton, too, in the platonic allegory of *Comus* and in *An Apology*, "the first and chiefest office of love, begins and ends in the soule, producing those happy twins of her divine generation knowledge and vertue."[43] But, as Eve herself has explained to Satan (651–54) and as Milton insists in *De doctrina*, the divine prohibition has "nothing to do with the law of nature" (*YP*, 6:373), which it supersedes. Milton's view accords with that of Arminius, who insists that eating the fruit in Eden, "an act in its own nature indifferent" and a transgression only because God forbade it, does not violate natural law: "From this shine forth the admirable benignity and kindness of God; whose will it was to have experience of the obedience of his creature, in an act which that creature could with the utmost facility omit, without injury to his nature, and even without detriment to his pleasure."[44] Satan wants Eve to see it differently: since this is not a moral law but merely a proto-ceremonial statute, its transgression will be unaccompanied by instinctive remorse. With a slight satanic push, an indifferent act becomes a positive good. Far from violating natural law, Eve, exercising virtue to acquire wisdom, fulfills it. As the angel in her dream has already told her, everybody wins if she eats the fruit: "since good, the more / Communicated, more abundant grows, / The author not impaired, but honored more" (5.71–73).

Continuing, Satan speaks of divine power and justice and of evil. Knowledge, whether of good or evil, must lead to a happier life:

> Of good, how just? Of evil, if what is evil
> Be real, why not known, since easier shunned?
> God therefore cannot hurt ye, and be just;
> Not just, not God; not feared then, nor obeyed:
> Your fear itself of death removes the fear.

> (698–702)

This sorites prepares Eve for the forthcoming presentation of a deity both malevolent and feeble, and it exploits traditional formulations of the problem of theodicy, specifically, of God's permitting evil to exist. As David Hume succinctly puts it: "Is [God] willing to prevent evil, but not able? then he is impotent. Is he able, but not willing? then he is malevolent. Is he both able and willing? when thence is evil?"[45] Lactantius in his thorough formulation of the problem quotes Epicurus:

> God . . . either wishes to take away evils, and is unable; or He is able, and is
> unwilling; or He is neither willing nor able, or He is both willing and able.
> If He is willing and is unable, He is feeble, which is not in accordance with
> the character; if He is able and unwilling, He is envious, which is equally at
> variance with God; if He is neither willing nor able, He is both envious and
> feeble, and therefore not God; if He is both willing and able, which alone is
> suitable to God, from what source then are evils? or why does He not remove
> them?[46]

Since Satan himself is the author of evil, he can hardly be expected to pose
without emendation the traditional questioning of his very existence. His
brazen strategy is to substitute for himself the simple, literal prohibition.
God may be good, both willing and able to remove the prohibition, and
indeed you will obey him best by eating the fruit. God may be omnipotent
but unjust, and an omnipotent tyrant ought not to be obeyed. Finally,
God may be both feeble and envious, but death means putting on immortality and becoming divine, so evil does not really exist apart from the
forbidder himself. These arguments questioning the authority of the divine command only superficially resemble those questioning the "high
permission of all ruling Heaven" (1.212) to suffer evil to exist.[47]

The final argument, bridging the two central, contradictory interpretations of the prohibition, is the most faithful to its source and for that very
reason may be the most important: "Your fear itself of death removes the
fear" (9.702). This verse, paradoxical and overdetermined, assures Eve
that her fear of punishment from God is unfounded, since any god who
would hurt her could not be God. Satan attempts to remove the objects of
Eve's fear—both death and the law—by proving that she has already removed them. The ambiguity and compression of "removes the fear" reflect Paul's frequent, urgent identifications of the law with death (Romans
7:7–8:13) and his own overdetermined plea: "who shall deliver me from
the body of this death?" (7:24). The source of Satan's verse is the Pauline
paradox "For I through the law am dead to the law" (Galatians 2:19).
Richard Sibbes explains that one's fear of the law itself removes fear of
the law:

> The covenant of works is taught to shew us our failing, that seeing our own
> disability to perform what the law requireth, we may be forced to the new
> covenant of grace. And therefore, saith Paul, "By the law I am dead to the
> law," Gal.ii.19. It is an excellent speech, "By the law I am dead to the law";
> by the covenant of works I am dead to the covenant of works. That is, by the
> law's exacting of me exact and perpetual obedience in thought, word, and
> deed, I come to see that I cannot fulfil it, and therefore am dead to the law;
> that is, I look for no salvation, for no title to heaven by that.[48]

The impasse that Paul reaches in this verse reflects the torment of his inability to perform the Mosaic law. To escape requires transformation, a radical change of perspective in which some newly gained knowledge brings about a changed way of understanding. If the "fear itself of death" is fear of the law, then only dying in Christ "removes the fear." Paul abandons his former identity, symbolized by law and epitomized as sin, in order to be "alive unto God through Jesus Christ" (Rom. 6:11). This, of course, is the language of conversion. In his temptation of Eve, Satan exploits the inseparability in Paul's thought of the end of the law and conversion. The Miltonic bard's strategy here is simple and brilliant: to conflate the Mosaic and Edenic law and then to rely on the extensive and persuasive arguments of the apostle of the annihilation of the law. What Paul did for Christianity in his mission to the gentiles, persuading them to be dead to sin by being dead to the law, Satan did for Eve.

The noonday devil, promising a "death to be wished," "putting off / Human, to put on Gods," assures Eve that in becoming divine her vision as well as her nature will be transformed:

> . . . your eyes that seem so clear,
> Yet are but dim, shall perfectly be then
> Opened and cleared, and ye shall be as Gods.
>
> (706–8)

To the serpent's argument in Genesis, "your eyes shall be opened, and ye shall be as gods" (3:5), Milton's Satan adds the idea of abandoning the dim, narrow, and blurred old way of seeing. The accounts of Paul's noonday experience on the road to Damascus employ the imagery of light and darkness that is standard in conversion.[49] Through the agency of Ananias, Saul learns the truth of his experience and "immediately there fell from his eyes as it had been scales" (Acts 9:18). Later Paul tells King Agrippa of "a light from heaven, above the brightness of the sun," and of his mission to the gentiles, "to open their eyes, and to turn them from darkness to light" (Acts 26:13 and 18). Satan joins the serpent's argument in Genesis with Paul's descriptions of transforming vision—although he quotes selectively, omitting, for example, the phrase that immediately follows "from darkness to light": "and from the power of Satan unto God" (26:18).

Satan's temptation of Eve is a social-science textbook example of conversion:

Conversions are transitions to identities which are proscribed within the person's established universes of discourse, and which exist in universes of discourse that negate these formerly established ones. The ideal conversion experience can be thought of as the embracing of a negative identity. The person becomes something which was specifically prohibited.[50]

The Pauline nature of the conversion becomes especially evident when one compares Milton's tempter with Joseph Beaumont's Ovidian serpent, who promises Eve

> A Death of Life, which will destroy you so
> That you no longer Creatures shall remain;
> But by this Metamorphosis shall grow
> Above your selves, and into Gods be slaine.

> (*Psyche*, 6:244)

Satan and Paul are themselves converts who attempt to reduce the inevitable cognitive dissonance that results from making hard decisions by adopting the classic solutions to postdecisional disconfirmation: proselytizing and exegesis.[51] Choosing to rebel against his creator, Satan knows that he should love him, but feels that he hates him. Painfully aware of the choices refused and the defects in the option exercised, Satan, in his soliloquy in book 4, evinces indecision although the decision has already been made. There he meditates on the law before his rebellion, when it was easy to keep:

> . . . nor was his service hard.
> What could be less than to afford him praise,
> The easiest recompense, and pay him thanks,
> How due! yet all his good prov'd ill in me,
> And wrought but malice; lifted up so high
> I sdein'd subjection, and thought one step higher
> Would set me highest, and in a moment quit
> The debt immense of endless gratitude,
> So burdensome, still paying, still to owe;
> Forgetful what from him I still receiv'd,
> And understood not that a grateful mind
> By owing owes not, but still pays, at once
> Indebted and discharg'd; what burden then?

> (4.45–57)

As John Reading points out, "The divell doth mainely labour to bring men downe the same way by which himselfe fell."[52] Satan candidly describes, first, his actual condition under a benign law that requires only a grateful mind, then, his conception of that law as burdensome, requiring eternal indebtedness, and underscoring the insufficiency of the poor debtor, and, finally, his attempt to escape in a moment from that law— nor was Godhead from his thought. Satan's subsequent career in Eden is a series of attempts to neutralize his torment by employing mechanisms that will appear to increase the attractiveness of his choice. He converts Eve, who imagines God's law to be more rigorous than it is, in the process substituting a spiritual reading of Genesis 2:17 for the literal prohibition. It is after the experience of disconfirmation that conversion provides essential social validation (if more people believe it, it must be true),[53] and, for Satan, exegesis is nothing but the continuation of war by other means.

Behind Satan's confession "yet all his good prov'd ill in me" lies Romans 7:7–12. There Paul distinguishes between the content of the Mosaic law, which is of divine origin and therefore good, and the effect of the law, which, through the machinations of Sin (here regarded as a quasi-demonic power), gives rise to sin and death. The argument of these verses is not simply that the law reveals sin, but that in some mysterious way the effect of this good law is to arouse sin.[54] The distinction between the nature and the effect of the law, as well as the many contradictory Pauline answers to the problem of the value of the Torah after the Christ event—these suggest permanently unresolved conflicts within Paul the Apostle who was once Saul the Pharisee.

Romans 7 furnishes Satan with the crucial argument that Eve is dead to the law. Paul begins the chapter, addressed "to them that know the law," by using an obscure aspect of rabbinic law in a completely new context. The obverse of his assertion "that the law hath dominion over a man as long as he liveth" (7:1) is the rabbinic maxim that a dead person is free from the duties of the law.[55] Paul uses this legal principle to carry the message that a convert need not worry about the law: the person who has died in Christ is dead to this aeon and has become free from the law (Rom. 7:6), for the messianic future era of the world has already begun. For Paul, as for the talking serpent, Torah has lost its status as *halakhah* (law), becoming instead *aggadah* (story) in the form of midrash, typology, or allegory. Satan transfers his struggle with God to the arena of textual politics, where "thou shalt not eat" becomes "eat" and where "thou shalt die" becomes a promise of divinity.

Moving farther away from the saving letter of God's command, Eve complains of her ignorance under a childhood of prescription:

> What fear I then, rather what know to fear
> Under this ignorance of good and evil,
> Of God or death, of law or penalty?
>
> (9.773–75)

Paul's references to the Mosaic law as schoolmaster (Galatians 3:23–25) and to those under the law as children (Ephesians 4:14) express his belief that only Christians have attained their majority. Calvin explains Paul's use of the word "childhood" to indicate "slenderness of understanding": "It was the Lord's will that this childhood be trained in the elements of this world and in little external observances, as rules for children's instruction, until Christ should shine forth, through whom the knowledge of believers was to mature."[56] Eve's Pauline view of God's command as one of his "little external observances," designed to keep her a child, fuses with the opinion of some Reformation expositors that, before their Fall, Adam and Eve romped naked like children. Wolfgang Musculus notes that nakedness before the Fall "was not subject to any filthynesse":

> The example whereof we see dayly in children, whiche be never so happy as when they be as it were in Paradise, without al care, not ashamed of their nakednes: but after they begin to grow to reason, immediately their eyes be opened to shame, as though they had eaten of the forbidden apple.[57]

If our first parents are children under the law, by sinning they "grow to reason." The Miltonic bard understands the danger of viewing Edenic law as primitive. Hence, Milton's God permits Raphael to unfold for Adam and Eve the "secrets of another world" (5.569), and the divine historian, through "friendly condescension," relates unsearchable knowledge (8.6–10). Prelapsarian intellect belies Eve's ultimately Pauline profession of ignorance.

Equally dubious is her characterization of saving knowledge as the grand act of simplification that she craves:

> Here grows the cure of all, this fruit divine,
> Fair to the eye, inviting to the taste,
> Of virtue to make wise; what hinders then
> To reach, and feed at once both body and mind?
>
> (9.776–79)

These last words before Eve's fall are ominous. They reveal Satan's success in driving a wedge between natural reason and divine revelation. The two contradictory answers to her final question "what hinders?," both "nothing" and "God's command," underscore the different imperatives of natural law and divine law, which, if not identical, coexist harmoniously before the Fall, when "God and Nature bid the same" (6.176). While Eve, professing ignorance, pretends interest in the separate vast topics she lists (good, evil, God, death, law, and penalty), she actually craves "the cure of all" "at once." She is self-centered, not much interested in the world's variety, which she lumps together as "all."[58] Eve does not want to earn her blessing, under long obedience tried, but to experience it without effort. Her faith that the fruit itself will grant the eater magic powers is a romantic myth. Leo Baeck describes faith in the romantic religion that he associates specifically with Paul:

> This faith is therefore decidedly not the expression of a conviction obtained through struggle, or of a certainty grown out of search and inquiry. Seeking and inquiring is only "wisdom of the flesh" and the manner of "philoso-

phers and rabbis." True knowledge is not worked out by man but worked in him; man cannot clear a way toward it; only the flood of grace brings it to him and gives him the quintessence of knowledge, the totality of insight.[59]

In the interval of silence between "what hinders" and her eating, it is necessary to remember that, in Milton's Hebraic Eden, Eve under the law is even at this moment guiltless. The proto-Mosaic law pronounces "Do this and live; do it not, and die." Eve is "yet sinless" because she has not yet disobeyed God's command. Although the "cure *of all*" will turn out to be the Fall, Eve's *craving* is not a transgression. Here Milton disagrees with most Puritan theologians, who are incapable of imagining a Hebraic dispensation. For William Ames, "Man was a sinner, before he had finished that outward act of eating. Whence it is that the very desire which *Eve* was caried with toward the forbidden Fruit, doth seeme to be noted, as some degree of her sin."[60] Ames recontextualizes the divine command of Genesis in the sermon on the mount:

> Ye have heard that it was said by them of old time, Thou shalt not commit adultery: but I say unto you, That whosoever looketh on a woman to lust after her hath committed adultery with her already in his heart. (Matt. 5:27–28)

Ames convicts Eve of desire, which is the first motion of disobedience. In Milton's Eden, the interdiction is itself Decalogic, the law "of old time, Thou shalt not" (Deut. 5:18), to which Christ refers specifically. Milton understands the divine command as ethically sublime and actualized sin as a transgression against this holiness. Before the Fall, the hellenized preference for an enlightened, philosophical religion of inwardness in contrast to the primitive superstition of an external, cultic, ceremonial commandment is satanic propaganda. The dietary prohibition must be taken literally as the prime example of "the Scriptures protesting their own plainnes, and perspicuity":

> to inferre a general obscurity over all the text, is a meer suggestion of the Devil to disswade men from reading it, and casts an aspersion of dishonour both upon the *mercy*, *truth*, and *wisdome* of God. . . . [T]o require strict, and punctual obedience, and yet give out all his commands ambiguous and obscure, we should think he had a plot upon us, certainly such commands were no commands, but snares. (*Of Reformation*, YP, 1:566)

Eve's first words upon eating complicate the plainness of the scriptural prohibition. Where Christian tradition parallels the tree of the cross and the tree of sin, Eve confuses them. She unconsciously evokes the Christ she does not know whose satisfaction her sin will require, displacing the gratitude due him upon the source of her woe:

> O Sovran, virtuous, precious of all Trees
> In Paradise, of operation blest
> To Sapience, hitherto obscur'd, infam'd,
> And thy fair Fruit let hang, as to no end
> Created; but henceforth my early care,
> Not without song, each Morning, and due praise
> Shall tend thee, and the fertile burden ease
> Of thy full branches offer'd free to all;
> Till dieted by thee I grow mature
> In knowledge, as the Gods who all things know.
>
> (795–804)

In one of the epic's rare references to the crucifixion, this book's lyrical prologue regards it as a topic hitherto "Unsung" (33). Now, as priestess, Eve will sing not of the cross or of the Son of God crowned with "Sapience" (7.195), but of the tree, "hitherto obscur'd, infam'd." Had it referred to the eventual source of life after the Fall, rather than to the source of death, Eve's complaint, "And thy fair Fruit let hang," might have come from the *Improperia* of the Good Friday liturgy or from Herbert's "The Sacrifice":

> O all ye who passe by, behold and see;
> Man stole the fruit, but I must climbe the tree,
> The tree of life to all, but onely me.
>
> (201–3)

Through justification, Christ's righteousness will be imputed to all believers so that subjection to due punishment will become instead remission, "a disburdening, a taking away, a removing."[61] Before the Fall, paradoxically, nature, "by disburd'ning grows / More fruitful" (5.319–20), and later, after Christ's mediation, the regenerate Christian in a state of Christian liberty will lay down an intolerable burden of sin and thereby grow more fruitful. Now Eve offers to ease the tree's burden, dispensing fruit as Christ will dispense grace, "free to all"—although she is actually dispensing universal death.

The tree is "a Sacrament of death,"[62] and Eve's desire to attain divine knowledge by eating (803–4) recalls Satan's appetite-whetting question: "And what are Gods that Man may not become / As they, participating God-like food?" (716–17). Both passages anticipate the Roman Catholic Mass. Milton distinguishes strenuously between the Lord's Supper and the Mass (*YP*, 6:552–62; *De doctrina Christiana*, 1:xxviii). The former is acceptable because it is merely commemorative; only faith can feed the believer, and the living flesh and blood of Christ is doctrine (553–57). Milton derides the Mass for promising eternal life through feeding, and he tries to reduce the sacrament to absurdity by tracing the passage of Christ's chewed-up body "through all the stomach's filthy channels," until it is shot out—"one shudders even to mention it—into the latrine" (560). The only two sacraments that Milton accepts, the Lord's Supper and Baptism, cast their shadows on this book. The first is an act of virtuous eating, in opposition to Eve's antisacrament. The second, a visible sign of Christ's satisfaction (*YP*, 6:542–52), stands behind Satan's promise that Eve will put off humanity to put on divinity. Baptism is the conversion rite that for Paul is "the central definition of the new Christian community, based on the Hebrew purity ritual of immersion, reinterpreted so that, once done, its purification powers last forever."[63] Since all who undergo baptism experience death and resurrection, being in Christ is a "death to be wished."

Following the Pauline paradigm outlined by Baeck, Eve praises "Experience," her "best guide" (807–8):

> For the romantic the living deed is supplanted by the grace whose vessel he would be; the law of existence, by mere faith; reality, by the miracle of salvation. . . . [H]e wants less to live than to experience—or, to use the German, he prefers *erleben* to *leben*. . . . [Religious romanticism proclaims] faith in a force of grace, entering the believer from above through a sacrament, to redeem him from the bonds of earthly guilt and earthly death and to awaken him to a new life which would mean eternal existence and blessedness.[64]

Before she sinned, Eve was guiltless and immortal. Whether or not she was experienced is a matter of some disagreement. Christine Froula, on Eve's side, reads her act of disobedience as a heroic quest for knowledge: "to cease respecting the authority fetish of an invisible power and to see the world for herself":

> That *Paradise Lost*, the story of the Fall, is a violent parable of *gnosis* punished attests to the threat that Eve's desire for experienced rather than mediated knowledge poses to an authority which defines and proves itself chiefly in the prohibition of all other authorities.[65]

Barbara Lewalski reads Eve's fall precisely as her acceptance of mediated knowledge over personal experience. Eve accepts the serpent's false report instead of judging "by what her own experience has taught her of God's beneficence."[66] Of course this assumes what Froula would not concede—Eve's felt knowledge that God's will is not inimical to her own. In a Reformation context, Eve's surrender of authority and responsibility constitutes implicit faith, a principle promulgated by the Inquisition and vehemently opposed by Milton.[67]

Doctrine, at least compared with poetry, usually offers interpretive certainty, although sometimes at an unaffordable price. Once Adam joins Eve in sin, Eden becomes doctrinally as well as poetically an interpretive no-man's-land, and it becomes difficult to locate the precise moment when a Hebraic ethos has yielded to a Christian one. The interval between Eve's sin and Adam's poses serious and perhaps insoluble interpretive problems—for example, should Adam now divorce Eve? pray for her? join her?—but at this point law still appears to dominate over gospel, making the passage more determinable, doctrinally if not poetically. Eve's romantic "agony of love till now / Not felt" (858–59)—"the pain of absence from thy sight" (861)—introduces Adam to New Testament diction, notably absent from her earlier speech, when work came first. Eve urges Adam to eat now,

> Lest thou not tasting, different degree
> Disjoin us, and I then too late renounce
> Deity for thee.
>
> (883–85)

The Miltonic bard, allowing irony free play, has Eve declare that, if necessary, she will become mortal for love, undergoing a *kenosis* like Christ's. The actual disjunction that now baffles conversation is not, as Eve intimates, between goddess and mortal, but rather between her vain gospel without Christ and a law that still offers Adam salvation. Adam dramatizes the disparity by judging Eve's sin according to the standards of the law and by not reacting at all to her good news, which he seems not to have heard.

Where Satan seduced Eve with the Pauline promise of "Internal" transformation (711; 1 Cor. 15:44–46), Adam submits her sin to the judgment of the Hebrew Bible. He invokes the visible creation ("God's works" [897]) and the law ("the strict forbiddance" transgressed [903]), and he alludes both to the cultic prohibition against violating a temple offering sacred to God (903–4) and to the Levitical law of the justice-ban, the sentence by the proper authorities on the idolater and the blasphemer. Eve, "to death devote" (901), falls under the ban: "None devoted, which shall be devoted of men, shall be redeemed; but shall surely be put to death" (Lev. 27:29; see also Exod.22:20).

Adam's remarkable next speech enumerates laws that Eve has already broken and those that he will momentarily break himself. The trajectory of their fall can be marked by their violation first of laws applying only to Israelites, then of those binding upon gentile converts to Christianity, resident aliens, and unaffiliated God-fearers. By the end of the speech, "manifold in sin," they will be pagans, stripped of all privilege, convicted by Pauline as well as Hebraic ethical systems. Adam begins by echoing Satan's praise of Eve's "dauntless virtue" (694):

> Bold deed thou hast presum'd, advent'rous *Eve*,
> And peril great provok't, who thus hath dar'd
> Had it been only coveting to Eye
> That sacred Fruit, sacred to abstinence,
> Much more to taste it under ban to touch.
>
> (921–25)

Eve has abandoned the lower law of obedience for the sake of some higher inward law, as Samson, moved by "intimate impulse," married the woman of Timna. But this passage will insist on the importance of that outward law, benign until, as a result of disobedience, it proliferates uncontrollably. Even now, to what was merely a prohibition against eating, Adam adds the sins of coveting, eyeing what belongs to another, and touching. By the end of the speech, the white light of the original prohibition will have been broken up into countless refractive prohibitions of every color, a spectrum of offenses.

For Paul, and for Milton in *De doctrina Christiana*, the tenth commandment, "Thou shalt not covet," represents the entire Decalogue. In Romans 7, trying to convince Roman Jewish Christians to break the ties that still bind them to the non-Christian Jewish community, Paul insists that the effect of the Mosaic law is to intensify the dominion of sin. Acknowledging the inherent goodness of the law but emphasizing its evil effects, he claims that through it comes concrete experience of sin. As has already been seen, Milton cites Paul's reading of the tenth commandment to prove that Christians are released from the entire Mosaic law, including the Decalogue:

> [7:7:] "I had not known sin but by the law," that is, the whole law, for the expression is unlimited, "for I had not known lust, except the law had said, Thou shalt not covet." It is in the decalogue that the injunction here specified is contained; we are therefore absolved from subjection to the decalogue as fully as to the rest of the law. (*CE*, 16:125)

By evoking Romans 7 as well as the Hebraic Decalogic prohibition (Exod. 20:17; Deut. 5:21), Eve's sin of coveting reinforces the connections between the Edenic and Mosaic laws. Those laws simultaneously evoke Paul and sever relations with his religious and ethical system, for, in Romans 7, Paul insists that to be baptized is to die to the law. Eve is not a Christian beyond the reach of the Torah. Her desire for the fruit underscores instead Paul's ultrapharisaic opinion that to violate one commandment is to break the entire law. Antedating Paul, and drawing on Stoic and Aristotelian views of desire and on rabbinic opinion regarding the tenth commandment, Philo intimates that the breaking of this commandment will ultimately lead to the breaking of all other commandments: "For plunderings and robberies and repudiations of debts and false accusations and outrages, also seductions, adulteries, murders and all wrongful actions" flow from "desire . . . , the fountain of all evils."[68] As Harry Austryn Wolfson points out,

> This list of wrongdoings is almost a summary of the things prohibited in the ten commandments. Philo seems to say that the reason why the tenth commandment prohibits one from desiring a neighbor's house or wife or manservant or maidservant or ox or ass or anything that belongs to him, is that such a desire will lead to the breaking of the commandments against murder and adultery and stealing and bearing false witness against one's neighbor and also the first five commandments which deal with things sacred.[69]

Philo relies on the tenth commandment for the argument that the Pentateuch requires virtuous character as well as virtuous action. He singles out desire as a voluntary emotion that "derives its origin from ourselves," inasmuch as its freedom has been implanted within us by God as a special gift.[70]

In book 9, after the Fall, the benign interpretation of Eden's Hebraic law gives way to the hostile view that led Paul to the impasse of Romans 7, but with no way to break that impasse. Eve was innocent until she ate the fruit, but, in the fallen world, one transgresses the tenth commandment as soon as desire is conceived in the heart. Milton makes this clear when he cites this prohibition as the first example of actual sin "By thoughts. Exod. xx. 17. 'thou shalt not covet [*ne concupiscito*] thy neighbor's house—' " (*CE*, 15:198–99). Although Raphael reproves Adam's desire for Eve ("In loving thou dost well, in passion not" [8.588]), it is sinless. After the Fall, by coveting, eyeing, and touching, Adam actualizes sin (9.1034–37), violating the tenth commandment's double prohibitions of *tahmod* ("covet," which requires possession) and *tit'aveh* ("desire," which only requires thought). He hints at the Decalogic nature of the prohibition when he boasts to Eve, "if such pleasure be / In things to us forbidden, it might be wish'd, / For this one Tree had been forbidden ten" (1024–26).

Immediately after acknowledging the sin of disobedience, Adam tests his first excuse on Eve:

> Perhaps thou shalt not Die, perhaps the Fact
> Is not so heinous now, foretasted Fruit,
> Profan'd first by the Serpent, by him first
> Made common and unhallow'd ere our taste.
>
> (928–31)

To eat food profaned first by the serpent, that towering idol of living gold (9.497–503), is to violate the thrice-repeated Apostolic Decree defining a minimum of practice for new gentile Christians: "We should not trouble those of the Gentiles who turn to God, but should write to them to abstain from the pollutions of idols." (Acts 15:20, 15:29, and 21:25). Satan is a demon-idol transformed into the "Image of a Brute" (1.371 and 9.507–8; Romans 1:23). Eve's idolatrous state after her sin is amply revealed by her invocation of the "Sovran" tree (9.795–833) and her homage to it in "low Reverence" (9.834–38). When Adam tastes what he believes has been twice foretasted, he uses food polluted by idolatry and thus violates a minimum standard of decency and ethical practice binding on non-Jews as well as Jews. The Apostolic Decree of Acts, recognizing that being in Christ does not always signify ethical seriousness, set down for gentile converts from paganism to Christianity moral requirements whose rejection, ipso facto, kept one outside the pale of salvation.[71]

Whereas the sin of covetousness violates the Decalogue, a Mosaic law governing Israel as a holy nation, Adam's sin of commensality, of a lower order, signifies his degeneration. This is a sin under Hebraic, rabbinic, and Christian dispensations. Behind the Apostolic Decree in Acts are the Levitical laws that apply to resident aliens (17–18) and the rabbinic Noachide laws, binding upon every living soul, which had been given to humankind before the special revelation on Mount Sinai, laws such as those proclaimed by Sophocles in the *Antigone* "that are not of today nor yesterday but are forever."[72]

As early as *Animadversions*, Milton notes that "to eat the good creatures of God once offer'd to Idols, is in Saint *Pauls* account to have fellowship with Devils, and to partake of the Devils Table" (*YP*, 1:687). In *Eikonoklastes*, he interprets broadly Paul's warning against using food after it had been offered to idols (1 Cor. 8). He rather cruelly derides the dead king's last prayer because it was lifted from "a Heathen fiction," "the vain amatorious Poem of *Sr Philip Sidneys Arcadia*." He asserts "that if only to tast wittingly of meat or drink offerd to an Idol, be in the doctrin of St. Paul judg'd a pollution, much more must be his sin who takes a prayer, so dedicated, into his mouth, and offers it to God" (*YP*, 3:362–64).

A less polemical and more literal interpretation of the warning against eating explicitly designated as a cultic act appears in the section on idolatry in *De doctrina*, where it is consistently linked with fornication:

We are commanded to abstain, not only from idolatrous worship itself, but from all things and persons connected with it. Acts xv.20. "that they abstain from pollutions of idols, and from fornication." v.29. "from meats offered to idols . . . and from fornication." Rev. ii. 14. "who taught Balak to cast a stumbling-block before the children of Israel, to eat things sacrificed unto idols, and to commit fornication." v. 20. "to commit fornication, and to eat things sacrificed unto idols." From a comparison of these passages, it would appear that the fornication here prohibited was a part of idolatrous worship. (CE, 17:143–45)[73]

In 1 Corinthians 10:7, Paul warns: "Neither be ye idolaters, as were some of them; as it is written, the people sat down to eat and drink, and rose up to play." After the Fall, Adam's famous words to Eve—"now let us play, / As meet is, after such delicious Fare" (9.1027–28)—are more than a newly debased courtier's invitation to dalliance. They clarify the nature of our first parents' participation, through food and fornication, in idolatrous celebration.

1 Corinthians 10 is Paul's response to a disputed question, whether one is allowed to eat meat offered to idols. Paul labels the two sides of the controversy the "strong" and the "weak." The strong, mainly gentile Christians, ignore the Mosaic dietary laws, adopting a weak-boundary position in their understanding of the relationship between the Christian community and the larger society. The "weak," mainly Jewish Christians, keep the laws and when in doubt eat only vegetables with their comrades. Paul considers himself one of the strong (Rom. 15:1), but for the sake of table fellowship outlines a diplomatic principle of conciliation, whereby the strong avoid foods that the weak despise.[74]

Christ in *Paradise Regained* rejects commensality in the banquet temptation. Where the biblical Daniel, resolving not to defile his ritual status by eating the king's food, had adopted the position of vegetarianism (Dan. 1:8–19) identified by Paul as "weak," Christ is even more careful. In a dream he sees himself "as a guest with *Daniel* at his pulse" (*PR*, 2.278), but awake he rejects food entirely, although Satan objects:

> nor mention I
> Meats by the Law unclean, or offer'd first
> To Idols, those young *Daniel* could refuse.
>
> (2.327–29)

Christ never suggests that he can eat foods unclean according to the Mosaic law. Later, on the pinnacle of the temple, he refuses to anticipate God's will. His final words in the brief epic, "Tempt not the Lord thy God" (4.561), constitute his own refusal to sin, an indictment of Satan, and a reversal of the first Adam's sin in Eden.

De doctrina Christiana, more directly than *Paradise Regained*, connects the prohibition against eating foods offered first to idols with that against tempting God. Three paragraphs after the condemnation of idolatry by means of food and fornication, Milton adds:

Another thing which is opposed to the invocation of God is the temptation of God. Exod.xvii.7: *they tempted Jehovah, saying Is Jehovah among us or not?* Psal. lxxviii.18, 19: *tempting the mighty God in their heart, and speaking obloquy against God. Can God, they said, raise up a table in this wilderness?*, and lxxviii.41: *they tempted God, and set limits to the Holy One of Israel*, and xciv.7: *saying, Jah does not see, the God of Jacob does not regard it. . . .* Matt.iv.7: *you shall not tempt the Lord your God*; 1 Cor. x.22: *do we provoke the Lord's jealousy? Are we stronger than He?* (*YP*, 6:695–96)

Adam's speech to Eve similarly conjoins the sins of commerce with idols and the temptation of God. His arguments limit the power of God and deny the effects of disobedience, revealing the culpability after the Fall of disbelief in God's wrath. Eve's earlier temptation of God is best glossed by scripture, Psalm 94:7, cited above. She imagines that God does not regard her sin: "And I perhaps am secret; Heaven is high, / High and remote to see from thence distinct / Each thing on earth" (811–13). Adam's version of the sin is more sophisticated, and it is thus appropriately glossed by scriptural hermeneutics. Reasoning from self that the fame of the creator depends on the fate of the creature,[75] he sets aside fear of destruction:

> Nor can I think that God, Creator wise,
> Though threat'ning, will in earnest so destroy
> Us his prime Creatures, dignifi'd so high,
> Set over all his Works, which in our Fall,
> For us created, needs with us must fail,
> Dependent made; so God shall uncreate,
> Be frustrate, do, undo, and labor lose,
> Not well conceiv'd of God, who though his Power
> Creation could repeat, yet would be loath
> Us to abolish, lest the Adversary
> Triumph and say; Fickle their State whom God
> Most Favors, who can please him long? Mee first
> He ruin'd, now Mankind; whom will he next?
> Matter of scorn, not to be given the Foe.
>
> (*938–51*)

William Ames identifies this sin as the "tempting of God":

This sinne doth oft times flow from doubting or unbeliefe: because he who seeks such *triall* of God, doth not sufficiently trust the revealed word of God. . . . It flowes also from a certaine arrogancy and pride, whereby we refusing to subject our wills to the Will of God, doe seeke to make his will subject to our lust. But it comes most often from presumption, whereby one is confident that God will doe this, or that, which he no where promised.[76]

Ames and Milton place Adam in exactly the same transitional situation—after Eve's act of disobedience and before his own—and both find him tempting God in the same way. Ames's Adam chooses a "tempting . . . of Man towards God, wherein he did in a certaine manner make triall of the truth and Grace of God: namely making triall, whether God would preserve him, although he did not cleave to him, or whether he would certainly doe what he had threatned."[77] Milton's Adam considers the same two possibilities: that God will not keep his promise by destroying them (938–51) and that he will (952–59). He chooses, come life or death, to "undergo like doom" with Eve. The unconscious ambiguity of Eve's immediate response to this decision figures forth the proliferation of sin:

> O glorious trial of exceeding Love,
> Illustrious evidence, example high!
> Ingaging me to emulate, but short
> Of thy perfection. . . .
>
> (961–64)

Eve knows much more than Adam does about the complexity and impurity of her own motives, so the apparent simplicity and purity of his love excite this outburst. But the lines mean more than she knows. The narrator has already celebrated Christ's future sacrifice ("O unexampl'd Love" [3.410]), so once again Eve unconsciously displaces the praise due him upon an unworthy object—and, in a Reformation context, the best paraphrase of the first line is "O vainglorious temptation of God." The fact that one can cite, without qualification, Reformation interpretations of the law's severity is the most reliable sign that, by this point in book 9, the benign Edenic law has been lost forever.

When Adam speaks doubtfully of the punishment of death although it was pronounced "most certainly," he separates mercy from justice:

> albeit men are oft perswaded that they sinne, yet . . . they are not perswaded
> of the justice of God against it: whereby the door is opened to sinne. Which
> is to make God an Idoll, in spoiling him of his justice; as if he were so all
> mercy, as he had forgotten to be just, when he is as well justice as mercy, as
> infinite in the one as in the other.[78]

Adam's sin of tempting God creates a breach in the Godhead, causing a debate between Father and Son with strategies that signal, however tactfully and sympathetically, distinct positions (however close)—a debate that anticipates the fuller separation to come, the Son's incarnation and passion. Before the Fall, in a monistic universe, divine mercy and justice, human obedience and faith are united. Now Adam banishes justice, thus, in a sense, exiling God the Father, fulfilling in an unexpected way the prologue's dire prediction of "Heav'n / Now alienated" (8–9)—by man.

Adam's argument (938–49) resembles that of the Son in debate, pleading with the Father to spare humankind (3.150–66). Surrendering power for love sounds more attractive in a Christian context than it does in the world Adam now inhabits, no longer edenically Hebraic, supporting power and love together, and not yet Christian.

Adam has so far considered violating the Decalogue, participating in idolatry, and tempting God. He concludes this speech, as he did the one preceding, by dissevering natural law from divine law, choosing love of Eve over obedience to God:

> no, no, I feel
> The Link of Nature draw me: Flesh of Flesh,
> Bone of my Bone thou art, and from thy State
> Mine never shall be parted, bliss or woe.
>
> (913–16)

> So forcible within my heart I feel
> The Bond of Nature draw me to my own,
> My own in thee, for what thou art is mine;
> Our State cannot be sever'd, we are one,
> One Flesh; *to lose thee were to lose myself.*
>
> (955–59; *my emphasis*)

Adam justifies his decision by appealing to his indissoluble unity with Eve, though, in the event, he causes only fragmentation, domestic unease, and a shattering of the original Edenic law into many pieces. Adam paraphrases Genesis 2:23 ("This is now bone of my bones, and flesh of my flesh") and then 2:24: "Therefore shall a man leave his father and his mother, and shall cleave unto his wife: and they shall be one flesh." Trying to understand Adam's predicament here, one can turn to the divorce tracts, where Milton cites these verses sixteen times, and to *De doctrina*, where he cites them four times. Considering the choices actually open to Adam, one ultimately finds interpretive uncertainty not only where one might reasonably expect it, in the gap between poetry and doctrine, but also within Miltonic doctrine, which offers contradictory solutions, Hebraic and Christian.

The poetry here insistently evokes the divorce tracts. Adam speaks to Eve fatalistically, "Submitting to what seem'd remediless" (919), and all four tracts offer divorce as the remedy of a sick marriage. Milton treats as a matter of choice what other writers on the same topic treated as a matter of necessity. Against the advice of patient submission, Milton all but shouts, "*Let not the remedy be despis'd*" (YP, 2:243): "God sends remedies, as well as evills; under which he who lies and groans, that may lawfully acquitt himself, is accessory to his own ruin" (YP, 2:341).

Citing the two beautiful verses from Genesis that institute Edenic marriage, Adam suggests that the perfection of his marriage with Eve is the greatest incentive to disobey God's command. Milton's own hermeneutic operations on these foundational verses are fairly violent; celebrating monogamy and indissolubility, the texts are obstacles to be overcome. In *De doctrina*, advocating polygamy, Milton insists that "one flesh" is neither law nor commandment, but only a description of intimate relationship in an unfallen state: "I have not said, as most people [writing on marriage] do, *between one man and one woman*. I have not done so, in order to avoid accusing the most holy patriarchs and pillars of our faith, Abraham, and others who had more than one wife, of constant fornication and adultery" (*YP*, 6:355–56). Milton insists on keeping the Hebrew verses describing prelapsarian life separate from New Testament interpretation, rejecting those expositors who read Genesis 2:24 by the monogamous light of Matthew 19:5 (*YP*, 6:356).

In the divorce tracts, Milton uses the debasement of marriage after the Fall as an argument in favor of the Mosaic law, which allows divorce and therefore eases the difficulties confronted in contemporary marriage, difficulties unforeseen in the verses in Genesis that appear to institute an indissoluble union. Milton objects to the use of Genesis 2:23–24 to restrain luckless marriage partners from improving their circumstances. Adam's cleaving to Eve shouldn't be one's "stern . . . command . . . to cleave to his error" (*YP*, 2:327) or to "cleav to calamity" (*YP*, 2:605). Against Adam's "bone of my bones and flesh of my flesh," Milton sets God's "I will make him a help meet for him" (2:8). A true marriage means that a wife is a meet help for her husband, and "*Adam* therfore in these words does not establish an indissoluble bond of marriage in the carnall ligaments of flesh and blood": "*Adam* spake like *Adam* the words of flesh and bones, the shell and rinde of matrimony; but God spake like God, of love and solace and meet help, the soul both of *Adams* words and of matrimony" (*YP*, 2:602–3). Adam, on the verge of sin, paraphrases Genesis 2:24, a text that Milton regards with conspicuous lack of sentiment. An earlier, wholly innocent Adam thanks God for Eve by paraphrasing the same verse, but with a significant addition:

> for this cause he shall forgo
> Father and Mother, and to his Wife adhere;
> And they shall be one Flesh, one Heart, one Soul.
>
> (8.497–99)

Milton devotes two chapters of *The Doctrine and Discipline of Divorce* to the "Idolatrous match" of a believer and an "idolatrous heretick" (*YP*, 2:259–68). Of special interest in these chapters is the treatment of a new theme that bears upon the reading of Adam's predicament:

the need to dissolve a happy marriage. Whereas a temperamentally un-
suited couple sets marriage above charity, an idolatrous match sets marriage above God (*DDD*, 260). Eve and Delilah haunt Milton's description of an idolatress as one who perverts her husband "by her enticing
sorcery" and "willingly allures him from the faith," setting "marriage
above God," "a doctrine of devils" (*DDD*, 260).

In spite of love, a believer is enjoined to divorce his idolatrous spouse
to avoid "seducement" and "spiritual contagion" (*DDD*, 262). Outlin-
ing the course of action to be followed by a Christian contemplating
union with an "idolatrous Heretick," Milton is implacable: "when it
comes into question . . . whether any civill respect, or natural relation
which is dearest, may be our plea to divide, or hinder, or but delay our
duty to religion, we heare it determin'd that father and mother, and wife
also is not only to be hated, but forsak'n" (*DDD*, 262–63). The argument
that one's marriage must be sacrificed to one's religion is repeated in the
tract (268).

When C. S. Lewis treats Adam's options in book 9, his tone is less
strident than Milton's, but his advice is similarly implacable. Adam's decision to fall would have been correct if conjugal love were the highest
value in his world:

> But if there are things that have an even higher claim on a man, if the uni-
> verse is imagined to be such that, when the pinch comes, a man ought to
> reject wife and mother and his own life also, then the case is altered, and then
> Adam can do no good to Eve . . . by becoming her accomplice.[79]

Both Milton's passage in the divorce tract and C. S. Lewis's explanation
of Adam's predicament virtually paraphrase the same scriptural verse
without referring explicitly to it: "If any man come to me, and hate not his
father, and mother, and wife, and children, and brethren, and sisters, yea,
and his own life also, he cannot be my disciple" (Luke 14:26).

Although Milton paraphrases Luke here, his principal support in these
chapters is Paul, whose warning against using food after it had been offered to idols helped us earlier to understand Adam and Eve's sin as participation in idolatry. Insisting that an idolatrous match leads to alien-
ation from God, Milton lends domestic specificity to Pauline verses that
in fact urge a general separation of the children of light from the children
of darkness (2 Cor. 6:14–17). By skillfully drawing on these verses
throughout the chapters, Milton is able to weight his domestic strictures
with the gravity of demonic implication. Paul enjoins the Corinthians to
resist union with the demonic in order to attain to unity with the divine:
"Be ye not unequally yoked together with unbelievers: for what fellowship hath righteousness with unrighteousness? and what communion
hath light with darkness? And what concord hath Christ with Belial? or
what part hath he that believeth with an infidel?"

Milton appropriates the polarity of these verses for his chapters on divorce from an idolatrous heretic: *"Mis-yoke not together with Infidels"* (*YP*, 2:262). The verses generate an image both cosmic and domestic of an idolatrous match as a marriage of heaven and hell: "For what kind of matrimony can that remain to be, what one dutie between such can be perform'd as it should from the heart, when their hearts and spirits flie asunder as farre as heaven from hell" (*YP*, 2:263).

An important reason for Milton's reinscribing Paul's general admonition within a domestic context is that more specific Pauline verses advise the partners in an idolatrous marriage to remain together. Indeed, bible scholars regard the insistence on radical separation in 2 Corinthians 6:14–17 as "strange to Paul,"[80] the apostle to the gentiles who elsewhere denies that the Corinthians should avoid the immoral of this world, the greedy and robbers, or idolaters, "for then must ye needs go out of the world" (1 Cor. 5:9–10). Only Paul's theology, not his sociology, is predicated on irreconcilable dualities; the letters reveal strenuous attempts, not always successful, to mediate among gentiles, Jews, and Christians.

Absent from the chapters on an idolatrous match are the definitive Pauline verses on the topic, for which Milton substitutes 2 Cor. 6:14–17. In *Tetrachordon* and *De doctrina*, Milton's readings of the relevant problematic verses offer two opposed solutions to Adam's dilemma: should he send away his his wife, an idolatrous heretic who has already vowed lifelong devotion to the tree and has called God "Our great Forbidder, safe with all his Spies / About him" (815–16), or remain with her? Paul advocates the latter:

> If any brother hath a wife that believeth not, and she be pleased to dwell with him, let him not put her away. And the woman which hath a husband that believeth not, and if he be pleased to dwell with her, let her not leave him. For the unbelieving husband is sanctified by the wife, and the unbelieving wife is sanctified by the husband: else were your children unclean; but now are they holy. (1 Cor. 7:12–14)

Milton's contemporaries attacked his divorce tracts for "bringing back *Christ* unto *Moses*,"[81] forcing Christ's rejection of divorce into compliance with the deuteronomic law. In *Tetrachordon*, Milton also refers Paul back to Moses. Arguing, against the majority view, that the Jewish law of divorce in Deuteronomy is a command and not a mere permission, he argues the obverse as well: that the problematic verses of 1 Corinthians 7 are a permission and not a command:

> That this heer spoken by *Paul*, not by the Lord [,] cannot be a command, these reasons avouch. First, the law of *Moses, Exod.* 34.16. *Deut.* 7.3.6. interpreted by *Ezra*, and *Nehemiah* two infallible authors, commands to divorce an infidel not for the feare only of a ceremonious defilement, but of

an irreligious seducement, fear'd both in respect of the beleever himselfe, and of his children in danger to bee perverted by the misbeleeving parent, *Nehem.* 13.24.26. (*YP*, 2:681).

Milton appears to reject Paul's assumption that, since Christians are united in the body of Christ, a believing husband will make his partner a believer as well and will make their children holy.

Paul cannot countermand the moral law of Moses, and to interpret his remarks in 1 Corinthians 7:12–14 as a command is to make the gospel a law of bondage. Milton insists on the perpetuity of that law and specifically of the moral Mosaic law requiring divorce from an unbeliever, to avoid seducement:

> The moral reason of divorcing stands to eternity, which neither Apostle nor Angel from heaven can countermand. All that [the majority of interpreters] reply to this, is their human warrant, that God will preserve us in our obedience to this command against the danger of seducement. And so undoubtedly he will, if we understand his commands aright; if we turn not this evangelic permission into a legal, and yet illegal command: if we turne not hope into bondage, the charitable and free hope of gaining another into the forc't and servil temptation of *loosing our selves*. (*YP*, 2:681; my emphasis).

To read Adam's dilemma in the distinctly Hebraic context of *Tetrachordon* is to urge him to take up the Mosaic law of divorce as an instrument of freedom. Adam's very last words before sinning are addressed to Eve: "to lose thee were to lose myself" (959). *Tetrachordon* tells him that only by separating himself from her can he avoid the servile temptation of losing himself. In this tract, "Submitting to what seem'd remediless" is like waiting submissively for grace that never comes, while the instrument of one's salvation is at hand, unused.

Milton turns again to 1 Corinthians 7:12–14 in his chapter on Christian liberty in *De doctrina Christiana*, in a paragraph asserting that the gospel abolishes the entire Mosaic law. Where earlier that law offered freedom, now constraint and slavery are as inseparable even from the moral law as liberty is from the gospel (*YP*, 6:535). Milton reads Paul's remarks entirely uncritically as an authoritative declaration, like Christ's:

> Christ himself broke the letter of the law, Mark ii.27: look at the fourth commandment, and then compare his words, *the sabbath was made for man, not man for the sabbath*. Paul did the same when he said that marriage with an unbeliever was not to be dissolved, contrary to the express injunction of the law. 1 Cor. vii.12: *I, not the Lord*. In interpreting both these commandments, the commandment about the Sabbath and that about marriage, attention to the requirements of charity is given precedence over any written law. The other commandments should all be treated in the same way. (*YP*, 6:532).

Miltonic doctrine offers two contradictory answers to Adam's dilemma that underscore their respective Hebraic and Christian contexts. The conflict between *Tetrachordon* and *De doctrina* can be read as exemplary of the larger conflict within this book between Genesis and the Pauline epistles. Book 9 begins in a Hebraic Eden, governed by a divine command and a covenant of works benign and easy to keep. Its primary literary source is Genesis 2, perhaps the most monistic of all Western texts, with no split between body and soul—a text that invites Milton's own passionate monistic response: "*living soul* [2:7] . . . :we must interpret this as meaning that man is a living being, intrinsically and properly one and individual. He is not double or separable: not, as is commonly thought, produced from and composed of two different and distinct elements, soul and body. On the contrary, the whole man is the soul, and the soul the man" (*YP*, 6:317–18).

Book 9 ends in a world of accusation, fruitlessness, self-condemnation, and vanity (1187–89), under the Mosaic law as Paul envisions it, "*a prison that shutteth up, the yoake of bondage, the power or force of sinne, the operation of wrath and of death, . . . the ministerie of death and condemnation, the killing letter.*"[82] Paul, an extreme dualist, sets up contradictions that would never have occurred to his contemporary believing Jews—between body and spirit, righteousness under the law and faith. Under a benign proto-Mosaic law, Adam and Eve know "Just confidence, and native righteousness, / And honor" (1056–57). After the Fall, there will be no native righteousness except for Christ's. Thomas Goodman cites Paul in protesting the inadequacy of human virtue:

> We are not to rest in graces or duties; they all cannot satisfy our own consciences, much lesse Gods Justice. If *Righteousnesse could have come* by these, then *Christ had dyed in vaine*, as *Gal. 2. ult.* What a dishonour were it to Christ, that they should share any of the glory of his righteousnesse? were any of your Duties crucified for you?[83]

When Paul's experience of the crucified and risen Christ overturned his pharisaic meaning system, native righteousness became impossible: "For Moses describeth the righteousness which is of the law, That the man which doeth those things shall live by them" (Rom. 10:5). To this promise of life under the Mosaic law (Lev. 18:5) Paul contrasts Deuteronomy 30:12–14, from which he derives midrashically the doctrine of "the righteousness . . . of faith" in Christ. The two passages that Paul perceives as mutually exclusive refer literally to Torah as revealed on Mount Sinai and are entirely compatible.

For the sake of coherence, one may segregate the Hebraic from the Pauline, thus emphasizing radical discontinuity in *Paradise Lost* between prelapsarian and postlapsarian worlds. Changing dispensations reveal God's changing ways with his faithful. This chapter began with Romans

7 and the doctrine of Christian liberty. For Barker, writing brilliantly but uncritically about the centrality of this doctrine in Milton's thought: " 'Christian liberty' nowhere appears in the later poems . . . because decorum and theology alike render it inappropriate in the representation of experience under pre-Christian dispensations. Yet 'Christian liberty' is what the poems are about."[84] Barker may well be correct, although there are aspects of the doctrine that he has not envisioned. Christian liberty imprisoned John Traske, and, in Satan's hands, it became a stunningly effective weapon against the law. The version of the doctrine that Eve found compelling necessitated and hastened Christ's redemptive sacrifice. In a Hebraic Eden, Christian liberty can only be damaging. Conversely, after the Fall, Satan's two principal arguments in his tempting of Eve will find their unparodic way into the Christian world of the poem: the dispensing of the ceremonial law (12.289–99) and the view of death as the gateway to a higher form of life (12.571).

Echoing his argument from *De doctrina*, Milton contends that the gospel could not possibly be more severe than the law: "*Thou shalt doe no manner of works* saith the commandment of the Sabbath. Yes saith Christ works of charity. And shall we be more severe in paraphrasing the considerat and tender Gospel, then he was in expounding the rigid and peremptory law?" (*YP*, 2:281). Satan offers Eve a version of the gospel, countering the divine command. But the ceremonial law she sets aside is itself considerate and tender, becoming rigid and peremptory (as in Rom. 7) only after the Fall.

Remembering that even Paul offers several contradictory answers to the value of the Torah, one might conclude by suggesting that the problem of law and gospel in Milton's thought remains permanently unresolved. In book 9, Milton offers a Hebraic critique of Romans 7, bringing Paul back to the benign law of Genesis. At the same time Milton filters the narrative of Genesis 2–3 through Romans 7, which is a central text in our understanding of the Fall:

> Is the law sin? God forbid. Nay, I had not known sin, but by the law: for I had not known lust, except the law had said, Thou shalt not covet. But sin, taking occasion by the commandment, wrought in me all manner of concupiscence. For without the law sin was dead. . . . For sin, taking occasion by the commandment, deceived me, and by it slew me. Wherefore the law is holy, and the commandment holy, and just, and good. (7–8 and 11–12)[85]

Had there been no commandment, there would have been no Fall. Satan is sin, using the commandment to deceive Eve. Yet the commandment apart from its effect is holy, just, and good. The passage conveys Paul's anxiety, the result of dissonance that follows hard decisions, such as the rejection of one's past. Paul's primary purpose, according to Watson, is to demonstrate to his Jewish Christian readers that the law's effect is to intensify disastrously the dominion of sin: "When they realize that the law was involved in the origins of sexual lust, its prestige will be greatly diminished."[86] But the verses can also be interpreted as Paul's apologia for the law. In Milton's brilliant adaptation of these verses, does sin take occasion to subvert Eve by the law or by the gospel?

The contradictory Miltonic interpretations of 1 Corinthians 7 in *Tetrachordon* and *De doctrina* point to a complex understanding of Milton's Hebraic and Pauline sensibilities engaged in unending dialectic. They suggest an alternative to coherence, in which lines of communication between prelapsarian and postlapsarian worlds, however attenuated, remain open despite the poet's attempts to close them. Milton, like Paul, rejected his Hebraic past, but muted Hebraic critiques occasionally bleed into even the extreme Christian doctrine of the epic's last books. At the point of Adam's dilemma, has Romans 7 already changed from a parodic text to a master text? Before the Fall, Eve fails to understand the benignity of the law. After the Fall, Adam is wrong to tempt God by not believing in the law's wrath. But, in this transitional moment, the law is no longer benign and not yet a minister of death and condemnation. One can feel the ground of interpretation shift as one moves closer to the catastrophe of *Paradise Lost*. Adam's dilemma takes one to the limits of doctrine, where choices between coherence and complexity, continuity and discontinuity, law and gospel coexist in tension, without resolution.

Just as the demonic consult in book 2 precedes its original, the heavenly council of book 3, so a parody of the New Testament in book 9 precedes its legitimate appearance in book 10, when the Son descends to pronounce a sentence that correctly interpreted is an evangelical promise. By that point in the poem, Christian typology has trivialized the Hebraic ethos of the Edenic books. But in book 9, it is the sanctity of Torah that must be preserved from contamination by the gospel. Satan's rhetoric in his temptation of Eve draws on a fund of images and ideas of Christ: his nativity, his setting aside the ceremonial law, and above all the transformations he effects—from obedience under the law to the experience of grace, from death to life, and from humanity to divinity. Eve, living according to a Torah that she mistakes for law, finds these irresistibly attractive, and in Milton's great epic the unfortunate redemption precedes the fortunate fall.

CHAPTER SIX

The Law in Adam's Soliloquy

IF ADAM, in his long soliloquy (*PL*, 10.720–844), feels that he is more miserable than he knows, at least we readers can find in Pauline theology the doctrine we need to keep pace with his experience. The soliloquy occurs in the interval of a double take, after the Son has pronounced sentence on the serpent, but before Adam has interpreted that sentence correctly as an evangelical promise. This interval belongs to the state of misery that follows innocence and precedes grace. Adam's opening antitheses—"O miserable of happy," (10.720) "Accurst of blessed" (10.723)—suggest that a glance at his former happy, blessed state will help us to measure his losses.

Adam's soliloquy dramatizes his creator's turning away from Torah after the Fall to meditate upon Romans and specifically upon the Pauline theme, begun in Galatians, that faith and law are contradictory. Although the law, good and holy, comes from God, it was never intended to last forever; rather, it was a temporary measure, valid only until the coming of Christ. Paul's own life story dramatizes the passing from Pharisaism to Christianity.[1] Milton's own life could serve as another example, since he had passed from Hebraic religious sympathy in the tracts of 1643–45 to the peremptory rejection of even the moral law in the Pauline chapters of *De doctrina Christiana*. The law of paradise contains the entire Mosaic law, and the mortal sin original transgresses it. It would be futile to maintain our first parents in a dispensation already violated in paradise and thus manifestly inadequate in the face of postlapsarian reality. So the Son appears as "mild Judge and Intercessor both" (10.96) even before the expulsion from the garden, at once fulfilling the benign law of paradise as judge and signaling a new dispensation as intercessor. Adam in his agony remains unaware of this mildness and of the supreme sacrifice it anticipates ("It is Christ that died . . . who is even at the right hand of God, who also maketh intercession for us" [Rom. 8:34]).

Turning to the soliloquy in book 10, one finds Adam lying under the weight of a Pauline conception of the law. Once Adam violates it, the law becomes "*a prison that shutteth up, the yoake of bondage, the power or force of sinne, the operation of wrath and of death, . . . the ministerie of death and condemnation, the killing letter.*"[2] Read in the context of Protestant commonplaces concerning the Mosaic law, virtually all of them deriving from Paul, the soliloquy becomes at once more ironic and more poignant.

Adam begins:

> O miserable of happy! is this the end
> Of this new glorious World, and mee so late
> The Glory of that Glory, who now become
> Accurst of blessed, hide me from the face
> Of God, whom to behold was then my highth
> Of happiness: yet well, if here would end
> The misery, I deserv'd it, and would bear
> My own deservings.
>
> (10. 720–27)

Adam, who replays Satan's "Me miserable!" (4.73), has already undergone a form of that death threatened in the interdiction. Wollebius makes this point explicit in the first rule of his chapter on misery: "God comprehended all mans misery under the name of death. Gen. 2.17."[3] Unsurprisingly, the four degrees of death he outlines resemble Milton's in *De doctrina Christiana*. The worst form of death is spiritual death, whereby the sinners are "forever excluded from the fellowship of God, and of the blessed. *Matth*. 25–41. Go from me ye cursed."[4] A comparison of Adam's plight with the state of spiritual death may seem exaggerated, until one recalls God's dialogues with the Son in books 3 and 11. There one learns that, without the free operation of grace (3.174–75)— without God's "motions" (11.91)—Adam would be "quite . . . lost" (3.173).

The soliloquy reminds the reader that God has not yet activated the machinery of grace. The various polarities Adam amasses here—misery and happiness (10.720), curses and blessings (723), life and death (729 and 731)—are brought into focus by a law that promises life but threatens death: "O voice once heard / Delightfully, *Increase and multiply*, /Now death to hear!" (729–31). God's primal blessing of humankind with fertility in Genesis 1:28, recounted first by Raphael (7.531–34) and then even more exuberantly by Adam (8.338–41), contains one imperative that stresses human kinship with the other animals through sexuality ("Increase and multiply") and another that stresses human superiority over them ("master . . . and rule"). Milton cites this blessing and commandment as proof that the "providence of God . . . which relates to [man's] prelapsarian state is that by which God placed man in the garden of Eden and supplied him with every good thing necessary for a happy life. . . . Gen. i.28" (*YP*, 6:351). Adam's peremptory devaluation of the Torah's first law derives from

Romans 7:10: "the very commandment which promised life proved to be death to me." Adam and Eve, now "manifold in sin" (10.16), will multiply curses and evil by multiplying progeny: "for what can I increase / Or multiply but curses on my head?" (731–32). Adam and Paul identify the Mosaic law, God's "voice once heard / Delightfully," with death and a curse. In one of *De doctrina Christiana*'s most thoroughly Pauline chapters (1.26), Milton cites Romans 7:7–13 as proof that the Mosaic law is an instrument through which humankind recognizes its depravity (*YP*, 6:518).

Paradise Lost, as well as the history of interpretation, suggests that proliferation can indeed be a curse. The original blessing of procreation could be both particular and universal, since unfallen Adam and Eve were the world's total human population. The Fall and the subsequent expulsion from paradise dissociate particularity from universality and thus create competition for privilege. The primordial blessing of Genesis 1:28 has been invoked to enforce value systems that deal explicitly in preference and implicitly in rejection. Human dominion over the animals becomes a metaphor of Israel's relation to the other nations of the world or of Christianity's dominion over Judaism. God's first, expansive blessing of humankind becomes, over the centuries, contested territory that opposing cultures struggle to appropriate. What was originally a blessing whose recipients were neither Jewish nor of the same gender becomes in rabbinic tradition a law applying only to free Jewish males. The oldest patristic reference to Genesis 1:28, in the *Epistle of Barnabas*, employs the verse polemically, so that the primordial blessing is addressed by God to his son Jesus, and it bespeaks the triumph of the church. For some Christian interpreters, the verse typifies the old law of the Jews, now obsolete. The world is already sufficiently populated, the Parousia is imminent, and procreation ranks noticeably below the ideal of celibacy. In a soliloquy that devalues life, law, and progeny, Adam cites a verse so thoroughly emptied of its original universality that a countertext eventually had to be found to authorize the settlement of the macrocosm by all the nations of the earth: "[God] did not create it a chaos, he formed it to be inhabited" (Isa. 45:18).[5]

Bereft of grace or the language of grace, Adam's soliloquy represents a law that works wrath in a language unremittingly legalistic. To end his misery, Adam would die, thus returning the gift of life he has received:

> if here would end
> The misery, I deserv'd it, and would bear
> My own deservings.
>
> (725–27)

> it were but right
> And equal to reduce me to my dust,
> Desirous to resign, and render back
> All I receiv'd, unable to perform
> Thy terms too hard.
>
> (747–51)

The terms of the one easy prohibition have become too hard to perform, like the Mosaic law described by the angel Michael: the ceremonial law cannot appease, "nor Man the moral part / Perform, and not performing cannot live" (12.298–99). The law that was easy is now impossible, and Adam cannot render back what he received because he is now utterly bankrupt.

Here is Bucanus trying to reconcile two apparently contradictory statements attributed to Jerome: "Cursed is hee who saith that God commanded impossible things: and cursed is he who saith, the law is possible":

> They are to be reconciled by a distinction of times and subjects. God did not commaund impossible things, namely, to our first parents before the fall, neither also to the regenerate, unto whom the Law is possible by grace. . . . But the Law is impossible, namely, to a man in this corrupt nature, in his owne strength and actions, and the Scripture feareth not to say concerning the observation of the Law, that it is, a yoak, which neither the Apostles, nor they which beleeved, neither the primitive Church, nor the fathers could beare.[6]

Before the Fall, then, Adam can easily fulfill the law on its own terms. After his justification, which imputes his sin to Christ and Christ's righteousness to him, he can fulfill it by believing in Christ. In what the reader, but not Adam, can recognize as the interval, Adam lies under the curse of a law that he was once able to perform through his own obedience. He and Eve are the only people both capable and incapable of performing the law. For the Reformers at least, God does not change the rules in the middle of the game. The game remains perfect, but not the player, who injures himself. Bucanus provides a less anachronistic context, using Adam's own legalistic terms, but with a certain ruthless efficiency:

> Is God therefore unjust, because he requireth these things of us which we cannot doe? Farre be it we should say so, for he asketh againe of us that which is his owne, and which before hee had given us: for hee gave to our first parents in their creation a power, and ability to performe the Law. Even as if one should lend any man money, and the debter should by his negligence and fault spend or lose it, and is no more able to pay, notwithstanding the creditor can not bee proved to deale unjustly, if he demaund the lent

money of him & his heires.[7]

By interpreting the law's efficacy in different ways before and after the Fall, Milton can present as logically separate ideas that in the New Testament sometimes coexist uneasily. Luke in Acts dismisses the Torah on the not wholly compatible grounds of its misuse by the Jews and of the impossibility of performing it.[8] By placing the law in paradise, however, Milton can suggest that Adam misuses it when he chooses to fall and that he is unable to perform it once he has fallen.

Although Adam at first articulates the assumption that his death can render back to God all he has received, he also, from the first, senses an even darker misery that would ensue should God call in his debts. Adam's fear that suffering can be protracted beyond the grave is too terrible to be expressed or even perceived all at once. It first approaches him, dimly and from afar, in the complaint that his posterity will curse him: "for what can I increase / Or multiply, but curses on my head?" (732). At this point, in a tone querulous rather than tragic, Adam recognizes that living infamy can be worse than death. The uneasy feeling that continuity is a curse grows slowly in the soliloquy, in phrases like "lasting woes" (742), "the sense of endless woes" (754), and "deathless pain" (775). Adam uses these phrases in a general way to increase the pathos of his current situation. The specific terror of their most literal meaning has not yet manifested itself.

Similarly undeveloped at this point is the split between divine and natural law, a topic not apparently related to perpetual torment. Adam contrasts the cause of his progeny's birth with that of his own:

> him not thy election,
> But Natural necessity begot.
> God made thee of choice his own, and of his own
> To serve him.
>
> (764–67)

The laws of nature lie behind the birth of a child, and these may not accord with a parent's choice: the existence of childless couples, unhappy parents, and unwanted children tells one that election does not always determine birth. How different from pro-choice paradise, where birth is a matter of election, in Eve's case by Adam as well as by God. God the Father's relationship with Adam before the Fall is like his relationship with the Son. According to Milton, the Son "is called God's own Son simply because he had no other Father but God, and this is why he himself said that God was his Father. . . . This particular Father begot his Son not from any natural necessity but of his own free will: a method more excellent and more in keeping with paternal dignity, especially as this

Father is God" (*YP*, 6:208–9). In paradise, where "God and Nature bid the same" (6.176), the terms of the interdiction and of nature's law were entirely compatible, a point Raphael emphasized near the end of his visit (8.561). The disjunction began after Eve tasted the forbidden fruit, when Adam chose to disobey the divine law for the sake of the natural: "I feel / The Link of Nature draw me" (9.913–14).

The key but problematic source of the rupture between nature and election is Galatians 4:22–30, the allegory of Hagar and Sarah, Ishmael and Isaac, and Sinai and Jerusalem, which reverses the iron law of primogeniture and asserts the primacy of the new. Paul contrasts Hagar the slavewoman and her son Ishmael, who was born in the course of nature, with Sarah the freewoman and her son Isaac, who was born as the result of election: "But he who was of the bondwoman was born after the flesh; but he of the free woman was by promise" (4:23). The two women—related as carnal to spiritual—and their two sons provide a lineage for the two peoples, the Jews and the Christians. They tell in a figure of the rejection of the Jews and the election of the Christians in their place, and Milton cites them frequently in the Pauline chapters of *De doctrina* to underscore the differences between the two covenants (*YP*, 6: 499, 522, 527, 530, 592, and 605). Adam reaches back beyond Hagar and Sarah to paradise, where election precedes natural necessity. By asserting the primacy of the original, he inadvertently and momentarily restores the balance upset by Paul.

The sudden fusion of two topics kept carefully separate—the duration of suffering and the split between the laws of God and Nature—detonates in Adam's imagination the mechanism of terror that was carefully set ticking early in the soliloquy. Nature offers rest, while the thunder of the law evokes the dreadful Sinai theophany:

> How gladly would I meet
> Mortality my sentence, and be Earth
> Insensible, how glad would lay me down
> As in my Mother's lap! There I should rest
> And sleep secure; *his dreadful voice no more*
> *Would thunder in my ears*, no fear of worse
> To mee and to my offspring would torment me
> With cruel expectation.
>
> (775–82; *my emphasis*)

Adam, like a pagan brought up on naturalism, wants to rest, but God's thunder will not let him. In *De doctrina Christiana*, Milton defines rest specifically as escape from the Mosaic law: "rest, that is, from the curse of the law. Hence the agitation in Paul's mind while he was under the curse of the law . . ." (*YP*, 6:519).

Adam's mortalism, a comfort when he considers the alternative, derives from his interpretation of natural law:

> though the Lord of all be infinite,
> Is his wrath also? be it, Man is not so,
> But mortal doom'd. How can he exercise
> Wrath without end on Man whom Death must end?
> Can he make deathless Death?
>
> (794–98)

> Will he draw out,
> For anger's sake, finite to infinite
> In punisht Man, to satisfy his rigor
> Satisfi'd never; that were to extend
> His Sentence beyond dust and Nature's Law,
> By which all Causes else according still
> To the reception of thir matter act,
> Not to th' extent of thir own Sphere.
>
> (801–8)

Adam relies on his body's frailty to thwart God's wrath. He finds consolation in natural law: since, according to this law, causes operate, not in proportion to their own power, but in proportion to the capacity of the object they work upon,[9] finite Adam will not suffer infinitely though he deserves eternal damnation. But Adam has transgressed a commandment divine rather than natural. He intends three questions to sound rhetorical—and they do—but they are not. The questions are posed in a way that suggests they will not take "yes" for an answer, but they do. Is God's wrath infinite? The immediate reply, "be it," concedes that it is. The infinite wrath of the Old Law was a commonplace among the Reformers. When Milton opposes the covenant of grace to the Mosaic law, he quotes Romans 4:15 ("The law worketh wrath" [*YP*, 6:518, 523, 528, and 533]), and, in *Paradise Lost*, wrath is used as a virtual synonym of law ("over wrath grace shall abound," [12.478]). Can God make deathless Death? He can according to the terms of a Mosaic law that operates absolutely as Paul believes it does, independent of human ability to perform it. Bucanus's legal metaphor now becomes ominous: even if the debtor is bankrupt, "the creditor can not bee proved to deale unjustly, if he demaund the lent money of him & his heires."[10]

John Marbeck's formulation is more direct: "it is impossible for a man to fulfill the lawe of his owne strength and power, seeing that we are by birth and nature, the heires of eternall damnation."[11] As Peter Bulkeley notes, "The covenant stands fast, but we have not stood fast in the covenant, but it is now become impossible to us, that we are unable to fulfill it, as the Apostle speaks, Rom. 8.3. Yea, it is the unchangeableness and stability of this covenant, which condemns all the world of sinful and ungodly men."[12] Fallen Adam's position under the law most closely resembles that of the Jews, who were given oracles, scriptures, and promises. God's faithfulness in making the promises is not invalidated by the failure of the Jews to keep their part of the covenant (Rom. 3:2–4 and 10–11). Calvin endlessly pursues the relentlessness of the law for those who do not accept Christ's grace:

> Doth the impossibilitie of dooing it, discharge us of our service which wee be bound to doe unto God? No. For the evil commeth of ourselves. . . . It is no marvel then, that God in his lawe shoulde have no regard to mans abilitie or unabilitie, but rather to the dutie which we owe him, or that he shoulde require the right that belongeth to him. . . . If wee had continued in our integritie, and not beene perverted and corrupted through sinne, then should we have beene able to have discharged all that God requireth of us in his lawe. That is certaine.[13]

The impossibility of performing the Mosaic law, then, is no objection to it, and Adam now sees himself paying through eternity a debt of suffering to a God of infinite wrath. This is worse than the "debt immense" of which Satan complains, "So burthensome still paying, still to owe" (4.52–53). Even the Son's "immortal love / To mortal men" (3.267–68) turns sinister in the soliloquy, proving as it does that God can after all exert immortal force on a mortal object.

It is clear that the Miltonic bard carries the Mosaic law back to Eden, identifying it with the first prohibition, and later, after the Fall, exploiting its power to evoke the terror of eternal condemnation. Adam faces directly the claustrophic terror of unextinguished sinful consciousness:

> endless misery
> From this day onward, which I feel begun
> Both in me, and without me, and so last
> To perpetuity: Ay me, that fear
> Comes thund'ring back with dreadful revolution
> On my defenseless head; both Death and I
> Am found Eternal, and incorporate both.
>
> *(810–16)*

The returning thunder that follows Adam's confrontation of his worst fear is the thunder of Sinai, which Hebrews 12:18–21 describes as unendurable, a symbol of the Mosaic law. Adam and death are incorporate and eternal, and one remembers Paul on sin and the Law: "O wretched man that I am! who shall deliver me from the body of this death?" (Rom. 7:24). Milton cites this verse in *De doctrina Christiana*, in the chapter on the Fall, where he connects the sin of our first parents with the body of death under the Law:

> Evil concupiscence is that of which our original parents were first guilty, and which they transmitted to their posterity, as sharers in the primary transgression, in the shape of an innate propensity to sin. This is called in Scripture "the old man," and "the body of sin". . . . "the body of death" . . . "the law of sin and of death." (*CE*, 15:193; compare *YP*, 6:389)

The law of God, which Adam disjoined from natural law when he chose to fall, now exacts vengeance on him by canceling even the small comfort of dissolution afforded by natural law.

Adam's entire soliloquy is a product of the Reformation. The speculations of Adam unparadised are not "by the mere light of nature," and his "intimation of unimmortality" is positively welcome compared with its alternative, interminable sinful consciousness beyond the grave.[14] David Paraeus describes the tribunal where God's justice prosecutes:

> Before [God's] tribunal we all stood guiltie of eternal death through sin: Gods revenging justice stood against us, requiring, that we should suffer temporal and eternal punishments, For what was committed by us against his infinite majesty: *For it is the judgement of God that they who commit such things are worthie of death* [Rom. 1:32]. Against us stood the law of God pronouncing cursings against the transgressours thereof: Our own evill conscience also, arguing and convincing us of eternall guiltinesse.[15]

In Milton's first outline for a tragedy on the theme of paradise lost, Moses and Justice are the first two "Persons." In the second plan, Moses is the prologue, followed immediately by Justice and Mercie, who debate "what should become of man if he fall," and, in the continuous scenario, "Adam unparadiz'd," in which Milton moves toward the actual method of the epic, Adam "is stubborn in his offence Justice appeares reason[s] with him convinces him."[16] Before Adam in the great epic relents and despairs, convicted of sin, he complains to God: "inexplicable / Thy Justice seems" (754–55). At that invocatory moment, Adam's conscience begins to speak to him in the second person ("thou," "thee," and "thy" appearing eleven times in ll.757–70). Adam has internalized the character Justice as a Mosaic superego:

> God made thee of choice his own, and of his own
> To serve him, thy reward was of his grace,
> Thy punishment then justly is at his Will.
> Be it so, for I submit, his doom is fair. . . .
>
> (766–69)

Adam will escape from God's infinite wrath in the implications of a phrase that terrifies him: will God "draw out / . . . finite to infinite / . . . to satisfy his rigor / Satisfi'd never"? (801–4). "Rigor / Satisfi'd" suggests "rigid satisfaction" (3.212), God's term for the necessary atonement in which infinite becomes finite. The Son of God offers to save Adam, thus satisfying a concept of justice that Paul and his Protestant interpreters would regard as inalienably Old Testament in character. The Son's faith stands in marked contrast to Adam's despair:

> Though now to Death I yield, and am his due
> All that of me can die, yet that debt paid,
> Thou wilt not leave me in the loathsome grave
> His prey, nor suffer my unspotted Soul
> For ever with corruption there to dwell.
>
> (3.245–49)

Adam, unaware of his allusion to Christ's atonement, ends the soliloquy convicted under the law, but before the book is over he will begin to interpret the judgment on the serpent as the promise that releases him from that law. If Adam's despair is an unbearable burden to him, his cruelty to Eve just after the soliloquy is painful for the reader. The pressure to dissolve the present situation increases, and the reader's desire for resolution meshes with Adam's longing for release from the law. The *protevangelium* promises that resolution and that abrogation—but at a price.

Adam under the law can never satisfy God's rigor. He may intend "to resign and render back / All [he] receiv'd (749–50), but God and his Son know that he is bankrupt: "Atonement for himself or offering meet, / Indebted and undone, hath none to bring" (3.234–35). Only Christ, infinite contracted to finite, obedient and capable of enduring punishment, fulfills both parts of legal justification:

1. Of *Obedience*, when all such things are done, as the Law commandeth. . . . He that does so is a just man.

2. Of *Punishment* or *Satisfaction*, when the breach of the Law is satisfied by enduring the utmost of such penalties, as the rigour of the Law required. For not only he who doth what the Law commandeth: but even he also that suffereth all such punishments, as the Law-giver in justice can inflict for the breach of the Law, is to bee accounted a just man, and reckoned after such satisfaction made, as no transgressor of the Law.[17]

Christ's satisfaction through torture and death ("on mee let thine anger fall" [3.237]) does not improve human nature, which is degraded after the Fall by Pauline anthropological dualism. Following the Torah of paradise, which was a way of life rather than merely an externally imposed code of restrictions, Adam described himself to Raphael as "free [to] /Approve the best, and follow what I approve" (8.610–11). In his soliloquy, anticipating Kant's antiparadisaic admonition against any rationalistic system of thought that issues in the pursuit of an ideal, Adam is the crooked timber from which no straight thing could ever be made:

> But from me what can proceed,
> But all corrupt, both Mind and Will deprav'd,
> *Not to do only, but to will* the same
> With me?
>
> (824–27; *my emphasis*)

Adam is the unclean fountain, the bitter root, the wild vine, the "*evill tree* [that] *cannot bring forth good fruite.*"[18] He has meditated on Romans 7:14–25: "for what I would, that do I not; but what I hate, that do I" (15) and "For the good that I would, I do not: but the evil which I would not, that I do" (19). Adam's self-assessment depends entirely on Paul's description of the Mosaic law as a code of restrictions that resembles Roman law rather than Torah. Human beings cannot obey that law because their physical bodies contain another law, which forces them to act against their will and prevents them from doing the good that is required by the Mosaic law. The anthropological dualism of a good soul in a weak, evil body can lead to a Marcion-like theological dualism that separates the bad creator-God of the Old Testament from the good redeemer-God found primarily in the Pauline epistles. As E. P. Sanders has noted, "anthropological dualism . . . denies a cardinal theological belief of Judaism: that God created the world and pronounced it good (Gen. 1:31)."[19]

Book 10 presents the epic's most grimly methodical devaluation of the laws of Moses and of nature (651–715), whose "growing miseries" (715) put Adam immediately in mind of his own misery. Philo comments on the biblical curses delivered against the transgressors of the Mosaic law (Deut. 28:15–68): "The story of Thyestes will be child's play compared with the monstrous calamities which those times of terror will bring about."[20] The Miltonic bard describes the terrible alterations in nature that are the consequences of disobedience: "At that tasted Fruit / The Sun, as from Thyestean Banquet, turn'd / His course intended" (687–89). The passionate hostility directed against the laws of nature and of Moses to which Milton had earlier appealed in the divorce tracts—laws that emphasized the human capacity for achievement—may represent the cynicism and disappointment of a disillusioned idealist. The ruining of paradise is also a compulsive, systematic spoiling of Israel, which had been Milton's model for England. Just as humankind can no longer find redemption even in the moral law, so can it find no saving knowledge in the laws of external nature—neither the signs of the Jews nor the wisdom of the Greeks, but only Christ crucified (1 Cor. 1:20–25; Rom. 1:16–17). One must be dead to one law and blind to the other.

Adam reprises his soliloquy later in the book, when Eve proposes suicide as a form of celibacy, to stop the production of children destined to feed death:

> doubt not but God
> Hath wiselier arm'd his vengeful ire than so
> To be forestall'd; much more I fear lest Death
> So snatcht will not exempt us from the pain
> We are by doom to pay; rather such acts
> Of contumacy will provoke the Highest
> To *make death in us live.*
>
> (1022–28; *my emphasis*)

Adam in this state of wrath solves the problem by carefully reinterpreting Genesis 3:15, understanding for the first time its promise of redemption. His reprise of God's primal blessing of humankind with fertility dramatizes the thinness of a Pauline conception of Torah.[21] Evoked before the Fall, Genesis 1:28 emphasized the mutual benefits of a covenantal relationship between humankind and the animals brought by God "to receive / From thee thir Names, and pay thee fealty" (8.344). Fallen Adam now reinterprets Genesis 1:28 as a promise of vengeance against the devil: "to crush his head / Would be revenge indeed; which will be lost / By death brought on ourselves, or childless days / Resolv'd, as thou proposest" (10.1035–38).

The shift after the Fall from a comprehensive to a monolithic interpretation of the law parallels what Waldock has described as the degradation rather than degeneration of Milton's Satan. According to a Reformation commonplace, the law places us "under the power of the divel . . . [and] in the lawe we finde death, damnation and wrath, moreover the curse and vengeance of God upon us."[22] More pertinently, Paul in Romans 7 regards sin as a quasi-demonic power that makes use of the divine commandment to further its own ends: "sin, taking occasion by the commandment, wrought in me all manner of concupiscence" (7:5). Paul occasionally blurs distinctions between the content of the law and the effect of the law, between a law that reveals sin and a law that arouses sin. For Paul, the Mosaic law and Satan would have more in common than their degradation.

When Adam begs for oblivion to provide escape from God's wrath (776–80), he belies the actual mildness of his judgment (10.96). Adam also misidentifies the benign law of paradise as the thunderingly negative Sinaitic law portrayed in the most doctrinally hostile texts of the New

Testament (Heb. 12:18–20 and 22–24). This is also the portrayal of the law in the epic's last books: "the voice of God / To mortal ear is dreadful (12.235–36).

The redemption dimly foreseen at the end of book 10 comes at a heavy price: the torture and death of Christ, an anthropological dualism that devalues human nature and denies the goodness of the created order, the degradation of the Mosaic law, a thin and factitious sense of history that does not merely replace and blot out the past but actively misrepresents it, and the squeezing of the dense poetry of prelapsarian paradise into a thin line of doctrine.

Despite its extreme Paulinism, Adam's soliloquy cannot suppress entirely the evocation of Milton's Hebraic paradise. The element of supersession in Pauline typology emphasizes the contrast between weak Old Testament types and their strong New Testament antitype. Paul's incursions against his own past require "forgetting what lies behind and straining forward to what lies ahead" (Phil. 3:13). But even the internalized voice of Justice, using the language of Calvin to contrast life before and after the Fall, reminds Adam of an original grace that does not require the death of the redeemer: "thy reward was of his *grace*, / Thy punishment then *justly* is at his Will" (10.767–68; my emphasis). Adam's soliloquy inadvertently reverses the dynamics of supersession by asserting the priority and authority of paradise: the covenant of grace precedes the covenant of works. Paul saw the events of the Hebrew Bible as "written down for our instruction, upon whom the end of the ages has come" (1 Cor. 10:11).[23] But *Paradise Lost* is a radically nostalgic work that looks back to election in paradise preceding natural necessity in the fallen world. In the Edenic books of the great epic, Torah is the antitype that precedes the law, and Genesis 1:28 celebrates fertility and amplitude rather than vengeance. Satan, preferring paradise over heaven, parodies the aggressively antithetical impulse of the typologist: "For what God after better worse would build?" (9.102).

Early in the soliloquy, Adam anticipates his children's curses:

> Who of all Ages to succeed, but feeling
> The evil on him brought by me, will curse
> My Head: Ill fare our Ancestor impure,
> For this we may thank *Adam*; but his thanks
> Shall be the execration.
>
> (733–37)

Adam's bitter question is unanswerable within Milton's Pauline Christian tradition, where only Christ, the second Adam, can reverse the sin of the first Adam that has spread to all of his children. The *Zohar* has an answer that, appropriately, lacks resolution, balancing Father Adam's perpetual anxiety about original sin against his assurance that he is not responsible for it:

> When a human being is about to depart from life, Adam, the first man, appears to him and asks him why and in what state he leaves the world. The man says, "Woe to you that because of you I have to die." To which Adam replies, "My son, I transgressed one commandment and was punished for so doing; see how many commandments of your Master, negative and positive, you have transgressed." . . . Adam appears to every man at the moment of his departure from life to testify that he is dying on account of his own sins and not the sin of Adam.[24]

CHAPTER SEVEN

The Price of Grace: Adam, Moses, and the Jews

THE MILTONIC bard withdraws his creative presence from most of books 11 and 12, abandoning the epic to Christian doctrine as expounded tactfully but relentlessly by Michael, the typologizing angel of the New Testament. Those enemies who attacked Milton for presenting a specifically Jewish theory and practice of marriage and divorce would be gratified by the evidence of his repentance here. Milton's conversionist mission in the final vision and narration harks back to his *Observations upon the Articles of Peace*: "while we detest *Judaism*, we know our selves commanded by St. *Paul, Rom.* 11. to respect the *Jews*, and by all means to endeavor thir conversion" (*YP*, 3:326). Adam after the Fall is an entirely negative type of the Christ who will supersede him and reverse the damage he has caused. In books 11 and 12, he is urged to obliterate every token of his identity, as if in accord with John Cotton's injunction:

> [I]f thy soul be not utterly lost, so long as it hath any root, or power in itself, it is not come to an utter self-denial: though I cannot work I will believe, and if I cannot believe, I can wait that I may believe, and so here is still the old root of Adam left alive in us, whereby men seek to establish their own righteousness.[1]

Michael expounds the typology of Moses to teach Adam the least severe of his lessons. The radically typological Epistle to the Hebrews is the principal thematic source of books 11 and 12. The biblical source of the vision-framework is suggested in that estimable fund of universal scholarship, *The Dunciad Variorum*. Book 2 of *The Dunciad* draws heavily on the last books of Milton's diffuse epic. The ghost of Settle prepares Theobald for the visions of Dulness:

> All nonsense thus, of old or modern date,
> Shall in thee centre, from thee circulate.
> For this, our Queen unfolds to vision true
> Thy mental eye, for thou hast much to view.
>
> $(2.51-54)$[2]

The reader's attention is called to these lines' "resemblance to that passage in Milton" where Michael purges Adam's sight (11.411–13, quoted in full), and one is informed that "there is a general allusion in what follows to that whole passage."[3]

The "general allusion" is apparent even in the disposition of scenes in the argument to book 3, where Settle is described taking Theobald to a "*Mount of Vision*, from whence he shews him the past triumphs of the empire of Dulness, then the present, and lastly the future." Settle prophesies the end, when "all shall return to their original Chaos: A scene, of which the present Action of the Dunciad is but a Type or Foretaste, giving a Glimpse or *Pisgah-sight* of the promis'd Fulness of her Glory; the Accomplishment whereof will, in all probability, hereafter be the Theme of many other and greater Dunciads."[4] With "Pisgah-sight," a term synonymous with "Type," "Foretaste," and "Glimpse," Pope establishes a typological perspective.

Pisgah is the mountain in Moab from whose top God showed Moses a vision of the land of Canaan. Moses was excluded from sacred ground because of his sin at Meribah (Num. 27:12–14), but he was later granted a mitigating vision of the place. The account of that vision and of Moses' death occupies most of the last chapter of the Pentateuch (Deut. 34). Some exegetes interpret Canaan as "the figure of our heavenly heritage."[5] Babington elaborates on the relation of Moses' vision to his death:

> But before he dye, and passe this way of all flesh, God will have him go into the Mountaine, and see the Land of Promise. This was done in sweet goodnesse, that with more readie will he might make an end. And assuredly, thus dealeth God with his loving children at their latter end, even give them a glimpse, a sight, and taste of the true Land of Promise, that heavenly Canaan which he hath prepared for them after death.[6]

The most frequent application of typology to the Pisgah vision occurs in discussions of the inferiority of the Mosaic law to justification by faith. The Pisgah vision, equated with the law, becomes the "glimpse," "sight," and "taste" of the gospel, and Moses' exclusion from that promised land signifies "that by the Law, whereof Moses was Minister, we may see, as it werre a farre off, eternal life and salvation, but never enter into it that way, because through corruption of our natures we are not able to performe it; which being not performed, shutteth us out, and subjecteth us to a Curse."[7] Milton relies on this tradition in *De doctrina*, when he offers a typological explanation for Moses' exclusion from Canaan:

> The imperfection of the law was made apparent in the person of Moses himself. For Moses, who was the type of the law, could not lead the children of Israel into the land of Canaan, that is, into eternal rest. But an entrance was granted to them under Joshua, that is, Jesus. (*YP*, 6:519)

Michael expresses humanity's need of Christian salvation in the poetic rendition of the passage just cited, in which the identities of Adam and Moses fuse into a symbol of fallen humankind:

And therefore shall not Moses, though of God
Highly belov'd, being but the Minister
Of Law, his people into *Canaan* lead;
But *Joshua* whom the Gentiles *Jesus* call,
His Name and Office bearing, who shall quell
The adversary Serpent, and bring back
Through the world's wilderness long wander'd man
Safe to eternal Paradise of rest.

(12.307–14)

With the addition of "Paradise" in the last line, Michael introduces the theme of the Fall to the subject of law and the gospel and produces the effect of uniting Adam and Moses. Jesus' triumph is seen as entry into the land of Canaan after long wandering in the desert and as a return to Eden. Adam and Moses are sinners excluded from sacred ground as a result of their sin, yet granted by God's grace a consolatory vision. At this moment, Adam recognizes his identity with Moses, although of course it is precisely this recognition of shared inadequacy and of the need for someone greater (whose birth is announced less than fifty lines later) that dissolves the relationship.

When Moses sins by the waters of Meribah, God tells him: "Because ye beleeve me not, to sanctifie me in the eyes of the children of Israel, therefore ye shall not bring this Congregation into the land which I have given them" (Num. 20:12). God's later addition of a vision makes Moses' fate more endurable: "Get thee up into this mount Abarim, and see the land which I have given unto the children of Israel. And when thou hast seene it, thou also shalt be gathered unto thy people, as Aaron thy brother was gathered. For ye rebelled against my Commandement" (Num. 27:12–14).

Moses' sin at the waters of Meribah is generally interpreted as "unbelief" or "distrust."[8] Milton regards the fetching of water from the rock as proof that "miracles have been sometimes wrought for unbelievers. . . . In this instance both he who worked the miracle, and those for whom it was worked, seem to have been in a state of unbelief at the time of its performance." (*CE*, 15:365; cf. *YP*, 6:460). He also cites the episode as an example of "distrust of God" (*CE*, 17:55; cf. *YP*, 6:658). In Milton's discussion of original sin in *De doctrina*, "that which our first parents, and in them all posterity committed," distrust and unbelief head his famous list: "For what sin can be named, which was not included in this one act? It comprehended at once distrust in the divine veracity, and a proportionate credulity in the assurances of Satan; unbelief . . ." (*CE*, 15:181; cf. *YP*, 6:383). In comparing the sins of Adam and Moses, one might note that Milton goes on to list fourteen additional sins included in Adam's "mortal Sin / Original."

Reformation expositors recognized the mingling of pain and consolation in the scriptural account of Moses' ascent to the Pisgah height, which begins the last chapter of the Pentateuch. Calvin sees a lesson here: "We must take notice of the consolation, which is here referred to, that the pain of his death was alleviated by the permission to behold the land of Canaan. For this reason he is commanded to get up into the top of the mountain. . . . For faith does not altogether deprive God's children of human feelings; but our heavenly Father in His indulgence has compassion on their infirmity."[9]

Moses' ascent is related typologically to the temptation of Christ by the devil. God's beneficence in the case of Moses is then underscored, for the devil's ocular presentation of empire to Christ is intended to subvert rather than to console. Lightfoot notes a significant difference in "the Lords shewing to *Moses* from a high Mount all the kingdomes of *Canaan*, and saying, *All these will I give to the children of Israel*, and the Devils shewing to *Christ* all the kingdomes of the earth, and saying, All these will I give thee."[10] Ainsworth amplifies this distinction:

> Thus Moses viewed the land after the order that Abraham did at the first. God here sheweth Moses all the Kingdomes, and glory of Canaan, from an high mountaine, for his comfort and strengthening of his faith, who saw the promises a farre off, saluted them, and died, as did his godly forefathers. On the contrary, the Devill taketh Christ up into an exceeding high mountaine, & sheweth him all the kingdoms of the world, and the glory of them, to draw him (if he had beene able) from the faith and service of God, unto the worship of Satan.[11]

Milton relies on the situational correspondence of Adam and Moses to give pointed force to his typological reference. When Adam ascends the "Hill / Of Paradise the highest," he is ignorant of the measure of grace he is receiving and of the trial which the Second Adam must undergo. The epic narrator makes certain that the reader is not:

> Not higher that Hill nor wider looking round,
> Whereon for different cause the Tempter set
> Our second *Adam* in the wilderness,
> To show him all Earth's Kingdoms and thir Glory.
>
> (11.381–84)

This is the poem's first indication that Adam's vision of the course of history is typologically related to the action of *Paradise Regained*, and Milton's readers are reminded that Satan "took / The Son of God up to a Mountain high"(*PR*, 3.251–52).

The recognition of an Adam-Moses relationship in the last books of *Paradise Lost* throws some light on the dramatic context of Adam and

Michael's last colloquy (12.214–314) before the announcement of Christ's birth. Adam, like Samson as described by Stanley Fish, "seems [at times] to make an advance toward understanding, only in the next minute to embrace in another guise the error he has rejected."[12]

Immediately after describing the climax of the Exodus, the overwhelming of Pharaoh's legions in the Red Sea, Michael turns to the wandering of the Israelites in the desert:

> the Race elect
> Safe towards *Canaan* from the shore advance
> Through the wild Desert, not the readiest way,
> Lest ent'ring on the *Canaanite* alarm'd
> War terrify them inexpert, and fear
> Return them back to Egypt, choosing rather
> Inglorious life with servitude; for life
> To noble and ignoble is more sweet
> Untrained in Arms, where rashness leads not on.
>
> (*12.214–22*)

Warburton's early note on these lines poses an extremely relevant question: "It is remarkable, that here Milton omits the moral cause (though he gives the poetical) of the Israelites wandering forty years in the wilderness; and this was their poltron mutiny on the return of the spies."[13] Warburton concludes simply that the substitution of a general reason for the circuitous route to the Red Sea (Exod. 13:17–18) in place of the literal cause of the Israelites' wandering (Num. 14)—the poetical for the moral, in his terms—derives from Michael's intention "to give such a representation of things, as might convey comfort to Adam." He might also have remarked Michael's exquisite sense of tact. Milton knew very well the literal reason for the wandering of the Israelites in the desert; indeed, "the murmurers. Num. 14" is one of the projected topics for a biblical tragedy in the Cambridge Manuscript in the library of Trinity College. A reference by Michael to the children of Israel as wandering sinners would have distressed Adam. The Israelites wander through "the wild Desert" (12.216), and Christ is found in *Paradise Regained* in "the Desert wild" (1.193; 2.109). Adam's part in all this desert wandering is made explicit by the Lutheran Daniel Brenius: "For the people of Israel, a type of Christ and his Church, were led into the desert, to that place to which Adam, who had been tempted in Paradise, had banished all his progeny out of the promised land. But Christ, the victor over the devil, has recovered paradise."[14]

Eschewing potentially disturbing comparisons, Michael continues the narrative with an account of the law and of Moses' mediatorial office, then describes the entry of the Israelites into Canaan. Suddenly, in a breach of the narrative pattern established in the last books, Michael turns back to provide a fuller account of the law and to describe the Israelites' entry into the promised land. This return is prompted by a statement and a question from Adam, which, from a typological perspective, are so dangerously wrongheaded that they require a reproof even from the most tactful of angels. Adam's interposition passes over the seventy-four lines devoted to Moses (12.169–242) and comes to rest on the promise made to Abraham "that all Nations of the Earth / Shall in his Seed be blessed" (12.147–48):

> now first I find
> Mine eyes true op'ning, and my heart much eas'd,
> Erewhile perplext with thoughts what would become
> Of mee and all Mankind; but now I see
> His day, in whom all Nations shall be blest,
> Favor unmerited by me, who sought
> Forbidd'n knowledge by forbidd'n means.
>
> (273–79)

Adam's disregard of Moses and his enthusiasm for "Just Abraham" (273) are hardly sinful, and the inevitable reverberations in the reader's mind of "Mine eyes true op'ning" are not to be urged against our first parent. At this point, the Christian reader's perspective is merely clearer than Adam's. Adam can see only as far as Abraham's day, while Milton's contemporary Christian reader remembers Christ's words: "Your father Abraham rejoiced to see my day: and he saw it, and was glad" (John 8:56). Of course, Adam's chronically enthusiastic assumption that he now understands everything and his definition of the sin as a reaching after knowledge underestimate the enormity of his act.

Now Adam—certain, no doubt, that his enlightenment is proceeding wonderfully—asks a question:

> This yet I apprehend not, why to those
> Among whom God will deign to dwell on Earth
> So many and so various Laws are giv'n;
> So many Laws argue so many sins
> Among them; how can God with such reside?
>
> (280–84)

How, indeed! Adam remembers Raphael's assurance in happier times that "God will deign / To visit oft the dwellings of just Men / Delighted" (8.569–71), and he is perplexed by God's inexplicable mercy to the children of Israel who need "so many Laws" for "so many sins." His own sin is single—almost excusable if regarded as a quest for knowledge. Adam complains to Michael from a position of privilege. Although he often acknowledges responsibility for his sin, he doesn't feel it yet. Hence the condescending question, which records his frank puzzlement.

Michael has tactfully omitted mentioning the sins of the Israelites, which Adam inferentially seizes upon in his question. The Angel is forced by Adam's interruption to check these ignorant assumptions and to draw the embarrassing comparisons between Adam and Moses and the children of Israel. Now Adam, with Michael as his guide, must wander in the desert, traversing the same ground, but with a difference this time. The subtlety and tact are not absent, but this time Michael moves inexorably toward a conclusion that will bind Adam and his sinful progeny:

> Doubt not but that sin
> Will reign among them, as of thee begot;
> And therefore was Law given them to evince
> Thir natural pravity, by stirring up
> Sin against Law to fight; that when they see
> Law can discover sin, but not remove,
> Save by those shadowy expiations weak,
> The blood of Bulls and Goats, they may conclude
> Some blood more precious must be paid for Man,
> Just for unjust.
>
> (285–94)

Michael begins his answer with the sort of direct injunction that is noticeably absent from the preceding account of the wandering: "Doubt not but that sin / Will reign among them, as of thee begot." Adam is to recall his own lamentable role as originator of mortal sin. If the Israelites require grace commensurate with their sin, so does Adam; and the last line of this excerpt recalls God's earlier request for love and charity "to redeem / Man's mortal crime, and just th' unjust to save" (3.214–15). Michael's use of the singular "Sin" and "Law" reminds Adam of his single disobedience of the single prohibition.

That the implied severity of Michael's next lines has gone unnoticed attests to the angel's tact. Indeed, William G. Madsen notes that only once in Michael's narration, in these lines, do we hear "the accent of sympathy for frail, erring humanity."[15] An understanding of the Adam-Moses typology should heighten one's apprehension of the accent of judgment as well:

> And therefore shall not *Moses*, though of God
> Highly belov'd, being but the Minister
> Of Law, his people into *Canaan* lead;

> But *Joshua* whom the Gentiles *Jesus* call,
> His Name and Office bearing, who shall quell
> The adversary Serpent, and bring back
> Through the world's wilderness long wander'd man
> Safe to eternal Paradise of rest.
>
> (*307–14*)

Michael has just joined Adam and the Israelites. Now identities merge when both are fused with Moses: "And therefore was Law given them" (287), "And therefore shall not Moses" (307)—the kinship is stressed by strong verbal and metrical similarities of the lines, which include the proximate position of Moses and the law and the common feminine caesural break between the upbeat and the downbeat of the fourth foot. The parody of Adam's awareness of kinship with his fallen progeny is Satan's awareness of kinship with his (book 2), and, perhaps, the fulfillment is the Son's willingness to relinquish privilege and to assume a fallen human nature.

Adam is being instructed, as were the Israelites, "that to God is no access / Without Mediator, whose high Office now / Moses in figure bears, to introduce one greater" (239–42). Adam can no longer remain aloof from this principle, since his new awareness of a shared inadequacy—exclusion by sin from sacred ground—prompts him to recognize as well the necessity of Christ's salvation. Moses' role is that of mediator, "to introduce one greater," and the announcement of the birth of Christ less than fifty lines later is theologically inevitable.

Michael excludes what Warburton would have called the "moral cause" of Moses' exclusion from Canaan in order to emphasize that Moses ("of God / Highly belov'd") is less guilty than Adam. God's impatience with his murmuring wanderers provokes him to broach to Moses his intention to "smite them with the pestilence, and disinherit them, and make of thee a greater nation, and mightier than they" (Num. 14: 12). Moses replies that the Egyptian enemy and the nations who have heard of God's fame will think that he has forsworn his promise to his people: "Now if thou shalt kill all this people, as one man, then the nations which have heard the fame of thee, will speake, saying, Because the Lord was not able to bring this people into the lande which he sware unto them, therefore he hath slaine them in the wildernesse" (14:15–16). God is sufficiently placated by Moses to alter the terms of his angry promise so that death will not come immediately, but rather after forty years' wandering in the desert (14:32–35). The bones of the Israelites will lie in the wilderness, and only Caleb and Joshua will be permitted entry into the promised land.

In book 9 of *Paradise Lost*, immediately before eating the fruit, Adam dismisses the possibility of his immediate death in an argument remarkably similar to the passage in which Moses argues successfully with God on behalf of the Israelites:

> Nor can I think that God, creator wise,
> Though threat'ning, will in earnest so destroy
> Us his prime Creatures, dignifi'd so high,
> Set over all his Works, which in our Fall,
> For us created, needs with us must fail,
> Dependent made; so God shall uncreate,
> Be frustrate, do, undo, and labor lose,
> Not well conceiv'd of God, who though his Power
> Creation could repeat, yet would be loath
> Us to abolish, lest the Adversary
> Triumph and say; Fickle their State whom God
> Most Favors, who can please him long? Mee first
> He ruin'd, now Mankind; whom will he next?
> Matter of scorn, not to be given the Foe.
>
> (9.938–51)

The different circumstances of the arguments of Adam and Moses underscore their different moral valuations. Adam, who assumes that God has created a universe entirely dependent on man, grounds his argument in selfishness. Moses, on the other hand, sees his own happiness depending on his people's survival, and his response to God's promise of personal glory is ample testimony of his love for the sinful Israelites. Milton cites Moses' argument in Numbers 14 as evidence that "LOVE OF GOD means love which . . . [i]s eager for his glory" (*YP*, 6:657). Michael's omission, then, of Moses' sin at the waters of Meribah in the wilderness of Zin may represent his intention to convey to Adam an even stronger sense of his own sinfulness. Even so, the Adam-Moses relationship is by far the most benign in the last books, reminding Adam of his sin and preparing him for his redeemer. Michael's other applications of typology go much further in degrading him.

If "no shadow" is the divine voice's first epithet for unfallen Adam (4.470), the only hope for fallen Adam in books 11 and 12 is to become someone else's shadow—as himself, the old Adam, the most potent symbol of sin under the law, he is lost. He is the eldest of all brothers, whose privilege, like that of biblical Israel, depends on an abrogated privilege based on birthright and temporal priority. By the reversal of primogeniture, he is overcome by his younger brother, the second Adam who is Christ. Adam's position is that of the Jews as illustrated by Tertullian through a typological reading of Genesis 25:21–23 ("Two nations are in thy womb . . . and the greater shall serve the less"):

> Since the "people" or "nation" of the Jews is anterior in time, and "greater" through the grace of primary favour in the Law, whereas ours is understood to be "less" in the age of times, as having in the last era of the world attained the knowledge of divine mercy: beyond doubt, as we learn through the edict of the divine utterance, the "prior" and "greater" people—that is, the Jewish—must necessarily serve the "less"; and the "less" people—that is, the Christian—must overcome the "greater." . . . [The Jews] have ever been depicted, out of the volume of the divine Scriptures, as guilty of the crime of idolatry; whereas our "less"—that is, posterior—people, quitting the idols which formerly it used slavishly to serve, has been converted to the same God from whom Israel. . . . had departed. For thus has the "less"—that is, posterior—"people" overcome the "greater people," while it attains the grace of divine favour, from which Israel has been divorced.[16]

Adam is like the Jews who fell off into idolatry—anterior in time and greater through the grace of primary favor in the law. Before the Fall, he was capable of keeping the great command: "Be strong, live happy, and love, but first of all / Him whom to love is to obey" (8.633–34). In book 12, having broken that command, and with faculties impaired, he evokes Raphael's earlier blessing, with Tertullian's remarks an ironic counterpoint:

> Henceforth I learn, that to obey is best,
> And love with fear the only God, to walk
> As in his presence, ever to observe
> His providence, and on him sole depend,
> Merciful over all his works, with good
> Still overcoming evil, and by small
> Accomplishing great things, by things deem'd weak
> Subverting worldly strong.
>
> (561–68)

Adam's praise is unconscious self-indictment, for he is the evil and strong whom Christ will overcome. Adam can become regenerate only when he accepts a relationship with Christ based not on bloodline (progenitor to progeny) but on grace (wretched sinner to redeemer). Somewhere between lines 564 and 565, Adam disappears as subject, relinquishing agency and identity, dying in Christ.

Michael activates the typological traditions associated with Abraham in order to strip Adam of the comfort that a parent whose life is a failure might take in the accomplishments of a successful child. Before the Fall, the Miltonic bard develops the Abraham-Adam parallel in book 8, where

Abraham's argument with God (Gen. 18:22–33) is the principal source of Adam's dialogue with God on the subject of a fit mate. The Hebraic and nontypological resemblances between the visit of the angels to Abraham at Mamre (Gen. 18:1–15) and Raphael's descent to paradise (book 5) are singular and unmistakable. They include the noontime approach, the deference of both Abraham and Adam in offering hospitality to angels, the human hosts' concern with preparing food for the feast, and the angels' promise of a blessed issue to the women. Adam's "Haste hither, Eve" (5.308) derives from Abraham's urging Sarah to "hasten" her food preparations (18:6). The overwhelming majority of Christian commentators focus their attention on the mystery of the trinity symbolized by the visit of the three angels; the Miltonic bard attends instead to Rashi's commentary, which concentrates on the literal details of the entertainment in Eden and which identifies the angel Raphael (lit., God's healing) as one of the visitors.[17] The entire episode reveals the inclusive spirit of the 1643–45 tracts and of Selden's scholarship. The comparison of Raphael with "*Maia*'s son" (5.285) points to Mercury's visit to Aeneas (*Aeneid* 4.238–78). Adam and Eve's simple and decorous banquet is identified as the archetype of Abraham and Sarah's graciousness at Mamre, and Adam becomes, like Abraham, an exemplar of Christian hospitality: "Be not forgetful to entertain strangers, for thereby some have entertained angels unawares" (Heb. 13:2).

When Michael recalls the promise that, in Abraham's seed, all nations shall be blessed (12.147–48), he is not referring to the original blessing of Genesis (18:8 and 12:3), but to Paul's typological reading of it in Galatians 3:8. Adam's response to the promise, "now I see / His day in whom all Nations shall be blest" (276–77), refers to John 8 as well as to Galatians 3. Both texts undo Jewish pride in being descended from Abraham. In Galatians 3, Paul argues that the true descendants of Abraham are those who have faith and that the promise applies to them and not to the Jews, his physical descendants. Christians share the faith that rendered Abraham acceptable to God before the making of the covenant and before he had any good deeds that he could offer to God. Paul disenfranchises the Jews by means of a Christian midrash on Genesis 15:6: "And he believed in the LORD; and he counted it to him for righteousness":

> Even as Abraham believed God, and it was accounted to him for righteousness. Know ye therefore that they which are of faith, the same are the children of Abraham. And the Scripture, foreseeing that God would justify the heathen through faith, preached before the gospel unto Abraham, saying, In thee shall all nations be blessed. . . . For as many as are of the works of the law are under the curse. (Gal. 3:6–8 and 10)

In his search for a precedent for gentiles who did not perform the ceremonial observances of the Torah, Paul finds Abraham, who risked sacrificing his son without the ordinances of Torah to guide him and who left his gentile home on a journey that brought him to God. Rabbinic Judaism as well as Christianity regard him as an example of conversion, although, as Segal observes, "[T]he later rabbinic stories of Abraham emphasize that he observed all the commandments in seeming polemic with the Christian view of the Abraham of faith."[18] Abraham's faithfulness consisted in his steadfast belief and in his observance of Torah. Instead of including Judaism as a religion of faith, Paul redefines faith as a quality inherent only in gentile Christianity, based on spiritual absorption into the risen Christ, involving a radical reorientation and commitment, in opposition to the Pharisaic observance of the law that carries a curse. In addition to stipulating a limiting definition of faith, Paul uses the potentially inclusive "all nations" of Genesis in the common technical sense of "the Gentiles" as distinct from "the Jews."[19]

Throughout the last books, Michael distinguishes between Abraham's seed and Adam's. "Seed" is an example of Paul's corporate language, the one including the many, just as, by "Christ," Paul often includes those who are in him. This conception of corporate identity is the Christian postlapsarian counterpart of the Edenic prohibition as the law containing all others. Abraham's progeny are all the heroes of faith and Christ himself. Adam's are all the evil of the world. The Pauline distinctions between loins and faith, body and spirit, Christians and Jews—all argue against privilege of any sort, individual, genetic, national, and all operate to strip Adam of the comforting title father of the human race.

Because they are projected on the epic screen of history, Adam sometimes forgets that the pictures Michael is showing him are home movies, crammed with relatives, directly descended, all of them resembling their ancestor, and all badly turned out. Judging the misbehavior of the "Sons of God," Adam observes that "the tenor of Man's woe / Holds on the same, from Woman to begin" (11.632–33). Michael responds immediately, "From man's effeminate slackness it begins" (634). More important, Noah's flood destroys *all* of Adam's children, the wicked majority of the world:

> How didst thou grieve then, *Adam*, to behold
> The end of all thy Offspring . . .
>
> . . . .
>
> . . . as when a Father mourns
> His Children, all in view destroyed at once.
>
> (11.754–55 and 760–61)

Noah, the flood's survivor, is not Adam's son but rather "the only Son of light / In a dark age" (11.808–9).

Michael repeatedly emphasizes blessed Abraham and his seed: "in his Seed / All Nations shall be blest" (12.125–26), "all Nations of the Earth / Shall in his Seed be blessed" (147–48), "that [not "thy"!] destin'd Seed" (233), "the Land / Promis'd to *Abraham* and his Seed" (259–60), and "Just *Abraham* and his Seed" (273). Adam rejoices at the news of the advent of Christ, "The Seed of Woman": "yet from my Loins / Thou shalt proceed" (380–81). Michael responds by returning to Adam's earlier allusion to Abraham in John 8 (12.276–77). There the Jews tell Jesus that they are descendants from Abraham and have never been in bondage to anyone. Jesus tells them that their father is the devil: "If ye were Abraham's children, ye would do the works of Abraham. . . . Ye do the deeds of your father. . . . Ye are of your father the devil, and the lusts of your father ye will do" (8:39–44). According to Michael, Christ will cure Adam's death wound

> Not by destroying *Satan*, but his works
> In thee and in thy Seed: nor can this be,
> But by fulfilling that which thou didst want,
> Obedience to the Law of God, impos'd
> On penalty of death.
>
> $\qquad\qquad\qquad\qquad\qquad\qquad$ (394–98)[20]

Adam, like the Jews, is of the devil's seed, under an unfulfillable law that carries a curse. Both lie under a penalty of death that extends to their progeny: "The penalty to thy transgression due, / And due to theirs which out of thine will grow." Only Christ can fulfill the law: "The Law of God exact [Christ] shall fulfil / Both by obedience and by love" (402–3). Conversion, and absorption in the risen Christ, is the only solution to human insufficiency under the Edenic-Mosaic law:

THE MOSAIC LAW WAS A WRITTEN CODE, CONSISTING OF MANY STIPULATIONS, AND INTENDED FOR THE ISRAELITES ALONE. IT HELD A PROMISE OF LIFE FOR THE OBEDIENT AND A CURSE FOR THE DISOBEDIENT. ITS AIM WAS TO MAKE THE ISRAELITES HAVE RECOURSE TO THE RIGHTEOUSNESS OF THE PROMISED CHRIST, THROUGH A RECOGNITION OF MANKIND'S, AND THEREFORE OF THEIR OWN DEPRAVITY. ITS AIM, ALSO, WAS THAT ALL WE OTHER NATIONS SHOULD AFTERWARDS BE EDUCATED FROM THIS ELEMENTARY, CHILDISH, AND SERVILE DISCIPLINE TO THE ADULT STATURE OF A NEW CREATURE, AND TO A MANLY FREEDOM UNDER THE GOSPEL, WORTHY OF GOD'S SONS. (*YP*, 6:517)

In Romans 9, Paul describes God's election of the spiritual Israel and distinguishes between "the children of the flesh" and "the children of the promise": "For they are not all Israel, which are of Israel: neither, because they are the seed of Abraham, are they all children" (6–8). The only "children of God" are the "children of the promise [who] are counted for the seed" (9). Similarly, Michael tells Adam of Christ's disciples:

> All Nations they shall teach; for from that day
> Not only to the Sons of *Abraham*'s Loins
> Salvation shall be Preacht, but to the Sons
> Of *Abraham*'s Faith wherever through the world;
> So in his seed all Nations shall be blest.
>
> $(446–50)$

Although "only" is a welcome surprise, "but to" rather than "but also to" suggests limitation, as does the Pauline interpretation of "all Nations." When Milton in *De doctrina* discusses God's calling the gentiles and abandoning the Jews, he joins Romans 9 with John: "*he came to his own, and his own did not receive him. He gave them the right to become sons of God; those, that is, who believe in his name.* The promise, therefore, is not to the children of Abraham in a physical sense, but to the children of his faith who receive Christ" (*YP,* 6:196). Adam's position is virtually identical to that of the Jews. According to Wollebius,

> As out of a venemous root, nothing can proceed that's wholsome, so all that are come of *Adam* naturally, are born guilty of that primitive sin. . . . Christ then is excepted from this guilt, for he was born of *Adam*, but not by *Adam*; not by natural generation, but by the vertue of the Holy Ghost.[21]

The distinction between the children of loins and of faith, used for millennia to disenfranchise the Jews from the promise of salvation, appears in England in the 1650s in tracts opposing the readmission of the Jews, who had been expelled in 1290 by an act of Edward I in his council. Edmund Gayton addresses an anti-Jewish poem to Menasseh ben Israel, "the cheife Agent for ye Introduction of ye Jewish Nation": "Welcome to us by what hard name so ever / Thou sonne of Abrams loynes (but Faith never)."[22] An anonymous conversionist tract seems to have been updated by adding Menasseh's name, which it then repeats endlessly in opposing his efforts to readmit the Jews into England. The tract begins by regarding the various promises God made to Abraham regarding his seed:

> As touching the Seed, it is evident, they cannot be all that naturally descended from *Abraham, Isaac,* or *Jacob,* or that should descend from their children, or childrens children in any age or time. For neither *Ishmael* nor *Esau* the first borne of *Isaac* were of the seed, nor any of all those that sinned and perished in the wildernesse. . . . So that it is evident, I suppose, unto you, *Ben-Israel,* as well as to us, that none of this sort of all the Tribes of Israel to

this day, are of that seed unto whom the promise was made, or that shall inherit . . . that good Land which God sware he would give them for an everlasting possession, and be their God. But that they are a far better sort of people which the Scriptures do distinguish from these. . . . And all this I hope *Ben-Israel* you understand also, and that the children of the promise are counted for the seed, and not the children of the flesh.[23]

The angel Michael's method in the final books resembles that of Menasseh's respondent, to read the Hebrew Bible typologically for the purpose of conversion: "But alas! what shall I say, or may some say unto me for all this? Doth *Ben-Israel* by his Book give us any cause at all to think that he or any of his brethren will regard these things?" He writes anyway, "for some of that remnants sake," "that they may consider and repent."[24]

The distinction between loins and faith that removes all privilege can be read in a contemporary political as well as religious context. Sir Robert Filmer, one of the most sensible and courteous of Milton's opponents, argues that the king's inheritance of the throne derives ultimately from Adam. Contemporary kings have inherited the "lordship which Adam by creation had over the whole world, and by right descending from him the Patriarchs did enjoy."[25] Before the Fall, Adam was a king, though the consecrated garden did not require for its enjoyment the overthrow of earlier inhabitants, as Canaan did. Adam would have transmitted traditions to his progeny, who would have gone on pilgrimage to visit him in his capital seat as the Jews visited Jerusalem:

> this had been
> Perhaps thy Capital Seat, from whence had spread
> All generations, and had hither come
> From all the ends of th' Earth, to celebrate
> And reverence thee thir great Progenitor.
> But this preëminence thou hast lost, brought down
> To dwell on even ground now with thy Sons.
>
> (11.342–48)

The distinction between the children of loins and of faith might have been on the mind of John Milton, whose surviving children gave him no hope of continued Miltonic greatness. His poems, the children of his faith, have given him immortality, for they "containe a potencie of life in them . . . as active as that soule was whose progeny they are." In paradise, pleasure, beauty, truth, and virtue flow along the same continuum, as "smiles from reason flow." The final books enforce radical disjunctions: pleasure and beauty are empty of all goodness (11.603–27). Adam's sin transmits only death, and believing Christians are the spiritual seed of

Abraham. The final books devalue the privilege of genetic transmission, choosing instead the discontinuities of conversion, baptism, faith, and grace. But the Pauline choice between loins and faith is not universally unavoidable. For the Pharisees and for the rabbis after them, there need be no contradiction between election (God's promise in choosing Israel) and the ancestry of the people.

The doctrine promulgated by Michael in the last books is meant to console Adam for the loss of paradise. The lost intimacy with God is entirely Hebraic:

> This most afflicts me, that departing hence,
> As from his face I shall be hid, depriv'd
> His blessed count'nance; here I could frequent,
> With worship, place by place where he voutsaf'd
> Presence Divine, and to my Sons relate;
> On this Mount he appear'd, under this Tree
> Stood visible, among these Pines his voice
> I heard, here with him at this Fountain talk'd:
> So many grateful Altars I would rear
> Of grassy Turf, and pile up every Stone
> Of lustre from the brook, in memory,
> Or monument to Ages, and thereon
> Offer sweet smelling Gums and Fruits and Flowers:
> In yonder nether World, where shall I seek
> His bright appearances, or footstep trace?
>
> (11.315–29)

Michael provides the ultimate correction of this Hebraic sense of holy place as external, separate, and enclosed when he explains the purpose behind the eventual removal and ruin of paradise:

> To teach thee that God attributes to place
> No sanctity, if none be thither brought
> By men who there frequent, or therein dwell.
>
> (11.836–38)

The verbs in the last line connect "Jerusalem laid waste" (PR 3.283) and paradise lost: Adam and Eve dwelled in paradise; priests frequented the temple in Jerusalem.

The difficulty for Christian readers of imagining a benign or gracious Mosaic law in paradise is dramatized by Northrop Frye's description of the difference between the comic and tragic modes. Where comedy moves toward freedom from time, nature, and arbitrary law, "tragedy presents the reverse theme of narrowing a comparatively free life into a process of causation."[26] According to Frye, any tragic mythos reenacts the Fall from freedom in paradise downward into time, causality, and an "epiphany of law."[27] But Milton's Adam falls from nature, history, and Torah as understood by the Hebrew Bible into the gospel's abrogation of the world, of temporality, and of the law as understood by typology. Since comedy often sets up an arbitrary law and then finds a way to break or evade it without penalty, the theme of law yielding to love and the elegant evasion of *felix culpa* should make *Paradise Lost* the supreme comedy of Christian liberty. Perhaps it is. But alongside the Pauline comedy is the Hebraic tragedy of Torah degraded into law, underscored by the damage wrought in historical time by the central biblical texts of book 12.

Notes

Introduction

1. *John Milton: Complete Poems and Major Prose*, ed. Merritt Y. Hughes (New York: Odyssey, 1957), p. 289. Parenthetic book and line references to Milton's poetry are to this edition.

2. *Christian Doctrine*, in *The Complete Prose Works of John Milton*, gen. ed. Don M. Wolfe (New Haven: Yale University Press, 1953–83), 6:515–20. Hereafter, parenthetic references to this Yale edition of Milton's prose will be abbreviated as *YP*.

3. Martin Luther, *Commentary upon Galatians* (1644), cited in *Puritanism and Liberty*, ed. A. S. P. Woodhouse (Chicago: University of Chicago Press, 1951), p. 221.

4. Milton's views on Christian liberty are more extreme than those of most orthodox Reformation theologians, who retain the moral component of the law, and also more than those of Luther, according to whom the moral law, while not binding, is at least "useful for self-examination" (Maurice Kelley, in *YP*, 6:521, n.).

5. In *The Art of Presence* (Berkeley and Los Angeles: University of California Press, 1977), Arnold Stein handles the devaluation of Eden with a degree of sensitivity and insight unmatched in current Milton studies.

6. William Guild, *Moses Unvailed: Or, Those Figures Which Served unto the Patterne and Shaddow of Heavenly Things* (London, 1620), p. 99; Samuel Mather, *The Figures or Types of the Old Testament* (Dublin, 1683), p. 408.

7. In his study of the Hebraic factor in seventeenth-century literature, *Jerusalem and Albion* (New York: Schocken, 1964), Harold Fisch considers the impact of the Scriptures as a firsthand imaginative experience rather than as merely a collection of "dogmas" (p.3). Fisch's book should appear on reading lists alongside of and as corrective to studies that reduce Milton to a Pauline paradigm. Those studies in turn can correct the imbalance in Fisch's own work, which refuses to acknowledge the capital importance of Pauline theology to Milton: "Milton . . . began from the book of *Genesis* and went on steadily forward to the Book of *Judges* and *Job*. Around those three works he wrote his major poems. One sometimes wonders whether he ever got as far as the *Epistles* of Paul, and he never wrote a full-length poem about the Crucifixion" (pp. 5–6). Fisch's failure to take into account the Pauline and Augustinian components of Milton's thought leads him to minimize the importance of the Fall in *Paradise Lost*. Fisch speculates that Milton implies a view of the Fall "as an offense serious indeed but remediable, just as the sins of backsliding Israel were felt to be remediable" ("Hebraic Style and Motifs in *Paradise Lost*," in *Language and Style in Milton*, ed. Ronald D. Emma and John T. Shawcross [New York: Ungar, 1967], p.50).

8. A. S. P. Woodhouse, "The Argument of Milton's *Comus*," *The University*

of Toronto Quarterly 11 (1941); 46–71; reprinted in *A Maske at Ludlow: Essays on Milton's 'Comus,'* ed. John S. Diekhoff (Cleveland: Case Western Reserve University Press, 1968), p. 19.

9. Woodhouse, *The Heavenly Muse: A Preface to Milton*, ed. Hugh MacCallum (Toronto: University of Toronto Press, 1972), p. 111.

10. Woodhouse, "Nature and Grace in *The Faerie Queene*," *ELH* 16 (1949); 194–228; reprinted in *Elizabethan Poetry: Modern Essays in Criticism*, ed. Paul J. Alpers (New York: Oxford University Press, 1967), p. 351.

11. See, for example, *YP*, 2:233, 259, 285, 287, 296–97, and 351. Milton is remembering the divine imperatives of the Hebrew Bible, such as "Speak unto all the congregation of Israel, and say unto them: Ye shall be holy; for I the LORD your God am holy" (Lev. 19:2). For Woodhouse, only Christians belong to the true congregation of Israel.

12. Woodhouse, "Nature and Grace," 352.

13. Gulielmus Bucanus, *Institutions of Christian Religion*, trans. Robert Hill (London: George Snowdon, 1606), p. 191.

14. The assumptions behind Stanley Fish's criticism of *Paradise Lost* and seventeenth-century literature derive from Woodhouse and Barker on Christian liberty. Paul is the ultimate guilty reader surprised by sin, and the Hebrew Bible is literature's supreme example of the self-consuming artifact, "the vehicle of its own abandonment." According to Fish on *Paradise Lost*, "the poem's operation is analogous to that of the Mosaic Law which, we are told in *The Christian Doctrine*, calls forth 'our natural depravity, that by this means it might bring us to the righteousness of Christ' " ("Discovery as Form in *Paradise Lost*," in *New Essays on Paradise Lost*, ed. Thomas Kranidas [Berkeley: University of California Press, 1969], p. 2). Substituting *Paradise Lost* for the Hebrew Bible, Fish reads the epic typologically, rejecting its literal narrative, "whose temporal structure, as many have observed, is confused" (p. 7). Fish asks about *Paradise Lost* "the obvious question" that Paul asks about the Hebrew Bible read merely as law: "if . . . the action is interior, taking place inside the reader's mind, what is the function of the exterior form? Why is it there?" (pp. 6–7). The answer to Fish's question, and to Paul's, is the same: to provoke an awareness of sin. Once that happens, the Hebrew Bible and *Paradise Lost* can be rejected: "the outer form of the poem is a 'scaffolding' which 'so soon as the building is finished' is but a 'troublesome disfigurement' that is to be cast aside" (p. 10). The literary thinness of such a reading is remarkable. Milton's great epic becomes one more seventeenth-century tract on the relations of law and gospel. Although Fish's rhetoric is bold and often dazzling, one wonders if his rejection of Milton's great epic as an independent entity would have been received so eagerly by Milton scholars if Woodhouse and Barker had not been his forerunners, preparing the way. For the continuing influence of Barker and Fish, see Joan S. Bennett, *Reviving Liberty: Radical Christian Humanism in Milton's Great Poems* (Cambridge: Harvard University Press, 1989).

15. Arthur E. Barker, *Milton and the Puritan Dilemma, 1641–1660* (Toronto: University of Toronto Press, 1942), p. 100.

16. Arthur E. Barker, "Structural and Doctrinal Patterns in Milton's Later Poems," in *Essays in English Literature from the Renaissance to the Victorian*

Age Presented to A. S. P. Woodhouse, ed. Millar MacLure and F. W. Watt (Toronto: University of Toronto Press, 1964), p. 172.

17. Barker, *Milton and the Puritan Dilemma*, p. 107. Barker, ignoring the deuteronomic text at the center of Milton's arguments for divorce, emphasizes instead "the basic principle of human good" that replaces the principle of divine prescription (p. 111): "for the plain immutability of divine prescription . . . is substituted the law written in the heart not only by the Spirit but by nature" (p. 112).

18. Barker, *Milton and the Puritan Dilemma*, pp. 98–120, and, on Christian liberty in particular, pp. 105–7.

19. Ibid., p. 236.

20. Anticipating the argument that the deuteronomic law of divorce is judicial rather than moral and may thus be abrogated, Milton argues for the perpetuity of the judicial Mosaic law: "It shall suffice them, that it was not a moral, but a judicial Law, and so was abrogated. Nay rather not abrogated because judicial; which Law the ministery of Christ came not to deale with. And who put it in mans power to exempt, where Christ speaks in general of not abrogating *the least jot or tittle*" (*YP*, 2:316–17). Christ came not to abrogate the moral and judical Mosaic laws but rather to "vindicate [them] from abusive traditions" (*YP*, 2:317). See also *YP*, 2:229, 264, 319, 325, 453, and 640.

21. Barker, *Milton and the Puritan Dilemma*, p. 105.

22. Ibid., p. 105.

23. Ibid. p. 366, n. 81.

24. See for example *YP*, 2:354: "If wee bee wors [than the Jews], or but as bad, which lamentable examples confirm wee are, then have wee more, or at least as much need of this permitted law, as they to whom God therfore gave it under a harsher covenant."

25. I owe this observation to an unpublished paper by Robert W. Ayers on *Doctrine and Discipline of Divorce* and ancient Jewish divorce law.

26. *An Answer to a Book, Intituled, The Doctrine and Discipline of Divorce* (London, 1644), p. 37.

Chapter One
Law and Gospel in *Paradise Lost*

1. Sifra, Kedoshim 8b; Sabbath 31a: "If a proselyte takes it upon himself to obey all the words of the Torah except one single commandment, he is not to be received."

2. See Alan F. Segal, *Paul the Convert: The Apostolate and Apostasy of Saul the Pharisee* (New Haven: Yale University Press, 1990), p. 120.

3. Worden, *The Types Unvailed, or, The Gospel Pick't Out of the Legal Ceremonies* (London, 1664), p. 19.

4. Ibid., pp. 19–20.

5. Sir Walter Raleigh, *The History of the World* (London: Walter Burre, 1614), p. 234. Milton's first entry on the topic of marriage in his Commonplace Book (*YP*, 1:411) consists of an approving reference to Raleigh's remarks on polygamy in the same chapter of the *History* as this definition of the law.

6. Raleigh, *History*, p. 232.

7. Ibid., p. 234: "The moral law commandeth this or that good to be done, and this or that evill to be avoided, in particular; as also it declareth, for whose sake it is to bee done; as, *Do this, for I am the Lord*, whereas the law of nature commands it but in generall."

8. Ibid.

9. John Calvin, *Sermons Upon . . . Deuteronomie*, trans. Arthur Golding (London: Henry Middleton, 1583), p. 946.

10. Calvin, *Institutes of the Christian Religion*, ed. John T. McNeil and Ford Lewis Battles (Philadelphia, 1960), 1:422. Similarly, Nicolas Hemmingsen, "an approved Author, *Melancthons* Scholler" (*YP*, 2:610), "highly esteem'd" (*YP*, 2:711), cites the same verse from James to refute the Roman Catholic position on the efficacy of works, in *The Way of Lyfe* (London, 1579), p. 28.

11. William Whately, *Prototypes, or, The Primarie Precedent Presidents out of the Booke of Genesis* (London, 1640), pp. 12–13. Andrew Willet, *Hexapla in Genesin* (London, 1608), p. 47, lists the many sins committed in paradise, including incredulity, unthankfulness, pride, wantonness, gluttony, disobedience, curiosity, presumption, concupiscence, homicide "in bringing death not only upon themselves, but all their posteritie," inordinate affection, and others that resemble in diction as well as substance the sins as listed by Milton. Willet introduces his list with an argument similar to Whately's: "Now because carnall men doe extenuate *Adams* sinne, that he was cast out of Paradise for eating an apple; I will briefly shew the greatnes of our first parents transgression, wherein many sins concurred."

12. Gulielmus Bucanus, *Institutions of Christian Religion*, p. 76.

13. Alexander Ross, *A View of the Jewish Religion* (London, 1656), p. 193.

14. For Newton and Verity, see James H. Sims, *The Bible in Milton's Epics* (Gainesville: University of Florida Press, 1962), p. 267. See also Hughes, ed., *John Milton: Complete Poems and Major Prose*, p. 377; Douglas Bush, ed., *The Complete Poetical Works of John Milton* (Boston: Houghton Mifflin, 1965), p. 369; John Carey and Alastair Fowler, eds., *The Poems of John Milton* (London: Longmans, 1968), p. 849.

15. See for example all of Deut. 27–32 and Lev. 26, or, to settle on a verse, Deut. 10:12: "What doth the Lord thy God require of thee, but to fear the Lord thy God, to walk in all his ways, and to love him, and to serve the Lord thy God with all thy soul, to keep the commandments of the Lord, and his statutes, which I command thee this day for thy good."

16. John Whitgift, *Works*, ed. J. Ayre (Oxford, 1822), 1:202 and 270.

17. This assertion anticipates my argument in the next chapter.

18. John Selden, *Opera Omnia*, ed. David Wilkins (London, 1726), 1, 2, cols. 1524–25 and 1674–75.

19. See Selden, *De Synedriis*, in his *Opera Omnia*, 1, 2, col. 1524, where, typically, he quotes, first in Hebrew and then in Latin, the Mishnah in question ("Rex non judicabat, nec judicabant alii ipsum; nec testimonium dabat forense, nec in ipsum testimonium dicebatur"), then cites his sources, which include both the Babylonian and Jerusalem Talmud, in the margin ("Gemar. Hierosolymit. ad tit. *Sanhedrin*, cap. 2 fol. 20 col. 1. Gemar. Babylon. ad tit. *Sanhedrin*, cap. 2, fol.

19), and finally quotes at some length Rabbi Joseph's explanation of the Mishnah ("Dixit Rab Joseph, non recipi hoc nisi de regibus Israel; [id est, regibus qui non ex stirpe Davidica; velut Hasmonaeis, qui ex tribu Levitica; nec enim de cunctis regibus Israel illud capiendum satis ostendunt alia quae e Talmudicis sequuntur de judiciis etiam regum Israel] sed reges domus Judae & judicabant ipsi, & judicabant ipsi, & judicabant alii ipsos."). He follows this with a marginal reference to "Maimonides Halach. Melakin Wemalchemoth, cap. 3 [sect.] 7. alii passim."

20. Selden, *De Synedriis* (*Opera Omnia*), 1, 2, cols. 1674–75.

21. John Salkeld, *A Treatise of Paradise* (London: Nathaniel Butter, 1617), p. 148. See also Vavasor Powell's *Christ and Moses Excellency, or Sion and Sinai's Glory* (London, 1650), p.186, which identifies "that prohibition to Adam (that hee should not eate of the forbidden fruit)" with "all the Morall Law, or Ten Commandements, afterwards given to Moses."

22. Tertullian, "An Answer to the Jews," *The Writings of Quintus Sept. Flor. Tertullianus*, trans. S. Thelwall (Edinburgh: T. & T. Clark, 1870), pp. 203–5. The Zohar (1:36a) similarly argues that the prohibition contains the Decalogue. *Genesis Rabbah* (16.5), retaliating upon Tertullian in *Adversus Judaeos* and upon other Christian apologists, remarks that Adam received the commandments concerning the observance of the Sabbath and the daily sacrifice. Christian apologists had attempted to prove the inferiority of such ceremonial laws as these from the fact that Adam, the creation of God's own hands, was not enjoined to observe them.

23. Joseph Beaumont, *Psyche, or Love's Mystery* (London, 1648), 6.246.

24. St. Bruno, on Rev. 12:3, in *Patrologia Latina*, ed. J.-P. Migne, 161:668A.

25. Nicholas Gibbens, *Questions and Disputations Concerning the Holy Scripture* (London: Felix Kingston, 1601), p. 116.

26. Gibbens, *Questions and Disputations*, pp. 116–17.

27. James Ussher, *A Body of Divinity* (London, 1649), p. 135.

28. William Whately, *Prototypes*, pp. 6–7.

29. Gibbens, *Questions and Disputations*, pp. 33–34.

30. Ibid., p. 133. Gibbens's *Questions and Disputations* was written at the same time as Shakespeare's *Hamlet*. The Prince's confession to Rosencrantz and Guildenstern (2.2.295–308) compresses Genesis 1–3, from the creation of heaven and earth and the sun placed "in the firmament of the heaven" (Gen. 1:14), to the creation of man in God's image (1:26) and the curse of Adam after the Fall ("thou art dust, and to dust shalt thou returne" [3:19]). Hamlet surveys "this goodly frame the earth" and "this brave o'erhanging firmament," and celebrates the culmination of creation: "What a piece of work is a man, how noble in reason, how infinite in faculties, in form and moving how express and admirable, in action how like an angel, in apprehension how like a god: the beauty of the world, the paragon of animals!" Hamlet's antitheses throughout his confession resemble Reformation contrasts of the earth, the air, and humankind before and after the Fall: the "goodly frame" is also a "sterile promontory," the "most excellent canopy" "a foul and pestilent congregation of vapors," and "the paragon" merely "this quintessence of dust."

31. Gibbens, *Questions and Disputations*, pp. 80–81.

32. Ibid., p. 100.

33. John Milton, *Poems, Reproduced in Facsimile from the Manuscript in Trinity College, Cambridge* (Menston, Yorkshire: Scolar Press, 1972), p. 35.

34. Cecil Roth, *A Life of Menasseh Ben Israel* (Philadelphia: Jewish Publication Society, 1934), pp. 94–95.

35. Menasseh ben Israel, *De Termino Vitae libri Tres* (Amsterdam, 1639); idem., *Of the Term of Life*, trans. Thomas Pocock (London: J. Nutt, 1699), p. 43.

36. Menasseh ben Israel, *Of the Term of Life*, p. 45.

37. Tractate Yoma, 72b. See also Deut. 32:47: "For [the Torah] is not a vain thing for you; because it is your life."

38. John Ball, *A Treatise of the Covenant of Grace* (London, 1645), pp. 9–10.

39. Lascelles Abercrombie's description of what epic poetry should be appears in Frank Kermode's great essay "Adam Unparadised," in his edition of *The Living Milton* (London: Routledge & Kegan Paul, 1960), pp. 86 and 123.

40. Calvin, *Institutes*, 1:241.

41. John Calvin, *Commentarie upon the first booke of Moses called Genesis*, trans. Thomas Tymme (London, 1578), p. 21.

42. Martin Luther, "Lectures in Genesis" [1535–36], in his *Luther's Works*, ed. Jaroslav Pelikan (St. Louis, Mo.: Concordia, 1958), 1:90.

43. Thomas Cartwright, "A Shorte Catechisme," in his *Cartwrightiana* [1611], ed. Albert Peel and Leland H. Carlson (London: Allen and Unwin, 1951), p. 159.

44. Ussher, *A Body of Divinity*, p. 125.

45. John Preston, *The New Covenant, or The Saints Portion* (London, 1630), p. 317.

46. Bucanus, *Institutions of Christian Religion*, pp. 210–11.

47. See E. P. Sanders, *Paul, the Law, and the Jewish People* (Philadelphia: Fortress, 1983), p. 17.

48. See, for example, the excellent discussion in Francis Watson's *Paul, Judaism and the Gentiles: A Sociological Approach* (Cambridge: Cambridge University Press, 1986), p. 150.

49. Calvin, *Sermons upon . . . Deuteronomie*, p. 4.

50. Martin Luther, *A Commentarie of M. Doctor Martin Luther upon the Epistle of S. Paul to the Galathians* (London, 1575), fols. 144v–45.

51. William Perkins, *Commentary . . . on . . . Galatians* (London, 1617), p. 200.

52. Ball, *Treatise of the Covenant of Grace*, p. 10.

53. *Treatise*, p. 10.

54. Arminius, *The Writings of Arminius*, ed. James Nichols and W. R. Bagnall (1853; reprinted Grand Rapids, Mich.: Baker Book House, 1956), 2:73.

55. ben Israel, *De Termino Vitae*, p. 43.

56. Milton's poetry advocates slow progress, "by degrees of merit rais'd," "at length," "under long obedience tri'd" (7.157–59). Sudden self-transformation is almost always to be resisted: don't sip from Comus's cup, don't eat the magic fruit in paradise (book 9) or in hell (book 10). See also the Miltonic bard's negative use of "transform'd" (4.824). Milton's skepticism about sudden, ecstatic transformation is close to the philosophical (Platonic, Philonic) and Jewish view that conver-

sion should be characterized by long training. Pagans and Jews disagreed with Christians about whether conversion should come slowly, the result of consistent moral progress, or quickly, the result of the miraculous power of the spirit. The most prominent examples of quick conversion are Paul (Acts 9:3–9) and Augustine (*Conf.* 6.7.11–12). Luke's description of Christian conversion as an instantaneous response to preaching left him open to the pagan charge that Christian conversion was simple-minded acceptance of outlandish claims made by hucksters. See Abraham J. Malherbe, " 'Not in a Corner': Early Christian Apologetic in Acts 26:26," *The Second Century* 5, no. 4 (1985/86): 193–210; Alan F. Segal, *Paul the Convert*, pp. 18–19 and 113.

57. Richard Baxter, *The Saint's Everlasting Rest* (London, 1650), pp. 44–45.

58. Wolfgang Musculus, *Common Places of Christian Religion*, trans. John Man (London, 1578), p. 75.

59. Matthew Poole, *Annotations Upon the Holy Bible* (1683; 3d edition, London: Thomas Parkhurst, 1696), Sig. B$_3$v.

60. Ibid., sig. B$_3$r.

61. *The Humble Advice of the Assembly of Divines, Now by Authority of Parliament Sitting at Westminster, Concerning a Confession of Faith* (London: Stationers Company, 1646), chap. 9, part 1 (n.p.).

62. Gervase Babington, *Certaine Plaine, Briefe, and Comfortable Notes upon Genesis* (London: Thomas Charde, 1596), p. 21.

63. William Pemble, *Vindiciae Fidei, Or A Treatise of Justification by Faith* (Oxford, 1629), pp. 148–53.

64. Ball, *A Treatise of the Covenant of Grace*, p. 8.

65. John Calvin, *A Commentarie on the Whole Epistle to the Hebrews* (London: Felix Kingston, 1605), pp. 5–6.

66. See Alan F. Segal, *Paul the Convert*, pp. 248–49.

67. John Wollebius, *The Abridgment of Christian Divinitie* (London, 1650), p. 98.

68. Frank Kermode, *The Art of Telling* (Cambridge: Harvard University Press, 1983), p. 172.

69. Nicolas Hemmingsen, *The Way of Lyfe* (London, 1579), Sig. B$_4$v.

70. Arnold Stein, *The Art of Presence*, p. 158.

71. For Paul's epistles as the source of the form and address of the tract's opening words—"To All the Churches of Christ and to All in any part of the world who profess the Christian Faith"—see *YP*, 6:117, 127, 227, and 577. Of the two proof texts quoted in Milton's introductory epistle (Rom. 16:17–18, Acts 24:14), one is by Paul, and the other is specifically attributed to him by Milton (*YP*, 6:123–24).

72. George Foot Moore, "Christian Writers on Judaism," *The Harvard Theological Review* 14 (1921): 197–254.

73. Bucanus, *Institutions of Christian Religion*, p. 191.

74. See, for example, Wiliam Perkins, cited in *YP*, 2:244, n. 9, who maintains that the Deuteronomic divorce law "was not morall, but civill, or politicke, for the good ordering of the commonwealth."

75. *An Answer to a Book, Intituled, The Doctrine and Discipline of Divorce* (London, 1644), p. 30.

76. Henry Hammond, *A Letter of Resolution to Six Quaeres, of Present Use in the Church of England* (London, 1653), p. 123.

77. Alexander Ross, *Pansebeia: or, A View of all Religions in the World, from the Creation, to These Times* (London, 1653), p. 400.

78. Theophilus Brabourne, *A Discourse upon the Sabbath Day* (London, 1628), p. 4.

79. Francis White, *A Treatise of the Sabbath-Day* (London: R. B., 1636), p. 1.

80. For more on Brabourne and other Sabbatarians, see David S. Katz, *Sabbath and Sectarianism in Seventeenth-Century England* (Leiden: E. J. Brill, 1988).

81. *The Early Lives of Milton*, ed. Helen Darbishire (London: Constable, 1932), pp. 23–24.

82. John Selden, *Table-Talk* (London: E. Smith, 1689), p. 20. Of course Milton's rejection of determinism and his relentless insistence on free will set him apart from most Puritans. But the specific argument from Christian liberty in the treatise *Of Civil Power* sounds exactly like those made by his contemporaries within a framework of Calvinist orthodoxy.

83. The point about the conjunction of the natural and Mosaic laws is reiterated constantly in this tract, most emphatically in *YP*, 2:237, 297–98, 328, 330, 343, and 346.

84. For citations of Cicero on law and nature (*De Legibus*, 1:6) and Plato on consistency ("The legislator must not give two rules about the same thing, but one only" [*Laws*, 4:710, trans. Jowett]), see *YP*, 2:310, nn. 8–9.

85. Barker, *Milton and the Puritan Dilemma*, pp. 116–17.

86. A. J. A. Waldock, *Paradise Lost and Its Critics* (Cambridge: Cambridge University Press, 1947), p. 82.

87. Georgia B. Christopher, "The Verbal Gate to Paradise: Adam's 'Literary Experience' in Book X of *Paradise Lost*," *PMLA* 90 (1975): 69–77. This quote appears in a revised version of the essay, in Christopher's *Milton and the Science of the Saints* (Princeton: Princeton University Press, 1982), p. 164, n. 25. Degraded under the pressure of Christopher's doctrinally based exposition, Eve's emphatic "*Adam*" in "Forsake me not thus, *Adam*" (10.914) becomes a wail, like Lou Costello's comically panic-stricken cry, "Abbott."

88. E. M. W. Tillyard, *Studies in Milton* (London: Chatto and Windus, 1956), p. 43; cited in Christopher, "The Verbal Gate to Paradise," 69.

89. Christopher, "The Verbal Gate to Paradise," 75.

90. *The Iliad of Homer*, trans. Richmond Lattimore (Chicago and London: University of Chicago Press, 1951), p. 164 (6.429–30).

91. Phyllis Trible, "A Human Comedy," in her *God and the Rhetoric of Sexuality* (Philadelphia: Fortress, 1984), pp. 166–99.

92. For the sinister casualness of that phrase, see David Daiches, "The Opening of *Paradise Lost*," in *The Living Milton*, ed. Frank Kermode (London: Routledge & Kegan Paul, 1960), pp. 58–59.

93. *Fathers According to Rabbi Nathan*, trans. Judah Goldin (New Haven: Yale University Press, 1955), chap. 14. Milton could have read Francis Tayler's Latin translation, *R. Natan tract. de patribus* (London, 1654), though there is no evidence that he did.

94. Henry Ainsworth, *Annotations Upon the Five Bookes of Moses, and the . . . Psalmes* (London: John Haviland, 1622), Sig. D3.

95. Ibid., Sig. Hh.

96. John Salkeld, *A Treatise of Angels* (London, 1613), p. 282.

97. Yeshayahu Leibowitz, "Hochhut's Error," in *Judaism, Human Values, and the Jewish State*, ed. Eliezer Goldman (Cambridge and London: Harvard University Press, 1992), p. 253.

98. Stein, *The Art of Presence*, pp. 52, 67–68, and 103.

99. I have, in this paragraph, drawn upon the discussion of Paul's nullification of the law in Hans von Campenhausen's *The Formation of the Christian Bible*, trans. J.A. Baker (Philadelphia: Fortress, 1972), pp. 25–36.

100. See, for example, Richard Sibbes, *The Faithful Covenanter* (London, 1639), in his *The Complete Works of Richard Sibbes*, ed. Alexander B. Grosart (Edinburgh: James Nichol, 1863) 6:4; John Preston, *The New Covenant*, p. 317; William Ames, *Conscience* (1639), reprinted in A. S. P. Woodhouse's *Puritanism and Liberty*, 2d ed. (Chicago: University of Chicago Press, 1965), p. 190; Joseph Mede, *Discourses on Divers Texts of Scripture*, in his *Works* (London: John Clark, 1648), p. 575.

101. William Pemble, *Vindiciae Fidei*, pp. 151–52.

102. Joseph Mede, *Discourses*, p. 575.

103. Jeremy Taylor, *Unum Necessarium, or The Doctrine and Practice of Repentance* (London: J. Flesher, 1655), pp. 2 and 5.

104. John Cotton, *The Covenant of Grace* (London, 1655), p. 114.

105. Raleigh, *The History of the World*, p. 232.

106. Ibid., p. 237. In his Commonplace Book (*YP*, 1:411), Milton quotes approvingly from this section of the *History*.

107. William Empson, *Milton's God* (London: Chatto and Windus, 1961), p. 147.

108. *Paradise Lost, Books I–II*, ed. J. B. Broadbent (Cambridge: Cambridge University Press, 1972), p. 51.

109. Carey and Fowler, eds., *The Poems of John Milton*, p. 51.

110. William Pemble, *Vindiciae Fidei*, p. 157. Pemble also distinguishes between the inherent righteousness of legal justification, applicable to Eden, and the imputed righteousness of evangelical justification, applicable to Christians in a fallen world (pp. 2–3). John Preston makes the same points in *The New Covenant, or The Saints Portion*, 9th ed. (London, 1639), pp. 314 and 317.

111. James Arminius, "Public Disputations," in his *The Writings of Arminius*, ed. James Nichols and W. R. Bagnall (1853; reprinted Grand Rapids, Mich.: Baker Book House, 1956), 1:547.

112. Bucanus, *Institutions*, p. 329.

113. Yet another of Bucanus's Hebraic, non-Pauline definitions of justification in his *Institutions* can be applied to the Miltonic bard: "[Justification] signifieth, to provoke and stirre up others unto righteousnesse, by teaching and instructing them, as *Dan.* 12.3. *They that justifie others*, that is, doe instruct them unto righteousnesse, or by their teaching and instruction doe make them just, *shall be as the stars in the firmament*" (p. 329).

Chapter Two
Milton's Hebraic Monism

1. Samuel Taylor Coleridge, *Table Talk*, 5 July 1834; in his *Coleridge's Miscellaneous Criticism*, ed. Thomas M. Raysor (London: Constable, 1936), p. 437.

2. Empson offers the medical analogy in *Milton's God*, p. 128.

3. On this point, see Stein, *The Art of Presence*, pp. 22–24.

4. Nathan A. Scott, Jr., "Poetry and Prayer," in *Literature and Religion*, ed. Giles B. Gunn (New York: Harper & Row, 1971), p. 201.

5. Balachandra Rajan analyzes Milton's *Of Education* as a monist curriculum culminating in poetry, which is superior because of its inclusiveness, "because among all the organic arts it has least outside its area of redemption" (p. 10). The self-transcendence of learning is evident in its end: the knowledge and imitation of God, which Rajan identifies with knowledge of the good "as the ground of a transforming militant goodness" (p. 9). See his essay "Simple, Sensuous, and Passionate," *The Review of English Studies* 21 (1945): 289–301; reprinted in *Milton: Modern Essays in Criticism*, ed. Arthur E. Barker (New York: Oxford University Press, 1965), pp. 3–20.

6. This is one of Harold Bloom's less controversial assertions in *The Book of J* (New York: Grove Weidenfeld, 1990), p. 176.

7. See *De doctrina Christiana*, CE, 15:230, and John Carey, "Translator's Preface," *YP*, 6:xv. Carey notes that the translation here is "plainly inadequate to Milton's purpose."

8. Arthur Barker, *Milton and the Puritan Dilemma*, p. 319.

9. Ibid., p. 323; my emphasis.

10. Ibid., p. 324.

11. Richard Overton, *An Arrow Against All Tyrants* (London, 1646), pp. 3–5.

12. Overton refers to Gen. 2:7 in the opening paragraph of *Mans Mortalitie* (London, 1644), p. 7. Like Milton's *Doctrine and Discipline of Divorce*, the first and second editions of Overton's *Mans Mortalitie* appeared in 1643 and 1644, respectively. Harold Fisch surveys the evidence of a connection between Overton and Milton in his edition of the tract (Liverpool: Liverpool University Press, 1968), pp. xxii–xxv.

13. Nemesius, *The Nature of Man . . . written in Greek by Nemesius, surnamed the Philosopher . . .*, trans. George Wither (London, 1636), p. 23; cited in Fisch's edition of *Mans Mortalitie*, p. xxi.

14. Rajan, "Simple, Sensuous, and Passionate," p. 9.

15. Augustine, *The First Catechetical Instruction*, trans. Joseph P. Christopher (Westminster, Md.: Newman Press, 1962), 4.8.

16. Jill Robbins, *Prodigal Son/Elder Brother: Interpretation and Alterity in Augustine, Petrarch, Kafka, Levinas* (Chicago: University of Chicago Press, 1991), p. 1.

17. See, for example, Alastair Fowler, who accepts a numerological theology of the divine monad promulgated chiefly by Pietro Bongo and compatible with orthodox trinitarianism. Fowler dismisses as "[r]idiculous" evidence of Arianism cited by A. W. Verity and Maurice Kelley. See *The Poems of Milton*, eds. Carey and Fowler, pp. 836–37. More recently, William B. Hunter, denying Milton's

heresies, denies as well his authorship of *De doctrina Christiana*, in "The Provenance of the *Christian Doctrine*," *Studies in English Literature* 32 (1992): 129–42.

18. See Segal, *Paul the Convert*, pp. 120 and 278. See also Hans Joachim Schoeps, "Paul's Misunderstanding of the Law," in *The Writings of St. Paul*, ed. Wayne A. Meeks (New York: Norton, 1972), p. 356: "this absolute opposition between faith, on the one hand, and the law, on the other, quite contrary to the continuous meaning of the biblical narrative, has always been unintelligible to the Jewish thinker."

19. Geoffrey H. Hartman, "Adam on the Grass with Balsamum," *ELH* 36 (1969); reprinted in Hartman's *Beyond Formalism: Literary Essays 1958–1970* (New Haven: Yale University Press, 1970), p. 131.

20. Ibid.

21. Sibbes, *The Faithful Covenanter* [1639], 6:4.

22. Pemble, *Vindiciae Fidei*, p. 151.

23. Friedrich Nietzsche, Morgenrote (Aphorism 84), in his *Werke*, ed. Karl Schlechta, 1:1067ff.; cited by Jill Robbins in *Prodigal Son/Elder Brother*, p. 11.

24. Ibid.

25. Jonathan R. Ziskind, "Introduction," in his *John Selden on Jewish Marriage Law: The Uxor Hebraica* (Leiden: E. J. Brill, 1991). Although much of my argument on Milton and Selden was completed before the appearance of Ziskind's edition, I have gratefully used his translation of the *Uxor* at appropriate places in this chapter, most especially in the section on divorce.

26. John Selden, *De Anno Civili et Calendario Veteris Ecclesiae seu Reipublicae Judaicae* (London, 1644), p. 9; cited in Ziskind, *John Selden on Jewish Marriage Law*, p. 17.

27. See Ziskind, *John Selden on Jewish Marriage Law*, p. 29: "How different Selden's understanding of Jewish marriage would have been if he had only attended a Jewish wedding!"

28. Frank E. Manuel, *The Broken Staff: Judaism Through Christian Eyes* (Cambridge: Harvard University Press, 1992), p. 85.

29. David S. Katz, *Philo-Semitism and the Readmission of the Jews to England* (Oxford: Clarendon, 1982), p. 3.

30. See Katz, *Philo-Semitism*, pp. 163–68.

31. Mark Twain, *Adventures of Huckleberry Finn*, ed. Henry Nash Smith (Boston: Houghton Mifflin, 1958), p. 180.

32. Ibid., p. 244.

33. Selden, *Table-Talk*, p. 11.

34. Ibid., p. 23.

35. Richard Helgerson, *Forms of Nationhood: The Elizabethan Writing of England* (Chicago: University of Chicago Press, 1992), p. 300.

36. Selden, *Table-Talk*, p. 23.

37. The pioneering work in this area includes Denis Saurat's *Milton: Man and Thinker* (London: Jonathan Cape; New York: Dial Press, 1925); Harris F. Fletcher's *Milton's Semitic Studies and Some Manifestations of Them in His Poetry* (Chicago: University of Chicago Press, 1926) and his *Milton's Rabbinical Readings* (Urbana: University of Illinois Press, 1930); and E. C. Baldwin's "Some

Extra-Biblical Semitic Influences Upon Milton's Story of the Fall of Man," *JEGP* 28 (1929): 366–401. The first edition of Poole's *Annotations* appeared in 1683; the Folger Library owns the third edition, published in London by Thomas Parkhurst in 1696.

38. Poole, *Annotations*, sig. B3r

39. *Pentateuch With Rashi's Commentary*, ed. and trans. M. Rosenbaum and A.M. Silbermann (London: Soncino, 1946), p.13.

40. John Aubrey, "Minutes of the Life of Mr. John Milton" (c. 1681), in *The Early Lives of Milton*, ed. Helen Darbishire (London: Constable, 1932), p. 6.

41. David Masson, *The Life of John Milton* (Cambridge: Macmillan, 1859–94), 1:200.

42. *Ascensio Isaiae Vatis* (Oxford, 1819); cited by Don Cameron Allen in "Milton and Rabbi Eliezer," *MLN* 63 (1948); 262.

43. Saurat, *Milton: Man and Thinker*, p. 280.

44. Seriatim: R. J. Z. Werblowsky, "Milton and the Conjectura Cabbalistica," *Journal of the Warburg and Courtald Institutes* 18 (1955): 90–113; Golda Werman, "Milton's Use of Rabbinic Material," *Milton Studies* 21 (1985): 35–47; and Samuel S. Stollman, "Milton's Rabbinical Readings and Fletcher," *Milton Studies* 4 (1972): 195–215.

45. George Newton Conklin, *Biblical Criticism and Heresy in Milton* (New York: King's Crown Press, 1949), pp. 54–61; Robert M. Adams, *Ikon: John Milton and the Modern Critics* (Ithaca: Cornell University Press, 1955), pp. 133–47; Stollman, "Milton's Rabbinical Readings and Fletcher," passim; Leonard R. Mendelsohn, "Milton and the Rabbis: A Later Inquiry," *SEL* 18 (1978): 125–35. Invariably, these critics begin by discrediting Fletcher et al. and end by discrediting Milton himself, although this devaluation of his scholarship is sometimes merely a byproduct of their critical procedure. Thus, for example, Conklin and Adams want to stress Milton's originality as a thinker and argue that he invented most of the material attributed to Jewish sources. The numerous rabbinic figures to whom Milton refers explicitly then become inconveniences, consigned to lexicons where, deprived of the persuasive intensity that only context can provide, they are powerless to violate his mind with the force of an idea.

46. Mendelsohn, "Milton and the Rabbis," 134–35.

47. This is the argument of my 1969 Brown University dissertation "A Revaluation of Milton's Indebtedness to Hebraica"; see also Harold Fisch, "Hebraic Style and Motifs in *Paradise Lost*," pp. 34–35.

48. Seriatim: Ben Jonson, "An Epistle to Master John Selden," in *The Complete Poetry of Ben Jonson*, ed. William B. Hunter, Jr. (New York: Norton, 1963), pp. 144–47; Grotius cited in Sir Eric Fletcher's biography *John Selden* (London: Quaritch, 1969), p. 15; John Lightfoot, *The Harmony, Chronicle and Order of the Old Testament* (London: John Clark, 1647), Sig. B3r. What Gibbon said of Lightfoot could be said of Selden as well, that he, "by constant reading of the rabbis, became almost a rabbi himself."

49. "A Catalogue of the books given by Mr Seldens Executors [in 1659] to the Library of the University of Oxford," Rawlinson MS 27837, Bodleian Library, Oxford; "Catalogus librorum Orientalium [impressorum] Seldenianorum" [1660], MS Selden 3473, Bodleian Library; and see Falconer Madan, *A Summary*

Catalogue of Western Manuscripts in the Bodleian Library (Oxford: Clarendon, 1922), 2.1:594–654 (Selden MSS., 1659).

50. See *YP*, 7:77, 233, 284, 288, 290–92, and 301.

51. *A Variorum Commentary on the Poems of John Milton*, 1:ii, ed. A. S. P. Woodhouse and Douglas Bush (New York: Columbia University Press, 1972), 101. See also *An Index to the Columbia Edition of the Works of John Milton*, ed. Frank Allen Patterson and French Rowe Fogle (New York: Columbia University Press, 1940), 2:1765.

52. Selden, *De Jure Naturali & Gentium*, pp. 551, 552, 557, 565, and 845. All but the last reference, which appears in *De Jure*'s last chapter, are found in book 5 (chapters 4 and 5), to which Milton refers directly in *Doctrine and Discipline of Divorce*.

53. Eivion Owen, "Milton and Selden on Divorce," *SP* 43 (1946): 233–57.

54. Masson, *The Life of John Milton*, 3:68.

55. Masson, 5:281; William Riley Parker, *Milton: A Biography* (Oxford: Clarendon, 1968), 1:480; 2:1052–53.

56. *Commonplace Book*, *YP*, 1:402.

57. Selden, *Uxor Ebraica*, 2, 28, p. 292. For Christianity as a reformed Judaism, see ibid., 2, 24, 235.

58. *Christian Doctrine*, *YP*, 6:378; *A Second Defence*, *YP*, 4:624–25.

59. *Uxor Ebraica*, 3, 33, pp. 620–21: ". . . Anglos nostros (qui gradus Consanguinitatis & Affinitatis Jure Pontificio praestitutos atque heic antiquitus receptos lege Parlamentaria centum amplius abhinc annos lata in eos laxarunt solos qui sacris in literis continentur, Pontificiorum um tamen interea de Divortiis doctrinam quasi integram etiam post Reformationem refinentes)."

60. Ibid., 3, 27, p. 547.

61. Plutarch, "Aemilius Paulus," in his *Lives*, trans. Bernadotte Perrin, Loeb Classical Library (London: Heinemann; Cambridge: Harvard University Press, 1943), 6:365. Milton's mistake is noted in *YP*, 2:348, n. 20.

62. See Selden, *Uxor*, 3, 33, pp. 617–18, which cites "*Petr. Suavis hist. concil. Trident. lib. 8. pag.* 609"; and *YP*, 2:300–1 and 492, n. 23.

63. Selden, *Uxor*, 1, 9, p. 63. See also Selden's rabbinic discussion of polygamy in his *De Jure Naturali*, 5 (chap. 6), pp. 563–64.

64. I have had access to *De Synedriis* only in Selden's *Opera Omnia*, 1, 2, cols. 761–1892.

65. Selden, *De Synedriis*, pp. VI–VII; cited in Ziskind, "Introduction," in his *John Selden on Jewish Marriage Law*, p. 18.

66. Cited in "Introduction" to *The Table Talk of John Selden*, ed. Samuel Harvey Reynolds (Oxford: Clarendon, 1892), p. xviii.

67. Mendelsohn, "Milton and the Rabbis," 125–35; Werman, "Milton's Use of Rabbinic Material," pp. 35–47; and Golda Werman, "Midrash in *Paradise Lost*: *Capitula Rabbi Elieser*," *Milton Studies* 18 (1983): 145–71.

68. The first two conclusions are from Mendelsohn, "Milton and the Rabbis," 134–35, the last two from Werman, "Milton's Use of Rabbinic Material," 44.

69. Mendelsohn, "Milton and the Rabbis," 129.

70. Sanhedrin, 19a. My translations from Sanhedrin are based on the text of the Vilna edition of the Talmud (1908), which belonged to my late father, Rabbi

M. D. Rosenblatt, and on the Hebrew translation by Adin Steinsaltz (Jerusalem, 1974). This elliptical narrative has elicited many responses to the problem of why Simeon ben Shetah asked Jannaeus to stand, since the litigants in a case are seated. Perhaps he was angered because Jannaeus did not wait for an invitation to sit, or the text may be speaking of the moment when the verdict is pronounced and everyone is required to stand. Or Simeon erred in this matter, and other colleagues on the court were in fact empowered to allow Jannaeus to stand. Indeed, if the court, out of respect for the Torah, can seat a scholar, then this applies all the more to a king. The RaN (on Sanhedrin 19a in the Vilna edition of the Talmud), R. Jonah (cited by Steinsaltz, p. 83), and the Rashbah (in *Hiddushei Aggadot ha-Shas* [Tel Aviv, 1966]) consider these and many more problems in their commentaries on the narrative.

71. Selden, *De Synedriis*, col. 1525.

72. Mendelsohn, "Milton and the Rabbis," 133.

73. Sanhedrin, 20b.

74. Mendelsohn, "Milton and the Rabbis," 129–30.

75. Sanhedrin, 21a–22a.

76. Rashi's commentary on *Parshath Melech*, which Mendelsohn claims would have resolved all doubt for Milton (130), consists simply of a seven-word reference to 1 Samuel 8. Here in its entirety is Kimchi's commentary on verse 9 of that chapter, which Mendelsohn claims Milton ought to have known if he could read the Buxtorf Bible (129–30): " 'R' 'Y' [Rav Jose, though my dictionary of abbreviations, *Ozar Rashe Tevot*, lists twenty-three other possibilities as well] says that a king is permitted to do all that is listed in the chapter of the king, while R. Judah says that this chapter intends only to frighten and alarm the people." Kimchi, commenting on a verse in 1 Samuel, does not discuss the possibility that the chapter of the king may be in Deuteronomy, nor does he mention that the discussion he is summarizing can be found in Sanhedrin.

77. Werman, "Milton's Use of Rabbinic Material," 40–41.

78. See for example *Colasterion*, where Milton taxes his anonymous detractor with "bearing us in hand as if hee knew both Greek and Ebrew, and is not able to spell it" (*YP*, 2:724). He continues: "I shall yet continue to think that man full of other secret injustice, and deceitful pride, who shall offer in public to assume the skill, though it bee but of a tongue which hee hath not, and would catch his readers to beleeve of his ability, that which is not in him" (725).

79. See, for example, *The First Defence* (*YP*, 4:349), where the dispute between Milton and Salmasius over royal privilege can be reduced to the single word *mishpat* in 1 Samuel 8:11, which in context means manner, the customary behavior of an oriental despot, rather than lawful procedure, the right of a king, as Salmasius would have it. In correcting Salmasius, Milton appeals to 1 Samuel 2:13, a description of the sacrilegious behavior of the corrupt sons of Eli, where the word *mishpat*, though often ambiguous, can only mean manner or custom: "This is not what kings should do, but what they wish to, and he was showing the people the procedure of the priestly sons of Eli, using the same word which . . . you, being a solecist in Hebrew too, call Mishpat." The attitude of the editor of *The Defence* toward Milton's Hebrew learning is consistently grudging, and he inexplicably sides with Salmasius here (*YP*, 4:349, n. 30).

80. Selden, *De Synedriis*, col. 1437.

81. See, ibid., cols. 1524–25, where Selden repeats the story of Alexander Jannaeus and cites the following sources: "*Sanhedrin*, cap. 2. fol. 19.1. Videsis etiam in Guil. Schickardi erratis ad finem lib. de Jure Regio, & in Jo. Cochii tit. *Sanhedrin*, pag. 168. *Aiin Israel*, tom. 2. fol. 996. &c."

82. Ibid., col. 1676. On col. 1677, Selden provides a lengthy quote from Salmasius on the question of whether a king can be judged by the court.

83. Ibid., col. 1676. What complicates matters here is that the order of this argument (Psalm 17, Barnachmani, Psalm 51) in both Salmasius and Selden may derive ultimately from Grotius's "*De Jure Belli ad Pacis*, lib. 1, cap. 3, section 20," scrupulously acknowledged by Selden, who always observes the scholarly courtesies. Perhaps more striking are the identical texts used by Selden and Milton regarding cases in which the Sanhedrin had a power of judging and the king had not: ibid., cols. 1670–71; *YP*, 4:408. See also col. 1677, where Selden quotes Josephus's commentary on Deuteronomy 17, which Milton cites in *The First Defence* (*YP*, 4:344).

84. This suggestion was made by David Wilkins in his life of Selden, in Selden, *Opera Omnia*, 1, 44. See also *The Life Records of John Milton*, ed. J. Milton French (New Brunswick: Rutgers University Press, 1949–58), 2:237.

85. Peter Du Moulin (?), *Regii Sanguinis Clamor* (The Hague, 1652), p.8; *Lettres de Gui Patin*, 2 (1846): 17–18, cited in Parker, *Milton: A Biography*, 2:962–63.

86. Werman, "Midrash in *Paradise Lost*," 145–71. Allen, "Milton and Rabbi Eliezer," 262–63. Vorstius's edition is called *Capitula R. Elieser* (Leiden, 1644).

87. Among Professor Werman's principal reasons for regarding the *Pirke* as an apt candidate for a source of the epic are the inherent interest of the Genesis material, the Arminianism of the translator, and the absence of anti-Christian polemic. Regarding the agreement of source and epic, Professor Werman compares the unapproachability of the *Shekhinah* [Divine Presence] in the *Pirke* with that of the "Begotten Son, Divine Similitude, / In whose conspicuous count'nance, without cloud / Made visible, th' Almighty Father shines, / Whom else no creature can behold" (*PL*, 3.384–87; Werman, 149). Yet this actually states—admittedly, in confusing syntax—not that the Son cannot be beheld, but rather that only in the Son can the Father be beheld, with the additional suggestion that only the Son beholds the Father. The notion that God laughs mockingly at his enemies, attributed to the *Pirke* (151), can of course also be found in Psalm 2:4: "The Lord shall have them in derision."

88. Werman, "Midrash in *Paradise Lost*," 155 and 170, n.

89. Werman, 170, n.

90. Selden, *Uxor Ebraica*, 2.12, p. 182ff. On this point alone Selden cites "Maimonides, *Halach Ishoth*, cap. 10," "*Shulcan Aruch lib. Aben haaezer*, cap. 54. section 2. vide Gem. Babylon. ad tit. *Cethuboth*, cap. 5. fol. 56.a." The related point that matrimony is effected from the moment the couple enters the bower elicits comments from, among others, "Maimonid. & autor *Shulcan Aruch*, loc. citat. & vide Magid Misna ad Maimonid. ibid. fol. 243.b. & Mos. Mikotzi Pracept. Affirm. 48."

91. See the lengthy discussion of *aperion, lectum conjugalem, fructificandi*

locum, or *huppah,* in Selden, *De Jure Naturali,* 5, 3, 545ff. Multiple rabbinic references here include "Gem. Bab. ad tit. *Sota,* cap. 1, fol. 12a & *Baal Aruch* in *aperion.* . . . J. Buxtorf. pater ad epist. Hebraic. lib. 2, ep. 7. Usurpatur *aperion* pro *huppah* seu *Thalamo* (sed templum innuitur) Cantic. Salom. 3.9." The nuptial bower is also discussed in Selden, *Uxor Ebraica,* 2, 15, pp. 192–98. See also the chapter heading, "De Sponsorum coronis, myrto ac palmarum ramis praeferendis," *Uxor Ebraica,* 2, 15, p. 192.

92. See, for example, Selden, *Uxor Ebraica,* 2, 13, pp. 184–86. But Selden's many references to specific chapters of "R. Eliaezer in *Pirke*" also appear in discussions of Adam and Eden (for example, his *De Jure,* 3, 13, 351, n; his *De Synedriis,* col. 1025). In fact, in the first volume alone of Selden's *Opera Omnia,* there are thirty-five references to *Pirke de-Rabbi Eliezer,* including both the Hebrew text and the translation by Vorstius.

93. For Maimonides, see *YP,* 2:257; on 238–39, Milton cites Fagius's *Thargum, Hoc Est, Paraphrasis Onkeli Chaldaica in Sacra Biblia* (Strassburg, 1546) and Hugo Grotius's *Annotationes in Libros Evangeliorum* (Amsterdam, 1641).

94. Milton, *YP,* 2:335; Selden, *De Jure Naturali,* 4 (chap. 8), 514–16, 4 (chap. 9), 530–34, 5 (chap. 4), 551–57, 5 (chap. 12), 615, and 7 (chap. 12), 845; idem., *Uxor Ebraica,* 3, 19, p. 434ff. See also Selden's *De Successione in Pontificatum Ebraeorum* (London: Richard Bishop, 1636), pp. 15–17.

95. Milton, *YP,* 2:257; Selden, *Uxor Ebraica,* 3, 19, p. 439ff.

96. Selden, *Uxor Ebraica,* 3, 18–3, 23, pp. 428–500; see especially pp. 458–60 for the positions of Hillel and Shammai. Regarding a wife who went out with clothes slit at the sides, bare arms, or an uncovered head, Shammai teaches that she could not be repudiated, Hillel that she could be.

97. Ibid., 3, 26, p. 522: "dum agitata est Hierosolymis controversia illa tam illustris de Divortiis inter Scholas Hillelianam & Sammaeanam, Christum docuisse non Licere uxorem dimittere quamlibet ob causam, seu graviter peccare & uxorem facere moechari qui eam dimiserit *extra causam fornicationis.*"

98. Ibid., p. 485. The question: "Anne fas est, Viro dimittere uxorem suam quacunque ex causa"; the answer: "Si dimiserit quis uxorem suam nisi ob Turpitudinem." Selden's persuasiveness here is the result of the conformity of both question and answer to talmudic formulae: *"'im rashai le'ish ligrosh 'ishto mishum kol davar?"*; " *'im yigrosh 'ish 'ishto v'lo mishum ervah."* Selden characterizes the language of the Mishnah in tractate Gittin as *"semi-Babylonica,"* "the Babylonian-like or Aramaic language . . . in use by the Hebrews at the time of Christ and for a long time before" (*Uxor Ebraica,* 3, 24, pp. 501 and 503). In those sections of Milton's writings influenced by Selden, Dr. Johnson's judgment may be true in a sense that he never intended: "[Milton] *wrote no language,* but has formed . . . a *Babylonish Dialect."* From *The Lives of the Poets* (1779), reprinted in *Milton Criticism: Selections from Four Centuries,* ed. James Thorpe (New York: Rinehart & Co., 1950), p. 86.

99. Selden, *Uxor Ebraica,* 2, 23, p. 496: "Cum igitur tum *porneia* tum *ervah* nomina fuerint aequivoca . . . nonne phrasis illa tunc temporis Scholastica *extra rationem Turpitudinis* quae adeo in disputationibus de Divortio tunc frequens erat, rite respondere potuerit *parektos logou porneias* in Graeca sive Evangelii sive Christi verborum versione?" Selden also explicitly identifies "fornication" in

Matthew 5:32 and 19:9 with *ervah* in Deuteronomy 24:1 ["fornicationis (id est *ervah*)"], in his *De Jure Naturali*, 7, 12, p. 845.

100. Selden, *Uxor Ebraica*, 3, 23, pp. 489–90. For the restrictive interpretation of the church fathers, see pp. 479–80. In *De Jure Naturali* (7, 12, p. 845), Selden had registered their opinion without comment: "praeter causam adulterii & praeter ex causa adulterii." [Selden's note: "Tertullian advers. Marcionem lib.4. cap.34."] For Demosthenes and Philo, see *Uxor Ebraica* 3, 23, pp. 480–81.

101. Sumner elides this phrase's central term in the Miltonic original ("multis Rabbinorum testimoniis"), so that it becomes in translation only "numerous testimonies" (*CE*, 15:171).

102. Selden, *Uxor Ebraica*, 3, 23, p. 482.

103. Ibid., 3, 21, p. 461: "melius suisse eam, si odio ita haberet, libello repudiare quam afflictam invisamque retinere." [Note: "*Sal. Iarch. ad dict. Malach locum.*"] See also 3, 19, p. 439.

104. Reynolds, ed., *The Table Talk of John Selden*, p. 109.

105. *A Concordance to Milton's English Prose*, ed. Laurence Sterne and Harold H. Kollmeier (Binghamton: Medieval & Renaissance Texts & Studies, 1985).

106. *An Answer to . . . The Doctrine and Discipline of Divorce*, p. 26.

107. "Anthony Ascham's 'Of Marriage' [1647–1648]," ed. John M. Perlette, *ELR* 3 (1973): 295. To this Jewish view Ascham opposes the law of "our saviour . . . a Lawe of God (not to be disputed by man)."

108. Christopher, *Milton and the Science of the Saints*, p. 38. See also an attack on "Papists" for their overemphasis on charity in Bucanus, *Institutions*, p. 358.

109. David Paraeus, *In Priorem ad Corinthios Epistolam S. Pauli Commentarius, Opera Theologicorum* (Frankfurt, 1628), 2:488; cited in *YP*, 2:352, n. 7.

110. Barker, ostensibly paraphrasing Milton on marriage, actually echoes Paraeus: "So far was Christ from introducing a new morality that his function was to release believers from the bondage of the Law" (*Milton and the Puritan Dilemma*, p. 105). Instead Milton repeats endlessly in these tracts "the promise of Christ & his known profession, not to meddle in matters judicial" (*YP*, 2:284; see also pp. 283, 303, 316, and 325). Regarding Christ's sermon on the mount: "if we marke the stearage of his words, what course they hold, wee may perceive that what he protested not to disolve . . . was principally concerning the judicial [Mosaic] law" (641).

111. Selden, *Uxor Ebraica*, 3, 22, p. 476.

112. John Halkett lists "prayer, forbearance, and an attempt to reform the offending partner" as ways recommended by English Protestants to deal with poor marriage choices (*Milton and the Idea of Matrimony* [New Haven: Yale University Press, 1970], p. 39). For James Grantham Turner, the divorce tracts are "authentically ugly" largely because of their "Old Testament sense of pollution" ("Intelligible Flame," from his *One Flesh: Paradisal Marriage and Sexual Relations in the Age of Milton* [Oxford: Clarendon, 1987]; reprinted in *John Milton*, ed. Annabel Patterson [London: Longman, 1992], p. 84). In an unpublished paper, "John Milton: 'Haile Wedded Love,' " presented at the fall 1992 Milton Seminar (Harvard University), Anthony Low considers Milton's "unforgiving" conception of spousal unfitness that resists "the universality of offered

grace and the freedom of every human will to reform itself" to be incompatible "with Christianity—whether Catholic, or Protestant, or extreme Puritan" (p. 12).

113. Selden, *Uxor Ebraica*, 3, 22, pp. 471–73: "Omnino constantes permanebunt conjugum convictus . . . quando in utriusque eorum genitura luminaria contigerit configurata esse concorditer. Hoc est, quando inter se ipsa triquetra aut sextili radiatione se respexerint & maxime cum vice versa. . . . Dissolvuntur vero levi occasione . . . atque invicem abalienantur omnino cum praedictae luminairium stationes vel in signis inconjunctis acciderint vel sint ex diametro vel quadrato." Selden cites Ptolemy's *Tetrabiblos*, cap. Peri Sunarmogon.

114. [I]oseph [H]all, *Resolutions and Decisions of Divers Practicall Cases of Conscience* . . . (London, 1649); cited by William Riley Parker, *Milton's Contemporary Reputation* (Columbus: Ohio State University Press, 1940), p. 79. Parker's list of printed allusions (pp. 69–119) includes numerous Presbyterian attacks on the licentiousness promulgated in Milton's divorce tracts.

115. Abraham Cowley, "A Vision Concerning his Late Pretended Highnesse Cromwell, the Wicked," *Cowley: The Essays and Other Prose Writings*, ed. Alfred B. Gough (Oxford: Clarendon, 1915), p. 87. *Mercurius Pragmaticus* 40–41 (26 Dec. 1648–9 Jan. 1649), cited in Katz, *Philo-Semitism and the Readmission of the Jews*, p. 178, connects Fairfax and the Council of War with contemporary Jews: "No marvell that those which intend to crucifie their *King*, should shake hands with them that crucified their *Saviour*."

116. Hammond, *A Letter of Resolution*, p. 123; Ross, *Pansebeia*, p. 400. Almost two-thirds of Hammond's chapter "Of Divorce," which attacks Milton for "bringing back *Christ* unto *Moses*," consists of a rebuttal of Selden's *Uxor Ebraica* (pp. 127–73).

117. For the influence of Jewish scholarship on Jerome, see Jay Braverman, *Jerome's Commentary on Daniel: A Study of Comparative Jewish and Christian Interpretations of the Hebrew Bible* (Washington, D.C.: The Catholic Biblical Association of America), pp. 4–9.

118. Ibid., p. xi.

119. Bucanus, *Institutions*, p. 193.

120. John Ziesler, *Pauline Christianity*, p. 99.

121. Sirluck on Milton sounds like Adolph von Harnack on Paul. Harnack asserts that Paul appeals to Scripture only as a concession to his adversaries; that he does not conduct exegetical arguments in his earliest letter (1 Thes.); and that he does not write biblical commentaries. See Harnack's "Das Alte Testament in den Paulinischen Briefen und in den Paulinischen Gemeinden," *Sitzungsberichte der Preussischen Akademie der Wissenschaften*, Philosophisch-historische Klasse (1928): 121–41. In *Echoes of Scripture in the Letters of Paul* (New Haven: Yale University Press, 1989), Richard B. Hayes challenges Harnack's view, maintaining that it fails to reckon sufficiently with the pervasiveness of scriptural allusion in Paul's discourse, including 1 Thessalonians (pp. 7 and 195, n. 16).

122. Wolfgang Musculus, *Common Places*, p. 382.

123. William Walywn, *The Compassionate Samaritane* (London, 1644), pp. 26–28; cited in *YP*, 2:566–67, n. 294.

124. R. G., "To the Reader," the translator's preface to Giovanni Diodati's

Pious and Learned Annotations upon the Holy Bible, 3d ed. (London, 1651), sig. A3v.

125. Musculus, *Common Places*, p. 373.

126. Musculus, *Common Places*, pp. 364 and 385. For two notable instances of Milton's attack on those who prefer mediated knowledge over personal experience, see the *Areopagitica*, YP, 2:543, on the subjective aspect of truth, and *Of True Religion*, where Milton sets against implicit faith "attentive study of the Scriptures & full perswasion of heart" (*YP*, 8:436).

127. Musculus, *Common Places*, p. 376.

128. Selden, *De Jure Naturali*, 1 (chap. 1), pp. 2 and 8: "*Et erit salus ubi multa consilia sunt . . . & salus in plurimis consiliariis.*"

129. John Drury, "Understanding the Bread: Disruption and Aggregation, Secrecy and Revelation in Mark's Gospel," in *"Not in Heaven": Coherence and Complexity in Biblical Narrative*, ed. Jason P. Rosenblatt and Joseph C. Sitterson, Jr. (Bloomington: Indiana University Press, 1991), p. 110.

130. Robert Baillie, *The Letters and Journals of Robert Baillie*, ed. David Lang (Edinburgh, 1841–42), 2:265–66; cited in Ernest Sirluck's "Introduction," YP, 2:125. In *A Dissuasive from the Errours of the Time* (London: Samuel Gellibrand, 1645), an attack on the tenets of the principal sects, "especially of the Independents," Baillie complained of "Mr *Milton* [who] . . . in a large Treatise hath pleaded for a full liberty for any man to put away his wife, when ever hee pleaseth, without any fault in her at all, but for any dislike or dyspathy of humour" (p. 116). He continues in a marginal note, "Mr *Milton* permits any man to put away his wife upon his meer pleasure, without fault and without the cognisance of any Judge."

131. Sidrach Simpson, *A Sermon Preached at Westminster before Sundry of the House of Commons* (London, 1643), p. 16.

132. See also a passage that in its defense of the national Mosaic law evokes the interdiction in paradise: "First the law, not onely the moral, but the judicial given by *Moses* is just and pure; for such is God who gave it. *Harken O Israel*, saith *Moses, Deut.* 4. *unto the statutes and the judgements which I teach you, to doe them, that ye may live*, &c. *ye shall not adde unto the word which I command you, neither shall ye diminish ought from it, that ye may keepe the commandements of the Lord your God which I command* you" (*YP*, 2:653).

133. For Milton's "eye towards Parliament's Erastian inclinations," see Michael Fixler, *Milton and the Kingdoms of God* (London: Faber and Faber, 1964), p. 113.

134. St. Haymo, *Opera Omnia*, in *Patrologiae cursus completus. Series secundo latina*, ed. J.-P. Migne (Paris, 1844–64), 116:539C.

135. Francis Barker, *"Areopagitica*: Subjectivity and the Moment of Censorship," in his *The Tremulous Private Body: Essays on Subjection* (London: Methuen, 1984); reprinted in *John Milton*, ed. Annabel Patterson (London: Longman, 1992), p. 67.

136. Selden's notes, in Sir John Fortescue's *De Laudibus Legum Angliae*, trans. Robert Mulcaster (London: The Stationers Company, 1616), pp. 7–9; cited by Paul Christianson, "Young John Selden and the Ancient Constitution, ca.

1610–18," *Proceedings of the American Philosophical Society* 128 (1984): 296. On Selden's rare wisdom in disputing the rival claims of English common law and Roman civil law, see Richard Helgerson, *Forms of Nationhood*, p. 68. J. G. A. Pocock's *The Ancient Constitution and the Feudal Law* (Cambridge, 1957; reprinted New York: Norton, 1967) provides indispensable analyses of the common-law mind and of the concept of the ancient constitution.

137. John Selden, *The Historie of Tithes* (London, 1618), pp. 124–25.

138. Selden, *Uxor Ebraica*, 1, 1, p. 2.

139. Jonathan Ziskind, *John Selden on Jewish Marriage Law*, p. 9.

140. Selden, *Uxor Ebraica*, 3, 23–25, pp. 499–514.

141. Ibid., 2, 18, p. 207. See also his *De Jure Naturali*, 2, 4, p. 162, for similar discussion: "Proselytus, ex quo fit Proselytus, velut infans, qui recens nascitur, habetur." Selden refers to "Gemar. Babylon. ad tit. Iabimoth, cap. 2 fol. 22a & cap. 11. fol. 97b. Maimon. halach. Iebom Wechalitza cap. 1. & Isuri bia cap. 14. Moses Mikotzi praec. affirm. 51. fol. 135. col. 4. Shulcan Aruch lib. Aben Haezer ca. 157. sect. 3."

142. Selden, *Uxor Ebraica*, 2, 16, p. 200.

143. Ibid. 2, 13, p. 187.

144. Ibid., 2, 21, p. 226: "Dii Conjugales qui sacris Nuptialibus invocati obiter memorantur, praeter Hymenaeum." Ibid., 2, 16, p. 202: "Eodem nomine apud veteres Ebraeos (Bereschith Rabba parash. 8) dicuntur Michael & Gabriel paranymphi Adae."

145. Selden, *De Jure Naturali*, 1 (chap. 10), p. 124.

146. Hugo Grotius, *De Jure Belli ac Pacis* (Leiden, 1625), 1:1 and 16.

147. *De Jure Naturali*, 1 (chap. 9), p. 109: "Aut scilicet intelligere eos ejusdem Juris capita tum in ipsis rebus initiis tum in ea quae fuit post diluvium instauratione Humano generi, ipsa Sanctissima Numinis Voce, fuisse imperata atque ad posteros per Traditionem solum inde manasse." See also 1 (chap. 6), p. 85: "Jus illud Naturale atque Universale, maxime quod sibi perpetuo constans est et numquam non obligat, petendum est." On the rabbinic discussion of Adamic laws promulgated in Eden, see 1 (chap. 10), p. 119.

148. Selden, *Opera Omnia*, 3: col. 2041. For Selden on natural law, see Richard Tuck, *Natural Rights Theories: Their Origin and Development* (Cambridge: Cambridge University Press, 1979), pp. 82–100; and J. P. Sommerville, "John Selden, the Law of Nature, and the Origins of Government," *The Historical Journal* 27 (1984): 437–47. In the course of a uniformly excellent survey of the topic, Sommerville corrects Tuck by pointing out that for Selden the "Noachide" laws go back not merely to a point after the Flood but in fact all the way back to Eden.

149. Selden, *De Jure Naturali*, 1 (chap. 9), p. 109; cited by Sommerville, "John Selden . . . ," 440.

150. Jeremy Taylor, *Ductor Dubitantium* (1660), *The Whole Works of the Right Rev. Jeremy Taylor*, ed. Reginald Heber (London: Longman, Green, 1862), 9:298.

151. Selden, *De Jure Naturali*, 1 (chap. 8), pp. 104–5.

152. Selden, *Table-Talk*; cited by Ziskind, *Introduction, Selden on Jewish Marriage Law*, p. 12.

153. Selden, *Uxor Ebraica*, 3, 22, p. 400; idem., *De Jure Naturali*, 5, 7, pp. 567–75, esp. p. 568.

154. Plato, *Symposium* (209A), trans. Walter Hamilton (Harmondsworth, Middlesex, England: Penguin, 1951), p. 90.

155. On the tripartite crescendo arrangement in Sonnet 23, see Leo Spitzer, "Understanding Milton," in his *Essays on English and American Literature*, ed. Anna Hatcher (Princeton: Princeton University Press, 1962), pp. 116–31.

156. Josiah Nichols, *Abraham's Faith* (London: Thomas Wight, 1602), p. 24.

157. Ibid., pp. 16, 19, and sig. B2v.

158. Selden, *Uxor Ebraica*, 2, 18, p. 207; idem., *De Jure Naturali*, 5, 4.

Chapter Three
Moses Traditions and the Miltonic Bard

1. Anne Davidson Ferry, "The Bird and the Blind Bard," in her *Milton's Epic Voice: The Narrator in Paradise Lost* (Cambridge: Harvard University Press, 1967), pp. 20–43; Louis L. Martz, *The Paradise Within* (New Haven: Yale University Press, 1964), pp. 105–10; and William G. Riggs, *The Christian Poet in Paradise Lost* (Berkeley and Los Angeles: University of California Press, 1972), passim.

2. James Holly Hanford, " 'That Shepherd Who First Taught the Chosen Seed', A Note on Milton's Mosaic Inspiration," *UTQ* 8 (1939): 403–19.

3. Ibid., 415.

4. Don Cameron Allen, *The Harmonious Vision: Studies in Milton's Poetry* (Baltimore: Johns Hopkins University Press, 1970), p. 136

5. Philo, *Questions in Exodus*, trans. Ralph Marcus, Supplement to *Philo*, Loeb Classical Library (London: Heinemann, 1964), 2:102. See also Flavius Josephus, *Jewish Antiquities*, trans. H. St. J. Thackeray, Loeb Classical Library (London: Heinemann, 1930), 4:289.

6. Augustine, *De Genesi ad Litteram*, in *Corpus scriptorum ecclesiasticorum latinorum*, ed. Joseph Zycha (Vindobonae: F. Tempsky, 1894), 28:203ff.

7. Henry J. Todd, ed., *The Poetical Works of John Milton* (London: J. Johnson, 1809), 4:5.

8. Philo, *De Vita Mosis*, trans. F. H. Colson, in *Philo*, 6:287–89. Colson notes that the regular school course of the Greeks would include grammar or literature and rhetoric.

9. Israel Baroway, "The Hebrew Hexameter: A Study in Renaissance Sources and Interpretation," *ELH* 2 (1935): 66–91. See also Don Cameron Allen in *Mysteriously Meant* (Baltimore: Johns Hopkins University Press, 1970). Allen examines the belief of the early Christian apologists that "Moses . . . is the source of all Greek philosophy" (p. 3), and he discusses Eusebius's identification of Moses with Musaeus and Hermes (pp. 108–9).

10. Flavius Josephus, *The Famous and Memorable Works of Josephus*, trans. Thomas Lodge (London, 1609), 1:252.

11. Philip Sidney, *The Defence of Poetry*, in *Sir Philip Sidney: Selected Prose and Poetry*, ed. Robert Kimbrough (New York: Holt, Rinehart and Winston, 1969), p. 110.

12. Andrew Willet, *Hexapla in Exodum*, 2:210.

13. William Attersoll, *A Commentarie Upon the Fourth Booke of Moses, called Numbers* (London, 1618), p. 847.

14. Harold Fisch, "Hebraic Style and Motifs in *Paradise Lost*," pp. 30–64; John T. Shawcross, "*Paradise Lost* and the Theme of Exodus," in *Milton Studies* 2 (1970): 3–26.

15. Philo, *De Vita Mosis*, in *Philo*, 6:357–59; see also 2:471–73.

16. That Philo was not alone in ascribing to Moses the tripartite office is proven by the exhaustive scholarship of Wayne Meeks in *The Prophet-King: Moses Traditions and the Johannine Christology* (Leiden: E. J. Brill, 1967).

17. Philo, *Jewish Antiquities*, 4:11.

18. Ibid., 4:13.

19. Jeremy Taylor, *Ductor Dubitantium*, his *Whole Works*, 9:296.

20. Eusebius, *Praeparatio Evangelica*, 9:29, in Eusebii Pamphili, *Evangelicae Praeparationis*, trans. E. H. Gifford (Oxford: Oxford University Press, 1903), 3:469. See also the account in Clement of Alexandria, *Stromata, Patrologiae . . . Series Graeca*, ed. J.-P. Migne (Paris, 1857), 8:902. For evidence of Milton's familiarity with Clement's *Stromata* in the edition of the *Opera* published by Carolus Morellus (Paris, 1629), see James Holly Hanford, "Milton's Private Studies," in his *John Milton: Poet and Humanist* (Cleveland: Western Reserve University Press, 1966), p. 86.

21. Eusebius, *Evangelicae Praeparationis*, 3:469–70. Here Moses is told that his mind will "survey all things in time, past, present, and to come." For Moses as a paradigm of the soul seeking heavenly mysteries, see Origen, *In Leviticum Homilia, Patrologiae . . . Series Graeca*, ed. J.-P. Migne (Paris, 1857–1912), 12:544; and, in the same volume, *In Numeros Homilia*, p. 630.

22. Isabel MacCaffrey, "The Theme of *Paradise Lost*, Book III," in *New Essays on Paradise Lost*, ed. Thomas Kranidas (Berkeley and Los Angeles: University of California Press, 1969), p. 58.

23. A topical gloss of the biblical passage, to which Milton would undoubtedly have assented, is provided by William Attersoll in his *Commentarie Upon . . . Numbers:* "Hee [Joshua] was too much addicted to the person of his master, as many hearers are to their teachers . . . as in our dayes, many conceive too highly of *Luther*, otherwise a very worthy man: howbeit *Moses* tendring the good of all the people more than his owne glory, reproveth his corrupt affection . . . and sheweth a contrary disposition in himselfe, desiring that all the Lords people could prophesie. . . . Heere we see what *Joshua* would have *Moses* do: he counselleth him to restraine them. A young man, young counsell" (pp. 540–42).

24. Mather, *The Figures or Types of the Old Testament*, p. 93.

25. See the citations of, inter alios, Jerome, Ambrose, and Gregory of Nyssa, in Andrew Willet's *Hexapla in Exodum* pp. 284–87 and 443–47; John Calvin, *Commentaries on Exodus*, trans. John King (Edinburgh: Calvin Translation Society, 1847), 3:315.

26. William Guild, *Moses Unvailed*, sig. A₃.

27. Thomas Taylor, *Christ Revealed* (London, 1635), p. 45.

28. *The Whole Book of Psalms, Collected into English Metre . . . Conferred with the HEBREW*, ed. Thomas Sternhold and John Hopkins (reprinted London: Stationers Company, 1682), title page.

Chapter Four
Angelic Tact: Raphael on Creation

1. St. Augustine, *De Genesi ad litteram libri duodecim*, ed. and trans. P. Agaësse and A. Solignac (Bruges: De Brouwer, 1972), 2.8.16; 1:169–70.

2. Rashi, *Commentary*, *The Pentateuch with the Targum and the Commentaries of Rashi and Ibn Ezra*, vol. 1 (Venice 1524–25), Gen. 1:5.

3. Luther, "Lectures in Genesis," *Luther's Works*, 1:22–23.

4. Willet, *Hexapla in Genesin*, p. 17.

5. Ibid., p. 18.

6. Guillaume Bartes, *Bartas, His Devine Weeks and Works*, trans. Joshua Sylvester (1605: facsimile reprint Gainesville, Fla.: Scholars' Facsimiles and Reprints, 1965), p. 245.

7. Luther, "Lectures in Genesis," 1:74.

8. St. Basil, *Exegetical Homilies*, trans. Sister Agnes Clare Way, C.D.P. (Washington, D.C.: Catholic University of America Press, 1963), p. 86.

9. St. Ambrose, *Creation, Paradise, Cain & Abel*, trans. J. J. Savage (New York: Fathers of the Church, 1961), p. 127

10. George Herbert, *The Works of George Herbert*, ed. F. E. Hutchinson (Oxford: Clarendon, 1941), p.51.

11. Willet, *Hexapla in Genesin*, p. 10.

12. St. Ambrose, *Creation*, p. 13.

13. Ibid., 13.

14. See, inter alios, St. Augustine, *The Trinity*, trans. Stephen McKenna (Washington, D.C.: The Catholic University of America Press, 1963), pp. 269–341; St. Thomas Aquinas, *Summa Theologica*, trans. by Fathers of the English Dominican Province (London, 1922), 4:272; Luther, *Works*, 1:63; Calvin, *Commentary on Genesis*, p. 42; Henry Ainsworth, *Annotations*, p. 7; John Diodati, *Pious and Learned Annotations upon the Holy Bible*, p. 3; John Salkeld, *A Treatise of Paradise*, pp. 88–89; Willet, *Hexapla in Genesin*, on Gen. 1:26. St. Thomas's commentary is typical: "We must not suppose that when God said Let us make man, He spoke to the angels, as some were perverse enough to think. But by these words is signified the plurality of the Divine Person, whose image is more clearly expressed in man."

15. Augustine warns against interpreting the creation account "in a childish way. . . . For he spoke, not with an audible and temporal word, but with an intellectual and eternal word, and the things were done." *de civ. Dei*, 11:8; cited by William A. Christian, "Augustine on the Creation of the World," *The Harvard Theological Review* 46 (1953):1–25.

16. Rashi, *Commentary*, 1:26.

17. Calvin, *Commentarie upon . . . Genesis*, p. 21.

18. Luther, *Works*, 1:90.

Chapter Five
Book 9: The Unfortunate Redemption

1. John Traske, *Treatise of Libertie from Judaisme, or, An Acknowledgement of True Christian Libertie* (London: N. Butter, 1620).

2. Ibid., p. 7.

3. Ibid., pp. 9–10.

4. Ibid., p. 5.

5. See Barker's powerful and persuasive essay "Structural and Doctrinal Pattern in Milton's Later Poems," pp. 169–94: "scholarship rightly associates the doctrine [of Christian liberty] chiefly with the radical Miltonic assertions of 'private or domestic liberty' and liberty of conscience" (170).

6. Traske, *Treatise*, p. 5. Although Traske seems to be addressing these words to himself, they constitute primarily an appeal to his readers to refrain from libelling him and to receive his treatise sympathetically.

7. Edward Norris, *The New Gospel, Not the True Gospel, or, A Discovery of the Life and Death, Doctrin and Doings of Mr. John Traske* (London: Henry Hood, 1638), p. 4.

8. See the account of Traske's persecution in Katz's *Philo-Semitism*, pp. 24–27.

9. Traske, *Treatise*, title page.

10. The translation of *non concupisces* in CE, 16:125.

11. Traske, *Treatise*, p. 21.

12. Ibid., p. 17.

13. Ibid., p. 29.

14. Ibid., p. 5.

15. Thomas Lorkin, in a letter dated 23 June 1618; cited in Katz, *Philo-Semitism*, p. 23.

16. Traske, *Treatise*, pp. 40–41.

17. Martin Luther, *Commentary upon Galatians* (1644), cited in Woodhouse, ed. *Puritanism and Liberty*, p. 221.

18. In the *Historia Augusta*, the author of the *Vita Claudii* uses this term, recalling Jewish sources such as Philo (*Mos.*1.156) and the *Sybilline Oracles*, where Moses is described as "the great friend of the most high" (2.245). See John G. Gager, *Moses in Greco-Roman Paganism* (Nashville, Tenn.: Abingdon, 1972), p. 22.

19. Thomas Blake, *Vindiciae Foederis; or a Treatise of the Covenant of God Entered with Man-kinde* (London, 1653), p. 13.

20. Arminius, *The Writings of Arminius*, 2:76.

21. Arminius, "ON THE NECESSITY OF THE CHRISTIAN RELIGION," in his *The Writings of Arminius*, 2:80.

22. Blake, *Vindiciae Foederis*, p.13.

23. Arminius, *The Writings of Arminius*, 2:80.

24. Bucanus, *Institutions of Christian Religion*, p. 76.

25. For a complete analysis of the shifts in mode and genre that occur at the Fall, see Barbara Kiefer Lewalski, *"Paradise Lost" and the Rhetoric of Liter-*

ary Forms (Princeton: Princeton University Press, 1985), pp. 36–38 and 220–53.

26. Milton calls the Edenic relationship with God a command (Heb., *mitzvah*) in chapter 10 of *De doctrina* (*YP*, 6:353) and a covenant (*"foedere"*) in chapter 11 (*YP*, 6:384). "Command" provides another link between the Noachide laws (*mitzvot*) of nature and the positive law of paradise (Gen. 2:16). Milton's reading of Genesis 2 in chapter 10 resembles Calvin's in the *Institutes* as explained by John S. Coolidge: "There is a promise of life attached to the command, . . . and if he does not observe that such an arrangement amounts to a covenant between God and man, the reason may be simply that the Bible does not call it a covenant. To do so would not appear to be in itself a substantial departure either from the Bible or from Calvin" (*The Pauline Renaissance in England: Puritanism and the Bible* (Oxford: Clarendon, 1970), p. 102).

27. Whately, *Prototypes*, pp. 8–9.

28. Whately, *Prototypes*, p. 67.

29. Ball, *A Treatise of the Covenant of Grace*, p. 15. See also Edward Leigh, *A Treatise of the Divine Promises* (London: George Miller, 1633), pp. 63–64.

30. Leigh, *A Treatise of the Divine Promises*, pp. 67–68.

31. Ball, *A Treatise of the Covenant of Grace*, p. 93.

32. Cotton, *The Covenant of Grace*, pp. 113–14.

33. Whately, *Prototypes*, pp. 6–7.

34. See William Ames, *The Marrow of Theology* [1629], ed. John D. Eusden (Boston: Pilgrim Press, 1968), pp. 53–54.

35. The ethos, if not the specific doctrine of the covenant of works in Eden, is sensitively described in an essential article on *Paradise Lost*, Barbara K. Lewalski's "Innocence and Experience in Milton's Eden," in *New Essays on Paradise Lost*, ed. Thomas Kranidas (Berkeley and Los Angeles: University of California Press, 1971), pp. 86–117. Comparing religious doctrine to literary convention, Lewalski looks beyond both to find Miltonic surprises in Eden, most of them having to do with physical, mental, and spiritual work. Labor is "not merely the expected ritual gesture, but a necessary and immense task" (90). Of special importance are the many connections drawn between work and good works: Adam and Eve are spiritual gardeners "responsible for perfecting their own natures" (93). Since the essay points out unconscious distortions imposed on the poem by various doctrines, including those of "the central Christian tradition" (87), its author might prefer not to have it co-opted as evidence of an Edenic covenant of works. Yet the essay seems to intuit such a covenant. Implicitly Hebraic in perspective, it characterizes Eden as "emphatically antiromantic, anti-Arcadian, anti-escapist" (116) and the Fall as a tragic event that blasted the opportunity to develop the "large potentialities of the human spirit" (117).

36. Martin Luther, "Lectures on Galatians," in *Luther's Works*, vol. 27, ed. Jaroslav Pelikan and Walter A. Hansen (St. Louis: Concordia, 1963); reprinted in Meeks, ed., *The Writings of St. Paul*, p. 248.

37. Leo Baeck, "Romantic Religion," trans. Walter Kaufmann in his *Judaism and Christianity* (Philadelphia, 1960); renamed "Paul's Romanticism" and reprinted in Meeks, ed., *The Writings of St. Paul*, pp. 336 and 346.

38. Maimonides, "Eight Chapters," 6, in *A Maimonides Reader* ed. Isadore Twersky (New York: Behrman House, 1972), p. 378.

39. John Selden, *Uxor Hebraica*, 3, 20, p. 449. For *bat kol* or *filiam vocis*, Selden refers to "Gemar. Hierosolymit. ad tit. Sanhedrin cap. 1 fol. 11a . . . Maimonid. in *More Nebochim* lib. 2. cap. 42." See also John Spencer's discussion of the *bat kol* as "an interpretive Voice from Heaven," identified as specifically Jewish and Talmudic, in *The Vanity of Vulgar Prophecies* (London, 1665), pp. 126–28.

40. John Selden, *De Jure Naturali & Gentium*, 1 (chap. 10), p. 122.

41. Ephesians 4:22–24, Colossians 3:9–10, 1 Corinthians 15:53 (cited by Douglas Bush in his edition of Milton's poetry), and Galatians 3:23–25.

42. Plato, *Symposium* (209A), p. 90.

43. Milton, *An Apology*, YP, 1:892; see also his *Animadversions*, YP, 1:719, and his *Comus*, 1003–11.

44. Arminius, "Public Disputations" (1609), in his *The Writings of Arminius*, 1:483.

45. David Hume, *Dialogues Concerning Natural Religion*, reprinted in *God and Evil: Readings on the Theological Problem of Evil*, ed. Nelson Pike (Englewood Cliffs, N.J.: Prentice-Hall, 1964), 10.22–23.

46. Lactantius, *A Treatise on the Anger of God*, trans. William Fletcher, in *The Ante-Nicene Fathers*, ed. Alexander Roberts and James Donaldson (Grand Rapids, Mich.: Eerdmans, 1975), 7:271.

47. Arminius's full and clear explanation of the permission of sin is astonishingly Miltonic in tone. See "An Examination of the Treatise of William Perkins Concerning the Order and Mode of Predestination," *The Writings of Arminius*, 3:429. After considering the problem that sin is both forbidden by law and yet permitted by God to exist, he warns: "Let no one think that God performs no act sufficient to prevent sin, when sin is not, in fact, prevented, and thence conclude that God wills sin; and again, let no one judge that, when God performs one or more acts, sufficient to prevent sin, that He unwillingly permits sin (429)." (Satan tells Eve first that God wants her to eat the fruit, then that he will permit it unwillingly.) Arminius declares two universal reasons for the permission of evil: "One is the freedom of the will. . . . The other is the declaration of the divine glory. . . . To which pertains that, which is beautifully said by Augustine, 'God has judged that it belongs to His own omnipotent goodness to bring good out of evil rather than not to permit evil to exist' " (439).

48. Sibbes, *The Faithful Covenanter*, 6:5.

49. For prooftexts employing such imagery, see Beverly Roberts Gaventa, *From Darkness to Light: Aspects of Conversion in the New Testament* (Philadelphia: Fortress, 1986).

50. Richard Travisano, "Alternation and Conversion as Qualitatively Different Transformations," in *Social Psychology Through Symbolic Interaction*, ed. Gregory P. Stone and Harvey A. Farberman (Waltham, Mass.: Ginn-Blaisdell, 1970), pp. 600–1.

51. See Leon Festinger, *A Theory of Cognitive Dissonance* (Evanston: Northwestern University Press, 1957); Leon Festinger, Henry W. Riecken, and Stanley

Schacter, *When Prophecy Fails: A Social and Psychological Study of a Modern Group that Predicted the Destruction of the World* (New York: Harper and Row, 1956). Disregarding the biblical severity of Auden's warning in "Under Which Lyre," "Thou shalt not sit with statisticians, / Nor commit a social science," scholars of religion have applied the theory of cognitive dissonance to the writings of Isaiah, Haggai, and Zechariah as well as Paul. See most notably Robert P. Carroll, *When Prophecy Failed* (New York: Seabury Press, 1979), and the appendix of Segal's *Paul the Convert*, pp. 285–300.

52. John Reading, *Moses and Jethro* (London: John Legatt, 1626), p. 4.

53. Festinger, *When Prophecy Fails*, p. 28.

54. See Watson, *Paul, Judaism and the Gentiles*, p. 156.

55. See Segal, *Paul the Convert*, p. 138. The relevant Talmudic sources cited by Segal are b. Shabbat 30a, 151b, b. Niddah 61b, b. Pesahim 51b, and j. Kilaim 9.3.

56. Calvin, *Institutes of the Christian Religion*, 2:10.454.

57. Musculus, *Common Places of Christian Religion*, pp. 33–34. For views similar to these, all at least indirectly influenced by Paul, see Luther, *Works*, 1:163–69; Gervase Babington, *The Workes . . . Containing Comfortable Notes upon the Five Bookes of Moses* (London, 1622), p. 15; Bartas, *His Devine Weekes and Workes*, p. 313.

58. On "all" in *Paradise Lost*, see William Empson, *The Structure of Complex Words* (1951; reprinted Cambridge: Harvard University Press, 1989), pp. 101–4.

59. Leo Baeck, "Paul's Romanticism," in Meeks, ed., *The Writings of Paul*, p. 343.

60. William Ames, *The Marrow of Sacred Divinity*, trans. John St. Nicholas (London: Edward Griffin, 1642), p. 49.

61. Ibid., p. 118.

62. Ibid., p. 48.

63. Segal, *Paul the Convert*, p. 137. For Milton, baptism signifies "OUR UNION WITH CHRIST THROUGH HIS DEATH, BURIAL AND RESURRECTION" (*YP*, 6:544).

64. Baeck, "Paul's Romanticism," pp. 337–38.

65. Christine Froula, "When Eve Reads Milton: Undoing the Canonical Economy," *Critical Inquiry* 10 (1983): 321–47.

66. Barbara K. Lewalski, "Milton, the Bible, and Human Experience," *Topoi* 7 (1988): 225.

67. For two notable examples, see the passage in the *Areopagitica* (*YP*, 2:543) that emphasizes the subjective aspect of truth, and *Of True Religion*, where Milton sets against implicit faith "attentive study of the Scriptures & full perswasion of heart" (*YP*, 8:436).

68. Philo, *The Special Laws* (4:84), in *Philo*, 8:61.

69. Harry Austryn Wolfson, *Philo: Foundations of Religious Philosophy in Judaism, Christianity, and Islam* (Cambridge: Harvard University Press, 1948), pp. 2 and 229.

70. In Philo's distinction, each of the other emotions "seems to be involuntary, an extraneous visitation, an assault from outside, [while] desire alone originates

with ourselves and is voluntary" (*The Decalogue*, in *Philo*, 7:77). See also Wolfson, *Philo*, 2:235.

71. W. D. Davies, *Paul and Rabbinic Judaism* (London: SPCK, 1955), p. 117.

72. Davies, *Paul and Rabbinic Judaism*, p.114; Segal, *Paul the Convert*, pp. 194–201 and 228–33; David Novak, *The Image of the Non-Jew in Judaism: An Historical and Constructive Study of the Noahide Laws* (Toronto: Edwin Mellen, 1983), p. 26. Novak discusses the view of some contemporary scholars that the Noachide laws originated in the diaspora as a regimen for God-fearers, the name given by Hellenistic Jews living outside of first-century Palestine to a group of gentiles who observed Jewish religious practices in varying degrees short of full conversion. As has been noted, John Selden's *De Jure Naturali et Gentium, Juxta Disciplinam Ebraeorum* is an exhaustive analysis of the seven Noachide laws.

73. See also *Animadversions*, on priests who "cast a stumbling-block before [God's] servants, commanding them to eat things sacrific'd to Idols, and forcing them to fornication" (*YP*, 1:706).

74. See Segal, *Paul the Convert*, pp. 235–36 and Watson, *Paul, Judaism and the Gentiles*, pp. 94–95.

75. Examining this speech, John Reichert asserts that Adam is "reasoning strangely well," and concludes, "[He] is, in large measure, right." Adam's failure to consider the price that must be paid by Christ for his redemption from death would probably not bother Reichert, who eschews theology. Like Adam, he reasons from self, and his conclusions are humane and consciously unrigorous. See his " 'Against His Better Knowledge': A Case for Adam," *ELH* 48 (1981): 99–100.

76. Ames, *Marrow of Sacred Divinity*, p. 267.

77. Ibid., p. 52.

78. Ussher, *A Body of Divinity*, p. 132.

79. C. S. Lewis, *A Preface to Paradise Lost* (1942; reprinted New York: Galaxy, 1961), p. 127.

80. See Meeks, ed., *The Writings of St. Paul*, p. 57, n. 3.

81. Hammond, *A Letter of Resolution*, p. 123.

82. Bucanus, *Institutions*, p. 191.

83. Thomas Goodwin, *Christ Set Forth in his Death, Resurrection, Ascension* (London: Robert Dawlman, 1645), p. 21.

84. Barker, "Structural and Doctrinal Pattern in Milton's Later Poems," p. 173.

85. When Milton asserts that "the Law is an instrument through which mankind recognizes its depravity," these verses are his prooftext. See *YP*, 6:518.

86. Francis Watson, *Paul, Judaism and the Gentiles*, p. 153.

Chapter Six
The Law in Adam's Soliloquy

1. On the Pauline theme of faith and law, see Segal, *Paul the Convert*, p. 181.

2. Bucanus, *Institutions*, p. 191.

3. Wollebius, *The Abridgment of Christian Divinity*, p. 86.

4. Ibid., p. 87.

5. Jeremy Cohen skillfully and patiently traces the proliferation of interpretations generated by this verse in *"Be Fertile and Increase, Fill the Earth and Master It": The Ancient and Medieval Career of a Biblical Text* (Ithaca, N.Y.: Cornell University Press, 1989).

6. Bucanus, *Institutions*, p. 194.

7. Ibid., p. 193. See also Ussher, *A Body of Divinity*, p. 145: "*But doth not God wrong to man, to require of him that he is not able to perform?* No: for God made man so that he might have performed it: but he by his sin spoiled himself and his posterity of those good gifts."

8. See Campenhausen, *The Formation of the Christian Bible*, p. 46.

9. See *Milton: Poetical Works*, ed. Douglas Bush (London: Oxford University Press, 1966), p. 417, n.

10. Bucanus, *Institutions*, p. 193.

11. John Marbeck, *A Booke of Notes and Common Places* (London, 1581), p. 615.

12. Peter Bulkeley, *The Gospel-Covenant* (London, 1615), Sig. 13v.

13. Calvin, *Sermons upon . . . Deuteronomie*, p. 946.

14. Kermode, "Adam Unparadised," in his edition of *The Living Milton*, pp. 117–18. In this essential article, Kermode regards Adam, "[d]eprived of Original Justice," as "merely natural" (118).

15. David Paraeus, *A Commentary Upon the Divine Revelation of the Apostle and Evangelist John*, trans. Elias Arnold (Amsterdam, 1644), p. 269. Also see Martin Luther, "Lectures on Genesis 1–5," in his *Works*, p. 240, on the "despair and blasphemy" begotten by Adam's "transgression of the command. . . . Man cannot do otherwise when no hope of forgiveness and promise of grace is available."

16. Milton, *Poems Reproduced in Facsimile*, pp. 35 and 40.

17. William Pemble, *Vindiciae Fidei*, p. 2.

18. Bucanus, *Institutions*, p. 362.

19. This entire paragraph relies on E. P. Sanders's discussion of dualism in *Paul* (Oxford: Oxford University Press, 1991), p. 93.

20. Philo *On Rewards and Punishments*, in *Philo*, 8:395. Milton might well have known the 1561 Latin translation: "quales ferútur epulae maćtatis Thyestae filiis, redeuntibus calamitatú priscarum tempo ribus."

21. On thinness as the recognition of only a narrow range of historical experience, see Mary Douglas, *Natural Symbols* (Harmondsworth: Penguin, 1970), pp. 40–41; cited by Gabriel Josipovici, *The Book of God: A Response to the Bible* (New Haven: Yale University Press, 1988), p. 270.

22. John Marbeck, *Notes and Common places*, p. 615, under the heading "How the lawe maketh us to hate God."

23. Herbert Marks demonstrates convincingly Paul's "drastic evacuation of the past into the present" in "Pauline Typology and Revisionary Criticism," *Journal of the American Academy of Religion* 52 (1984): 79.

24. "Bereshith," in *Zohar* [thirteenth century] (Vilna, 1894), 1:57b.

Chapter Seven
The Price of Grace: Adam, Moses, and the Jews

1. John Cotton, *The New Covenant* (London, 1654), p. 182.

2. Alexander Pope, *The Dunciad Variorum*, in his *The Poems of Alexander Pope*, ed. John Butt (New Haven: Yale University Press, 1963), p. 404.

3. Ibid.

4. Ibid., pp. 348–49.

5. Ainsworth, *Annotations*, p. 122; Joseph Hall, *Contemplations Upon the Principall Passages of the Holie Storie*, in his *Works*, Part 2 (London, 1625), p. 939.

6. Babington, *Workes*, p. 125.

7. Ibid., p. 125. See also Ainsworth, *Annotations*, p. 22.

8. Luther, *Lectures on Deuteronomy*, in his *Works*, 9:299; Babington, *Workes*, p. 124; Joseph Hall, *Works*, ed. Josiah Pratt (London, 1808), 3:84.

9. John Calvin, *Commentaries on the Last Books of the Bible*, trans. Charles William Bingham (Edinburgh, 1855), 4:377. See also Ainsworth, *Annotations*, on Deut. 3:27, p. 22.

10. Lightfoot, *The Harmony of the Foure Evangelists* (London, 1647), 2:29.

11. Ainsworth, *Annotations*, p. 166.

12. Stanley Fish, "Discovery as Form in *Paradise Lost*," p. 4.

13. Todd, ed., *Poetical Works Of John Milton*, 4:317–18.

14. Daniel Brenius, *Breves in Vetus & Novum Testamentum Annotationes*, in his *Opera Theologica*, II (Amsterdam, 1666), fol. 5.

15. William G. Madsen, "The Idea of Nature in Milton's Poetry," in Richard B. Young, W. Todd Furness, and William G. Madsen, *Three Studies in the Renaissance*, Yale Studies in English, 138 (New Haven: Yale University Press, 1958), p. 267. See also Martz, *The Paradise Within*, p. 161. Even J. B. Broadbent, in *Some Graver Subject* (London: Chatto & Windus, 1960), interrupts his mordant censure of book 12 to praise these lines (p. 286).

16. Tertullian, "An Answer to the Jews," in his *Writings*, pp. 202–3.

17. For more on the Abraham-Adam relationship in book 5, see Jason P. Rosenblatt, "Celestial Entertainment in Eden: Book V of *Paradise Lost*," *The Harvard Theological Review* 62 (1969): 411–27.

18. Segal, *Paul the Convert*, p. 333, n. 8.

19. Wayne Meeks makes this point in *The Writings of St. Paul*, p. 16, n.4.

20. In "Abraham, Adam, and the Theme of Exile in *Paradise Lost*," (*PMLA* 80 [1965]: 365–71), Mother Mary Christopher Pecheux expresses the more upbeat majority opinion on the Abraham-Adam association in the final books: "In the coming of the Savior [Adam] himself has a part to play, for he is father of the race, as Abraham is father of the Chosen People" (369). And regarding Adam and Eve: "Ancestors of Abraham and of the King Messiah, custodians of the faith which unites the elect, they can . . . look towards the future" (371).

21. John Wollebius, *Abridgment of Christian Divinity*, p. 76.

22. Edmund Gayton, "Upon Rabbi Manasses ben Izrel"; cited in Katz, *Philo-Semitism*, p. 249.

23. Anon., *To the Learned Jew, Menasseh Ben Israel of Amsterdam* (London, 1651), pp. 2, 4, and 6.

24. Ibid., p. 53.

25. Sir Robert Filmer, *Patriarcha*, chap. 3, in his *Patriarcha and Other Political Works of Sir Robert Filmer*, ed. Peter Laslett (Oxford: Blackwell, 1949), p. 8.

26. Northrop Frye, *Anatomy of Criticism* (Princeton: Princeton University Press, 1957), p. 212.

27. Ibid., p. 208.

Index of Biblical References